AF552942

THE FLAG ART FOUNDATION

2008–2018

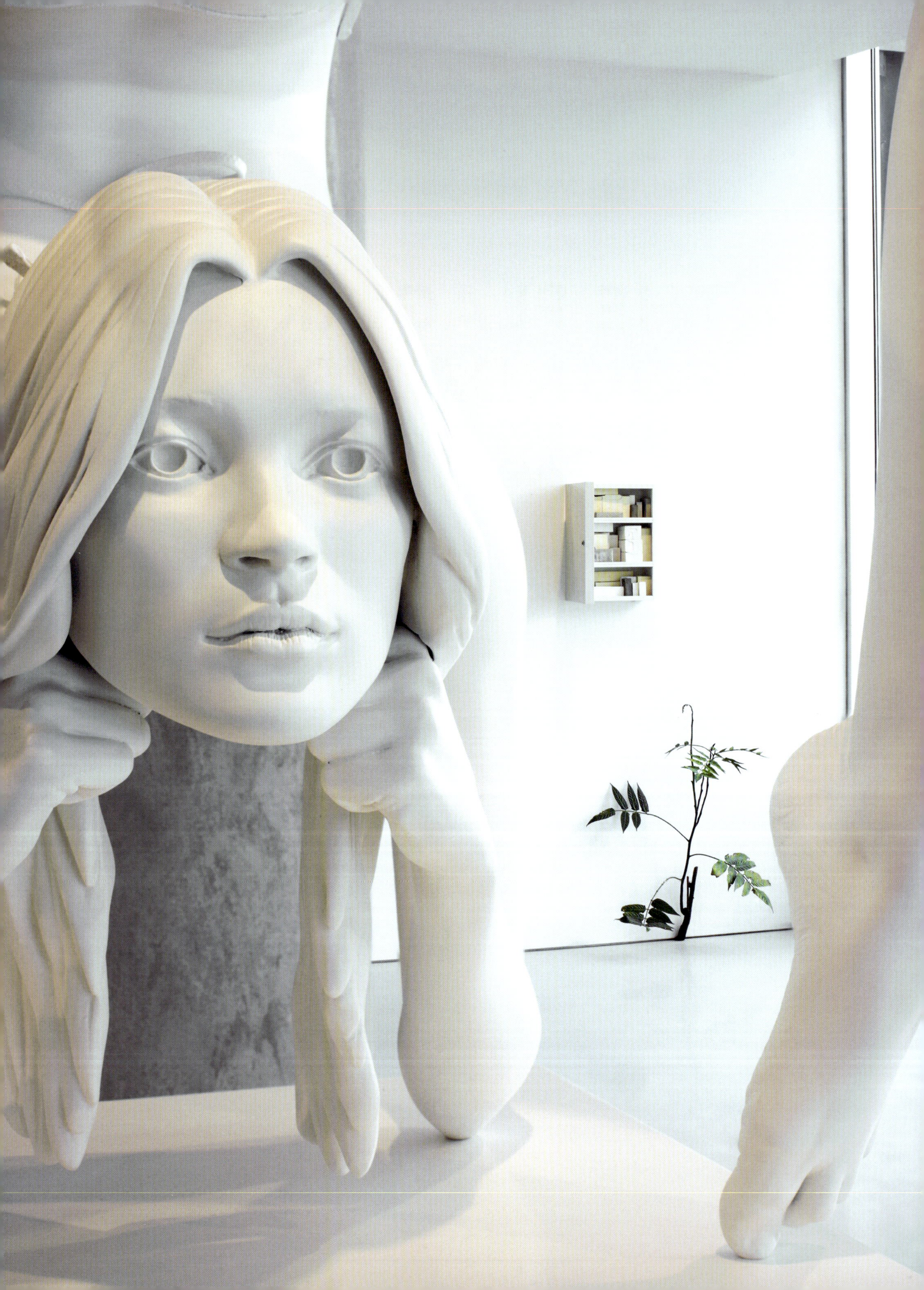

THE FLAG ART FOUNDATION

2008–2018

With contributions by

Ashley Bickerton, Delia Brown, Chuck Close,
Patricia Cronin, Cynthia Daignault, Lisa Dennison, Sarah Douglas,
Elmgreen & Dragset, Awol Erizku, Eric Fischl, James Frey, Ewan Gibbs, Louis Grachos,
Stamatina Gregory, Prabal Gurung, Jane Hammond, Hilary Harkness,
Jim Hodges, Philae Knight, Cary Kwok, Josephine Meckseper, Shaquille O'Neal,
Richard Patterson, Jack Shear, Carolyn Twersky, Lesley Vance, Rebecca Ward,
Linda Yablonsky, and Heidi Zuckerman

THE FLAG ART FOUNDATION and GREGORY R. MILLER & CO.

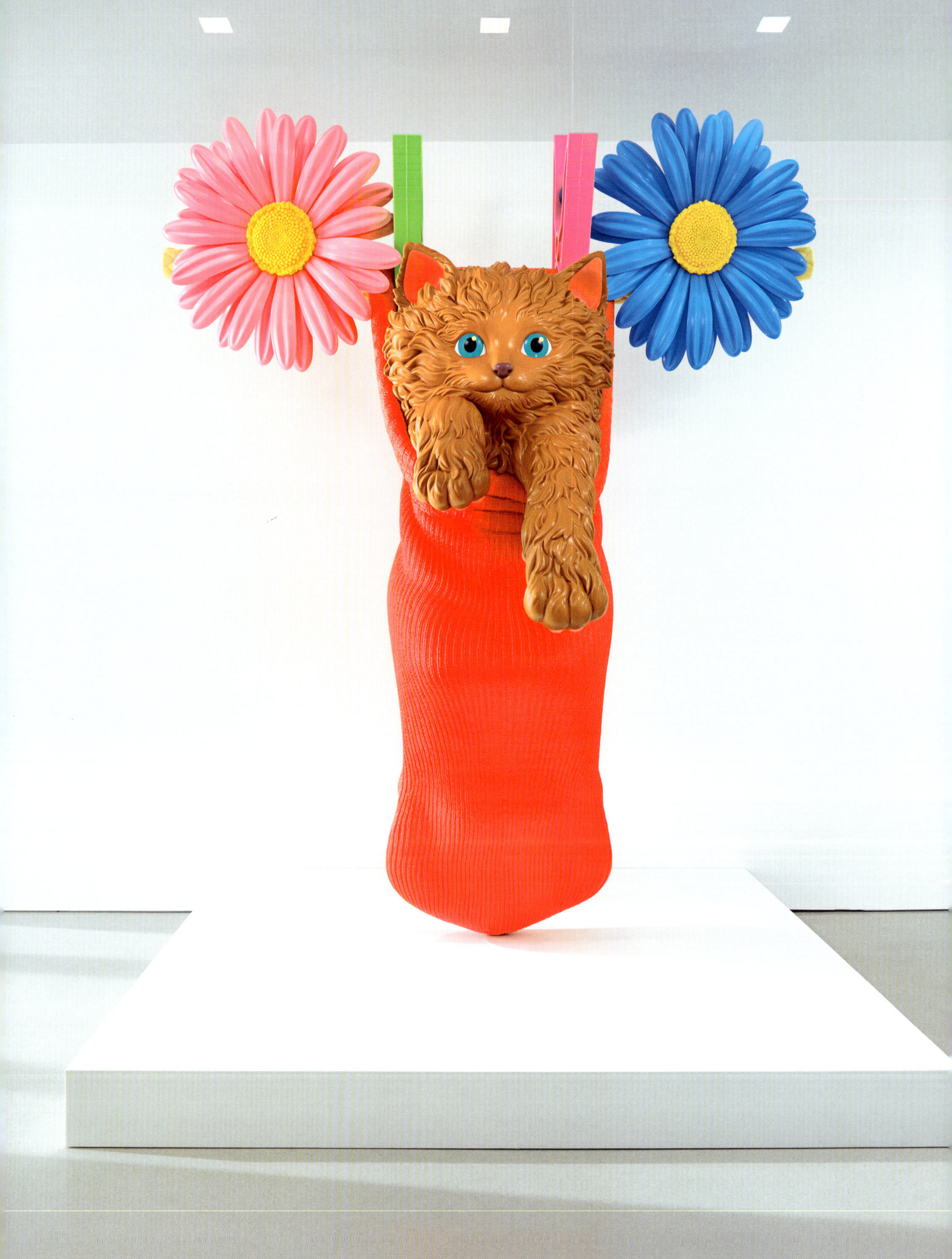

CONTENTS

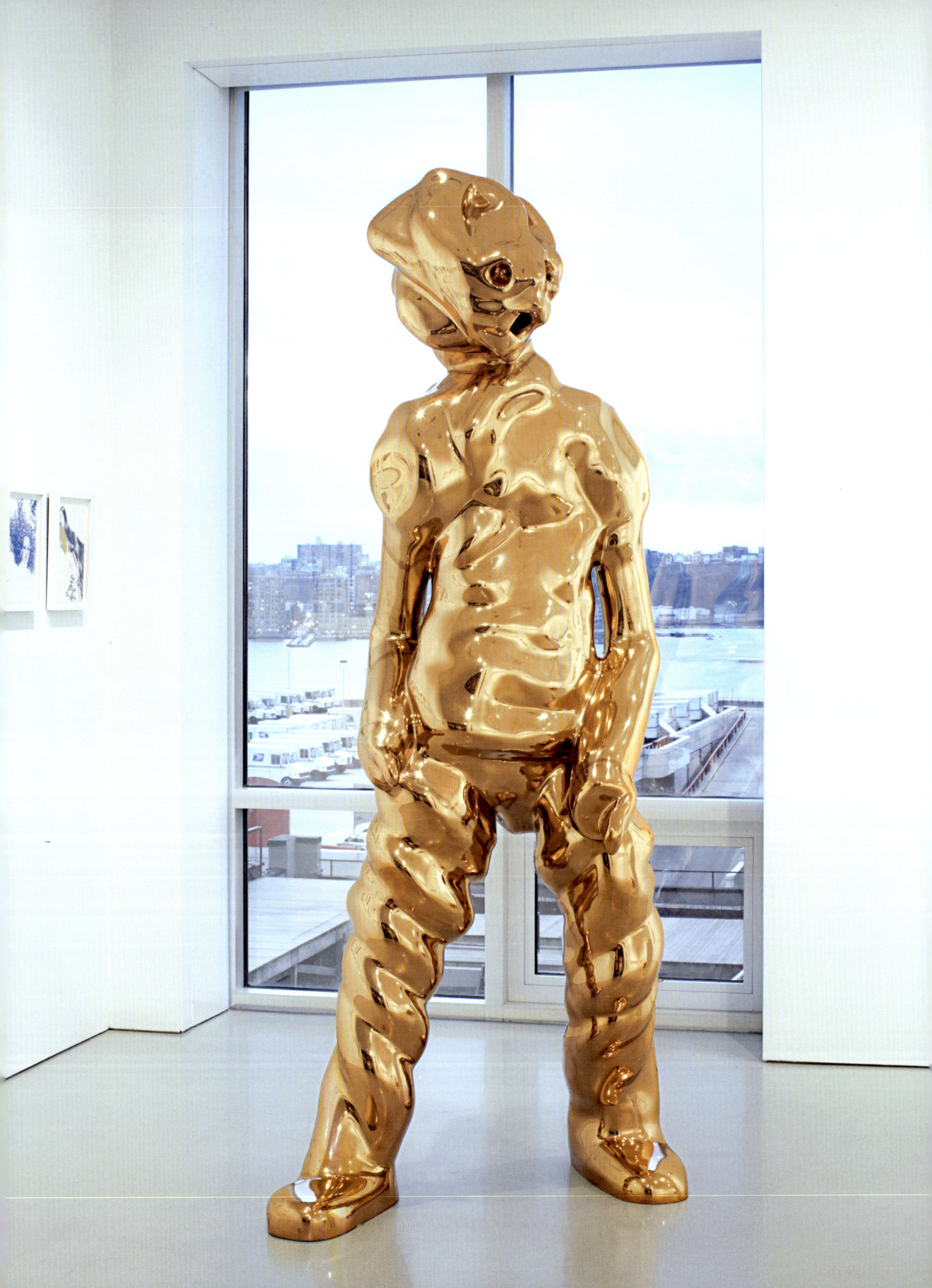

FOREWORD

Glenn Fuhrman

The FLAG Art Foundation emanated from my love for collecting contemporary art and the desire to share that joy with the public at large. For more than twenty-five years, I have cultivated an in-depth approach to collecting the art of my lifetime, which has allowed me to forge strong and sustained relationships with artists throughout the evolution of their careers. Additionally, I've developed close relationships with curators, gallerists, museum directors, and other collectors, all of whom tremendously enrich my life. It was my hope that in creating FLAG, I could work with these creative and inspiring individuals in new and different capacities and build a program that would honor artists and engage viewers.

FLAG's ten-year history now includes 50 exhibitions with 467 different artists and 18 curators. Many artists have appeared in multiple shows: Louise Bourgeois, Mark Bradford, Jennifer Dalton, Awol Erizku, Tom Friedman, Ewan Gibbs, Robert Gober, Felix Gonzalez-Torres, Ellsworth Kelly, Steven and William Ladd, Charles Ray, Gerhard Richter, Cindy Sherman, Ken Solomon, and Jim Torok have each been in at least five exhibitions. Jim Hodges has appeared in ten, and in 2009, he curated a beautiful show pairing his work with that of Gonzalez-Torres. We were especially excited when Jim allowed us to use two of his wonderful mirrored works for the cover of this catalogue.

Over the past decade, FLAG has worked with curators ranging from artists to athletes, fashion designers to museum directors. We strive to make our exhibitions and programming accessible to anyone with an interest in contemporary art. Our commitment to using outside curators was based on the idea that each show would have a unique vision, a changing perspective that would lead people to come back time and again.

Opposite: Installation view of *Going International*, showing Thomas Schütte, *Grosser Geister, #1*, 2003

Since FLAG's inception, we have presented solo, two-person, and group exhibitions, featuring both established and emerging international artists. More recently, we expanded our program to work with individual artists, such as Ashley Bickerton, Patricia Cronin, and Cynthia Daignault, to develop solo shows of new work or to present a body of work never before seen in New York. Many artists have been invited to explore ideas relevant to their practices through curatorial projects, including Chuck Close, Awol Erizku, Eric Fischl, Ewan Gibbs, and Hilary Harkness, among others.

My personal story has grown alongside FLAG's with the addition of my wonderful wife, Amanda, and our three children. Amanda is an enthusiastic supporter of mine, our family, and our art endeavors. In 2009, she curated a stellar exhibition in partnership with Philae Knight titled *Re-Accession: For Sale by Owner*, which featured artists negatively affected by the economic recession that shuttered countless galleries and caused significant budget cuts for museums and galleries. When our children were born, Amanda and I created "Baby Art History," which brought toddlers and their parents into FLAG for art projects and activities related to art and art history. I have wonderful memories of the floor of the foundation covered with small children coloring in Roy Lichtenstein coloring books during our show of his work, *Roy Lichtenstein: Nudes and Interiors* (curated by Hilary Harkness and Ewan Gibbs in 2014).

I want to recognize FLAG's stellar team led by Stephanie Roach, who has been an incredible thought-partner and skilled director from the very beginning. I first met Stephanie when she was a freshman at the University of Pennsylvania, my alma mater, and after a brief sojourn working in Spain after graduation, she agreed to move to New York in 2006 to open FLAG and become its first director—it's hard to believe she started this job in her early twenties. FLAG would not be anything close to the success it is today without her efforts. Stephanie's passion for art and her pride in getting things done the right way, along with her ability to work with artists from all over the world, have consistently been vital to FLAG's achievements. I would like to recognize Jonathan Rider, Associate Director, and Risa Daniels, former Exhibitions and

Programs Manager, amazing partners; they have worked at FLAG for almost half of its history, and their efforts and contributions are impossible to overestimate. I would also like to thank Rebecca Streiman, who played an important role in FLAG's earlier years, and Caroline Cassidy, who recently joined our team to help us embark on our second decade. I want to recognize the long and vibrant list of interns, art handlers, and security staff, all of whom have helped build FLAG into what it is today.

I would like to thank the artists who are at the very heart of everything we do and express my utmost gratitude to them, the curators, and the colleagues who shared their words and experiences for this catalogue. Reflecting on the past decade, I'm extremely proud that FLAG could be a space that brought so many brilliant voices together.

While our first exhibitions included many artworks drawn from my collection, as FLAG's ambitions grew over the past decade, so too did the scope of our shows. I want to thank the esteemed lenders and private collections who have shared an extraordinary range of contemporary artworks with us. I want to especially thank the institutions and museums that have lent their masterworks, including the American Folk Art Museum, New York; the Cleveland Museum of Art; the Hirshhorn Museum and Sculpture Garden, Washington, D.C.; the Museum of Modern Art, New York; the San Francisco Museum of Modern Art; and the Whitney Museum of American Art, New York, among others.

Finally, as with most things in my life, I would like to thank my parents, who first introduced me to the world of contemporary art, whether it was on purpose or by accident. My childhood room had a Roy Lichtenstein poster, and I knew who Helen Frankenthaler, Alex Katz, David Hockney, and Tom Wesselmann were way ahead of anyone else in my elementary school, since we had posters or lithographs by them on our walls. My parents have been true champions of all my efforts at FLAG and have attended almost every event we have put on.

As FLAG moves into its second decade, we are excited to work with new artists, new curators, and new ideas, while we continue, of course, to work with old friends along the way. I look forward to seeing you at the next opening.

PREFACE

Stephanie Roach

When I reflect on the first decade of The FLAG Art Foundation, a colorful amalgamation of experiences with artists and curators comes to mind: reviewing images of artworks with basketball superstar Shaquille O'Neal in Cleveland for *SIZE DOES MATTER*—I will never forget his expression upon seeing Ron Mueck's oversized hyperrealistic sculpture *Big Man* (2000), and when he exclaimed, "I want that in the show!"; sampling a variety of hard candies with Jim Hodges for Felix Gonzalez-Torres's *"Untitled" (Rossmore II)* (1991) before ultimately deciding on a custom green apple flavor; meeting Dorothy Lichtenstein at Roy's hallowed former studio with artists Hilary Harkness and Ewan Gibbs, who selected drawings to feature in the exhibition they curated, *Roy Lichtenstein: Nudes and Interiors*; seeking refuge from a rainstorm in Venice in the sixteenth-century church of San Gallo and being overcome with emotion by Patricia Cronin's poignant *Shrine for Girls*, which a year later would travel to FLAG; and discussing with Awol Erizku a new series of photographs completed during a trip to his home country, Ethiopia, which would eventually become his solo exhibition *New Flower | Images of the Reclining Venus*.

Before these memories were woven into FLAG's history, I fortuitously intersected with Glenn Fuhrman at the Institute of Contemporary Art at the University of Pennsylvania, when I was an undergraduate. This meaningful connection led to a substantive conversation about his plans to start FLAG, and in 2006, Glenn enlisted me in this exciting endeavor. At that time, the space was literally under construction and FLAG was still an idea. I had the honor of working alongside him to shape what it has become today. Developing a new contemporary art organization required the ability to navigate uncharted territory with a combination of curiosity, adaptability, and open-mindedness. Glenn's prescient words—"What we both lack in experience we will make up for with enthusiasm and passion!"—were a constant and guiding force that has proven true time and again over the past decade.

When FLAG opened to the public in January 2008, Glenn and I were just beginning to define its role within New York's cultural landscape and the art world. The first five years were primarily dedicated to exhibitions by rotating curators, whose distinct voices and appreciation of contemporary art informed their diverse approaches: Lisa Dennison selected more than seventy artists who explored Ed Ruscha's inimitable influence; Shaquille O'Neal brought a larger-than-life presence and a sense of humor to his exploration of the miniature, the gigantic, and everything in between; Prabal Gurung utilized his sensibility as a fashion designer to interpret Cary Kwok's elaborate drawings; Linda Yablonsky's meditation on trees was a beautiful and unexpected take on this subject matter; Eric Fischl mined his family history, American suburbia, and artists' fascination with dolls, toys, and mannequins to shape a psychologically charged panoply of works. Each exhibition was a collaboration—a process of adapting to varied personalities and working styles—and an opportunity for interesting individuals to realize unique visions and address relevant issues.

In 2011, FLAG broadened its program to focus on in-depth solo exhibitions of artists at pivotal junctures in their careers: Josephine Meckseper's exhibition marked the first time we supported the fabrication of new work; Jane Hammond's *Fallen* (2004) was a profound and timely tribute to U.S. soldiers killed in Iraq, for which she inscribed each fallen soldier's name onto a colorful handmade leaf (4,455 in total); Hilary Harkness presented the first comprehensive exhibition of her intricate "cross-section" paintings—the only occasion that many works from this series had been seen together; after receiving his MFA from Yale, Awol Erizku had his first solo exhibition at FLAG; and Cynthia Daignault's exhibition introduced new paintings that included collaborations with thirty-six emerging and established artists. We were honored to give Wayne Lawrence, Richard Patterson, and Rebecca Ward their New York solo exhibition debuts.

FLAG turns to artists for their perspectives during watershed moments in society, and two key thematic group exhibitions bookend the past decade: *Re-Accession: For Sale by Owner*, a direct response to the 2008 economic downturn in which many artists lost the support of gallery representation; and *The Times* (2017), which featured over eighty artists who used the "paper of record" to address social issues in the wake of the 2016 election. We hosted open calls for both exhibitions, providing a platform for the broadest range of artists to respond to the cultural climate.

In addition to FLAG's vibrant exhibition program, accessibility and engaging with our audience are vital parts of our spirit and ethos. Among the numerous museum and school groups we have welcomed over the past decade, the Harlem Children's Zone has been one of our most fulfilling and sustained relationships; their students have offered brilliant insights on topics ranging from Maurizio Cattelan's controversial sculpture of upside-down police officers (*Frank and Jamie*, 2002) to the 2016 presidential election. Artist conversations with Lawrence Weiner (complete with a Scotch tasting), Jeff Koons, Sean Scully, and Cynthia Daignault, among others, revealed personal anecdotes as well as insights about their oeuvres. FLAG has hosted various memorable events from concerts to benefits to Will Cotton's figure drawing party, which filled our space with artists and friends hard at work at easels as nude models struck poses. Each of these experiences has contributed to our evolution.

The core of FLAG's mission is to support emerging and established international artists, and the relationships we have cultivated are integral to our success. Ultimately, our history is a shared one. I am immensely grateful to all the individuals who have made the past decade truly remarkable and are a special part of FLAG's family. I would like to thank them for their indelible contributions:

To the artists, for their infinite creativity and inspiration.

To the curators, with whom it was an honor to work together to make their dream a reality.

To the community of galleries, museums, collectors, and artists, for their generosity in lending works to our exhibitions.

To our loyal viewers, whose curiosity and loyalty are the lifeblood of what we do.

To the art handlers, for their time and expertise; the photographers, designers, and interns, for their work behind the scenes and their attention to detail; and to Maureen Sullivan, for creative strategy and public relations.

To the awesome team we collaborated with to realize this catalogue—Miko McGinty and her designers, Rita Jules and Claire Bidwell; our editor, Kate Norment; and our co-publisher, Greg Miller—each of whom helped shape this book into a fantastic marker of our tenth anniversary.

I owe a debt of gratitude to the other members of the FLAG team: Associate Director Jonathan Rider; the former Exhibitions and Programs Manager, Risa Daniels; and the current Exhibitions and Programs Manager, Caroline Cassidy, who recently joined us. Their diligence, heart, and enthusiasm have been integral to the pursuit of FLAG's mission, and it has been a great pleasure to work with them.

I would like to acknowledge Glenn as a true visionary and extraordinary mentor; his dedication to and support of art and artists are unparalleled. In working with him, I have learned as much about life as I have about art.

Finally, I would like to thank my parents, Jill and Dennis, for providing me with invaluable exposure to art throughout my life, and my husband, John, for sharing my love of art.

Being at the helm of this organization has been exciting, challenging, and rewarding. I am continually invited to open my eyes and mind to the universal and transformative power of art. As I look toward the future, I am proud to say that FLAG's unwavering commitment to contemporary art and its community is stronger than ever.

THANK YOU

James Frey

Thank you
Thank you
Thank you
FLAG
For
Quiet
Peace
Stillness
Solitude
For a place
To look
And think
And feel
For a place
To contemplate
And disappear
Thank you
FLAG
For doing
What you do
For the sake
Of doing it
Show after show
Year after year
No admission fees
No crowds
No dealers
Sending follow-up emails
Just art
Paintings
Photographs
Sculpture
Video
Digital
Mixed media
For the sake of it
In quiet peace stillness and solitude
I remember
Sitting on the floor marveling at Cattelan's little
elevator opening and closing

Being dwarfed by Therrien's table and chairs
Being awed by
Richter
Mehretu
Grotjahn
Hammond
Laughing at Jeff Koons laughing with Jeff Koons
Turned on by Cecily Brown
I remember
Ellsworth Kelly simple elegant eternal I
disappeared into color
Cindy Sherman I disappeared into identity
I remember
Josephine Meckseper too smart for me
Damien Hirst golden drugs I do understand those
I remember
Mark Bradford and Tara Donovan
Awol Erizku and Robert Gober
Hilary Harkness and Jim Hodges and Roni Horn
(so many H's)
Richard Patterson and Paul Pfeiffer and
Richard Prince (so many P's)
I remember Cy Twombly
A giant late painting taking an entire wall
awesome and humbling it lit my heart on fire
I remember
A tiny portrait of the Obamas I saw through a
microscope awesome and humbling it lit my
heart on fire
I saw them all
In quiet
Peace
Stillness
Solitude
With no admission fees
Crowds
Dealers sending follow-up emails
Thank you
Truly

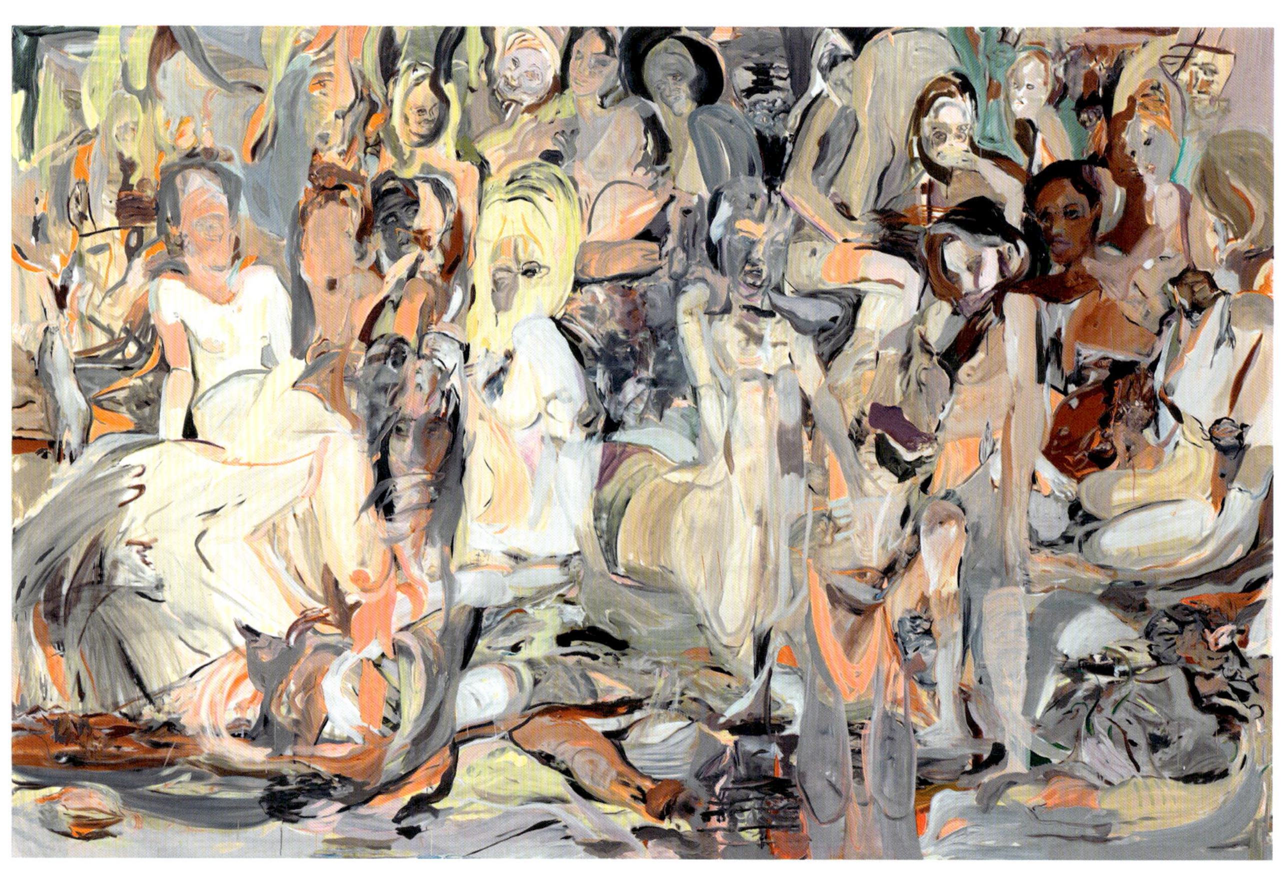

Cecily Brown, *Untitled (Blood Thicker Than Mud)*, 2012

Thank you
For so much
Beauty
Intellect
Feeling
Emotion
Humility
Awe
Inspiration
Thank you
For doing it
Without any agenda
Plan
Idea
Or motivation
Beyond
Wanting to share
Art
Art
Art
With me
With New York
With everyone who walked through your doors
With the world
Thank you
Thank you
Thank you
FLAG
For so much Beauty Intellect Feeling Emotion
Humility Awe Inspiration Art
Paintings
Photographs
Sculpture
Video
Digital
Mixed media
For the sake of it
Thank you

CHRONOLOGY OF EXHIBITIONS, 2008–2018

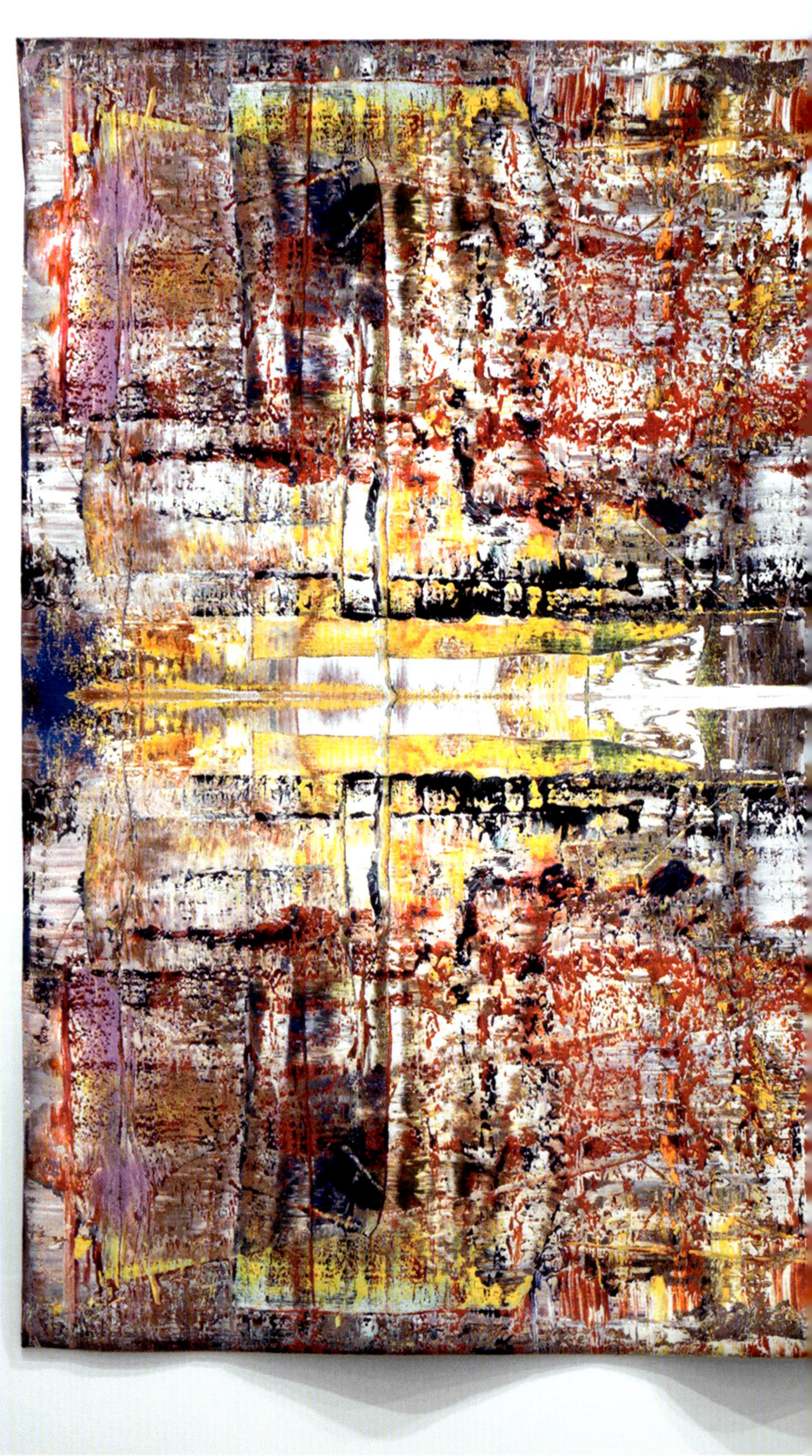

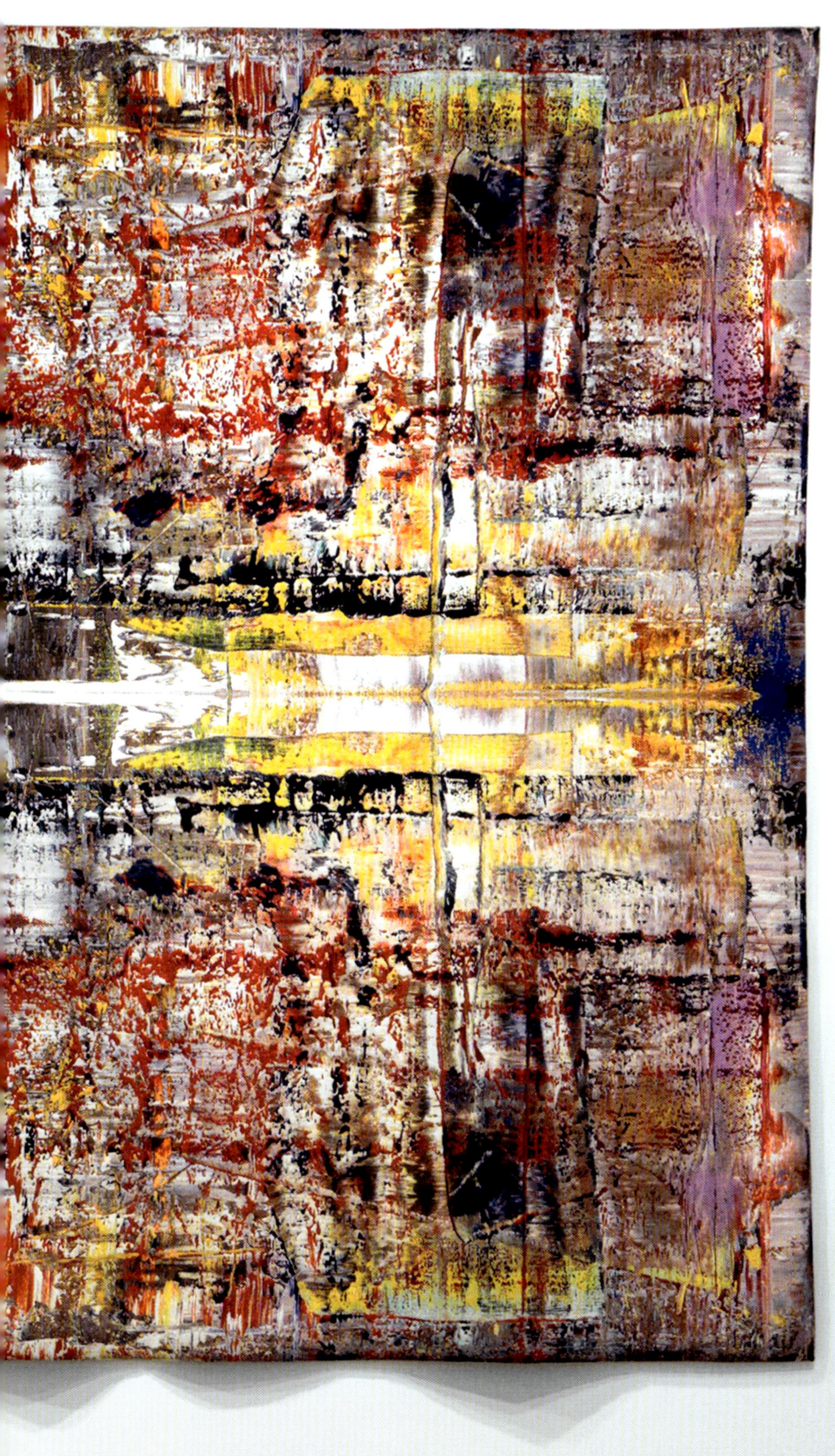

ATTENTION TO DETAIL

January 5–August 1, 2008
Curated by Chuck Close

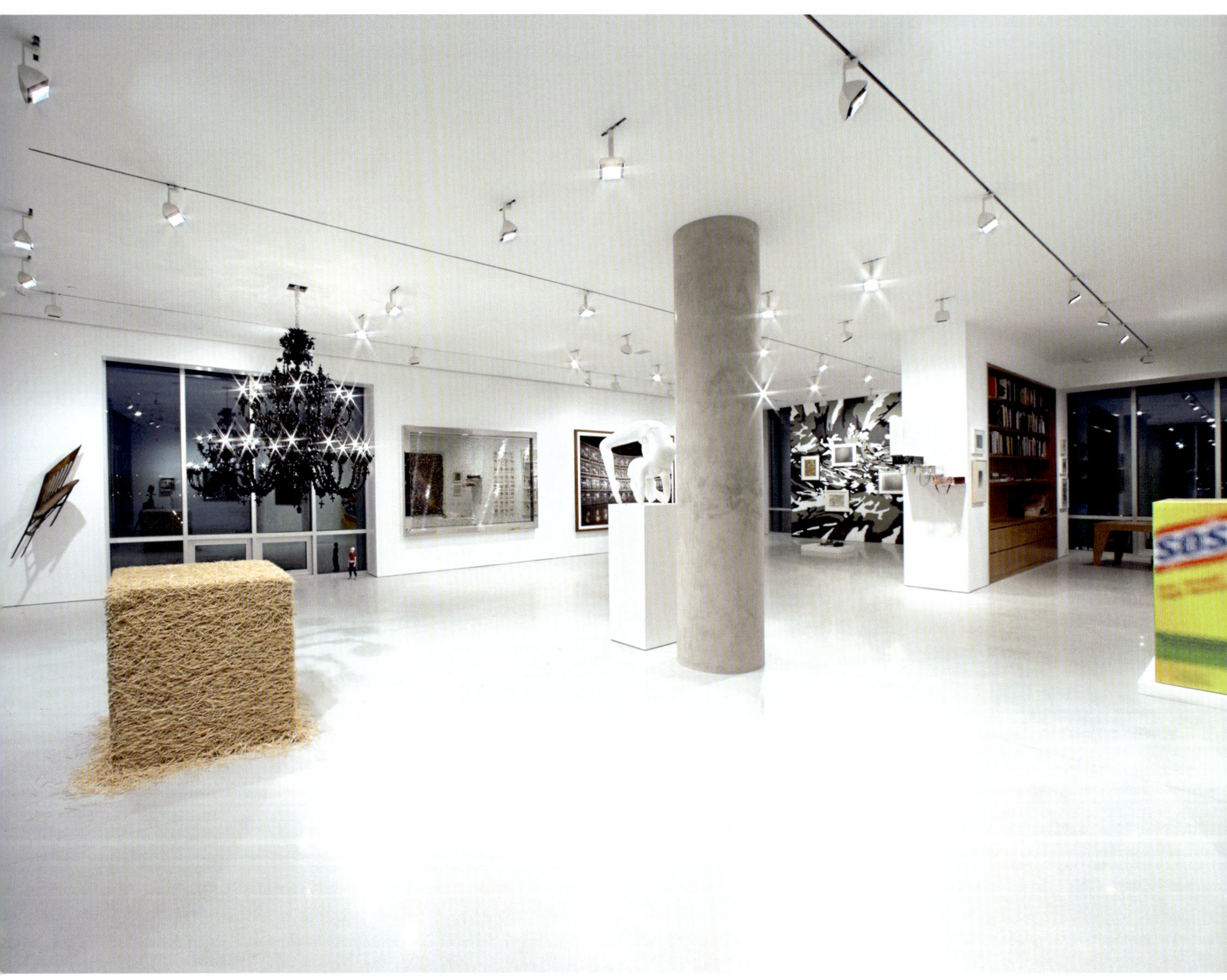

Installation view

As I look back at *Attention to Detail* a decade later, I see the show as a tribute to Glenn and his diverse collection; he collects interesting artists, and we share similar tastes.

I like many types of art, and when I curated an exhibition at the Museum of Modern Art (*Chuck Close: Head-On/The Modern Portrait* [1991]), I thought I could select my favorite pieces from its vast collection. But what good would that be? It's the mix that makes for a rich and complicated dialogue between works that have never been seen together before, and probably shouldn't be. No one would ever choose to combine the works in *Attention to Detail*, but that is the art of the impossible—what can we do with what we've got?—which I find fascinating.

To me, curating is not only about the relationships among works of art, but also about sharing someone's personal sensibility. When Shaquille O'Neal curated his show for FLAG, *SIZE DOES MATTER* (2010), I was interested to see what he would come up with. Certain pieces, such as Robert Therrien's oversize table and chairs (*Untitled [Table and Six Chairs]*, 2003), are wonderful because they change everything else in the space.

FLAG is so interesting because each show has a particular curator's input, and the results are completely different each time. But why they're different and how they're different are really what it's all about. I love the program, and I love seeing what other people do with it.

Chuck Close

Artists

Louise Bourgeois
Delia Brown
Glenn Brown
Maurizio Cattelan
Vija Celmins
Jennifer Dalton
Thomas Demand
Tara Donovan
Olafur Eliasson
Dan Fischer
Tom Friedman
Ellen Gallagher
Tim Gardner
Franz Gertsch
Ewan Gibbs
Robert Gober
Andreas Gursky
Damien Hirst
Jim Hodges
Naoto Kawahara
Ellsworth Kelly
Cary Kwok
Robert Lazzarini
Graham Little
Christian Marclay
Brice Marden
Tony Matelli
Ron Mueck
Richard Patterson
Richard Pettibone
Elizabeth Peyton
Richard Phillips
Marc Quinn
Alessandro Raho
Gerhard Richter
Aaron Romine
Ed Ruscha
Cindy Sherman
James Siena
Ken Solomon
Thomas Struth
Tomoaki Suzuki
Yuken Teruya
Fred Tomaselli
Jim Torok
Mark Wagner
Rachel Whiteread
Fred Wilson
Steve Wolfe
Lisa Yuskavage

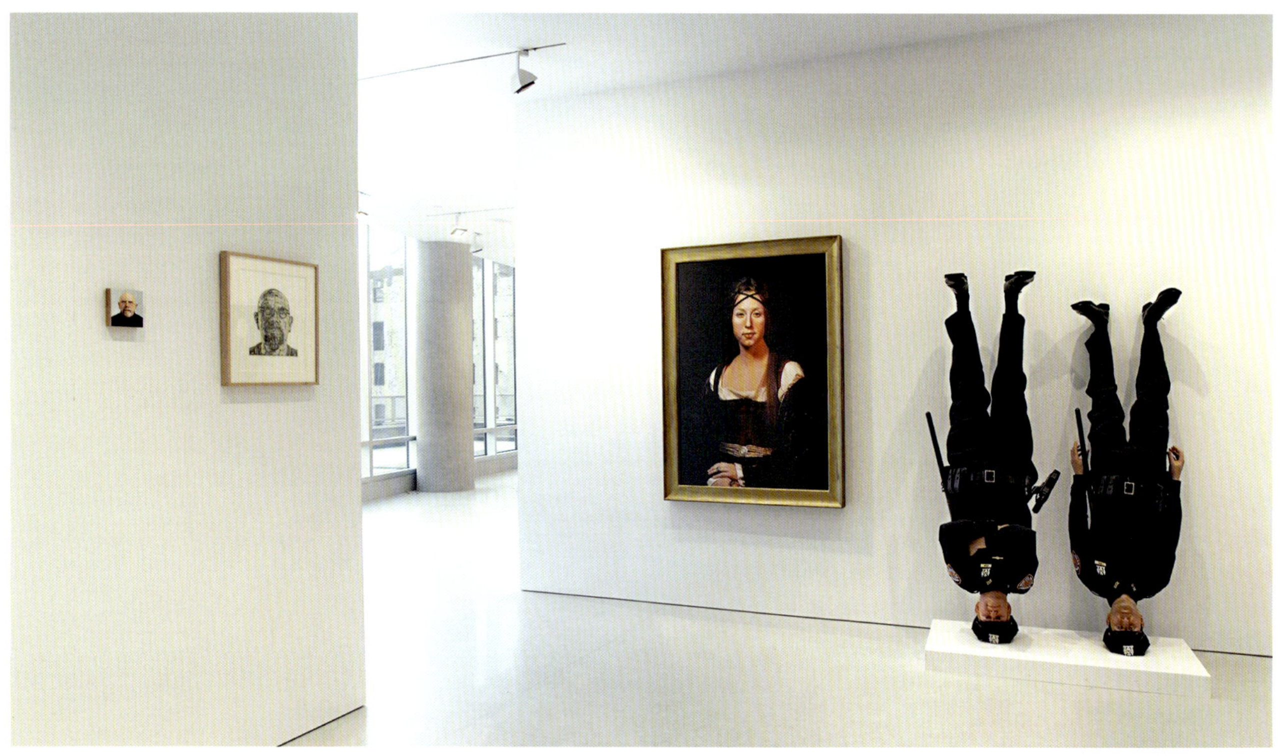

Left to right: Jim Torok, *Chuck Close*, 2004–5; Mark Wagner, *Chuck*, 2005; Cindy Sherman, *Untitled (#209)*, 1989; Maurizio Cattelan, *Frank and Jamie*, 2002

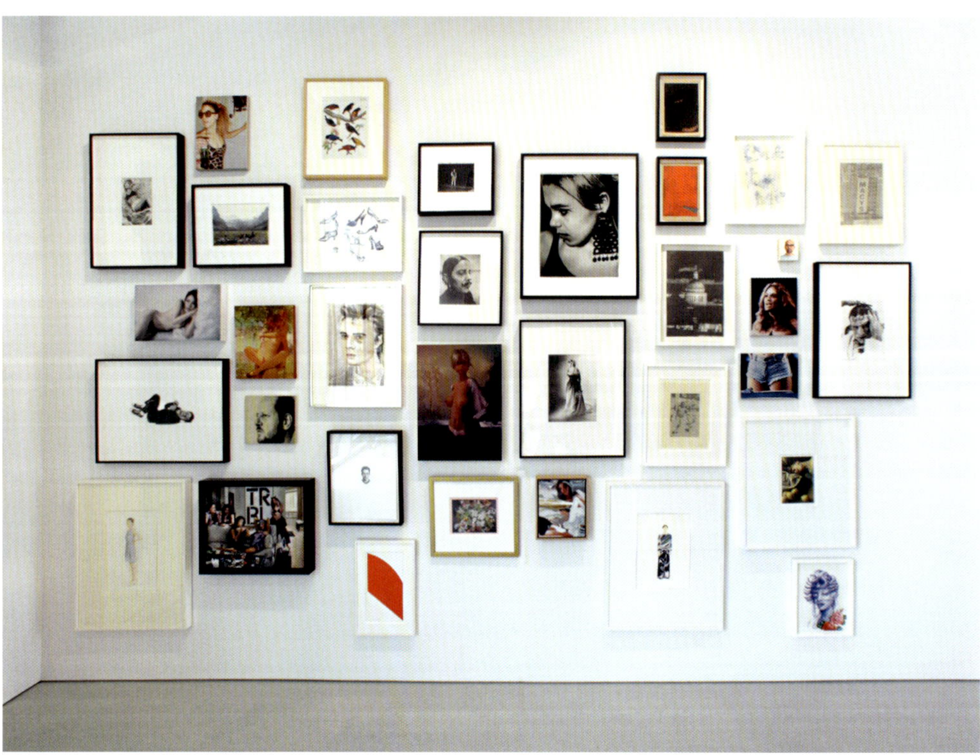

Installation view

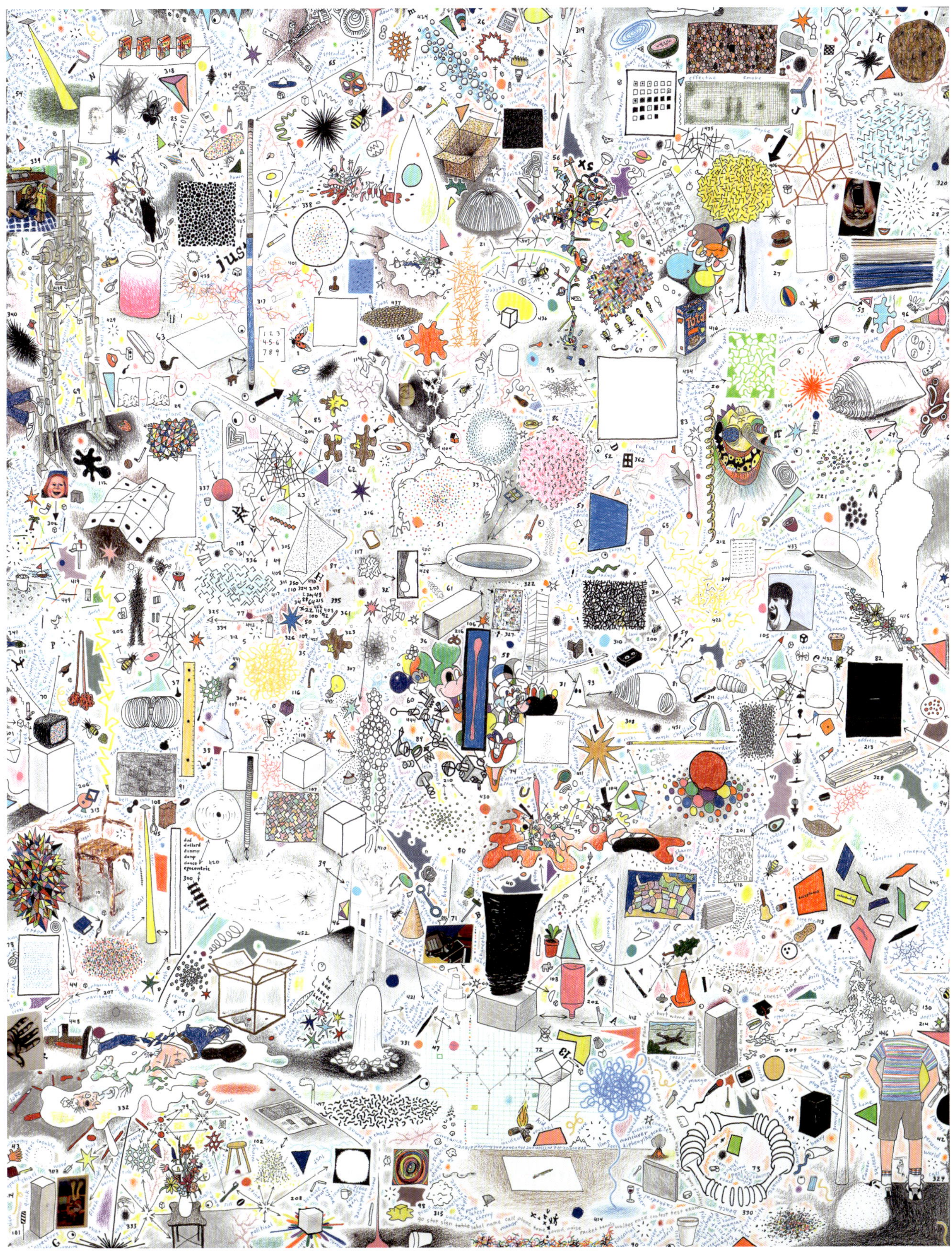

Tom Friedman, *75-03*, 2003

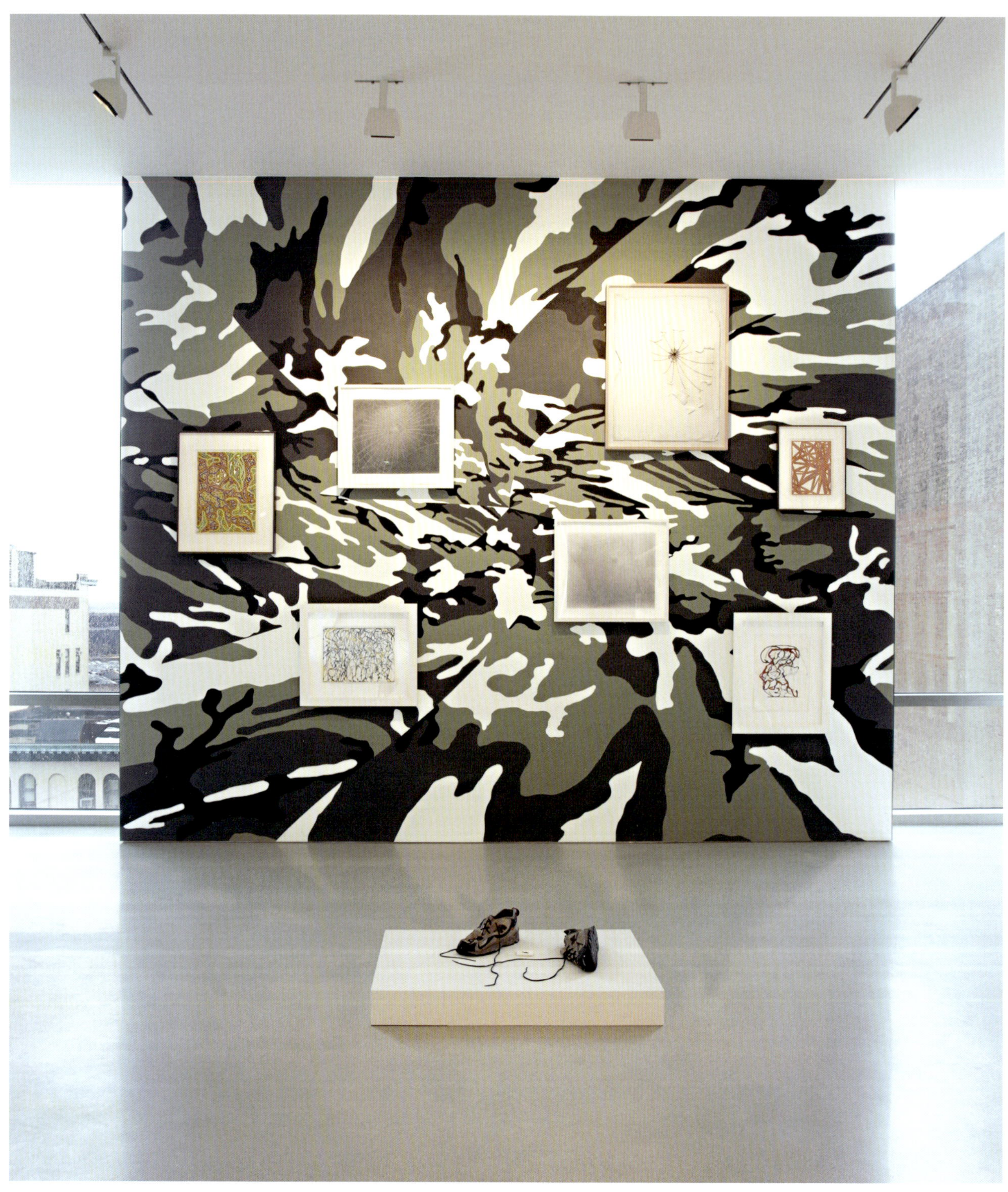

Background: Jim Hodges, *Oh Great Terrain I*, 2005; clockwise from left: James Siena, *Cell of Unknown Title*, 2006; Vija Celmins, *Web #3*, 1999; Jim Hodges, *No More Dreams/Everything From Here*, 1994; James Siena, *Shifted Lattice*, 2005; Brice Marden, *Butterfly Wings 2*, 2005; Vija Celmins, *Web #9*, 2006; Brice Marden, *Vertical Red Rock Drawing 2*, 1999; foreground: Tom Friedman, *Untitled (Sneakers)*, 2005

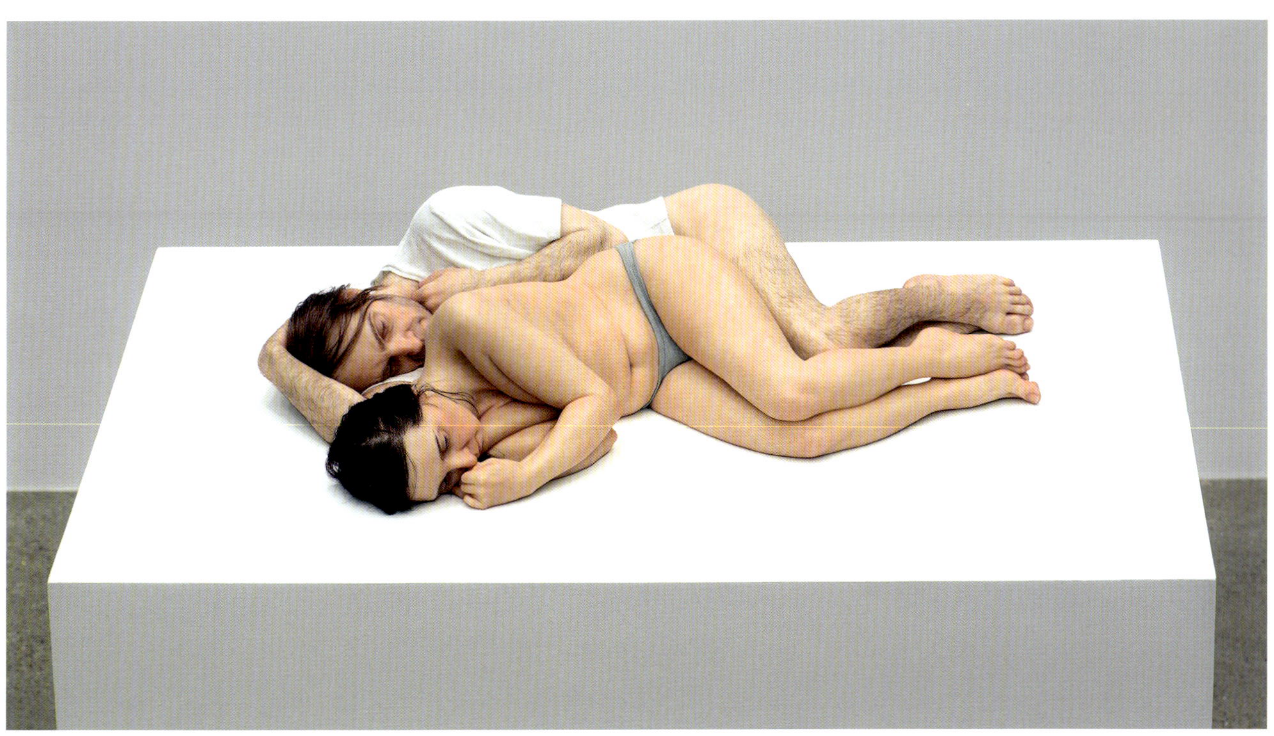

Ron Mueck, *Spooning Couple*, 2005

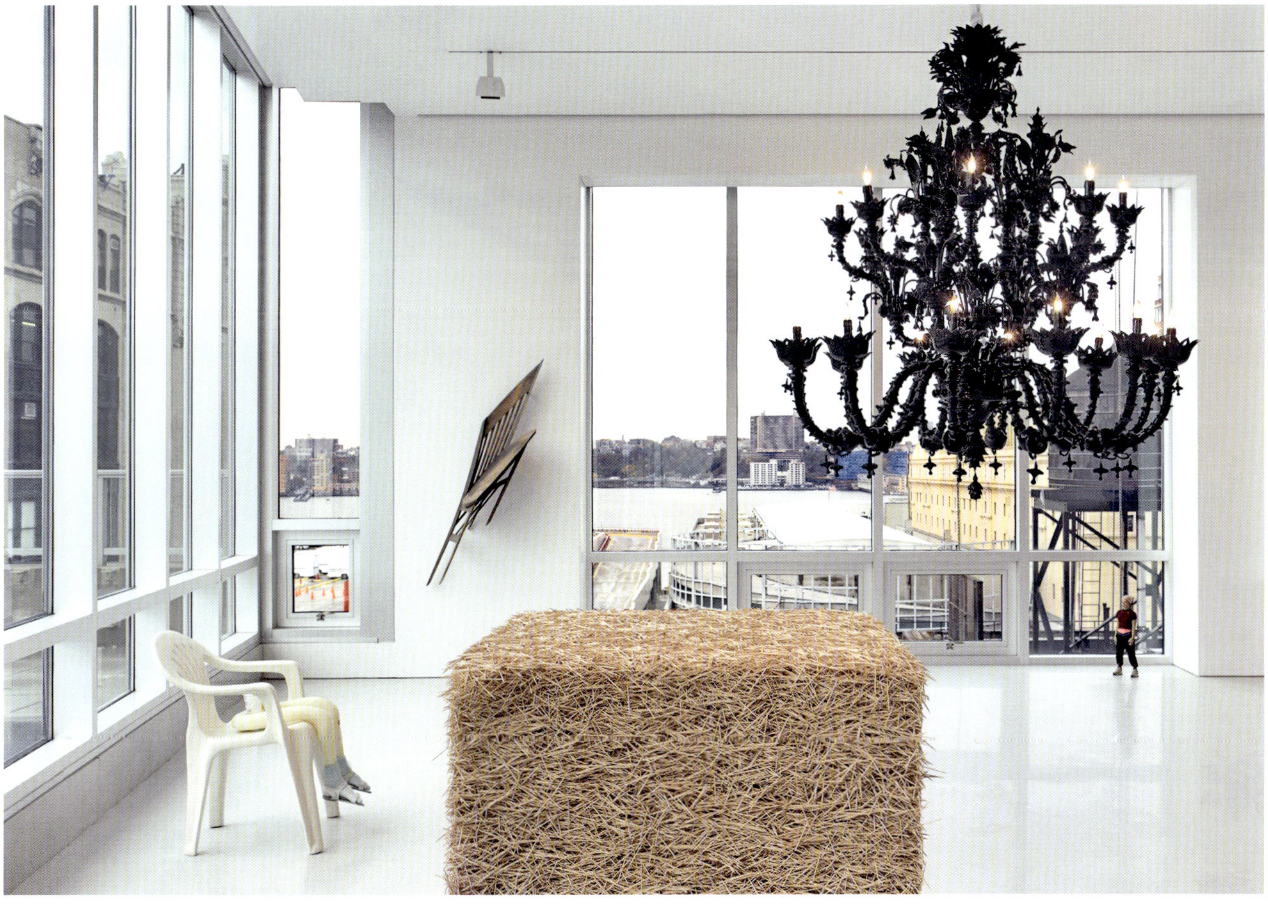

Left to right: Robert Gober, *Untitled*, 2005–6; Robert Lazzarini, *Walnut Chair*, 2000; Tara Donovan, *Untitled (Toothpicks)*, 2004; Fred Wilson, *Chandelier Mori: Speak of Me as I Am*, 2003; Tomoaki Suzuki, *Natascha*, 2001

DRAWN TOGETHER

April 1–June 30, 2008

Artists
Mark Bradford
Dan Fischer
Ewan Gibbs
Jim Hodges
Ellsworth Kelly
Brice Marden
Richard Phillips
Charles Ray

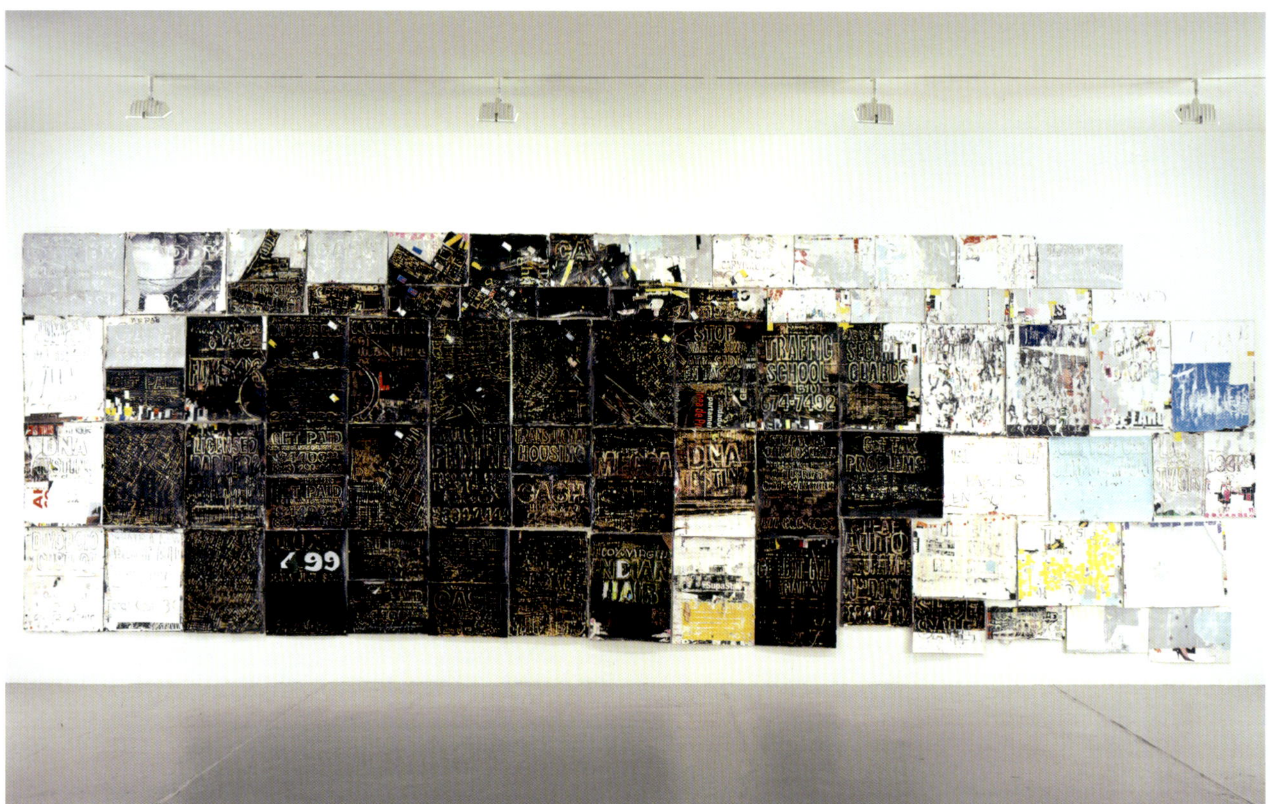

Mark Bradford, *Ridin' Dirty*, 2006

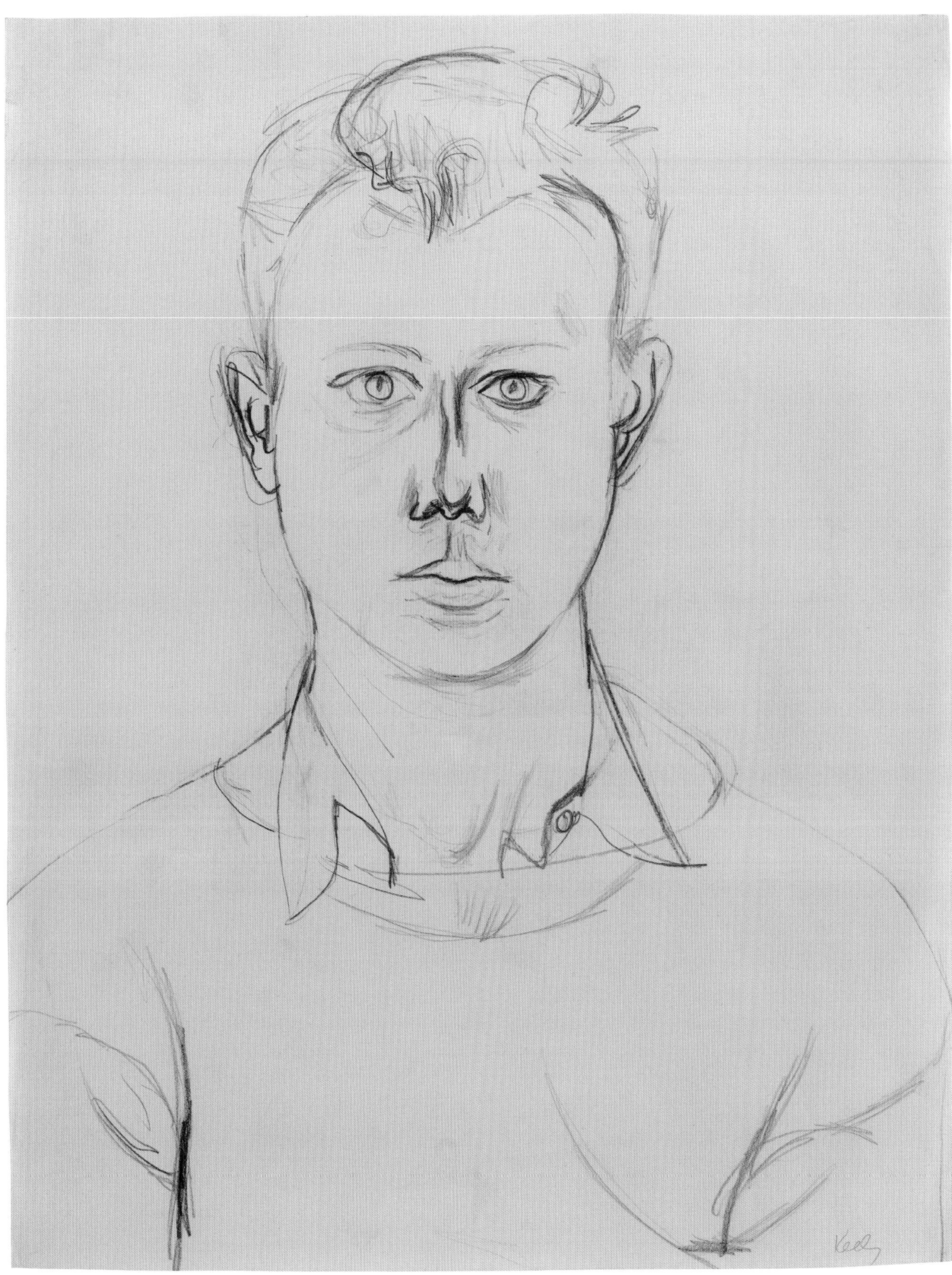

Ellsworth Kelly, *Self-portrait,* 1948

WALL ROCKETS: CONTEMPORARY ARTISTS AND ED RUSCHA

October 3, 2008–April 18, 2009
Curated by Lisa Dennison

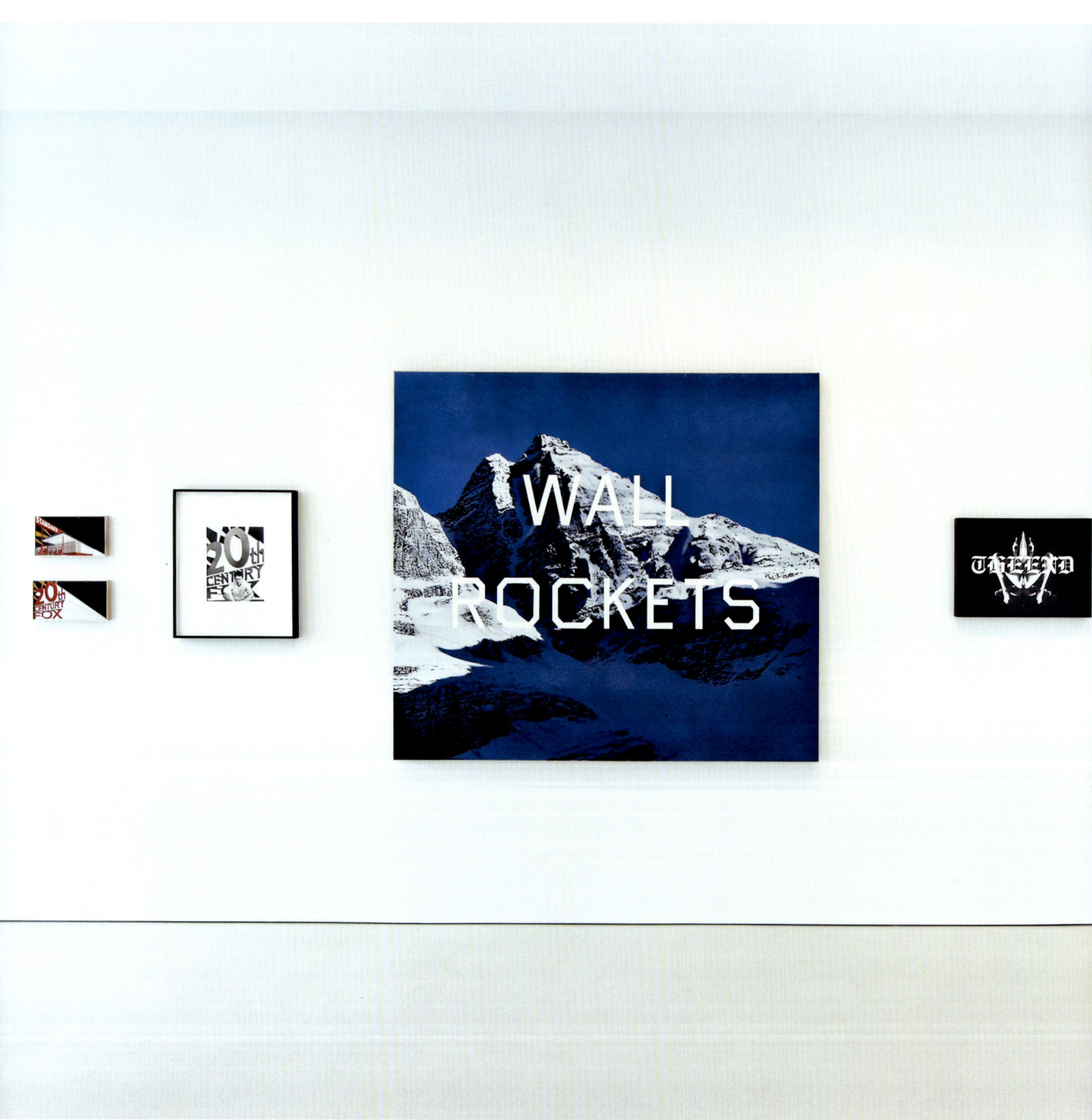

Left to right: Richard Pettibone, *Ed Ruscha 'Standard Station, Amarillo, Texas', 1963*, 2006; and *Ed Ruscha 'Large Trademark with Eight, Spotlight', 1962*, 2006; Dan Fischer, *Ed Ruscha*, 2006; Ed Ruscha, *WALL ROCKETS*, 2000; Kendell Geers, *THEEND (Tulsa Slut)*, 2008; Peter Cain, *Untitled #5*, 1996

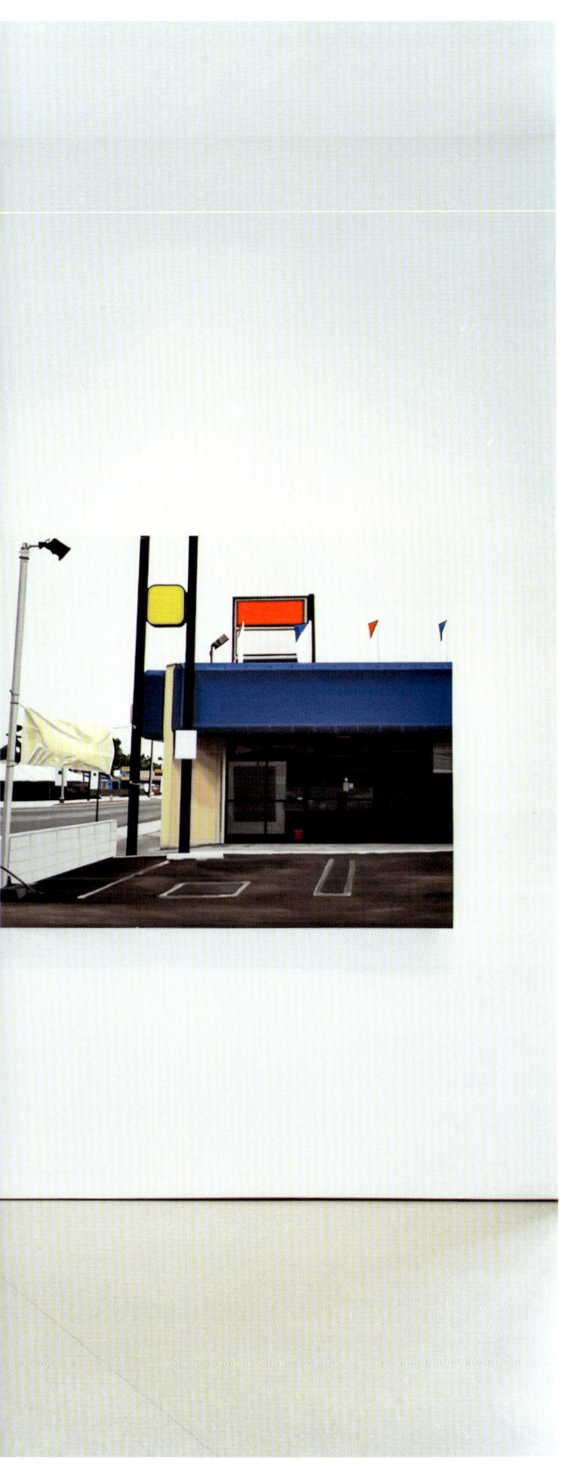

Artists

Amy Adler
Noriko Ambe
Kamrooz Aram
Tonico Lemos Auad
Conrad Bakker
John Baldessari
Jeremy Blake
Mark Bradford
Delia Brown
Jeff Burton
Peter Cain
Ingrid Calame
Peter Coffin
George Condo
Will Cotton
Jennifer Dalton
Thomas Demand
Amie Dicke
Iris van Dongen
Sante D'Orazio
James Esber
Dan Fischer
Tom Friedman
Barnaby Furnas
Francesca Gabbiani
Kendell Geers
Ewan Gibbs
Joe Goode
Joseph Grigely and Amy Vogel
Nir Hod
Jim Hodges
Dennis Hopper
Roni Horn
Barbara Kruger
Cary Kwok
Inez van Lamsweerde
Louise Lawler
Robert Lazzarini
Graham Little
Mads Lynnerup
Marco Maggi
Florian Maier-Aichen
Robert Mapplethorpe
Christian Marclay
McDermott & McGough
Jean-Luc Moerman
Paul Morrison
Richard Patterson
Richard Pettibone
Richard Phillips
Richard Prince
Alessandro Raho
Charles Ray
Ugo Rondinone
Danna Ruscha
Ed Ruscha
Eddie Ruscha
Thomas Scheibitz
Michael Scoggins
Ken Solomon
Billy Sullivan
Juergen Teller
Yuken Teruya
Robert Therrien
Fred Tomaselli
Jim Torok
Rosemarie Trockel
Keith Tyson
Aya Uekama
Julia Venske & Gregor Spänle
Mark Wagner
Lawrence Weiner
Terry Winters

In 2007, in a move that astonished the art world, I left the Solomon R. Guggenheim Museum after a nearly thirty-year curatorial career, for Sotheby's, to become Chairman, North and South America, focused on international business development and the Impressionist/Modern and Contemporary markets.

To my surprise, a year later I was approached by Glenn Fuhrman about a project we had discussed during my Guggenheim tenure. One of the early exhibitions of his newly created FLAG Art Foundation was to be a show about Ed Ruscha. While at the museum, I was asked to contribute to the catalogue (permission denied!), but now I was being asked to actually curate the presentation. To my further surprise, Sotheby's gave me their blessing, not seeing a conflict in an auction house executive overseeing an exhibition at a nonprofit founded by a major collector. And so the journey began. You can take the girl out of the museum, but you can't take the museum out of the girl!

The show already had a concept and even a number of works secured for loan. It would center on a significant mountain painting of Ed's that Glenn owned titled *WALL ROCKETS* (2000), and artists were invited to pay homage to the great master through existing works or newly created ones.

At first I was confounded by the idea of using Ed's language in the literal sense. My understanding of his work was that he didn't use words to say things or send messages per se, but rather that they were more like structural devices, giving shape to his compositions. But when asked, Ed had told Glenn that a wall rocket is a "powerful work of art that shoots off the wall," so I decided to go with the flow. My dual criteria for selection were: 1) Is this work a wall rocket? and 2) Does this work in some way "emulate, embrace, challenge, deconstruct, or lampoon" some aspect of his practice? And about seventy-five works later, thirty-three of them newly created, we had a collective portrait of a profoundly great and influential artist.

The show landed me on the cover of *Art and Auction* in October 2008 in a story titled "Rocket Woman," which thankfully did not bear the heavy connotations it does in this era of Trump tweets. It extended my history with Ed—truly a pleasure—as I had acquired the Guggenheim's first Ruscha in 2002 and was instrumental in selecting him for the 2005 Venice Biennale in a show that was deftly overseen by Donna De Salvo.

We met in the mountains of Aspen, appropriately enough, where Ed's ideas helped give substance and texture to a beautiful exhibition concept.

So the question is: Ten years later, does Ruscha's influence still prevail as strongly as ever? Indeed it does. Every single work in the *WALL ROCKETS* show still feels incredibly relevant, and one of the greatest pleasures of the project was getting to know artists who had previously been unfamiliar to me. Ed's particular fusion of Pop, Minimal, and Conceptual art resonates even more powerfully today than it did then. There is rumor of a Ruscha retrospective at MoMA in the not-too-distant future, and I have had the pleasure of bidding on, and in many cases placing, numerous works in collections worldwide through our contemporary sales, most recently a particular canvas called *Light Leaks* (1993), which fittingly bears the words "The End."

—Lisa Dennison

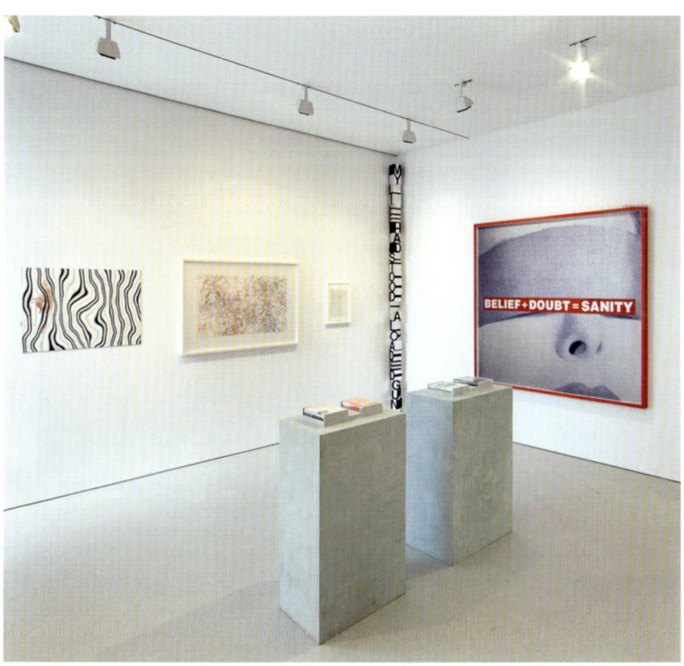

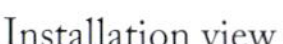
Installation view

Left to right: Sante D'Orazio, *ED RUSCHA*, 2006; Inez van Lamsweerde, *Ruscha*, 2008

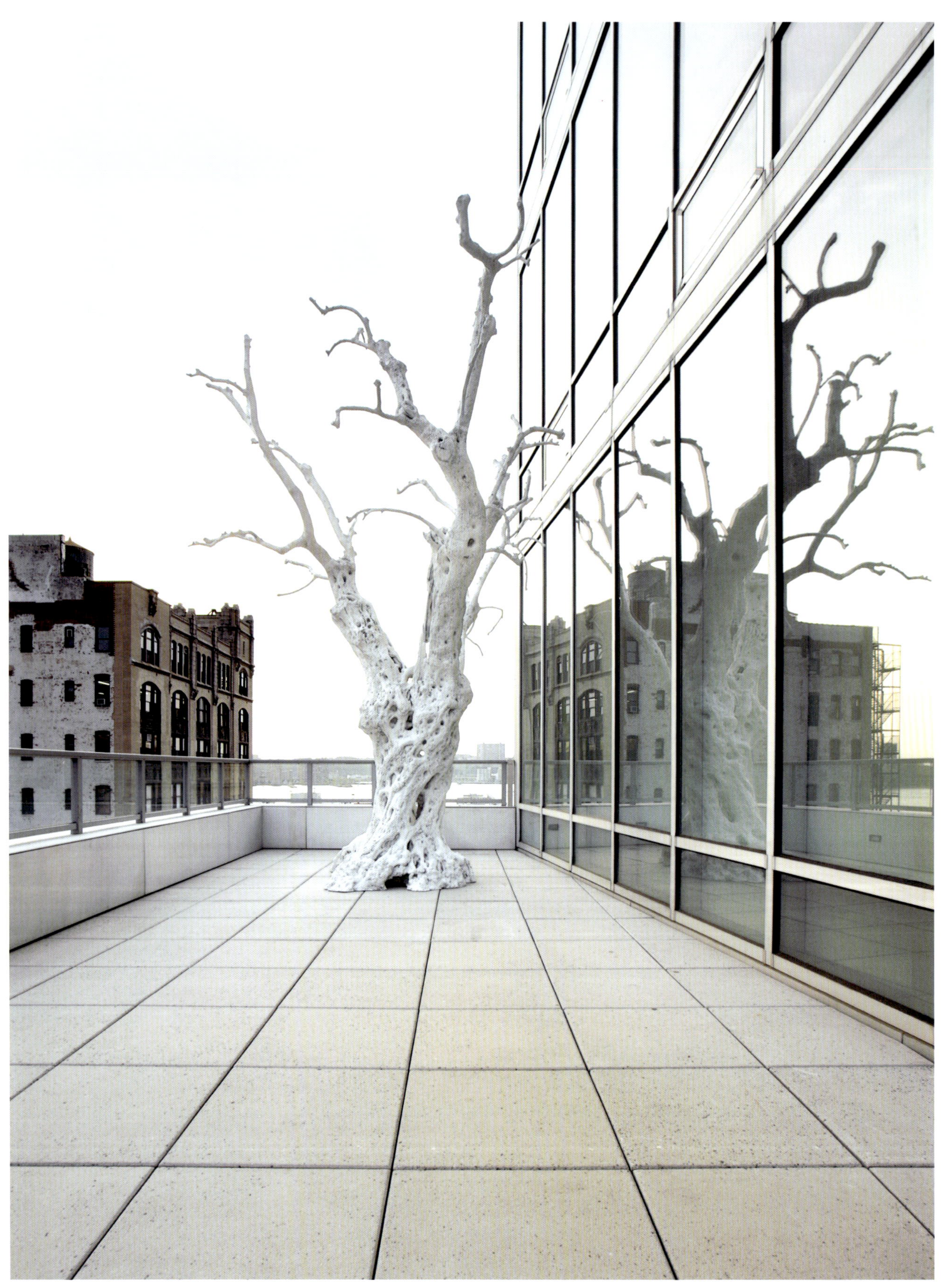

Ugo Rondinone, *get up girl a sun is running the world*, 2006

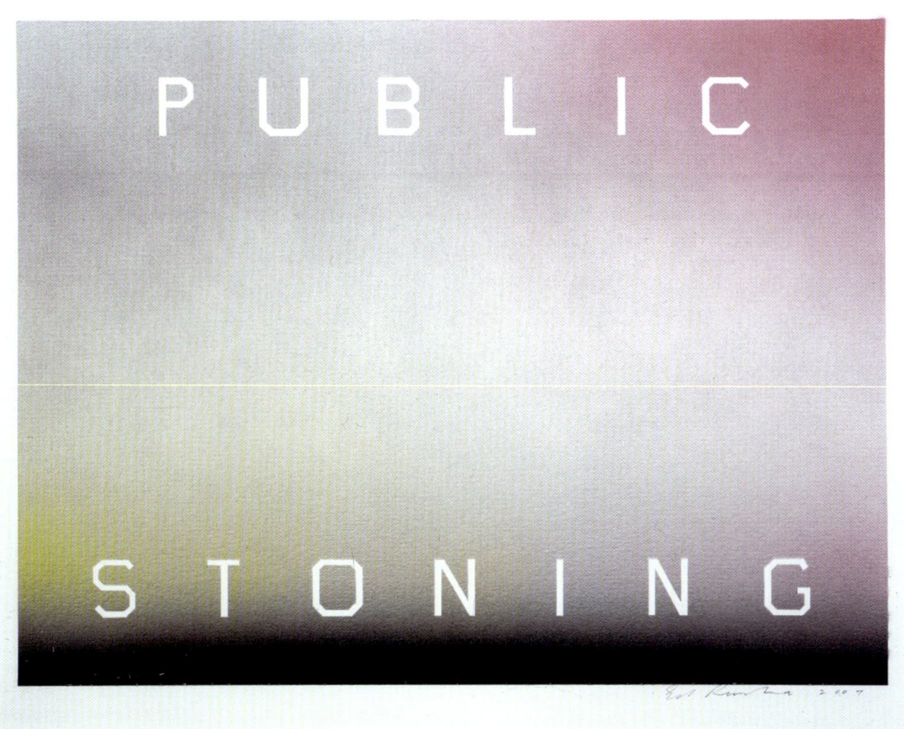

Ed Ruscha, *Public Stoning*, 2007

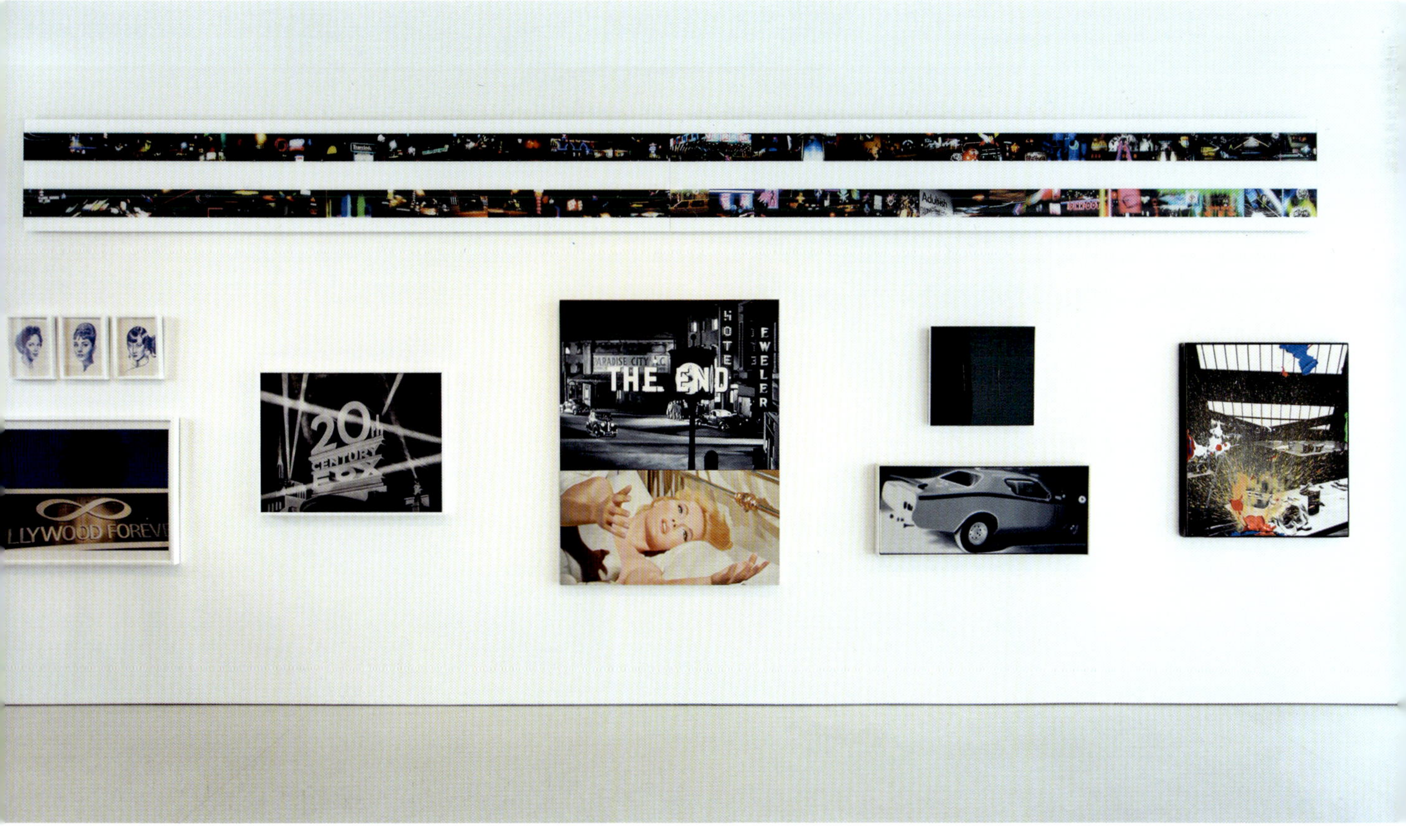

Installation view

VAGUE TERRAIN: ANALOGUES OF PLACE IN CONTEMPORARY PHOTOGRAPHY

May 8–September 1, 2009
Curated by Stamatina Gregory

Artists
Oliver Boberg
James Casebere
Gregory Crewdson
Thomas Demand
Joan Fontcuberta
Barry Frydlender
Noriko Furunishi
Andreas Gursky
Beate Gütschow
An-My Lê
David Levinthal
Aleksandra Mir
Cindy Sherman
Jeff Wall
Jason Wee
James Welling

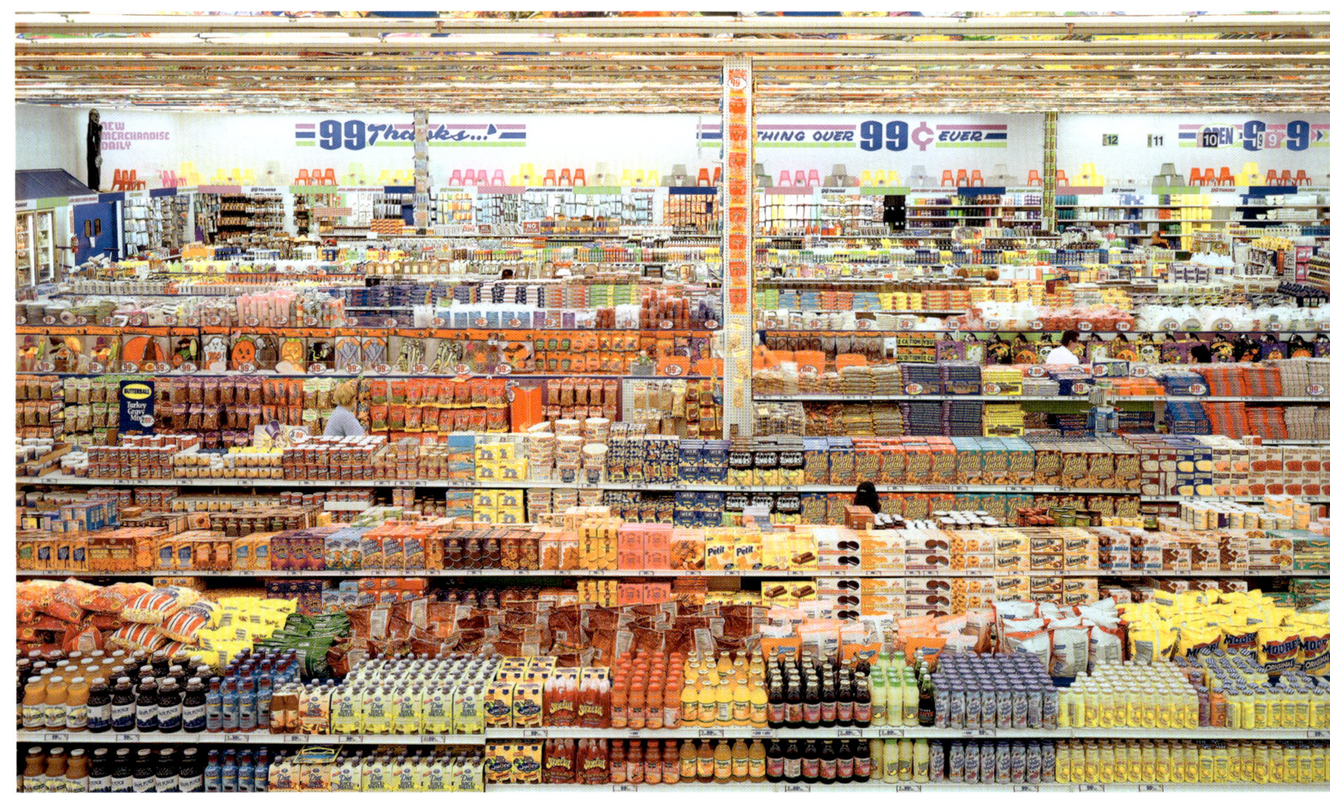

Andreas Gursky, *99 Cent II, Diptychon*, 2001

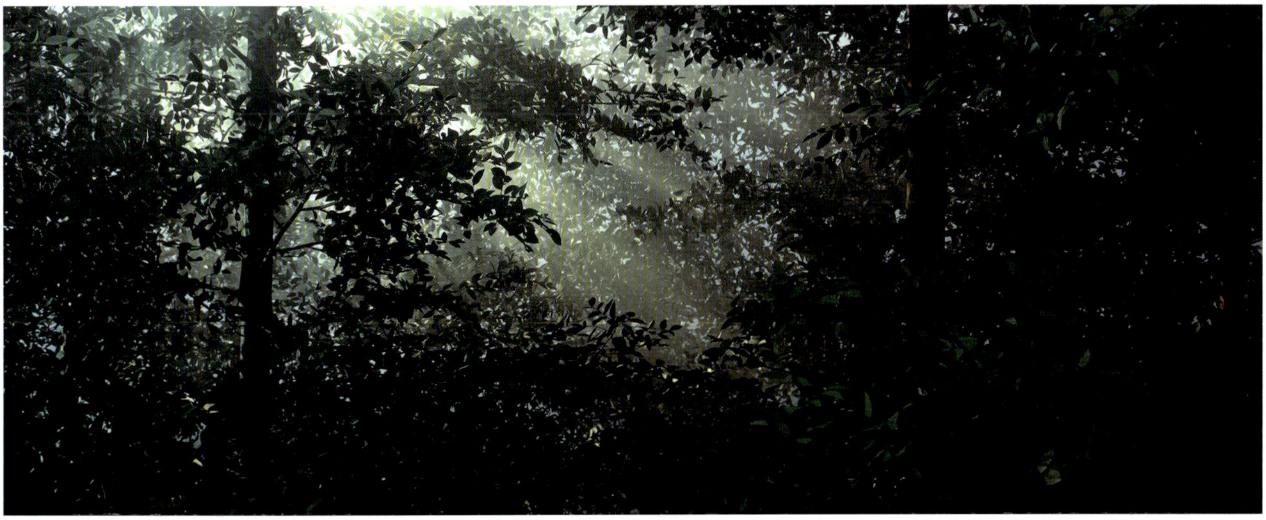

Thomas Demand, *Clearing*, 2003

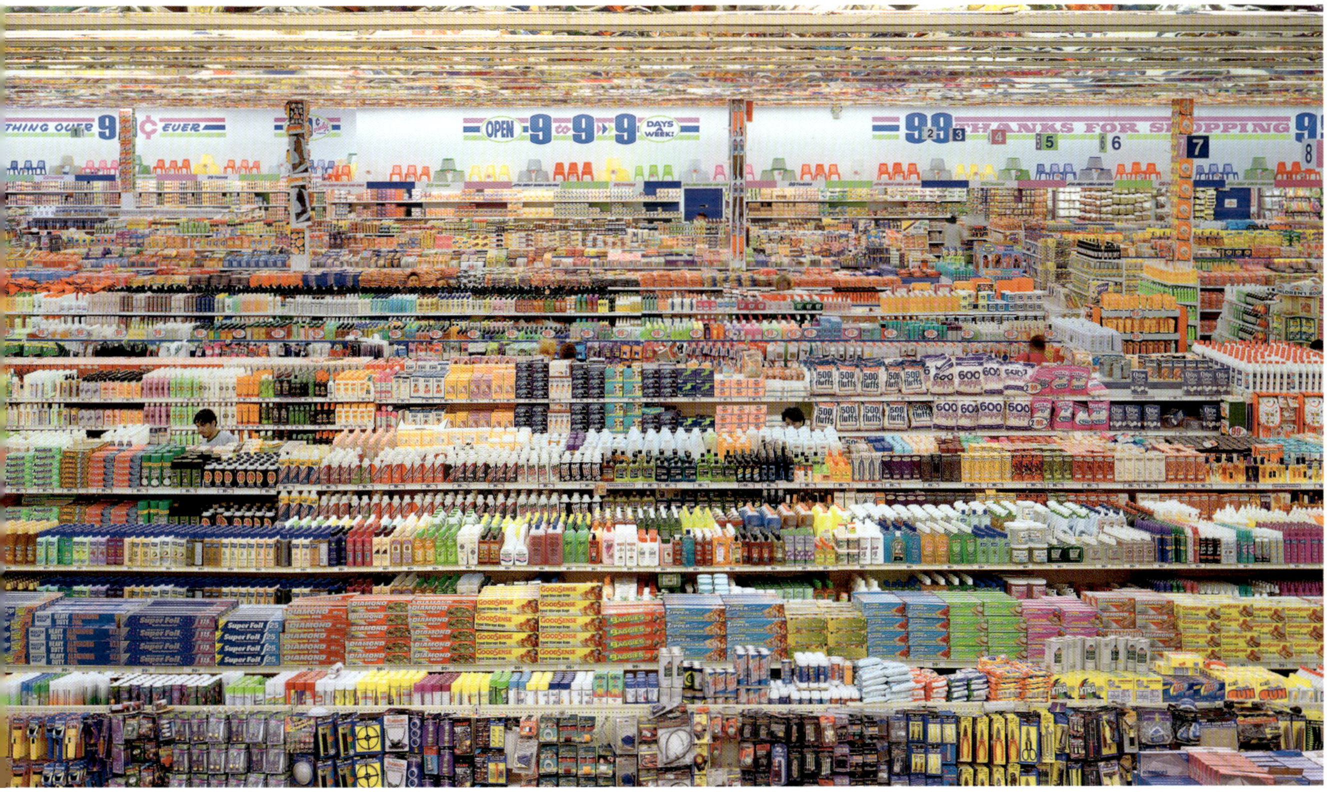

In 2009, I organized an exhibition at FLAG titled *Vague Terrain: Analogues of Place in Contemporary Photography*. As a curator and art historian, I wasn't just interested in photographic constructions of fictive space. In a banal way, all spaces presented through photography are a fiction (and I'm not talking only about pictures of real estate). Even places that photographers most often tend to reconstruct—once-bloody battlefields, childhood bedrooms, colonized vistas—point to just one way in which reality is inevitably a negotiation, with photography as simply one more tool.

I wanted to trace a trajectory from a studio-based, postmodern self-awareness of photography's constructed-ness (James Welling's flaky dough and velvet drape landscapes, James Casebere's flooded rooms) to the deliberate process of scenic construction as social critique. An-My Lê's images of dedicated Vietnam War reenactors in the forests of Virginia gesture to the reprocessing of collective trauma in both private lives and national politics; Barry Frydlender's composite image, integrating hundreds of individually shot and edited scenes, becomes a veritable point-by-point guide to the stage management of the disengagement of a Gaza settlement by the Israeli government for the Western media. Works by Jason Wee and Aleksandra Mir ask, in radically different ways, how we can return to history as a raw material, using elements of the past to create a performative, liberatory future.

At the time of their making, many of the images in the exhibition undertook a serious critique of indexical truth claims, in addition to exploring the ways in which we hold, process, and reimagine cultural imagery. While the latter remains a rich vein of inquiry, the former has been utterly demolished. At a political moment in which photographs are, at best, irrelevant to facts (if not to "alternative facts"), why embrace more fictions? Why, when even astute citizen journalism and raw footage of innocent civilians being murdered by police isn't enough to indict murderers or save lives, should we pay attention to photography's conceptual narratives?

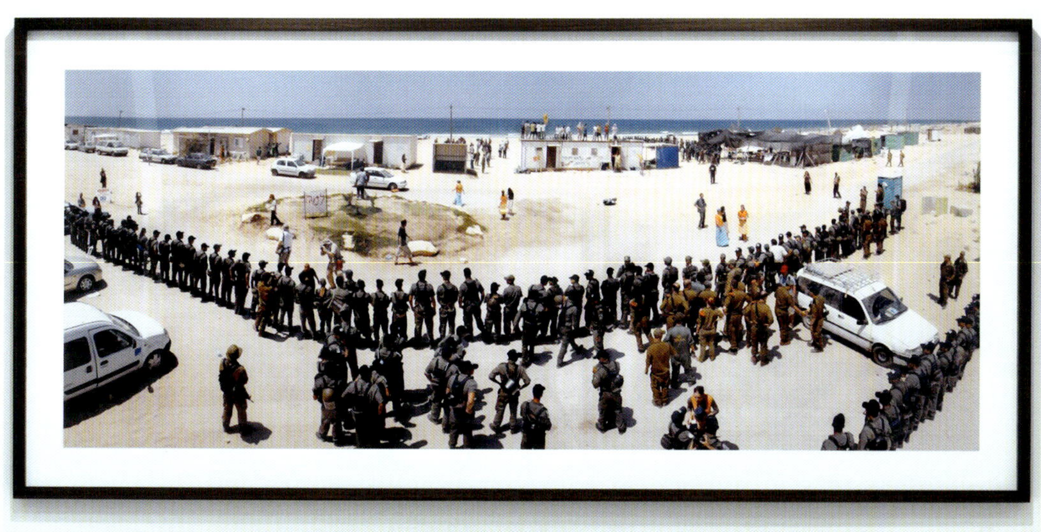

Barry Frydlender, *Shirat Hayam (End of Occupation? Series #2)*, 2005

Given the speed at which today's media images enter (and vanish from) our consciousness, their importance is measured in millions of clicks and views, instead of how long they linger in our collective memory. The works in this exhibition still resonate with me. But nearly a decade later, they seem most remarkable in their slowness, and in their singular ability to parse the power relationships between viewer and viewed, photographer and subject, exposure and redaction, the spectacle and the suppressed.

—Stamatina Gregory

RE-ACCESSION: FOR SALE BY OWNER

June 23–September 1, 2009
Curated by Philae Knight and Amanda Fuhrman

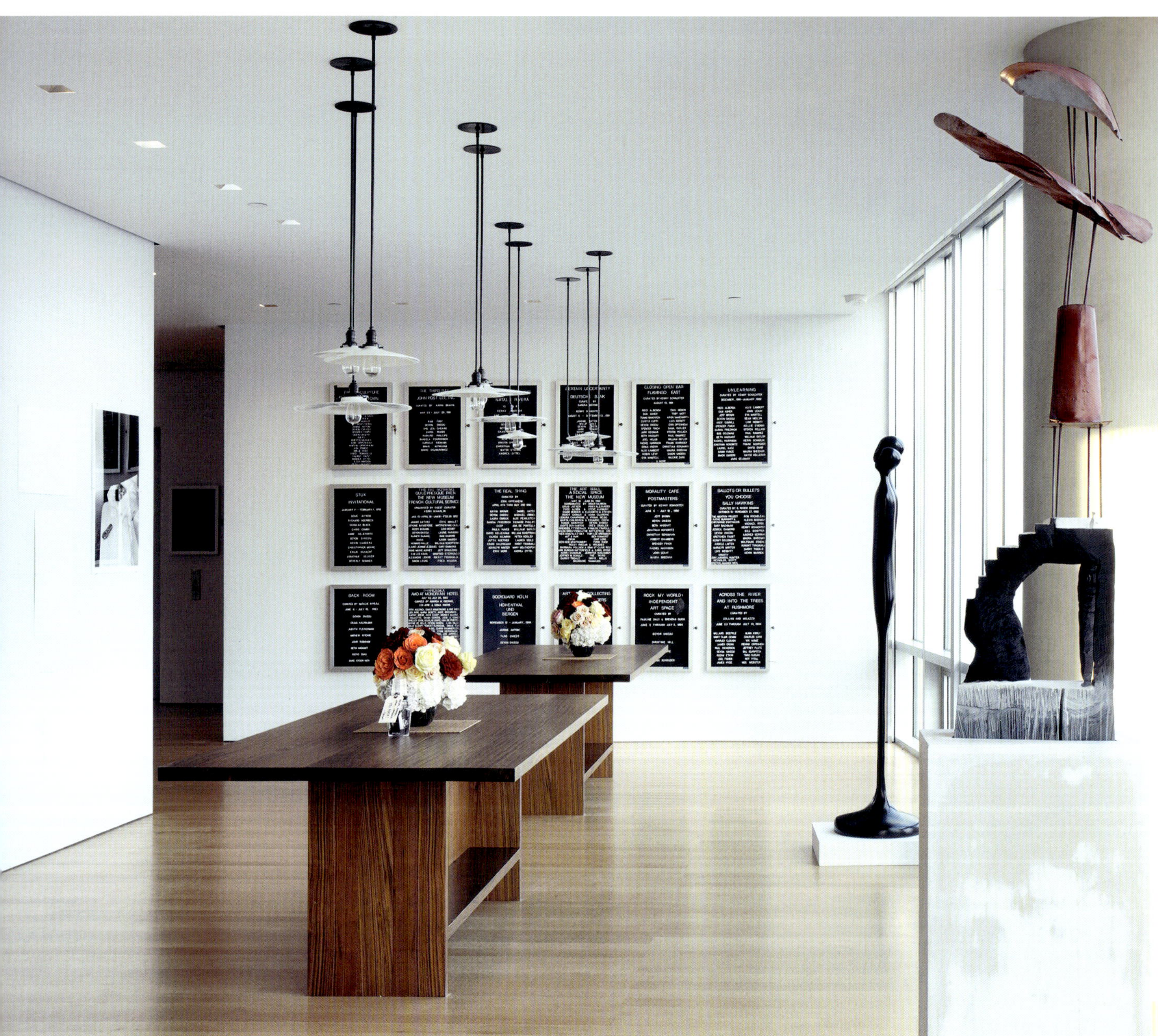

Installation view

At the end of 2008, the world was rippling with the intensity of loss. Fear came in waves with expressions like "subprime mortgage crisis," "Lehman Brothers collapse," "credit default swaps," "AIG bailout," and "Great Recession." The art-world news headlined gallery closures. Along with Glenn and Amanda on those last days in December, we wondered how artists would fare without representation.

At that time, I did not know how deeply foreshadowing this global financial descent was for me personally. I was struck by how differently my family felt over Christmas 2008, our patriarch shattered by the layoffs he had administered. The effects were palpable, and the chatter in my head tic'ed like a banner: "He looks so old, tired. That's what stress'll do to you." On New Year's Eve, there was a blackout. What a timely exclamation point, a poignant ending to the year. And then my dad died on January 1, 2009, his heart giving in to the duress of failure and hopelessness.

Ugh. The universality of humanity confronting loss ranges from devastation and betrayal to longing and nostalgia. Eventually, all that emptiness sort of evaporates. Glenn called in June 2009 with a resolution, an invitation to curate a show for the artists whose galleries had shuttered. Loss began its transformation, both personally and metaphorically.

The word "re-accession" came to me as a divergence from "de-accession." Amanda and I wanted to turn the notion of loss upside-down and deactivate the suffering exposed during a recession. "De-" and "re-" are like each other, opposites that attract; one cannot exist without the other. Artists, financial markets, and even our emotions, all exist on a continuum that cycles around and around. Now that I've passaged through that era of firm, gripping grief, I see that what time exposed for me is a fluidity and flow that I have an awareness of. The angst of hard times dissipates, and sometimes becomes invisible until we are confronted with it again. The rewards are maturity and resilience.

—Philae Knight

Artists
Conrad Bakker
Jan Baracz
David Baskin
Dana Bell
Erik Benson
Rebecca Bird
Sebastiaan Bremmer
Christopher Brooks
Frank Brunner
Mary Carlson
Jennifer Dalton
Jay Davis
Devon Dikeou
Bill Durgin
Yukari Edamitsu
Laura Gilbert
Tim Hailand
David Hardy
EJ Hauser
Claire Jervert
Ted Jessup
Steven and William Ladd
Dietrich Lafferty
Andy Lane
Oliver Michaels
Paul Pagk
Danica Phelps
Anna Pietrzak
Lisa Marie Schilling
Matt Tackett
Conrad Ventur

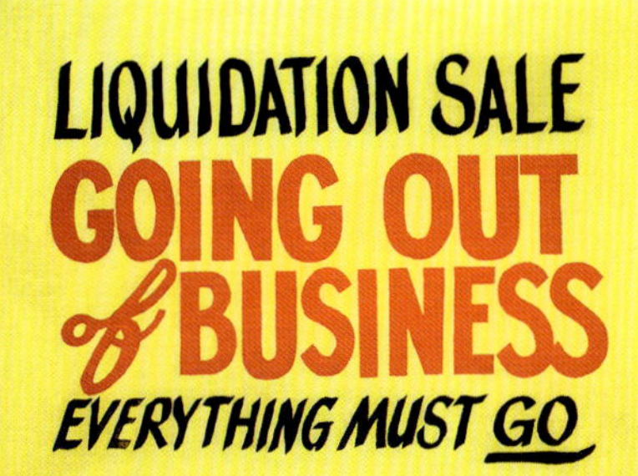

Conrad Bakker, *Sign [GOING OUT OF BUSINESS]*, 2009

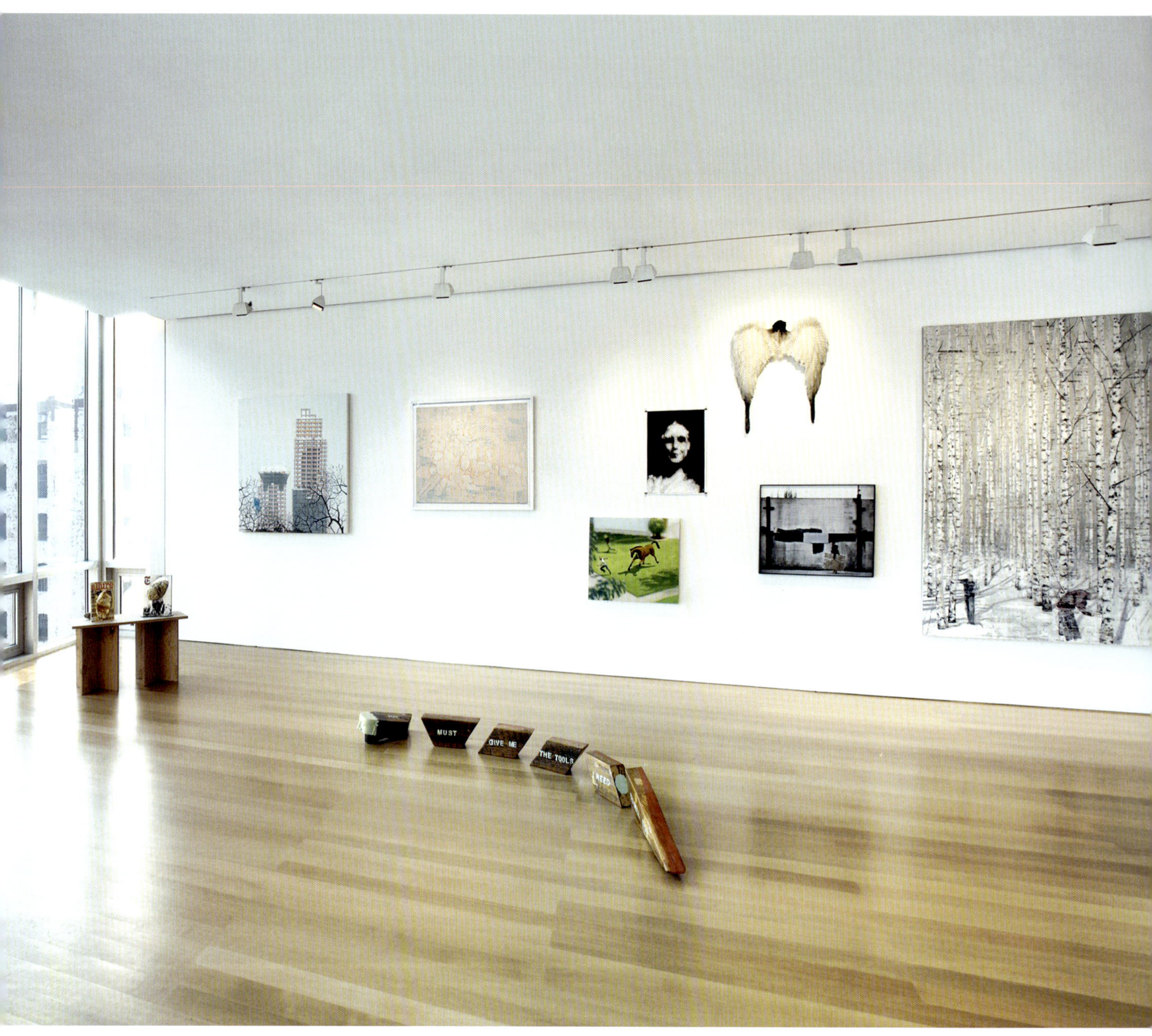

Installation view

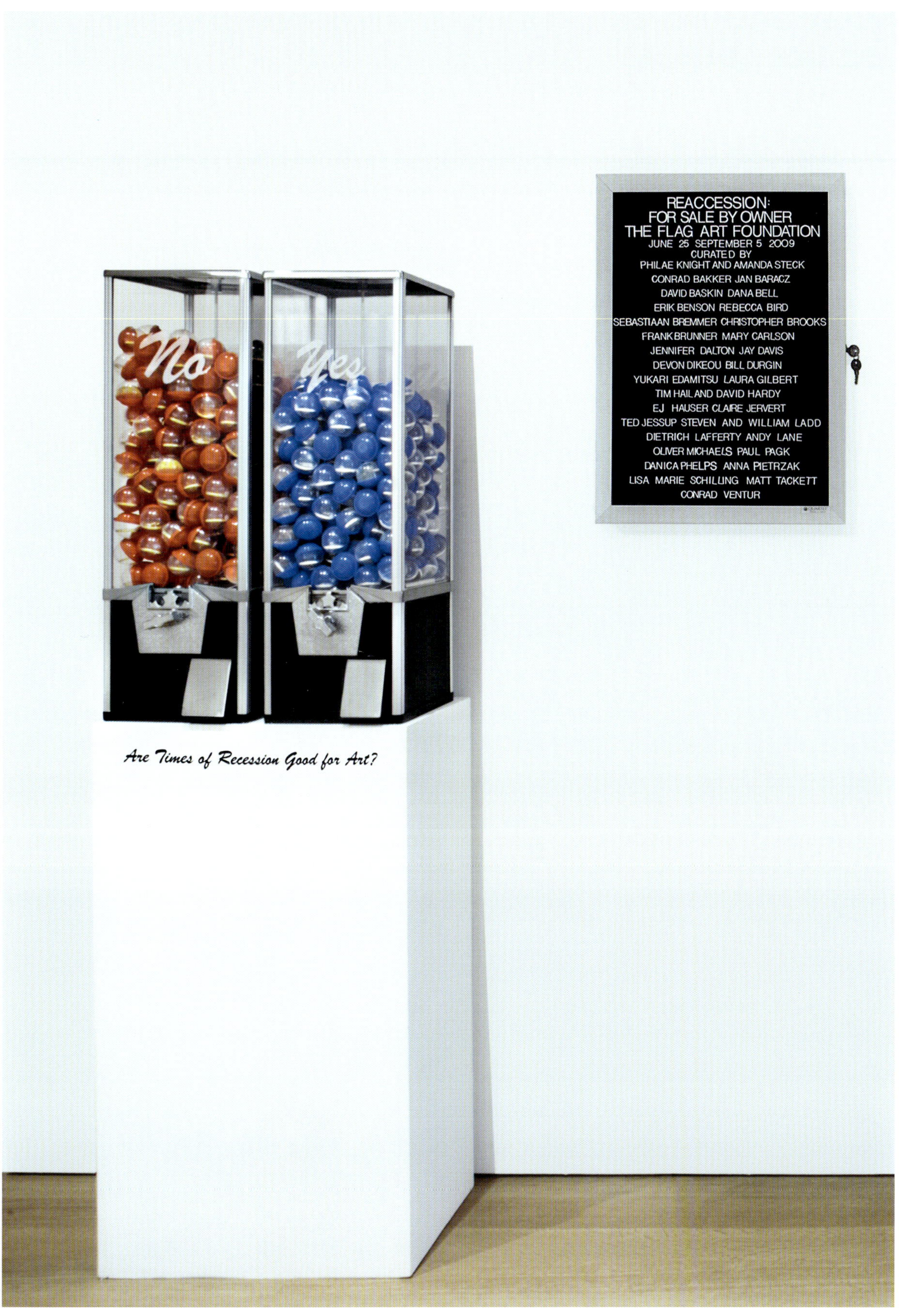

Jennifer Dalton, *Are Times of Recession Good for Art?*, 2008

FLOATING A BOULDER: WORKS BY FELIX GONZALEZ-TORRES AND JIM HODGES

October 1, 2009–January 31, 2010
Curated by Jim Hodges

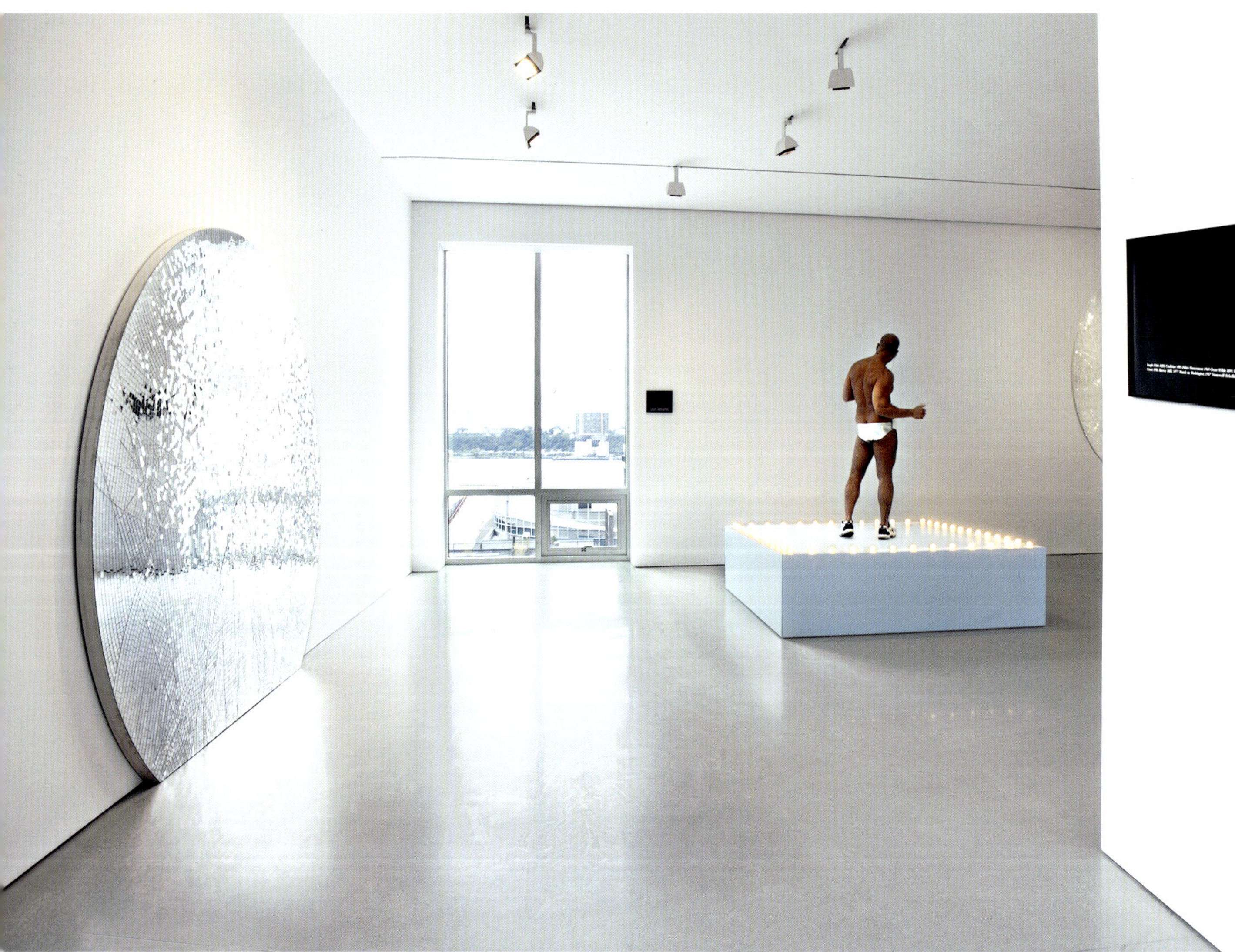

Left to right: Jim Hodges, *Movements (Stage II)*, 2006; Felix Gonzalez-Torres, *"Untitled" (1988)*, 1988; *"Untitled" (Go-Go Dancing Platform)*, 1991; and *"Untitled"*, 1989

Today, Floating a Boulder *comes down. Sometime today a dancer will appear in the gallery, wearing a silver lamé swimsuit, a little too small to cover the beauty of his body, muscled and tattooed. He'll be focused on the sound of music only he can hear. He'll enter the gallery with purpose; he'll ignore anyone who is there. He'll be inside the music, and he'll dance for himself. Everyone else will disappear; he'll become a dream, a physical reality of a thought, of an idea. For a few short minutes he will be the thought. He will contain the energy of meaning. He will move atop a pale blue surface and curve rhythmically in a warm glow of light. He will see the whiteness of the walls, hints of reflection glistening from pixeled mirrors through half-open eyes. He'll dance and the music will lift him into the air; he will move beyond the platform; he will be a projection of the artist's imagination, dancing there in that space of blue becoming the sky, traveling beyond the walls and windows, merged music and movement dissolving over the horizon; and then he will vanish, leave as he came, silently, self-contained, eyes fixed on his destination, without a sound. The platform will stand empty, with the aura of the dancer haloed in the space he had filled.*

Connecting these remarks to the closing lines above from my exhibition catalogue essay, "What Was," is a way of attempting to make contact with a spirit that was generated during the many months leading up to the exhibition *Floating a Boulder*—to occupy that time and to share a vision with you, and in so doing set the stage for the words that follow. I want to conjure the room and the experience from the inside and somehow magically transport us there, spirit us away. Believing as I do that once this spell is cast and we are traveling together, the journey back in time will illuminate itself and my words will align into the story that wants to be told—the story that today glistens in fragments across the surface of memory that I turn to in order to divine the narration. I want to dip into that well of memories and re-enliven, re-remember the time, to share these reflections that are glimpsed on the surface and to dive under them to the heart of something.

It was probably a year before *Floating a Boulder* opened at FLAG that Glenn invited me to take on the challenge of curating an exhibition of work by Felix Gonzalez-Torres and myself. It was such an extraordinary offer and one I had never anticipated receiving. He took me by surprise, and in my surprised haze I immediately said yes, without even thinking about what it would mean. I count that reflexive response as a blessing, since the experience of working so closely with Glenn and

Stephanie and all the others who joined forces to realize what we made was one of those life-changing events that happen before we know what's going on, synching with life as we are dizzily regaining our footing and finding bearings. Tempos and rhythms are synchronized to produce and create. Negotiating numerous participants and orchestrating all of the materials to put on a show like *Floating a Boulder* was a major effort by all who took part in it, and the initial conversations and meetings I had with Glenn revealed a commitment and willingness that had no limits. Nothing that I proposed was rejected or not considered. Not once did I hear or sense Glenn doubting or hesitating. He was right there by my side every step of the way, and when we ran into roadblocks and dead ends, he never stopped believing and with fierce will did all he could to see that our vision would be realized fully.

Such dedication and belief are basic requirements when attempting to realize visions. Manifesting dreams into physical experiences that can be shared is an artist's job and duty. One is in service to the vision, and once committed to it, all rational limitations fall away and creative forces merge to power the mechanics that generate the art reality.

FLAG is a realized vision in the process of becoming. Each time Glenn invites someone to use the space to conjure an art reality, the process is reinitiated to an end and everyone benefits. Giving is embedded in the nature of creation. Generosity surges through the process like blood through veins, as necessary and serious and with stakes as high as life and death. Fearlessness and doubt go hand in hand to energize the terrain that one occupies along the way. All this effort, belief, commitment, rigor, and sweat still don't guarantee success. Failure lurks in the shadows always. It plays a part in the drama of making and occasionally even takes the starring role. Failing happens inside success, and here lessons are learned and gathered up and saved for the next adventure. One builds an archive internally that one travels with. Our histories become the materials that we make from. The blessing of a long life is the wealth of one's rich history that gets dragged along the way—treasure chests of experiences that radiate with usefulness, potential, and meaning.

For ten years, FLAG has been at the service of imaginations. For ten years, Glenn and Stephanie have joined forces with a spectrum of thinkers and dreamers to generate questions for all of us to experience and respond to. The spirit of giving lives in the body of creation, and that spirit is nourished and offered to all who cross the threshold of FLAG.

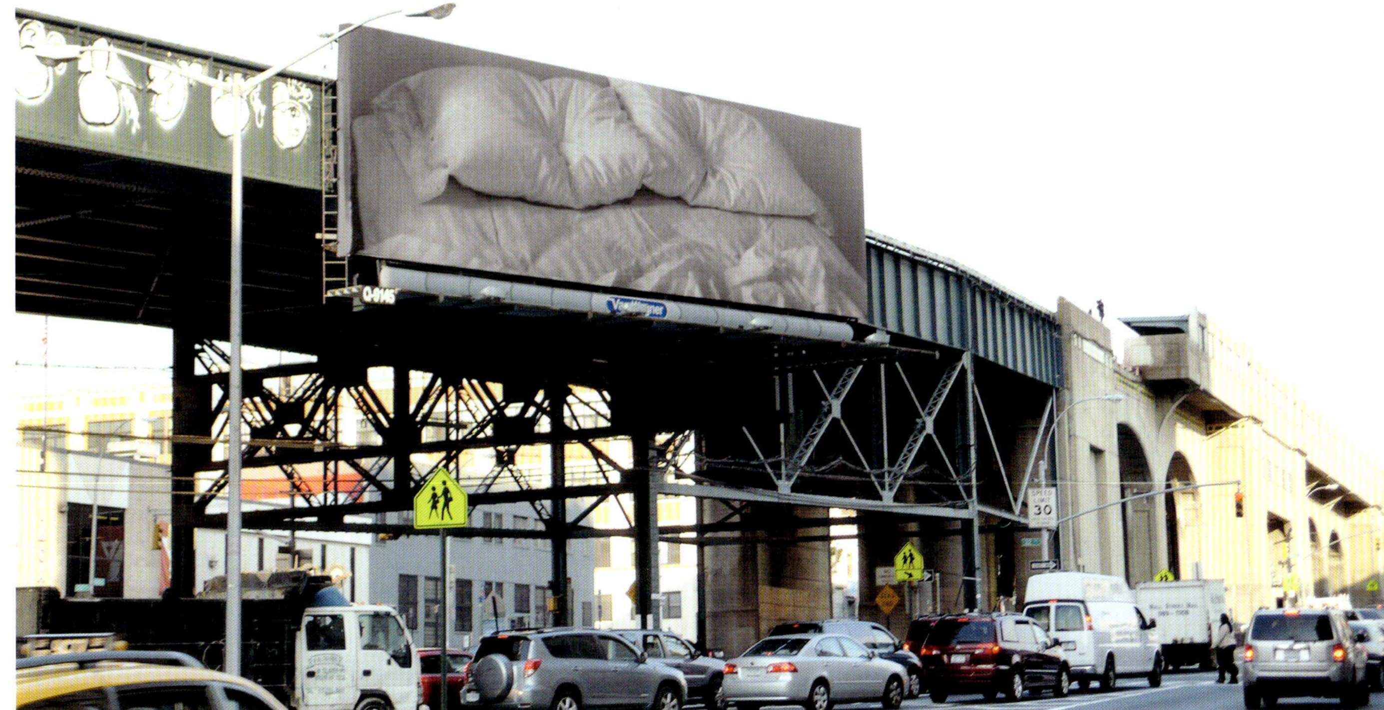

Felix Gonzalez-Torres, *"Untitled"*, 1991

Artists invent and manifest form to carry intention to share with others. In the process, an artist can disappear and from a place of invisibility generate major life-changing experiences. The hiding places allow one to vanish while the show happens all around, building beyond the limits of physical space.

Pulling Glenn from his place in the wings, I want to shine a light on him, to shower him with thanks for introducing his dream to us and inviting us to join him to make FLAG as it is becoming. The heart of a place is constructed from the love of its inventor. Without it, an idea will never come to life, or won't have a future. The effort to maintain intention over time is not something that just happens. It takes continual reevaluation and adjusting; like a bird in flight, every slight shift of air must be responded to in order to keep soaring. To reach great heights, thousands of adjustments and constant effort are required. A great view is worth all that it takes to get there.

Thank you, Glenn, for ten years of believing and loving. For ten years of curiosity and fearlessness. For ten years of friendship and community. Thank you for ten years of proof that promises another ten years to come. Here we are in this in-between place with so much magic behind us. What a joy to turn toward the openness of what's still to come and imagine the wonder that awaits...

Just imagine it!

—Jim Hodges

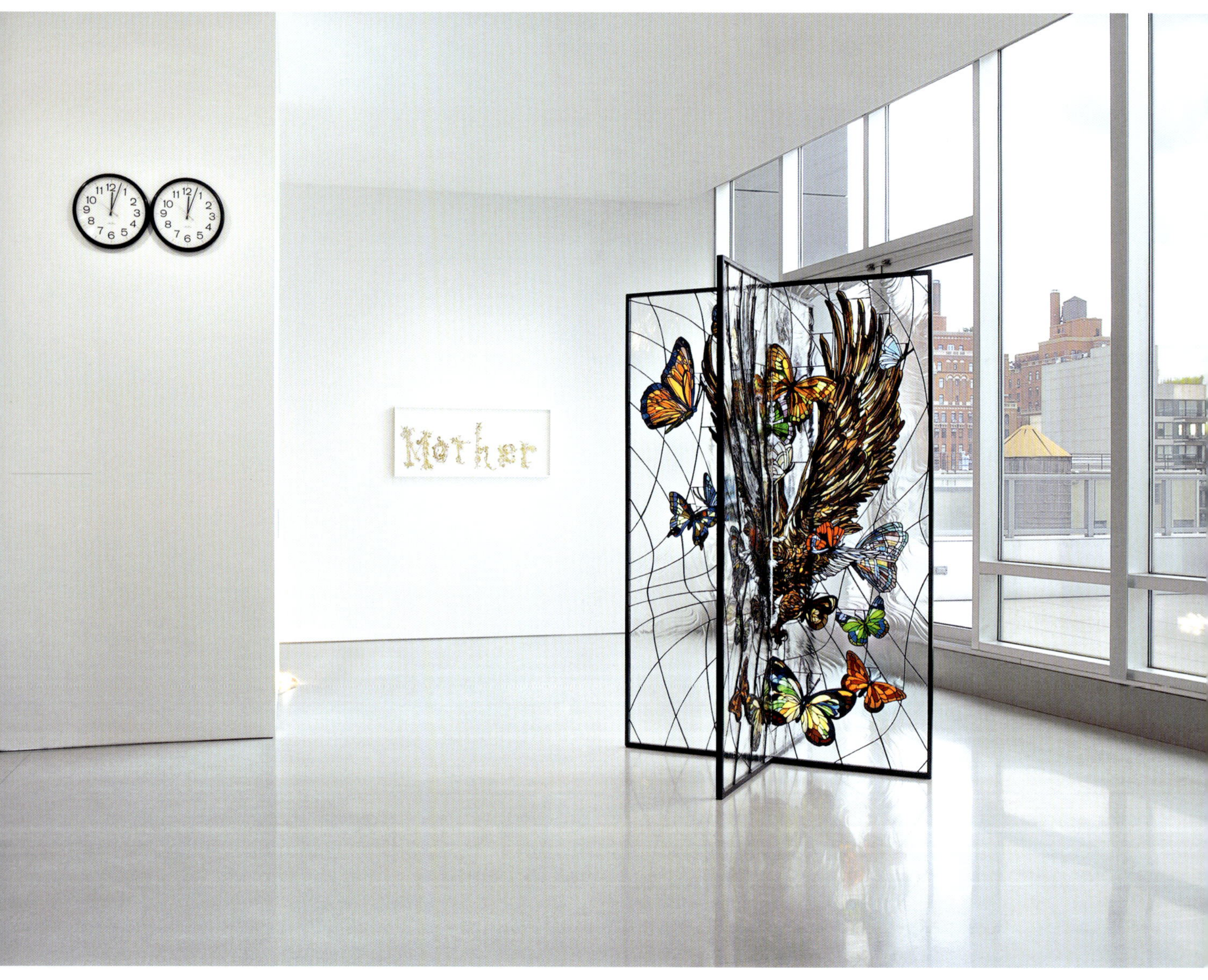

Left to right: Felix Gonzalez-Torres, *"Untitled" (Perfect Lovers)*, 1987–90; Jim Hodges, *Monument*, 2007; and *When I Believed, What I Believed*, 2008

Opposite, background: Jim Hodges, *In Blue*, 1996; foreground: Felix Gonzalez-Torres, *"Untitled" (We Don't Remember)*, 1991

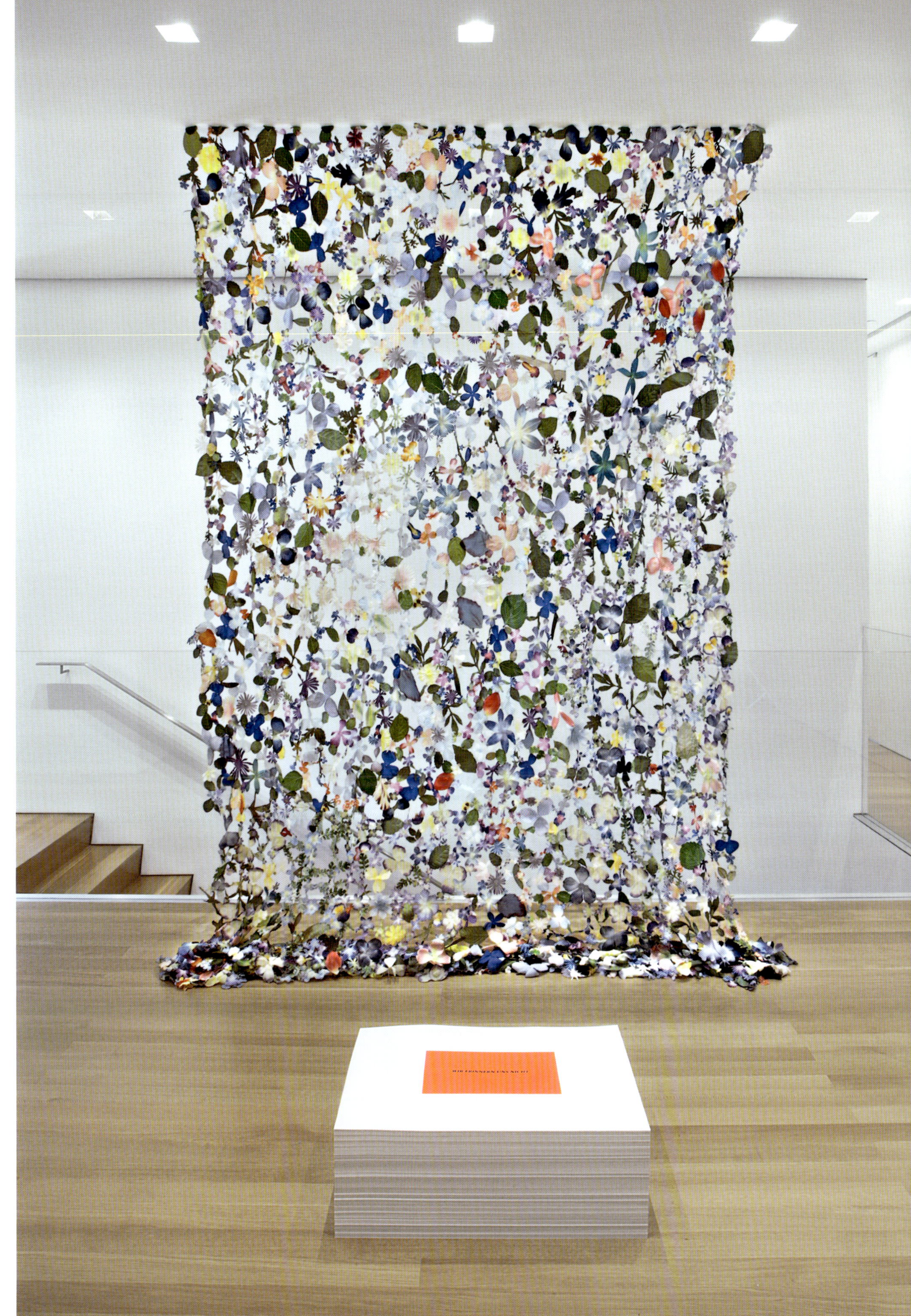
WIR ERINNERN UNS NICHT

SIZE DOES MATTER

February 19–May 27, 2010
Curated by Shaquille O'Neal

Artists
Conrad Bakker
Delia Brown
Don Brown
Maurizio Cattelan
Chuck Close
Richard Dupont
Joe Fig
Tom Friedman
Franz Gertsch
Andreas Gursky
Tim Hawkinson
Brian Jungen
Anselm Kiefer
Jeff Koons
Dr. Lakra
Inez van Lamsweerde
Charles LeDray
Peter Max
Cathy de Monchaux
Ron Mueck
Juan Muñoz
Richard Patterson
Evan Penny
Richard Pettibone
Elizabeth Peyton
Paul Pfeiffer
Richard Phillips
Charles Ray
James Rieck
Ugo Rondinone
Thomas Ruff
Cindy Sherman
Yinka Shonibare MBE
Ken Solomon
Tomoaki Suzuki
Robert Therrien
Jim Torok
Mark Wagner
Corban Walker
Willard Wigan
Kehinde Wiley
Fred Wilson
Ivan Witenstein
Lisa Yuskavage

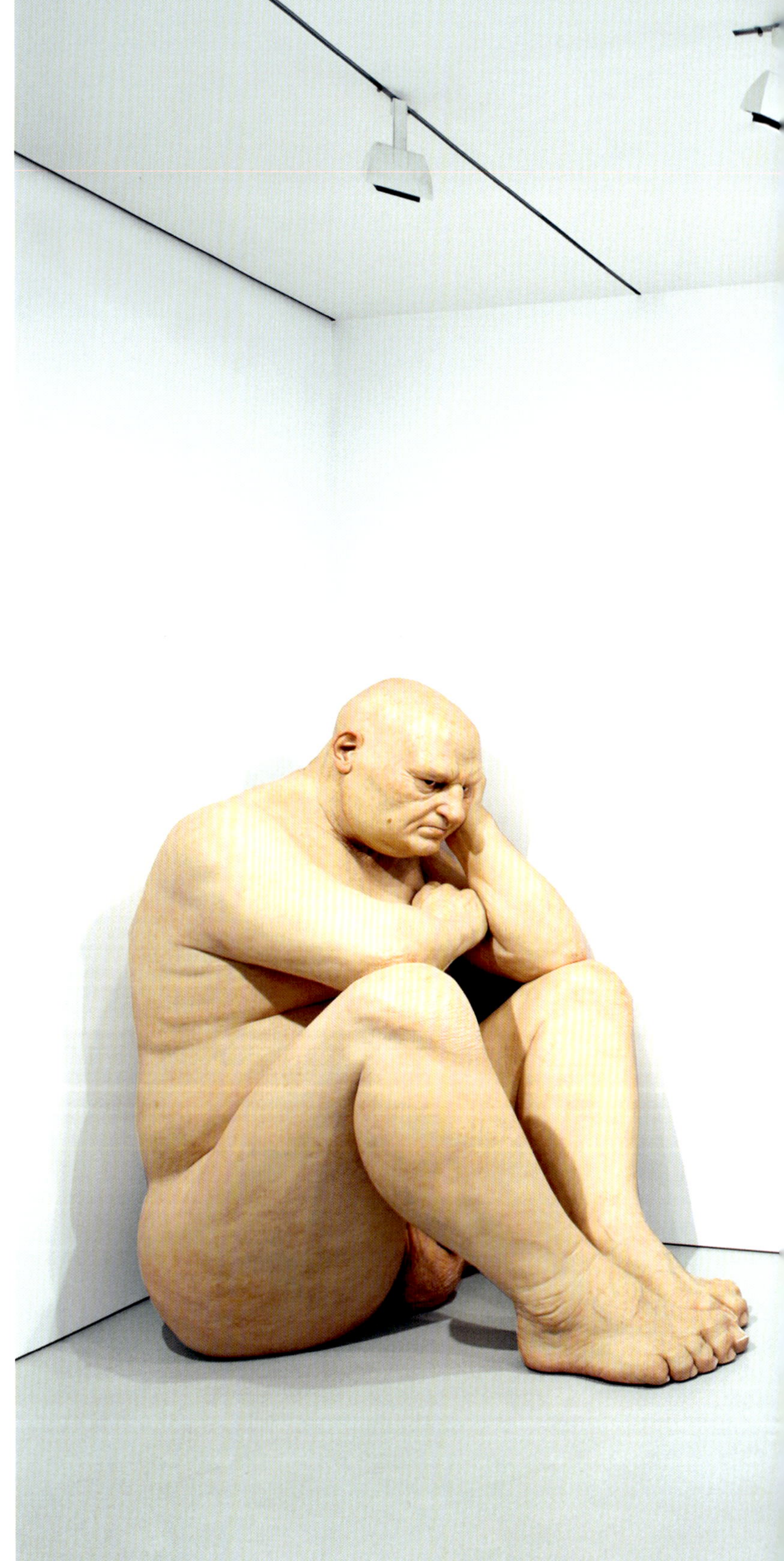

Left to right: Ron Mueck, *Big Man*, 2000; Richard Patterson, *Cheerleader*, 2001

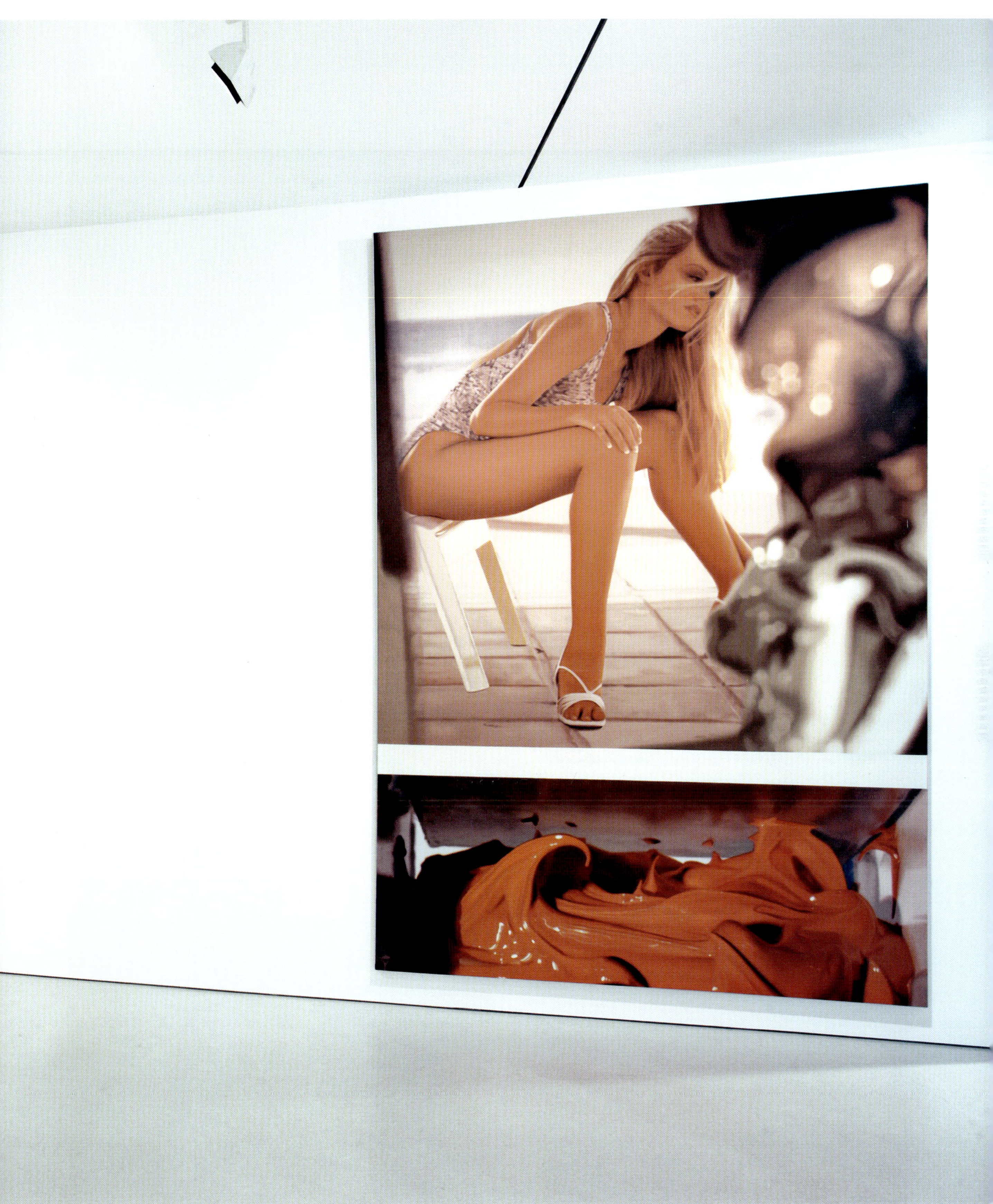

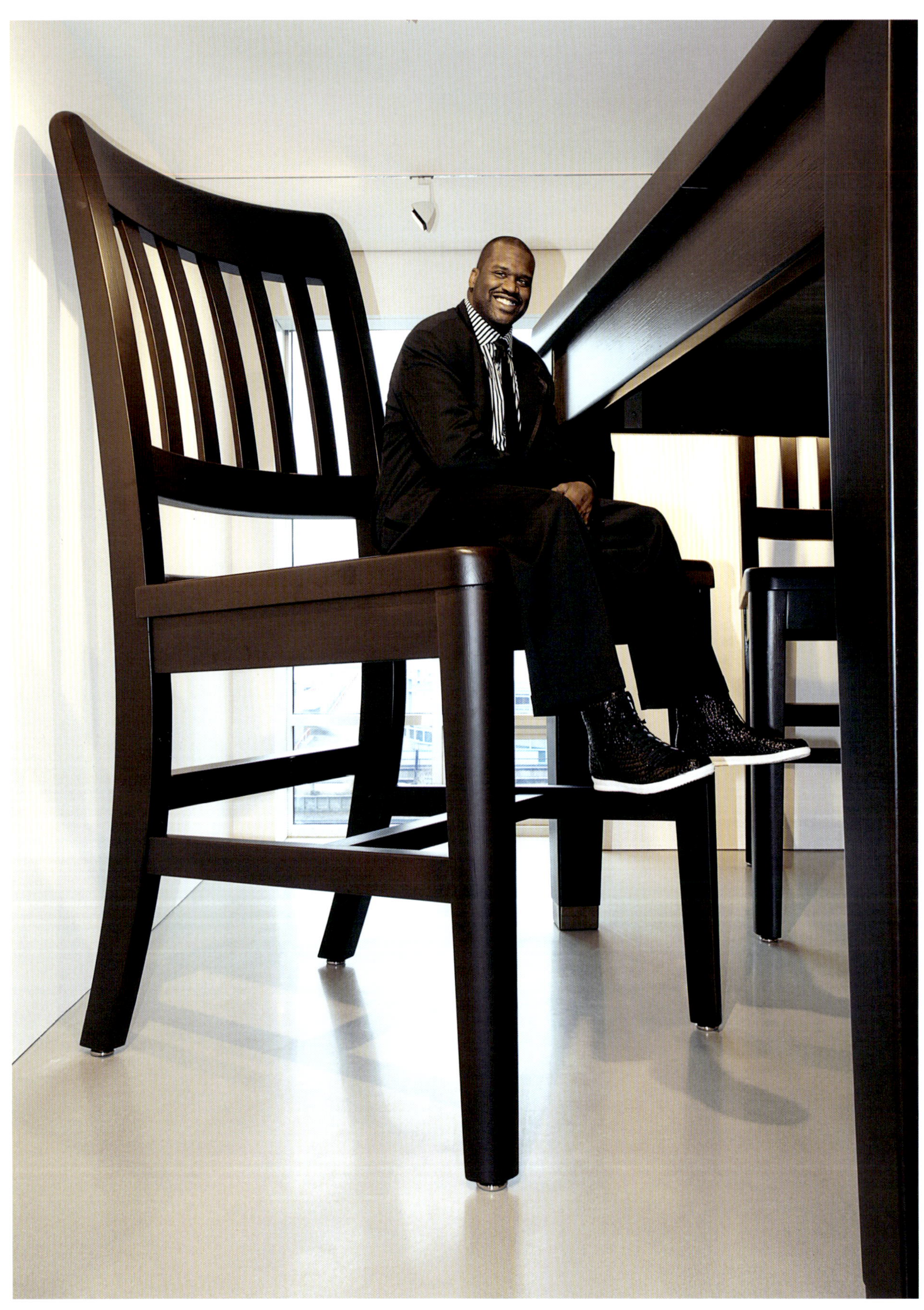

Shaquille O'Neal with Robert Therrien's *Untitled (Table and Six Chairs)*, 2003

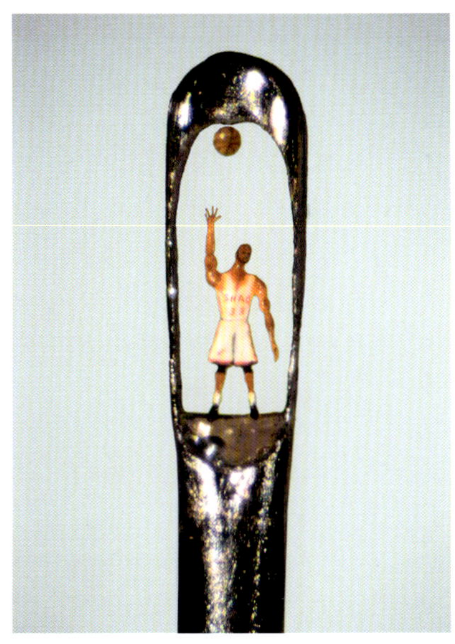

Willard Wigan, *Micro Shaq*, 2010

As someone who is seven feet tall, my life revolves around my relationship to size and the reactions from people that I experience both on and off the court. Sometimes I get a laugh out of standing in the middle of a busy sidewalk, just to see how people will respond to me. With that in mind, *SIZE DOES MATTER* was an opportunity to explore my own fascination with scale and to show people that I love art.

The biggest and the smallest works in the show captivated me the most. When people look at Ron Mueck's *Big Man* (2000), they may think, "big miserable man," "man who's thinking," or "big man, what are you looking at?" I like this piece because it makes me feel small; I'm 7′1″, 350 pounds, and this guy is 12′ and 700 pounds. I also included Robert Therrien's massive table and chairs (*Untitled [Table and Six Chairs]*, 2003) to shock people, since the work barely fit in the space. When I first saw Willard Wigan's work, he told me how he made it, and I thought, "There's no way he could do that!" If you think about how small his work is, that it's literally in the eye of a needle—well, that's art right there. When something is so big or so small, it becomes beautiful in a way that inspires people to take a second look.

Ultimately, *SIZE DOES MATTER* was meant to reimagine perceptions of scale through humor, surprise, and the endless creativity of the artists I included. I enjoy looking at art that allows my imagination to fill in the blanks. Some of the works in the show reminded me of experiences I've had while in the middle of a game, about to make a shot. Others just made me think of how it feels to be big and beautiful out in public. Really everything we do in our life is art.

—Shaquille O'Neal

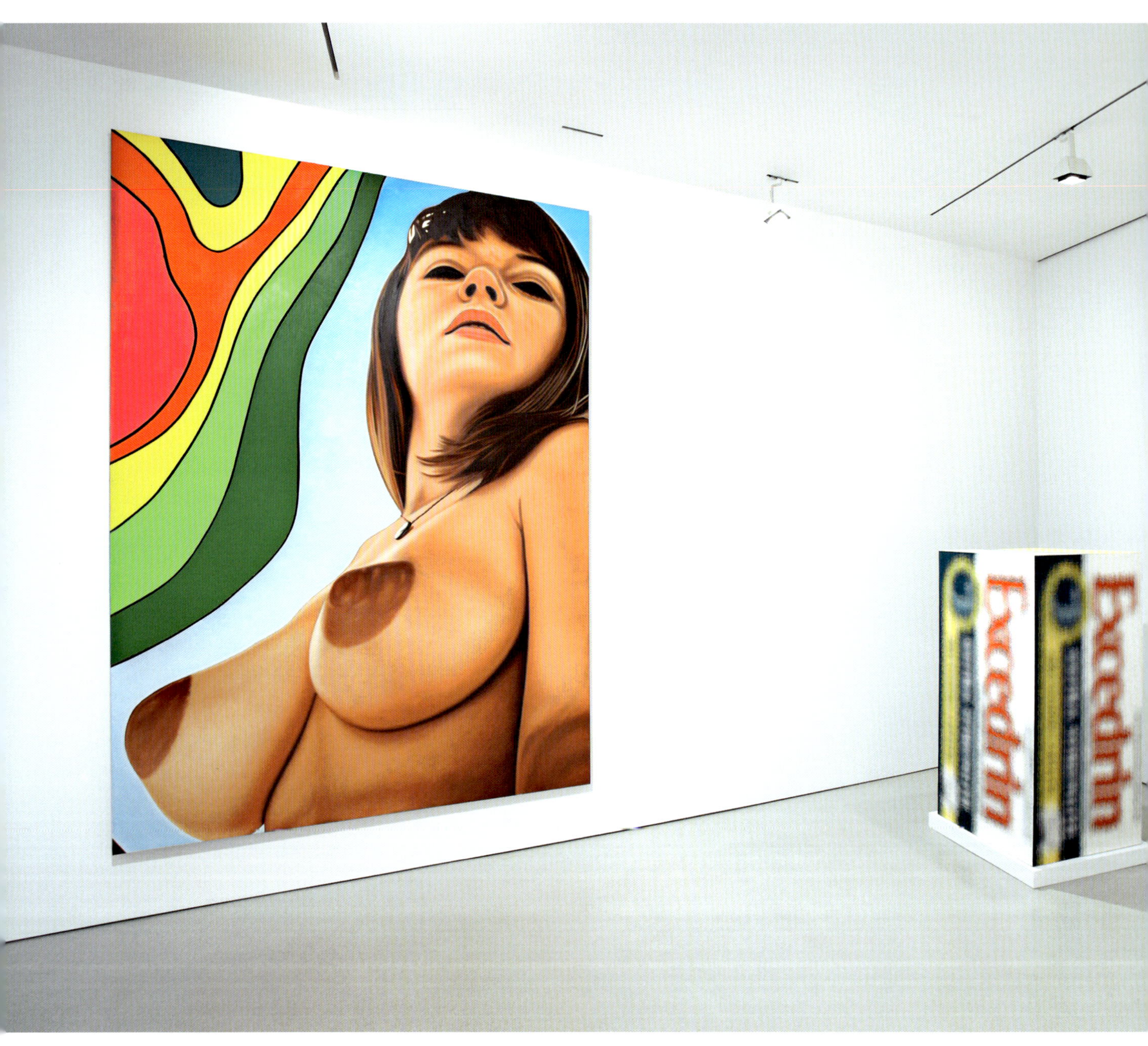

Left to right: Richard Phillips, *Michelle Angelo*, 2010; Tom Friedman, *largeexcedrinbox*, 2006

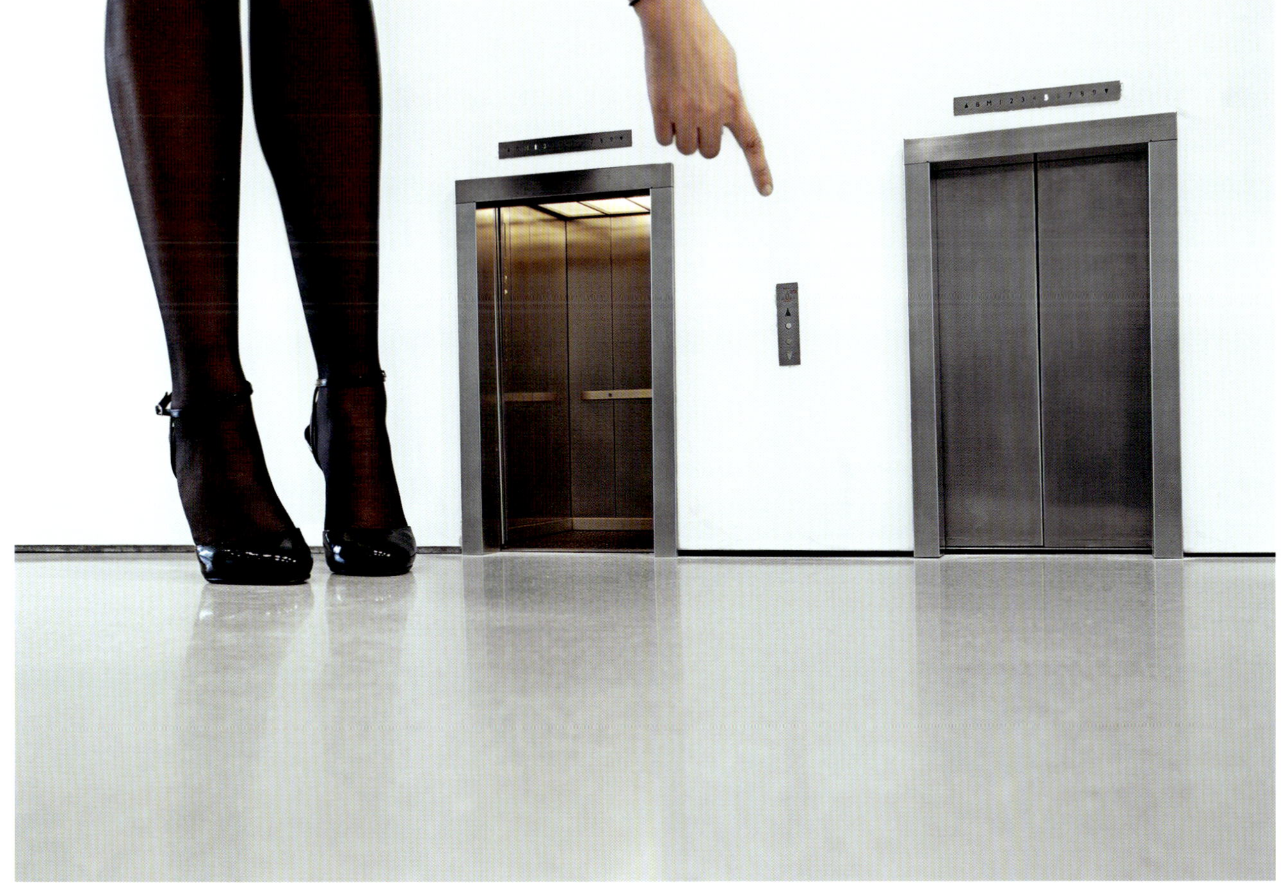

Maurizio Cattelan, *Untitled*, 2001

SUMMER @ THE FLAG ART FOUNDATION

June 30–September 10, 2010

Artists
Noriko Ambe
Jennifer Dalton
Robert Lazzarini
Magnum Photos

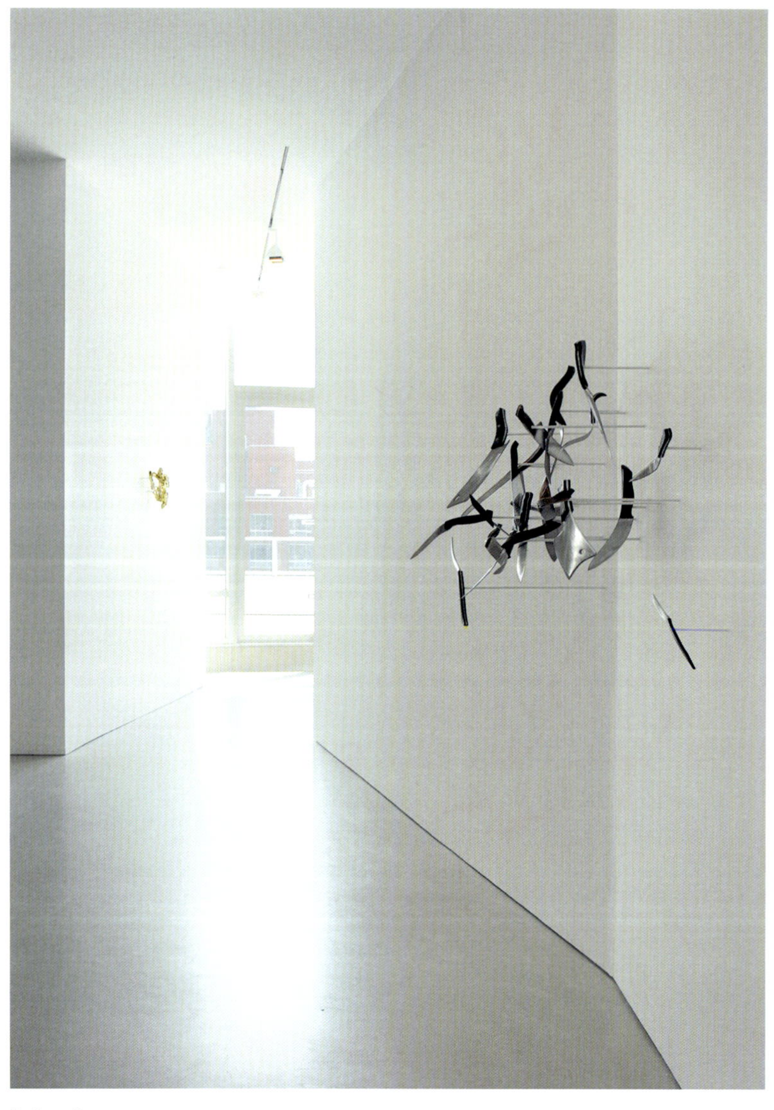

Robert Lazzarini, *Knives*, 2008

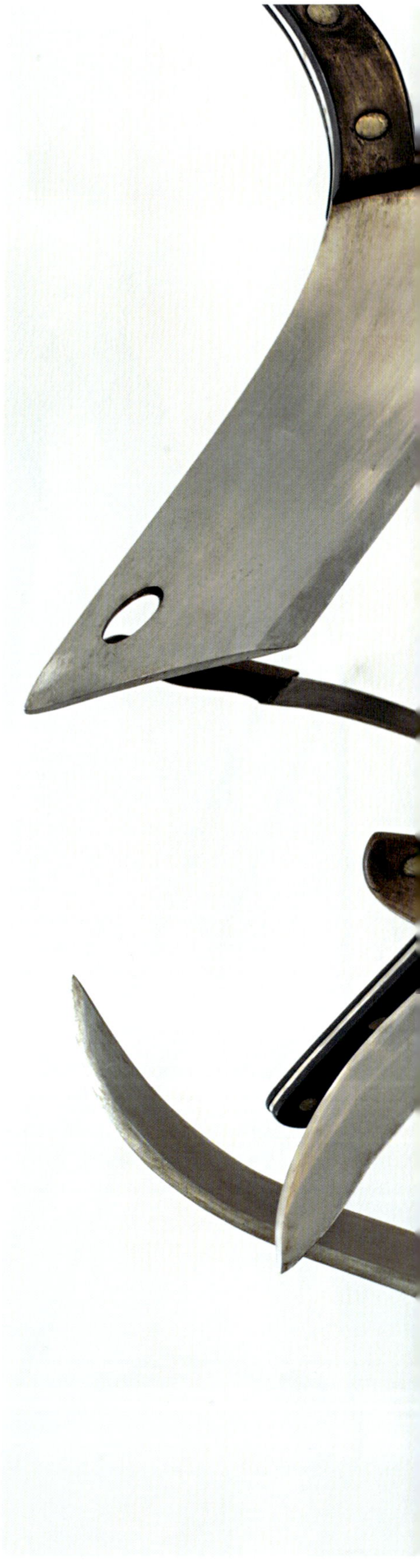

Detail, Robert Lazzarini, *Knives*, 2008

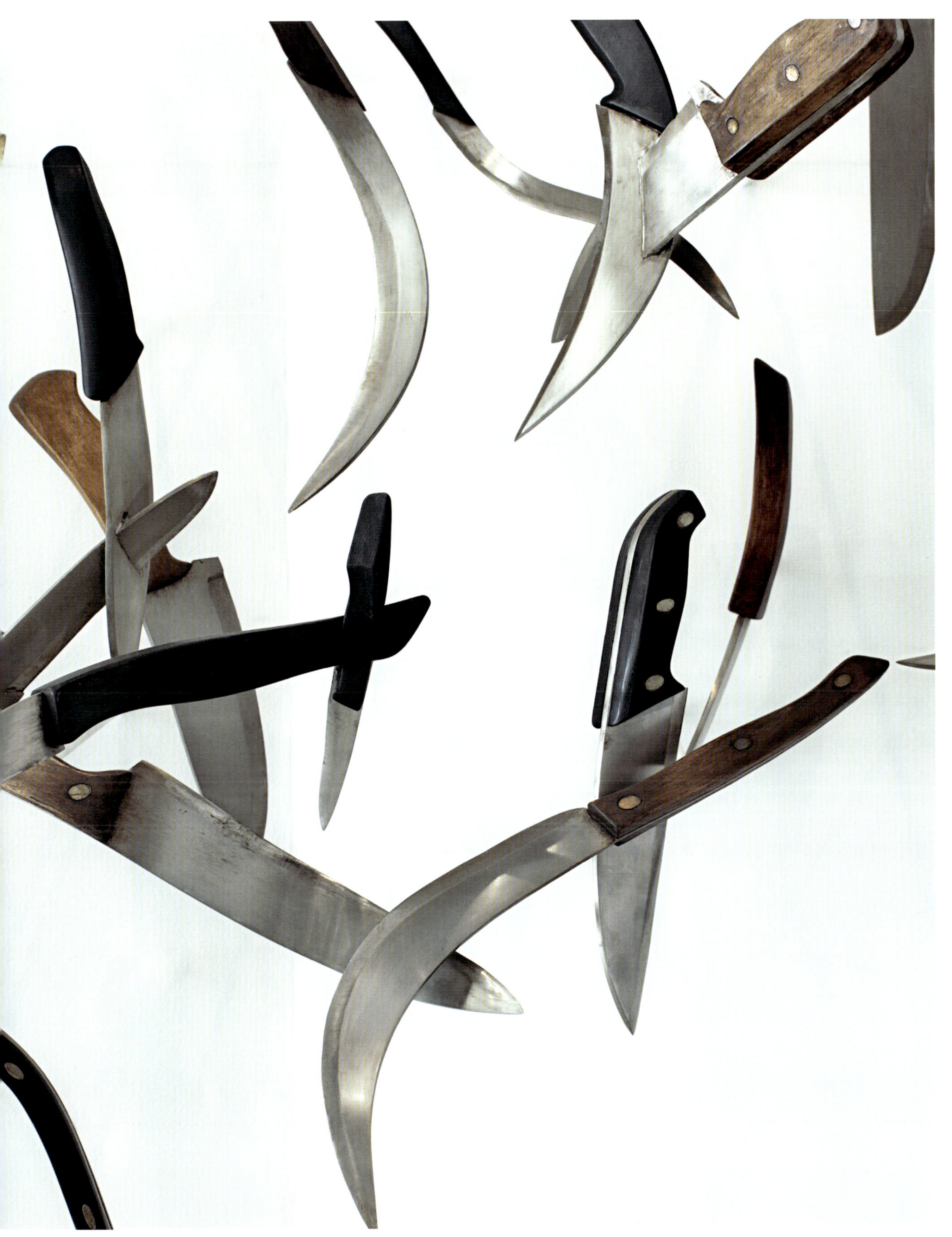

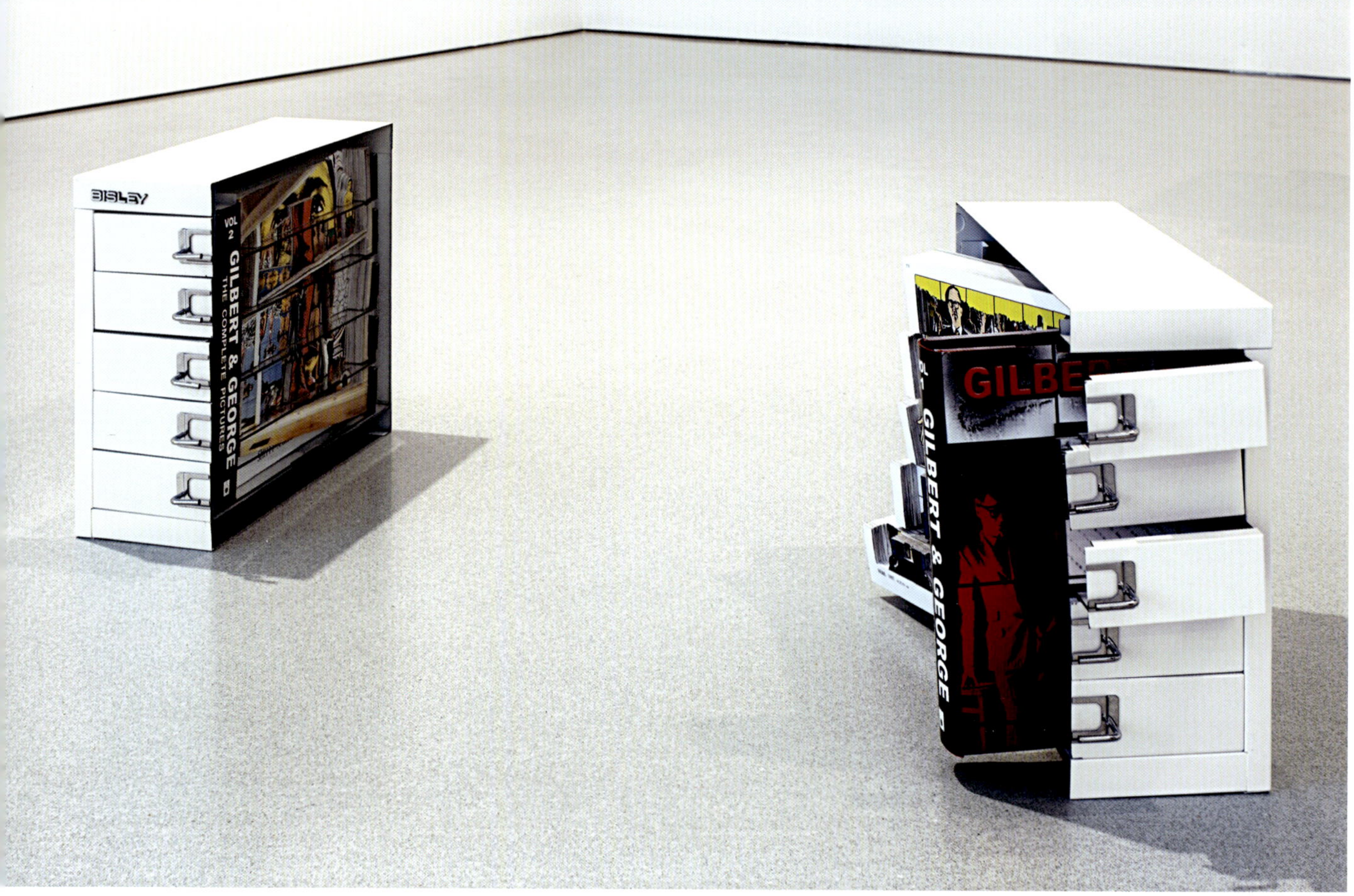

Noriko Ambe, *Double Sides: Gilbert & George*, 2010

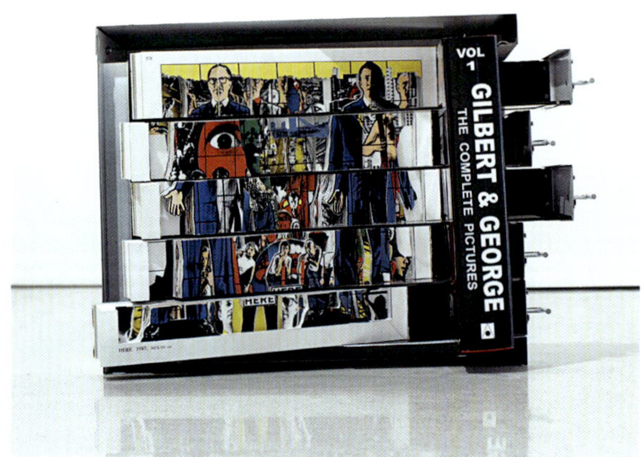

Detail, Noriko Ambe, *Double Sides: Gilbert & George*, 2010

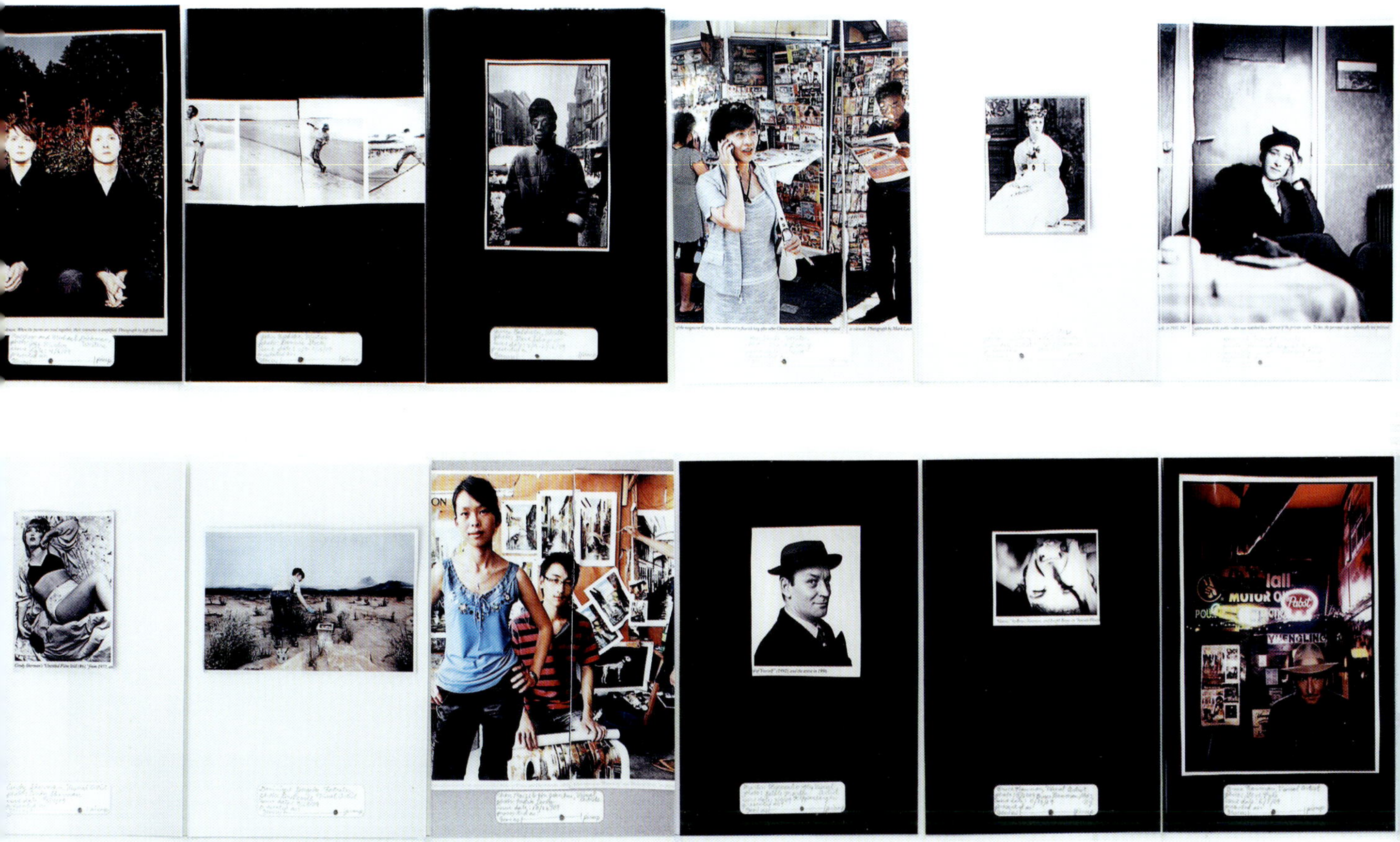

Detail, Jennifer Dalton, *What Does an Artist Look Like? (Every image of an artist to appear in the New Yorker magazine 1999–2001)*, 2002

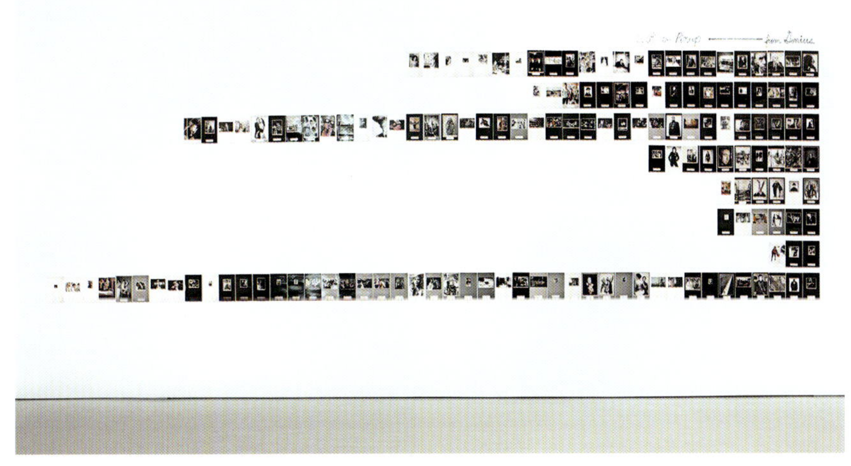

Jennifer Dalton, *What Does an Artist Look Like? (Every image of an artist to appear in the New Yorker magazine 1999–2001)*, 2002

CARY KWOK: OBSESSION

November 18, 2010–January 29, 2011
Curated by Prabal Gurung

Art has always been a core part of my brand; it's thought-provoking and intriguing, and I often draw inspiration from a variety of different artworks when designing a collection. Glenn and Amanda are longtime friends, and in 2009, I showcased my first collection at FLAG. Not only is the space beautiful, but I loved being able to present the collection in a venue that celebrates such incredible art, and in the midst of New York's greatest galleries.

I was later asked to curate an exhibition of Cary Kwok's meticulous ballpoint-pen drawings and saw that task as an extension of how I style and edit a collection. His work celebrates so many of the same notions and brand ideals that we do: women, colour, depth, detail, sensuality—the list goes on.

As a fashion designer, I create a breadth of pieces—so much work goes into each and every garment—but ultimately, it's important to tell a cohesive story that fits into a larger narrative. Art creates challenging and layered conversations, addressing society in such a thoughtful way, and my role as a designer is to help translate and manifest this dialogue into something tangible. For me, it's always a creative and exploratory curation, regardless of the final product, whether art or fashion.

—Prabal Gurung

Opposite: Installation view

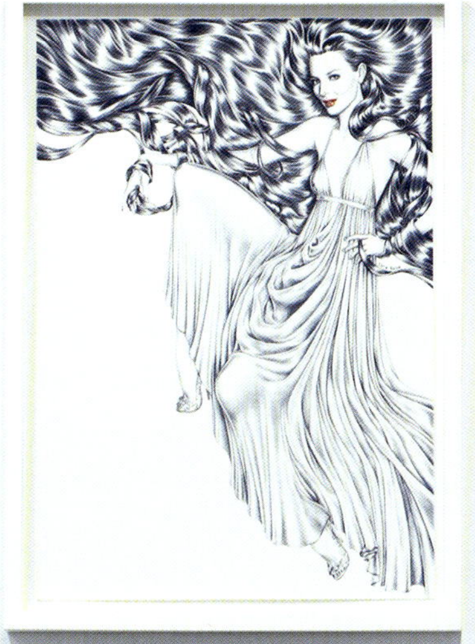

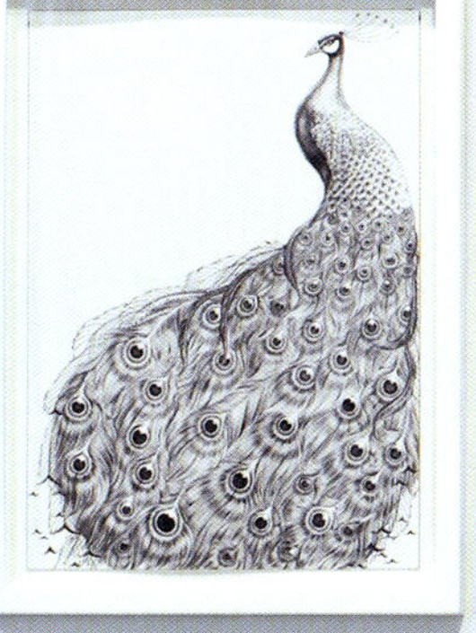

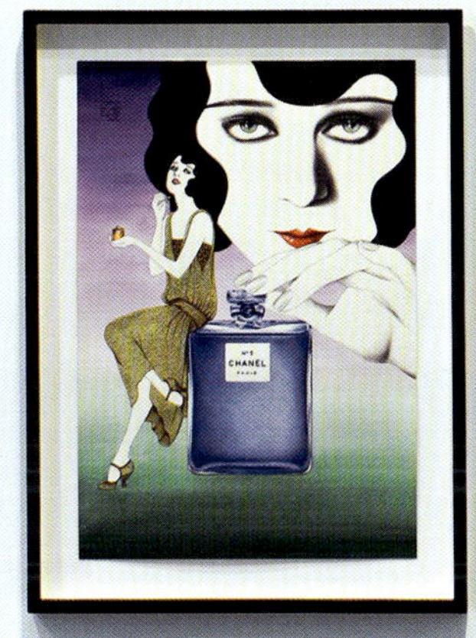
CHANEL

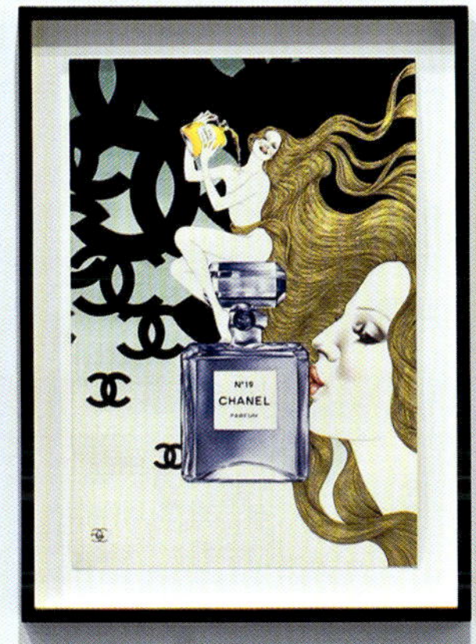
N°19
CHANEL
PARFUM

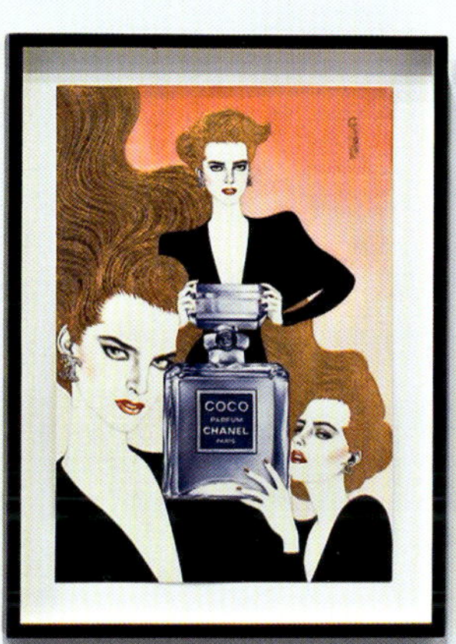
COCO
PARFUM
CHANEL

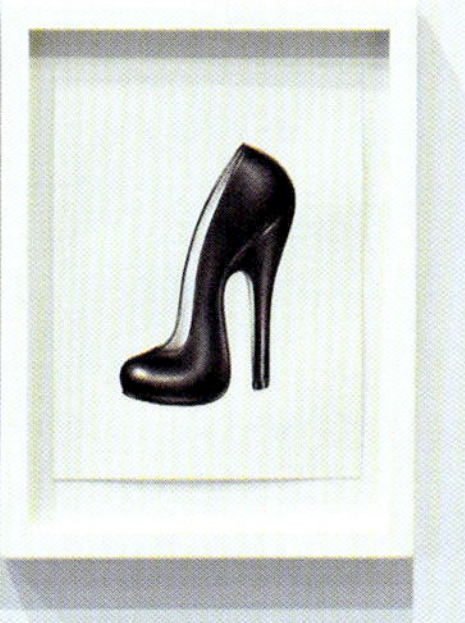

I first met Glenn in 2007 at Art Basel Miami Beach when I cut his hair as part of my hairstyling performance with my gallery, Herald St. He's not only one of my most important patrons but also one of the nicest people I know. Glenn's passion for contemporary art is admirable, and in 2010, he suggested I do a solo show at FLAG. I was very grateful for the opportunity.

"Obsession" is a play on words that I thought would be a funny title for my show. It represents my meticulous attention to detail and my analysis of subjects I'm passionate about. I also happen to share the same initials as the famous fashion designer who launched the perfume Obsession.

I use ballpoint pen, which is one of the easiest and most accessible media—it renders beautifully. I've always been attracted to things that are ordinary with the potential to be extraordinary. It's like my theory of fashion and style: you can look amazing in the most ordinary clothes if you have a good understanding of style, your body type, and your proportions. If you know how to put clothes together, you can make something ordinary extraordinary. This has been my belief since my teens, and it was the theory behind my MA fashion graduation collection for Central Saint Martins College of Art and Design in London.

Fashion and art influence each other, and I'm fascinated by how beauty is perceived. I explore past trends and art movements, especially those influenced by intercultural appreciation and the desire to know and understand foreign ideas, objects, and ideals of beauty. People have a curiosity and desire for novelties, and novelties often have significant and unforeseen impacts on culture, ways of thinking, aesthetics, and people's lives. Clothes are a statement of how a person expresses oneself, one's individuality, social status, intellectual background, etc. I draw inspiration from different cultures and past eras—it's the fantasy and romance of the past that attracts me.

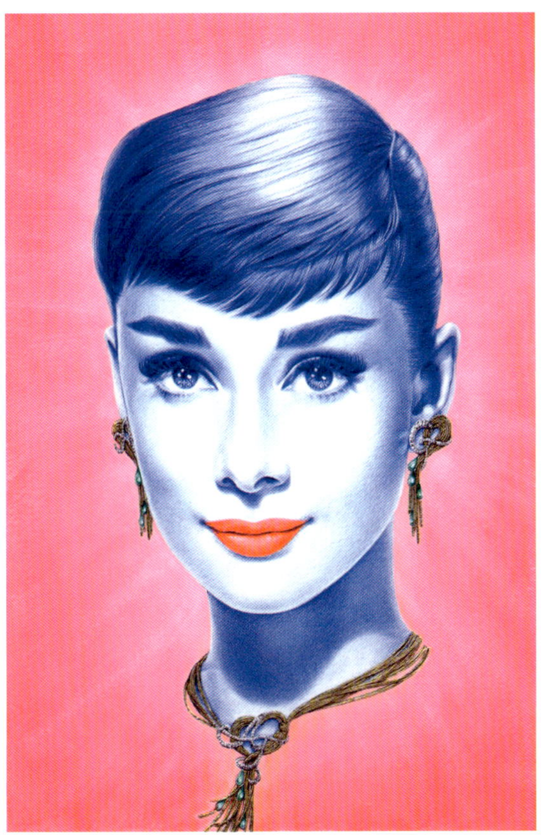

Cary Kwok, *Audrey Hepburn*, 2009

Some of my negative experiences of living in the West as an "ethnic" person have inspired me to become a person who appreciates people's differences. The message I try to communicate through my work is that although we are all culturally diverse, with different customs and languages, we share many similarities. If we can allow ourselves to be influenced by our surroundings, surely we can encourage both ourselves and the people around us to become more thoughtful, considerate, and empathetic. Equality is progress, regardless of gender, ethnicity, sexuality, age, or anything else: that's what I try to say through some of my work, sometimes with a sense of humor, I hope.

—Cary Kwok

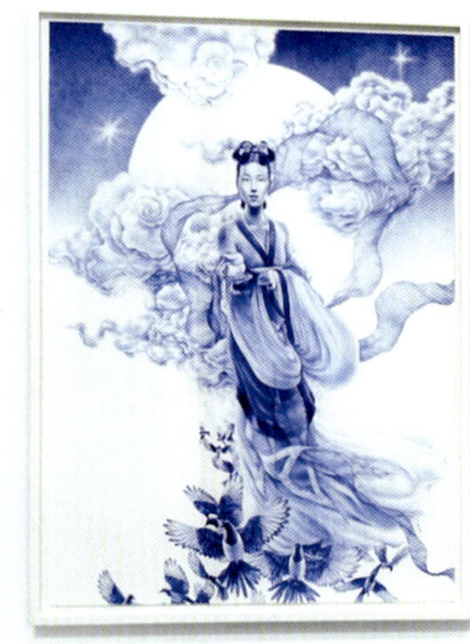

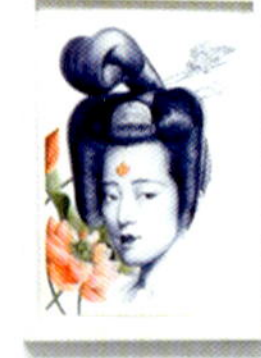

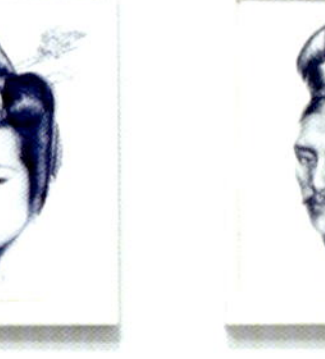

Installation view

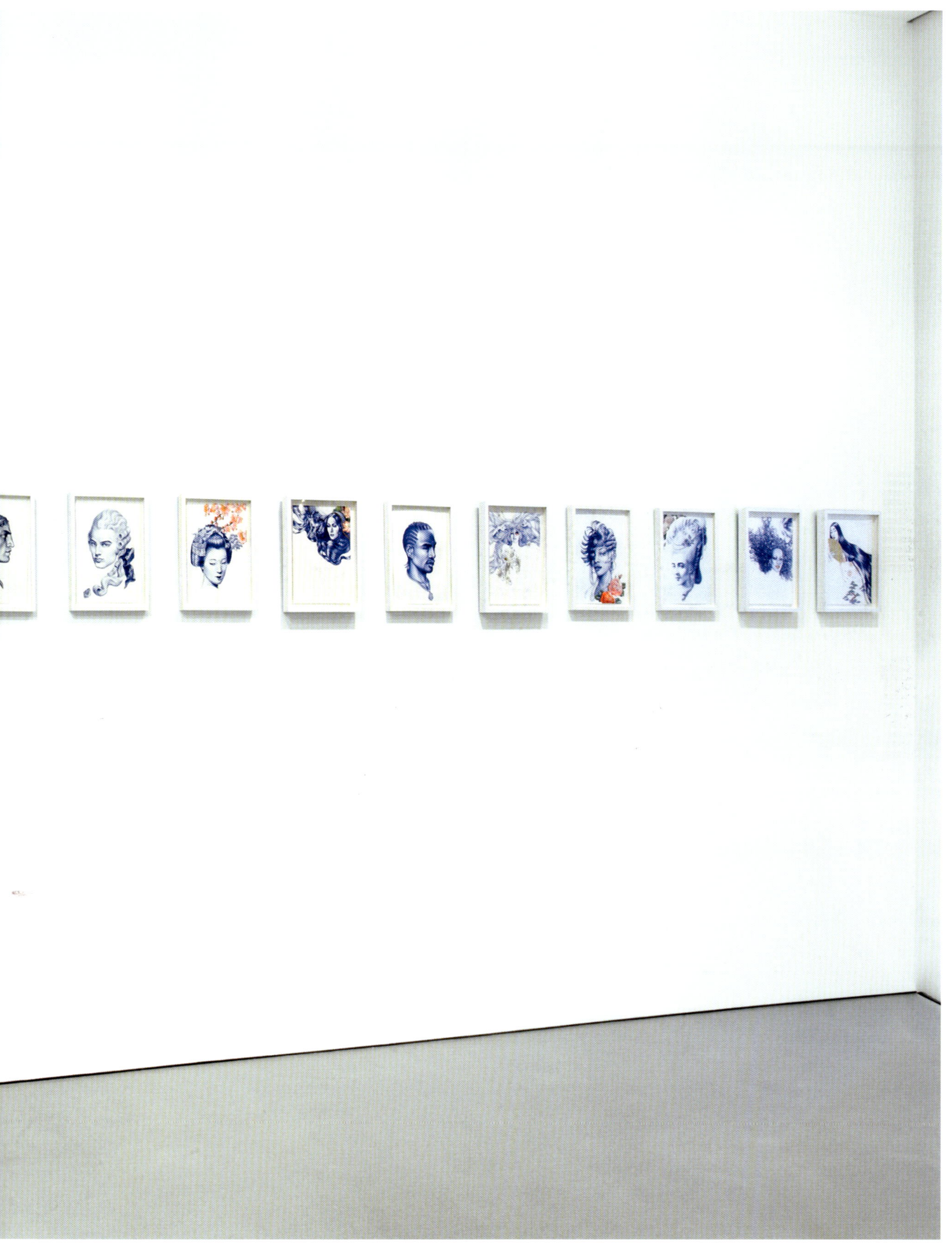

JOSEPHINE MECKSEPER

February 23–May 26, 2011

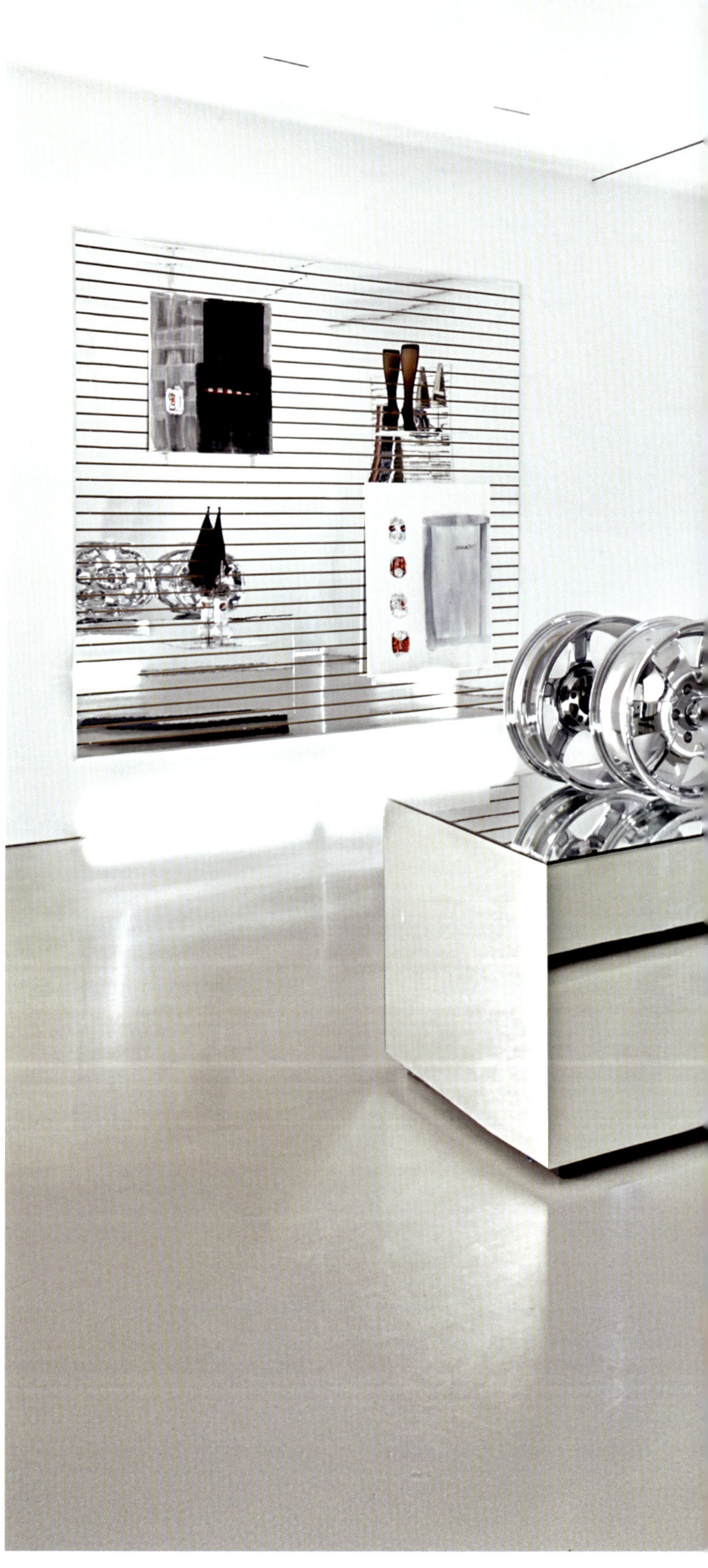

Installation view

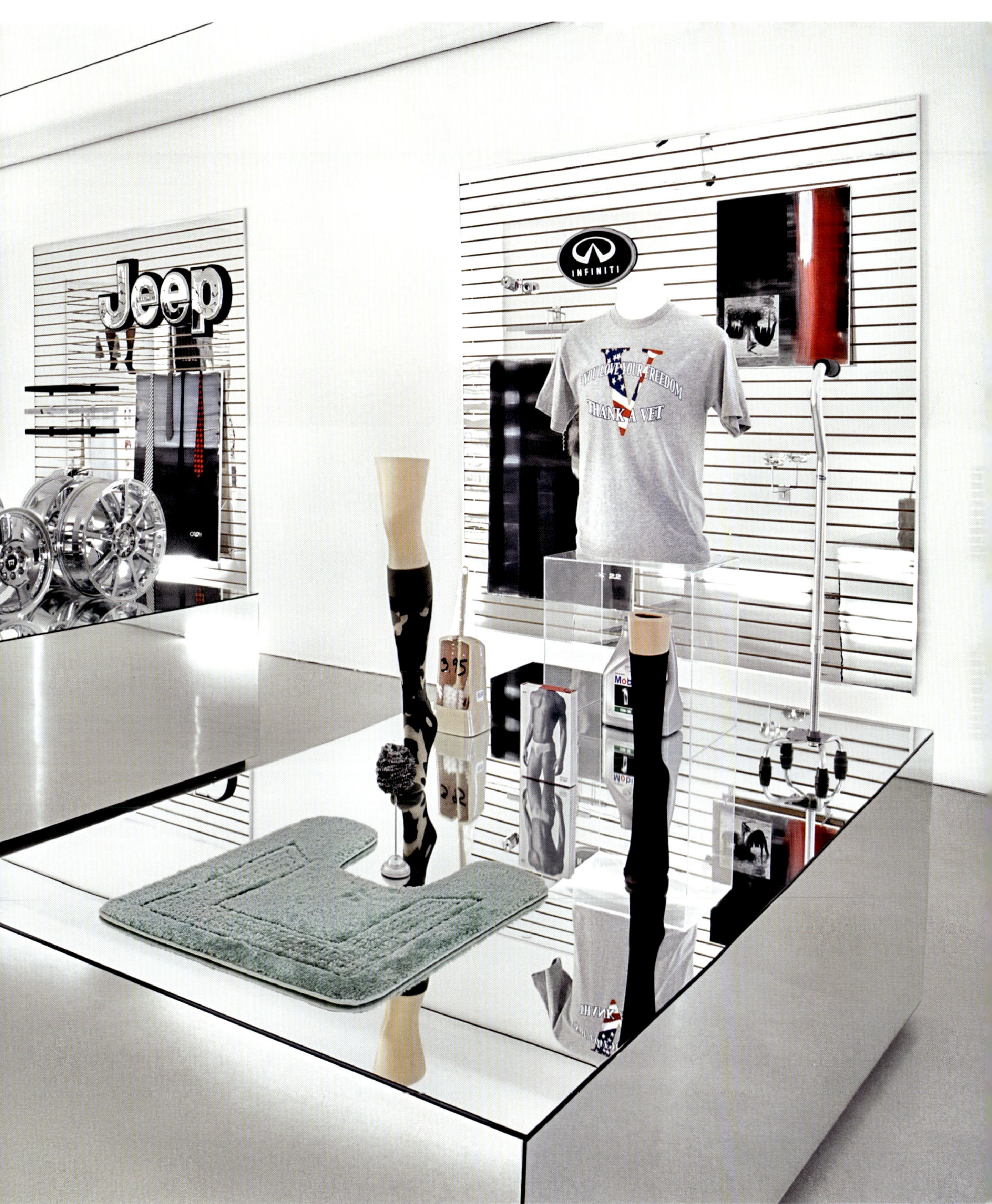
Jeep
INFINITI
THANK A VET

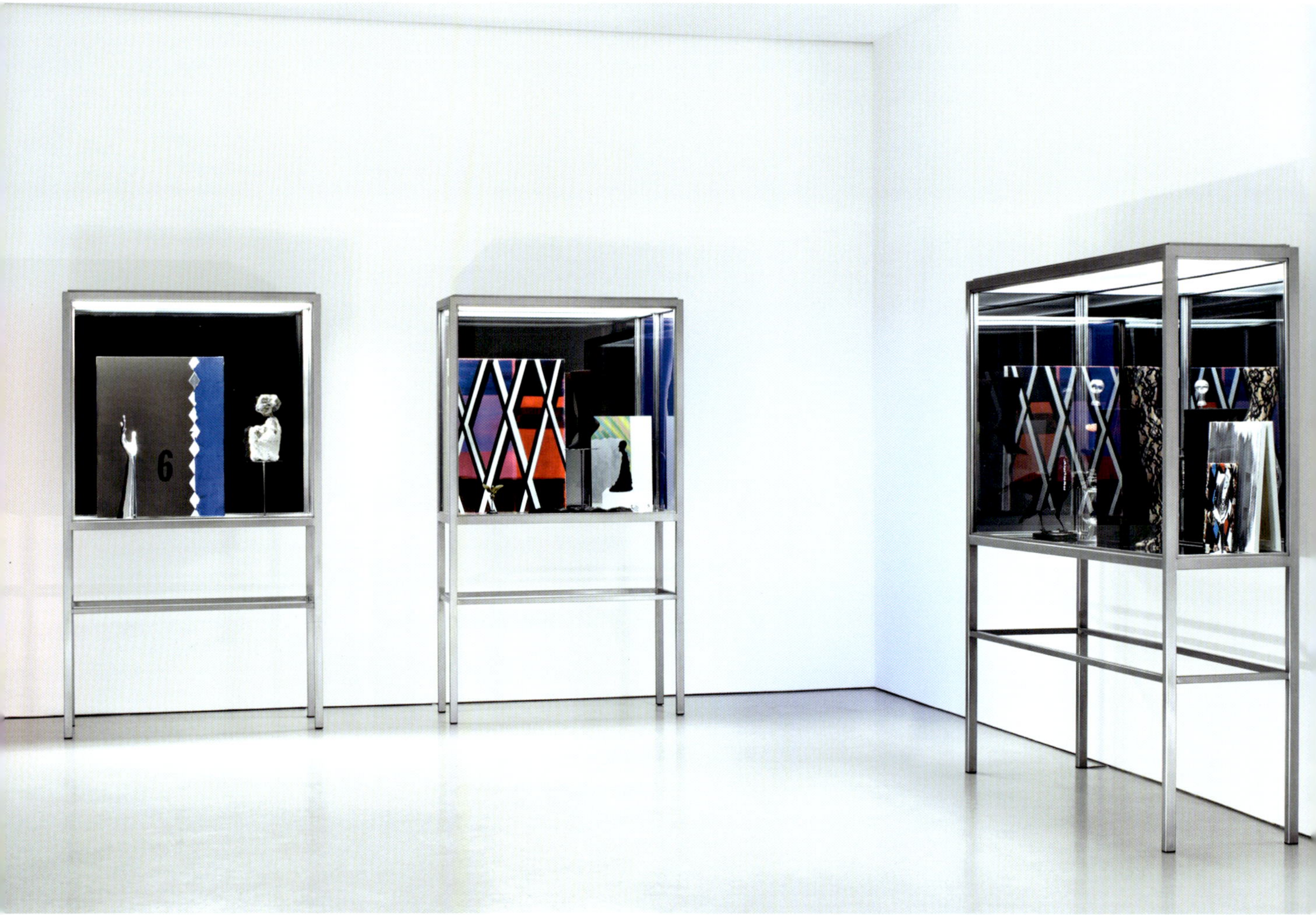

Left to right: Josephine Meckseper, *6*, 2011; *Emirates Palace*, 2011; and *Afrikan Spir*, 2011

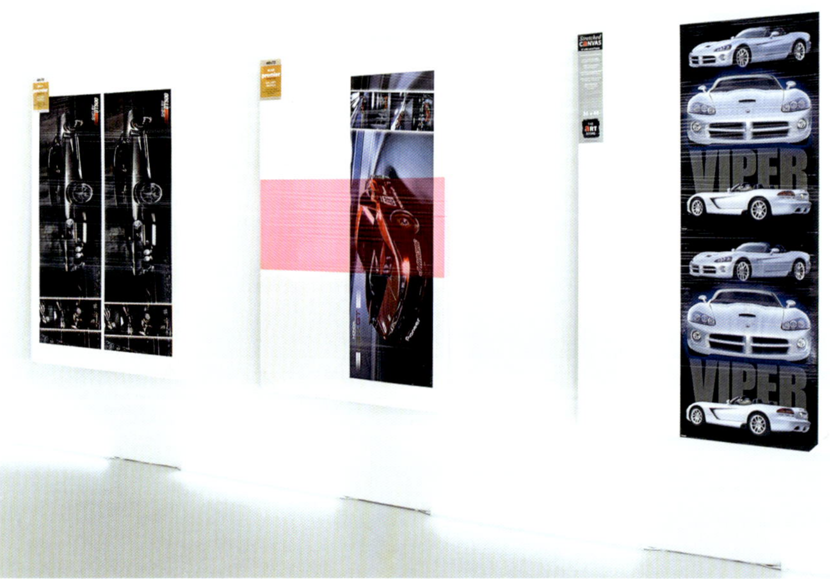

Left to right: Josephine Meckseper, *Shelby GT500 (Grey, double)*, 2009; *Honda NSX GT*, 2008; and *Viper*, 2009

It's hard to imagine an art world without Glenn and Amanda Fuhrman. Their passion for and support of the arts encompass a wide range of remarkable examples. Anyone who has had the privilege of visiting Glenn and Amanda's home, with their incredible collection, knows that the Fuhrmans care deeply about art. Their warmth, generosity, and genuine connection to artists and their works are profound.

I was thrilled when Glenn invited me to present a solo exhibition at FLAG in 2011. It was a uniquely collaborative process, in which the ambitions of the show were met with kindness and thoughtfulness. Walls were literally moved, under Director Stephanie Roach's superb stewardship, and I could not have been more pleased with the result.

The exhibition included some of my favorite works, which were in dialogue with each other, evoking retail environments and concepts of industrial display. The pieces ranged from sculpture to four large mirrored wall panel assemblages, industrially shrink-wrapped canvases of sports cars, and a video work titled *Shattered Screen* (2009). A signature work was the large steel and glass vitrine titled *Afrikan Spir* (2011), named after a nineteenth-century Russian philosopher who studied the essential properties of individual and universal identity. The vitrine recalls early modernism, housing disparate objects such as a taxidermied raven and an image of actress Tippi Hedren in Alfred Hitchcock's *The Birds* (1963). The piece is now in the collection of the Solomon R. Guggenheim Museum, while other works that were in the show are now in other great collections, including that of the Perez Art Museum Miami and Glenn's own.

The catalogue published by FLAG on the occasion of the show was another testament to Glenn's extensive long-term vision. Our mutual friend, writer James Frey, economist Stephen Roach, curator Francesco Bonami, and the *New Yorker*'s John Cassidy contributed meaningful texts to the catalogue.

Since then, with Glenn's continued support, works from my show at FLAG have been included in various museum exhibitions, such as my exhibition at the Parrish Art Museum (Watermill, New York) in 2013, and my first large public commission, *Manhattan Oil Project*, came to life near Times Square in 2012.

In these uncertain times, it is a certainty that with every coming year FLAG will continue to surprise and inspire us with its thoughtful and committed program dedicated to a diverse spectrum of artists' voices.

—Josephine Meckseper

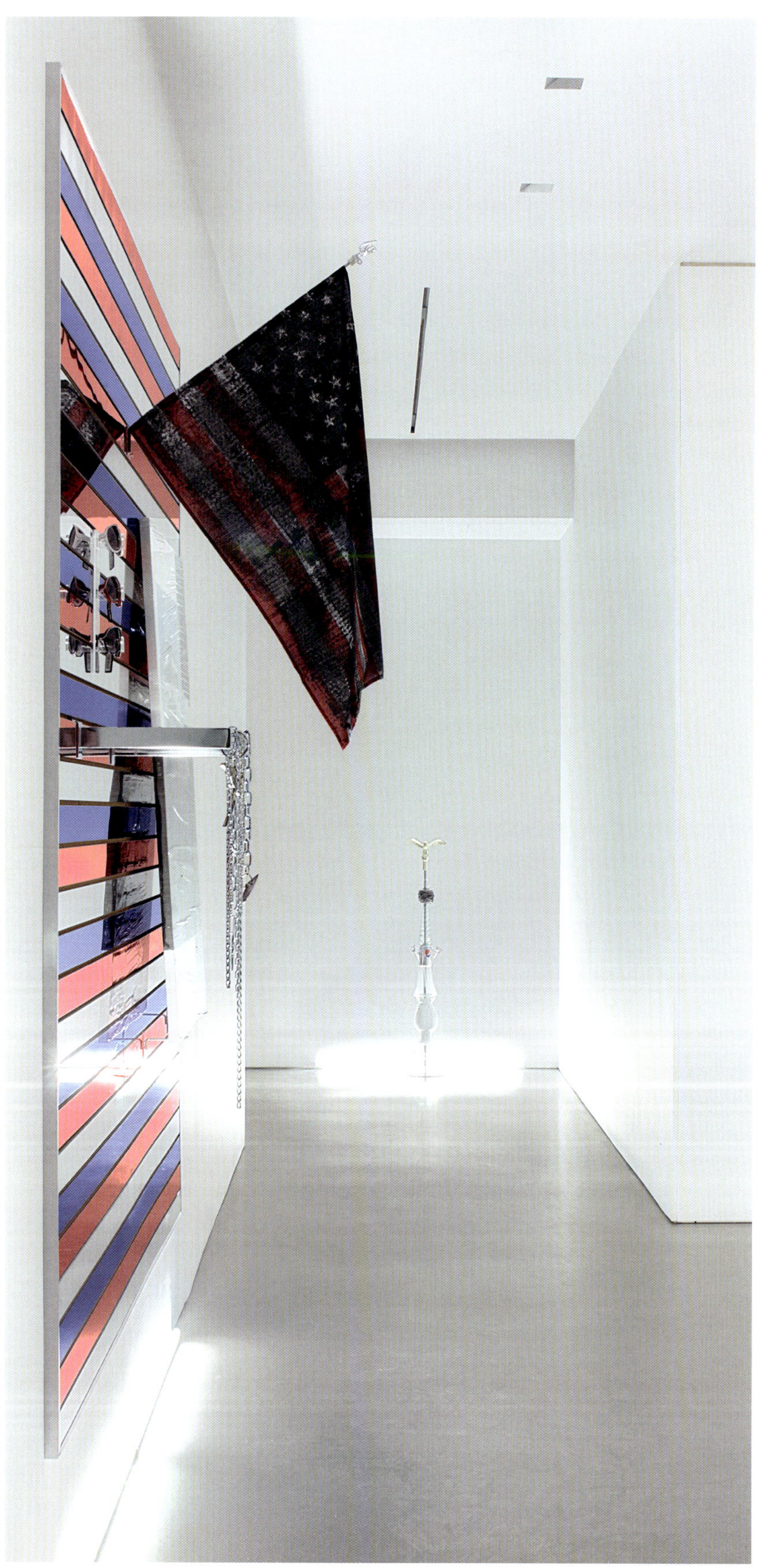

Left to right: Josephine Meckseper, *Cobra*, 2011; and *Der Wille zur Macht*, 2011

Opposite: Josephine Meckseper, *Cobra*, 2011

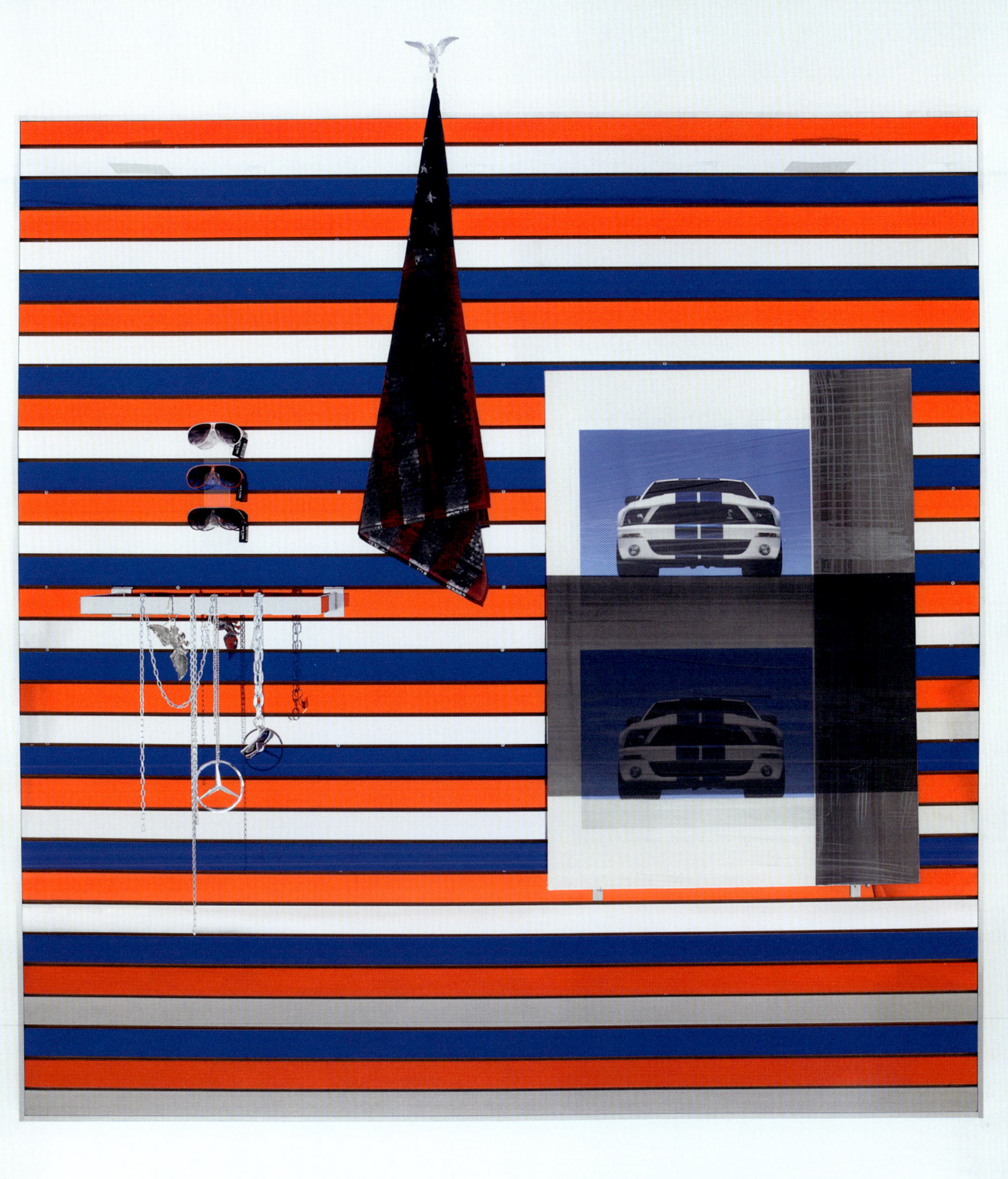

GERHARD RICHTER: SINBAD

February 23–May 26, 2011

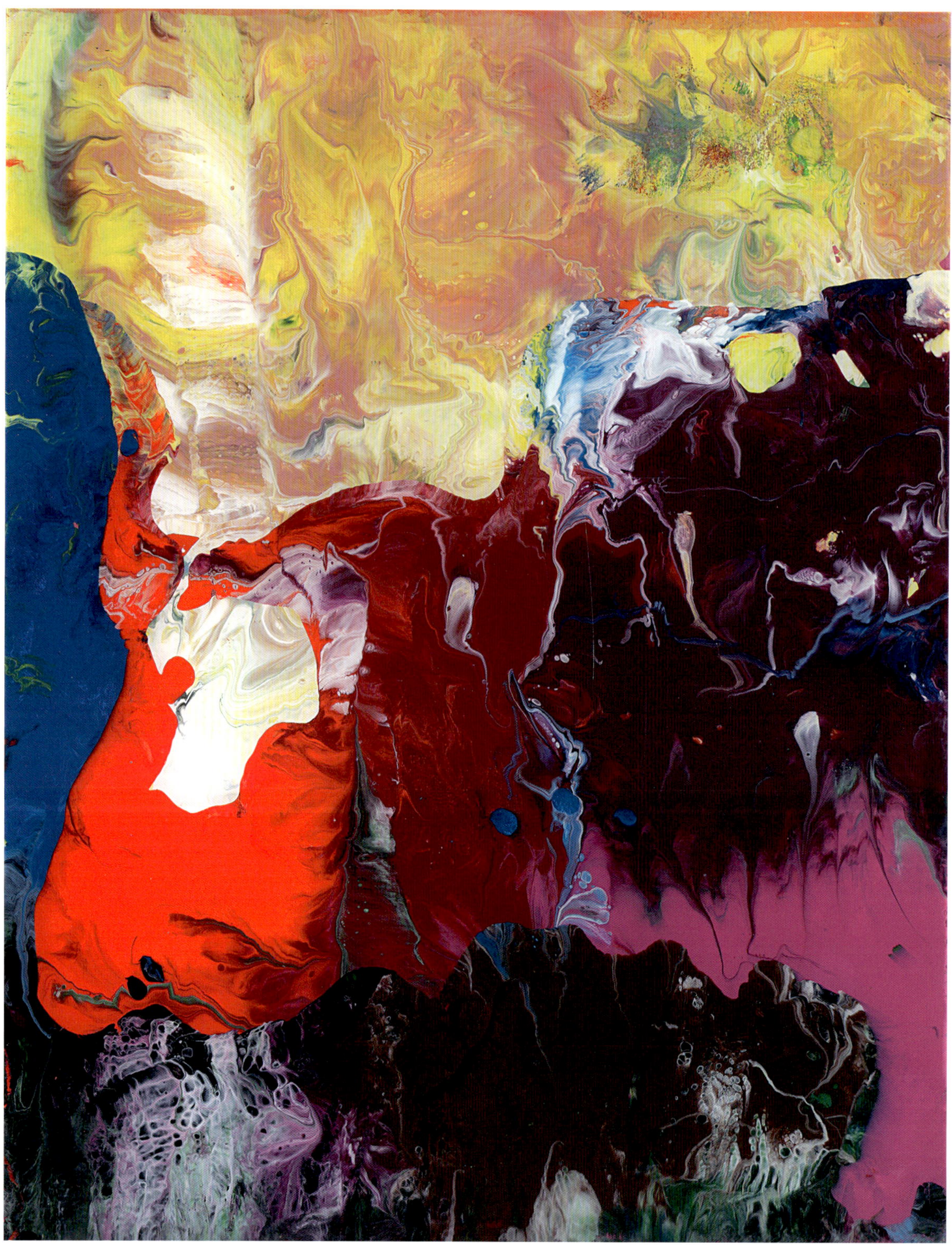

Detail, Gerhard Richter, *Sinbad*, 2008

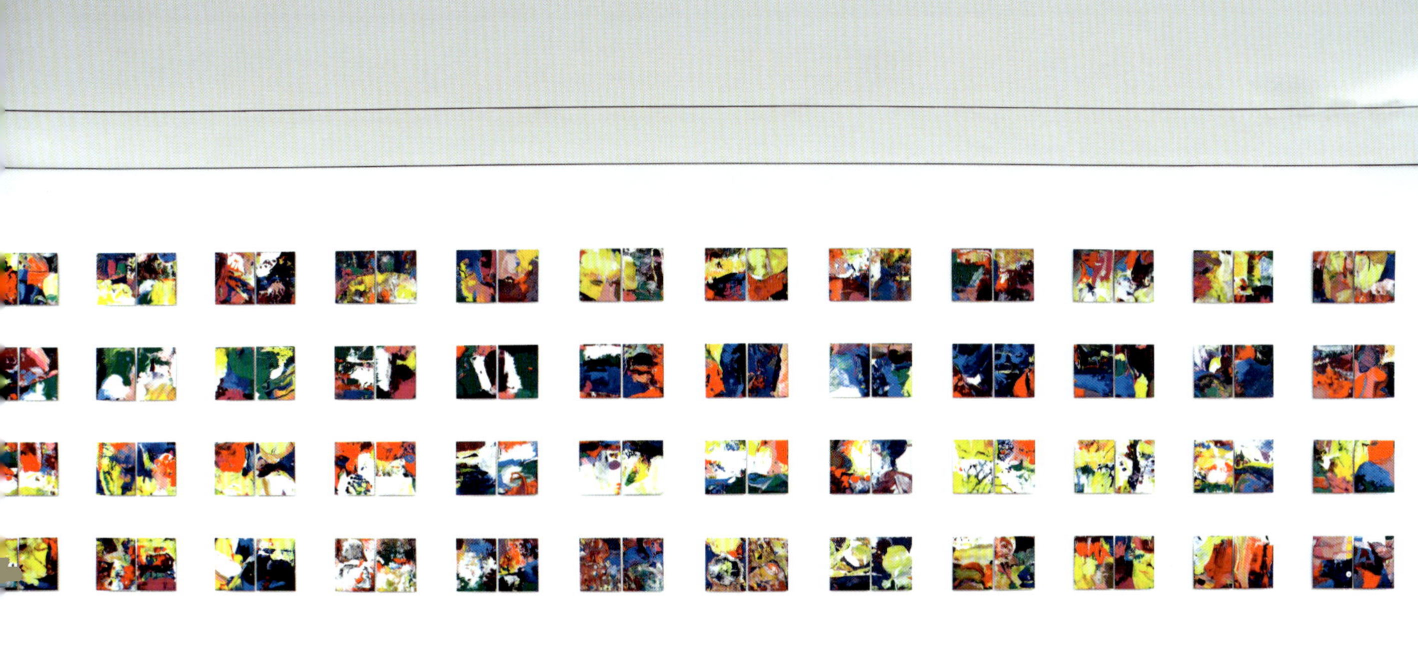

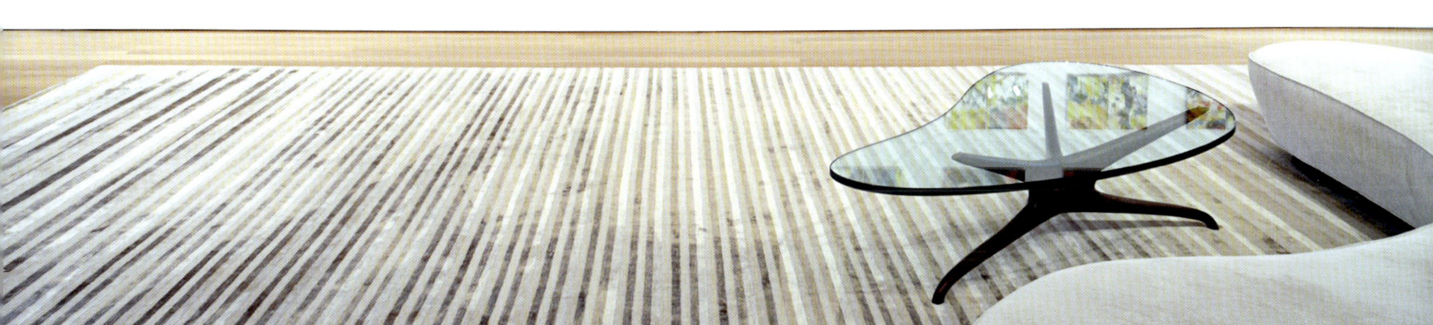

Installation view, Gerhard Richter, *Sinbad*, 2008

RONI HORN: DOUBLE MOBIUS

June 29–August 31, 2011

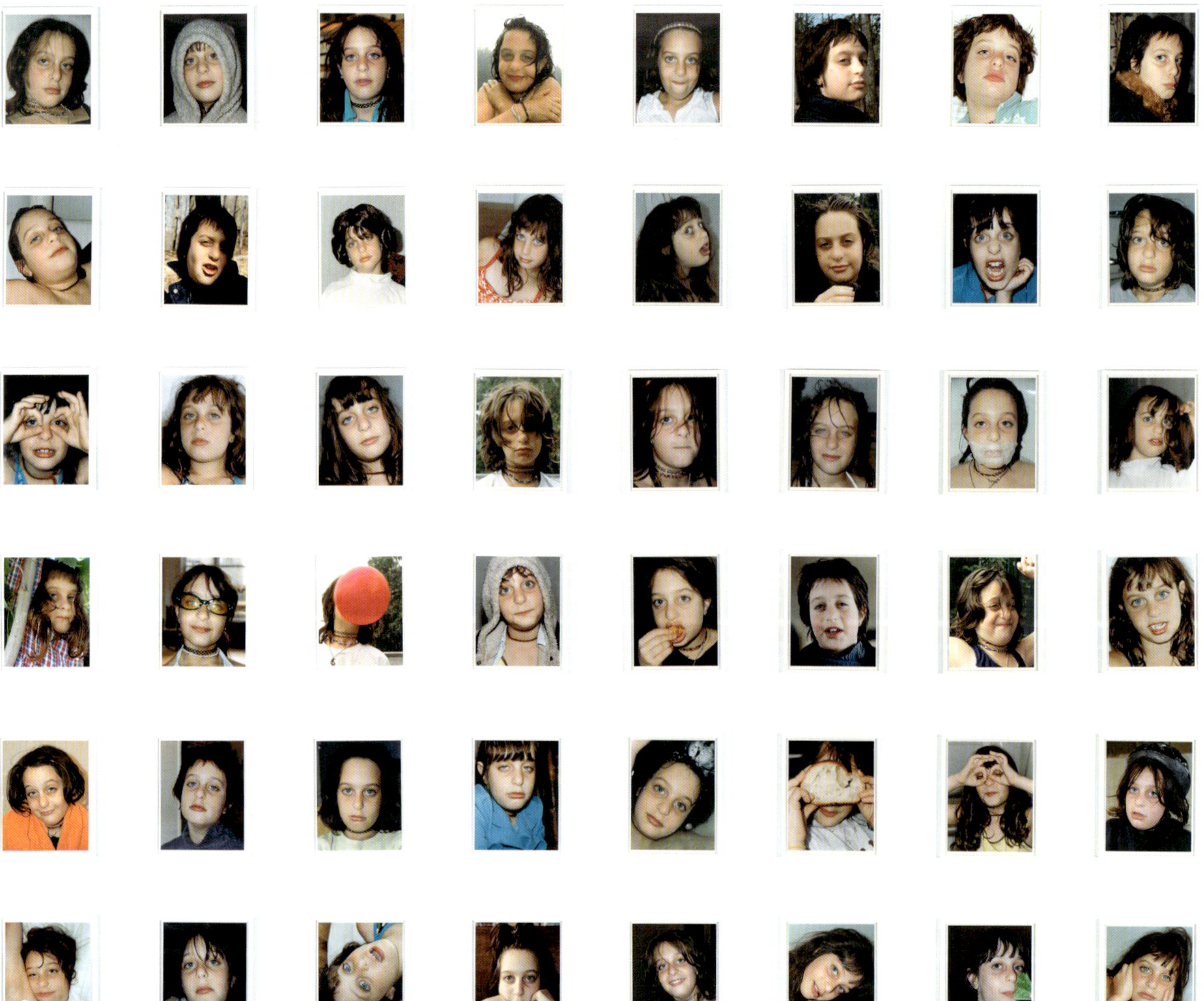

Detail, Roni Horn, *This is Me, This is You*, 1997–2000

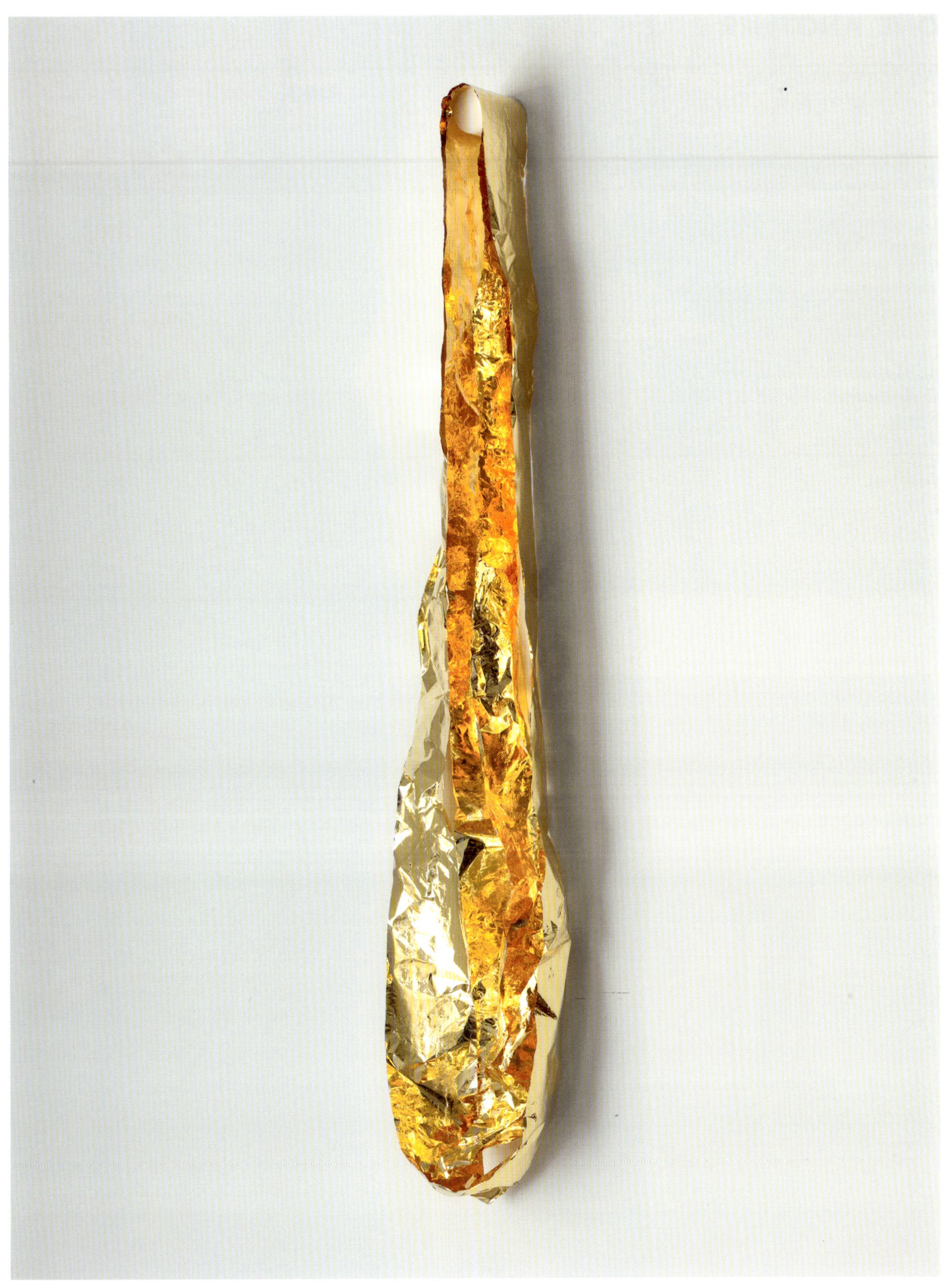

Roni Horn, *Double Mobius v. 1*, 2009

ART²

September 23–December 17, 2011

Artists
Barry X Ball
Delia Brown
Glenn Brown
Marc Dennis
Awol Erizku
Roe Ethridge
Hilary Harkness
Deborah Kass
Naoto Kawahara
Roy Lichtenstein
Duane Michals
Tom Molloy
Chris Ofili
William Pacak
Richard Pettibone
Richard Prince
Ken Solomon
Ena Swansea
Terri Thomas
Jim Torok
Kehinde Wiley

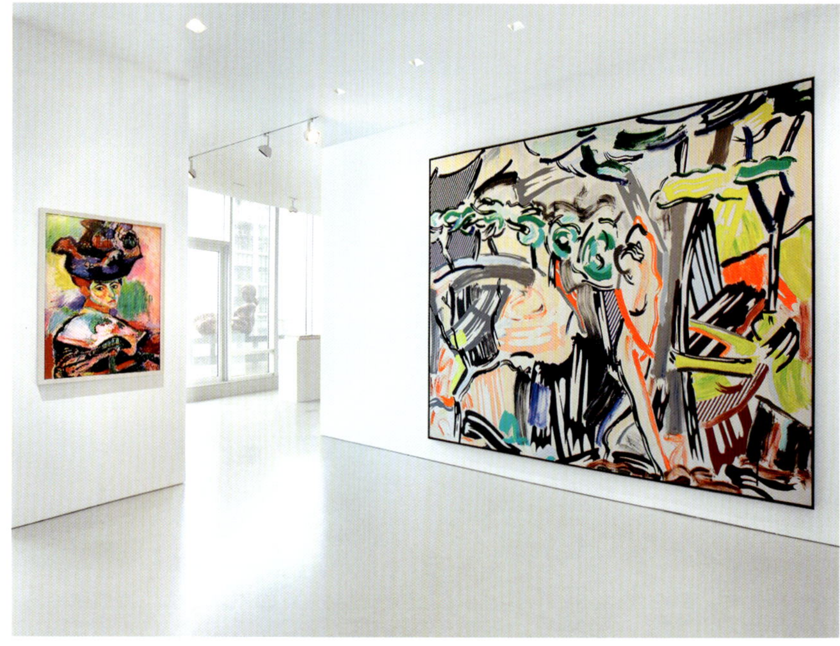

Left to right: Roe Ethridge, *Untitled*, 2009–11; Roy Lichtenstein, *Figures in Landscape*, 1985

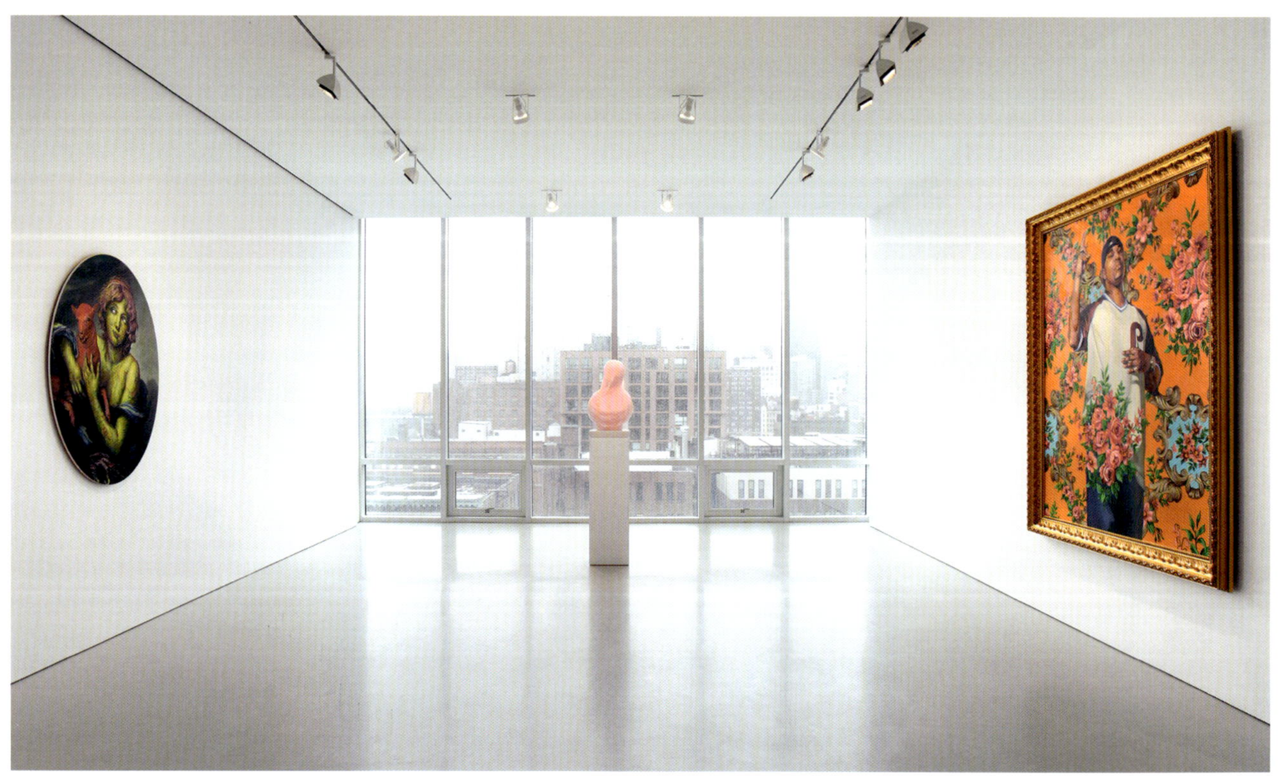

Left to right: Glenn Brown, *Wild Horses*, 2007; Barry X Ball, *Purity*, 2008–11; Kehinde Wiley, *The Blessing Christ*, 2007

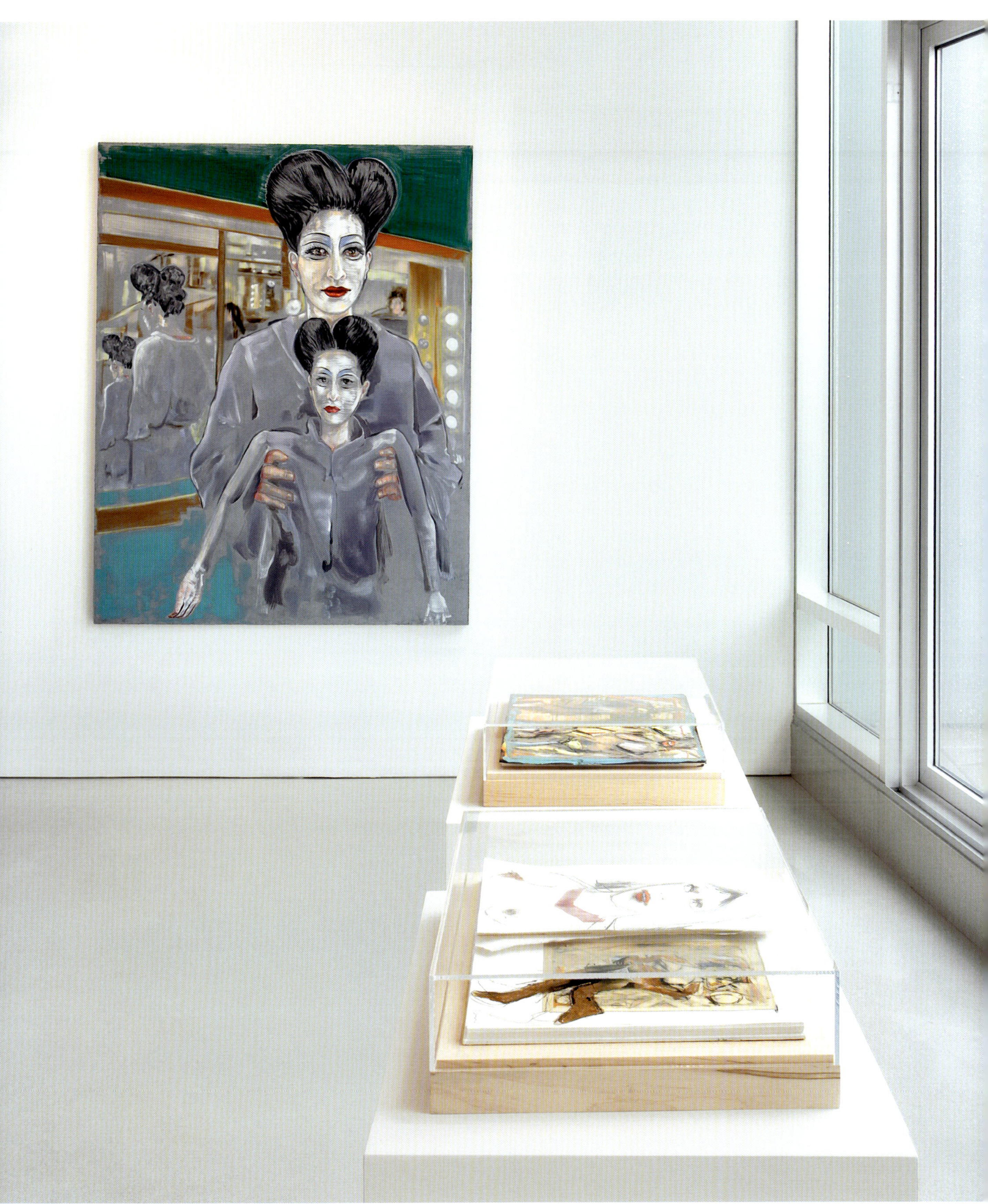

Clockwise from top: Ena Swansea, *backstage*, 2011; Richard Prince, *Untitled (de Kooning)*, 2007; and *de Kooning Collage and Drawing*, 2005

I've had the profound privilege to have known Glenn Fuhrman since I first moved to New York sixteen years ago. We were connected by Christopher D'Amelio, my gallerist at the time. I was looking for swanky art collectors' residences where I could perform the photo-shoot parties that were the basis for my guerrilla lounging paintings, and Chris recommended Glenn (with whom he'd overlapped at Penn) as an adventurous young art collector who would likely be game to let me run wild in his expansive apartment, which was filled with bold and ambitious artworks. My jaw dropped as I entered a light-filled living room with impressive works by Cindy Sherman, Ed Ruscha, and Gerhard Richter—and then I proceeded to open all the champagne in his fridge and went to town, clowning with friends and snapping pics. Many paintings came out of this afternoon on the Upper East Side (which were the subject of my final show at Margo Leavin Gallery in LA), and a lifelong friendship with Glenn emerged.

Since that winter day in 2002, much has happened in both of our lives. In addition to marrying the whip-smart, hilarious, and beautiful Amanda Fuhrman and having three gorgeous children, Glenn opened the art space of his dreams: The FLAG Art Foundation. He had always wanted to share his prodigious collection with others, so that they might enjoy them as he does.

I was fortunate to be included in two of the three exhibitions in FLAG's first year: *Attention to Detail* (2008) and *WALL ROCKETS* (2009). For *WALL ROCKETS*, an homage to Glenn's favorite artist, Ed Ruscha, I created a piece that drew upon our friendship and familiarity. I asked Glenn to allow me to pose as his wife, and had his niece pose as our daughter, and I created a portrait of the three of us seated under a Ruscha painting that Glenn owned. I have long been interested in the patron/artist relationship as a stand-in for other, more primal, interdependent relationships—I also explored this by posing as Margo Leavin's daughter, and by posing as the mother of another of my collectors' children—as well as the way disparities in income lead us to convey ourselves in different ways. (In this case, I was interested in how I might dress and pose differently if I were the wife of a banker, living on the Upper East Side.) To me, it says so much about Glenn's generosity that he is so often willing to open himself to participating in the production of works by the artists he supports, even if the request is awkwardly intimate or just plain goofy.

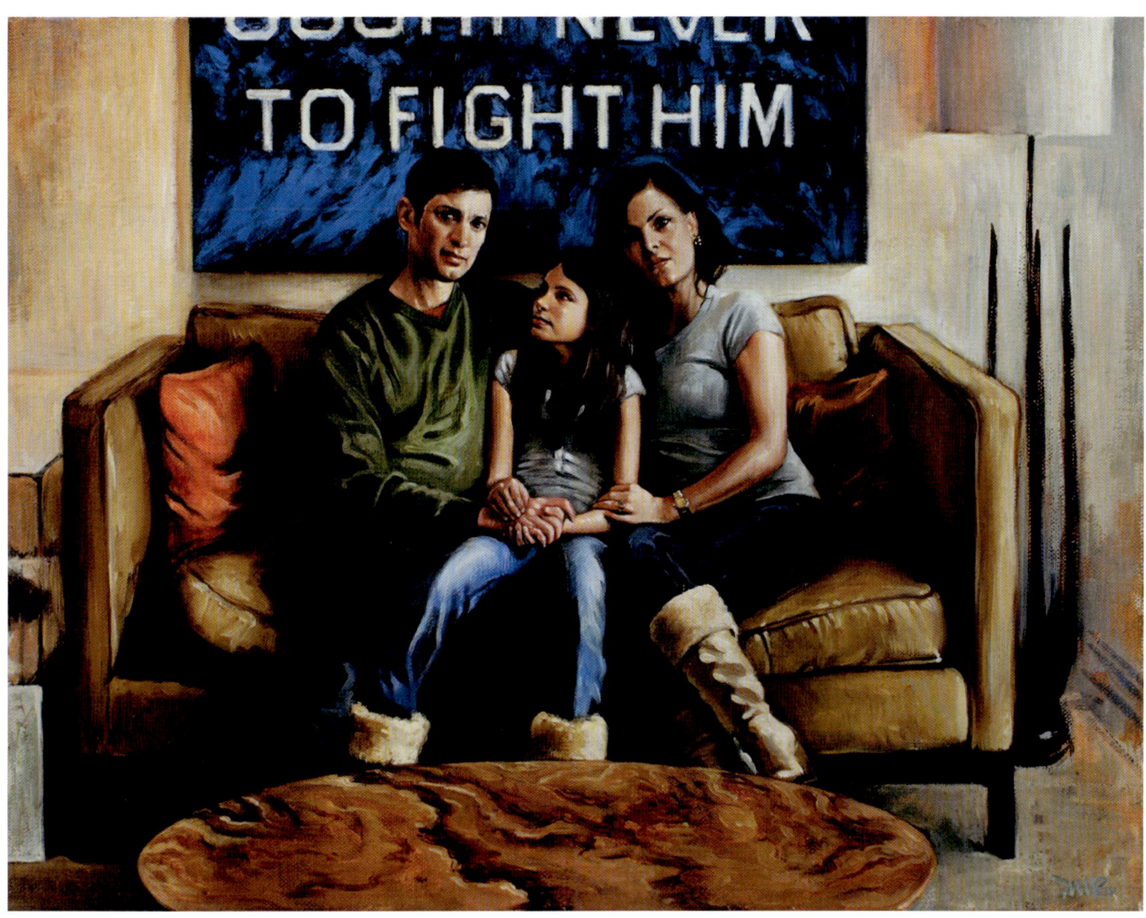

Delia Brown, *A Young Collector with His Wife and Daughter in Their New York Apartment*, 2008

I had the pleasure of being included in two more shows at FLAG, *Art²* (2011) and *SIZE DOES MATTER* (2010) (the show amusingly curated by Shaq)—and to see many more exhibitions of incredible scope and quality, all open to the public, free of charge.

But perhaps the most moving experience I've had at FLAG was when Glenn and Amanda held a private performance by singer Rufus Wainwright to support me and celebrate my just having overcome cancer. The concert was held on the second floor of the space, in the middle of Betty Tompkins's one thousand paintings of the language people use to refer to women (*Betty Tompkins: WOMEN Words, Phrases, and Stories*). Stephanie, Risa, Jon, and the whole FLAG gang went over the top to make it a magical night, and indeed it was like a dream—glistening with sweet music, great art, and love.

—Delia Brown

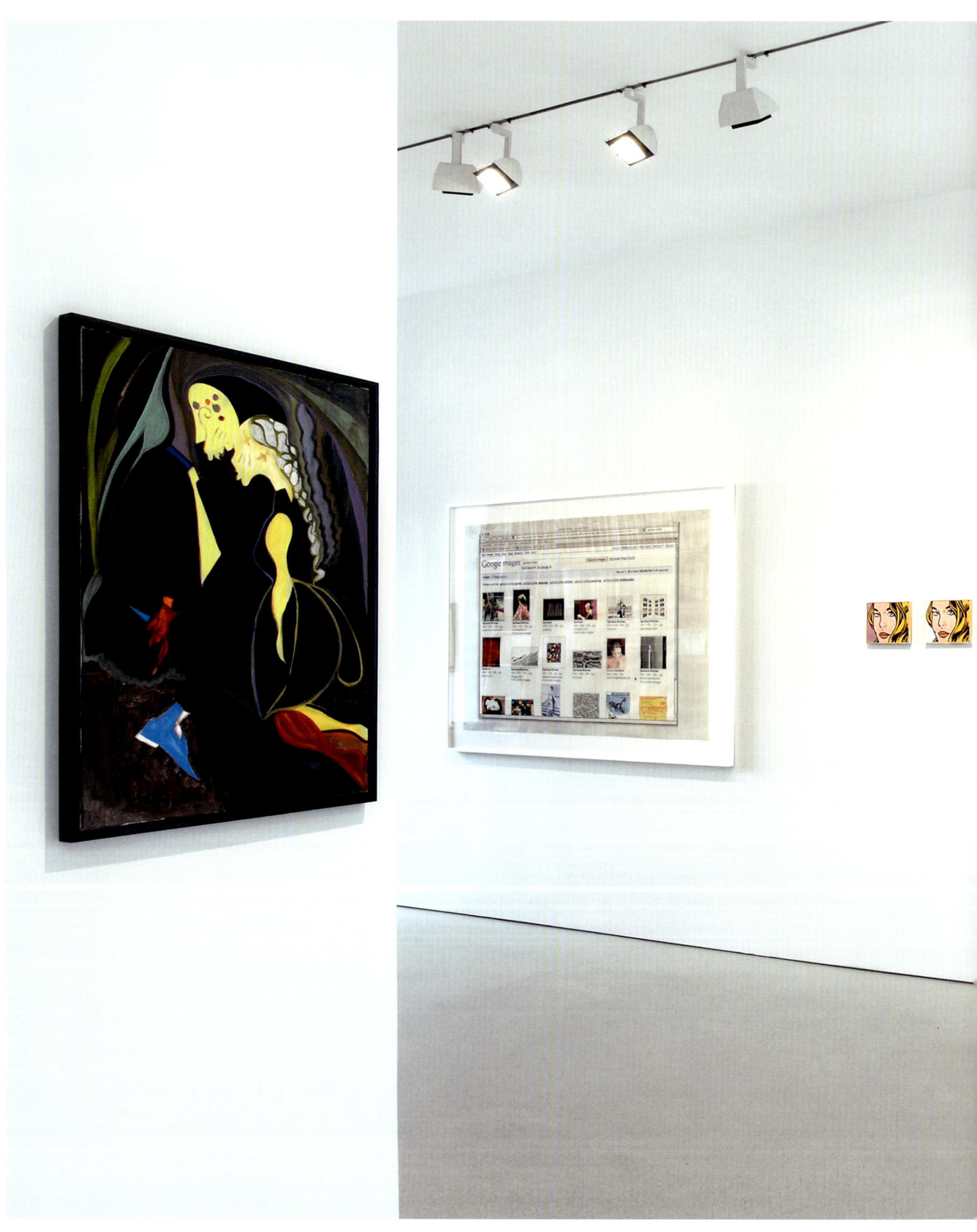

Left to right: Chris Ofili, *Dancers (red hand)*, 2007; Ken Solomon, *Google Portrait: Gerhard Richter–Page 1*, 2011; Richard Pettibone, *Roy Lichtenstein, 'Seductive Girl', 1964, Yellow-Purple*, 2009; *Roy Lichtenstein, 'Seductive Girl', 1964, Yellow-White*, 2009; *Roy Lichtenstein, 'Seductive Girl', 1964, Purple-Yellow*, 2009; and *Roy Lichtenstein, 'Seductive Girl', 1964, White-Yellow*, 2009; Marc Dennis, *Koons' Dog at The Metropolitan Museum of Art*, 2010; and *Untitled*, 2010

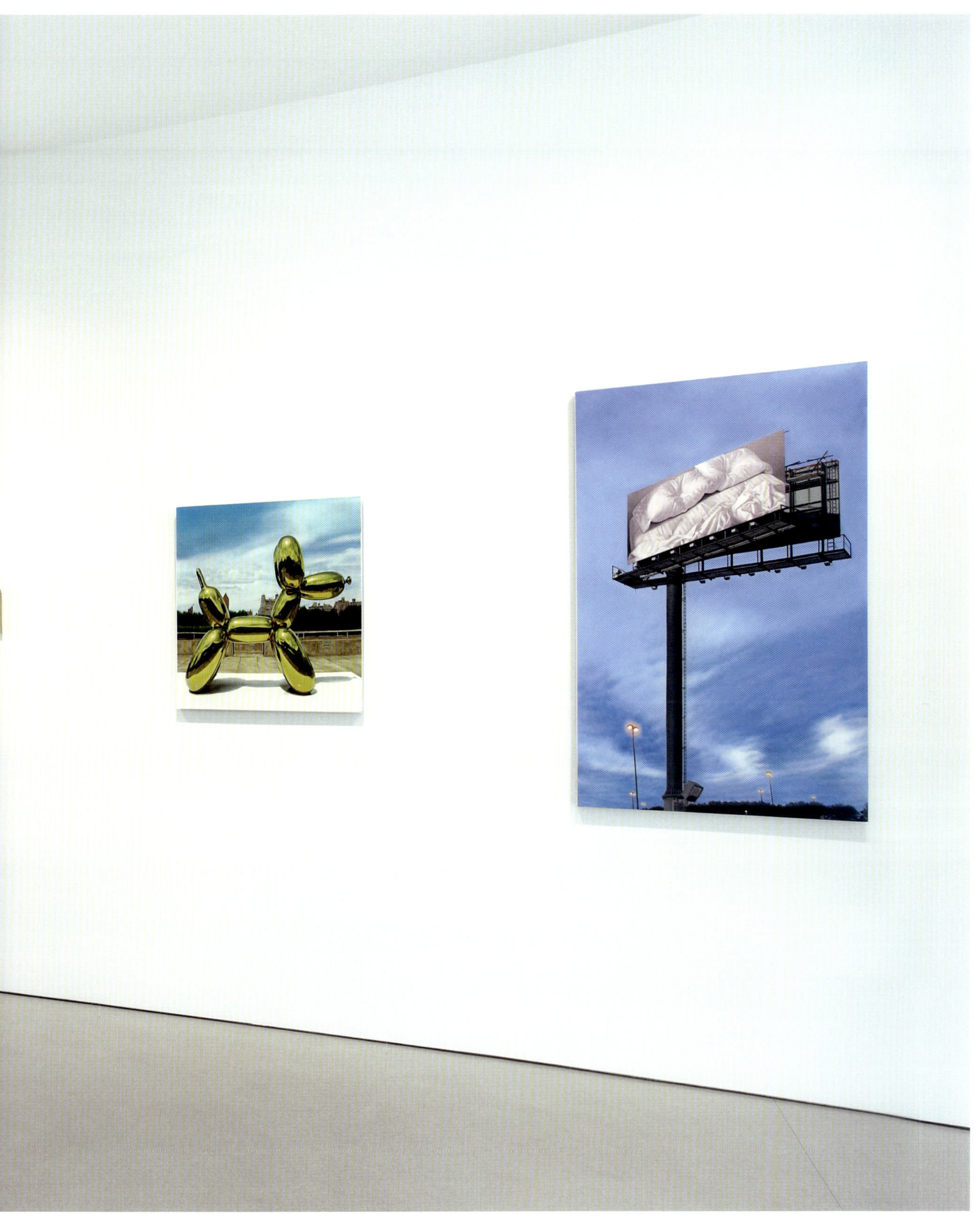

JANE HAMMOND: FALLEN

September 23–December 31, 2011

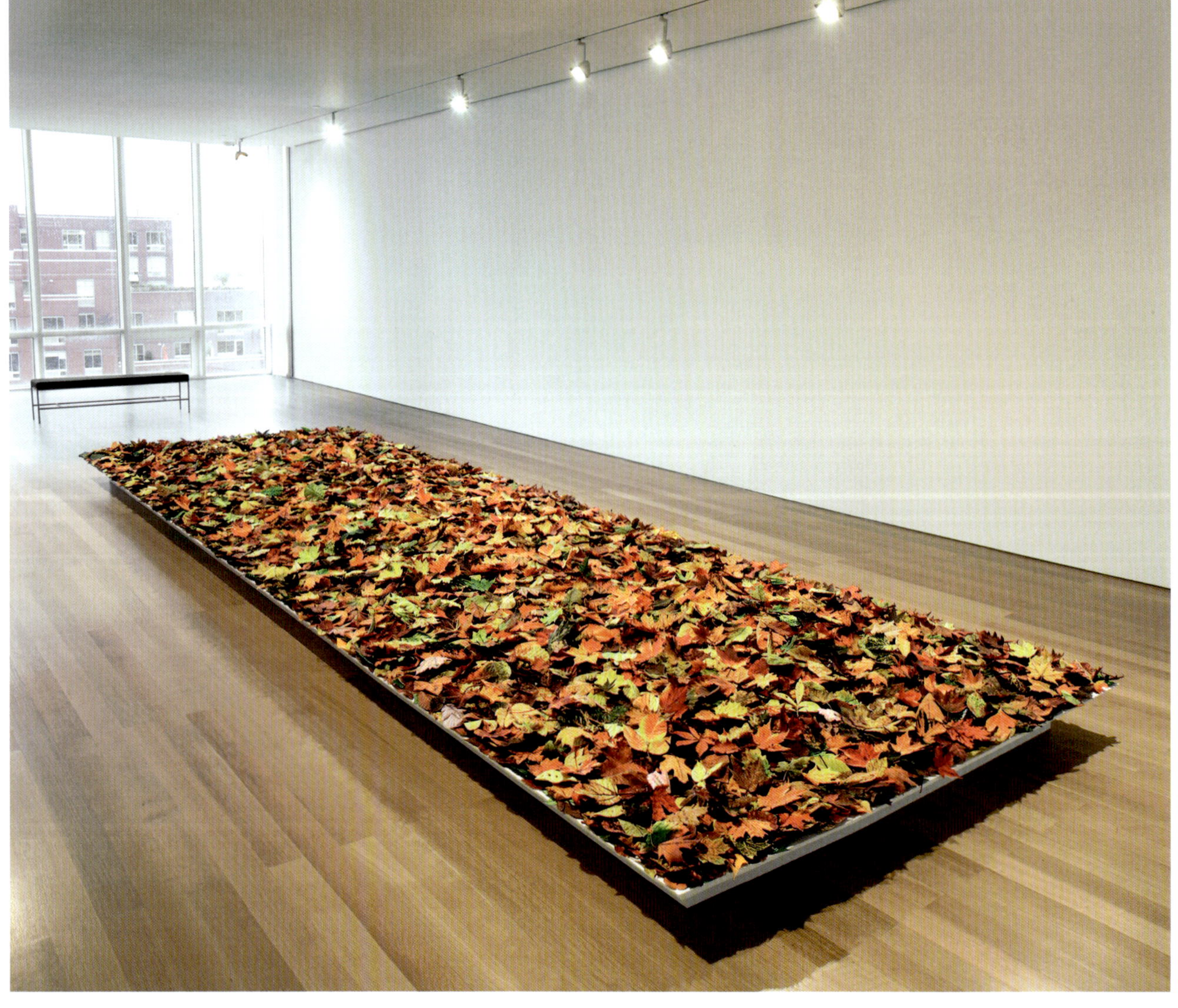

Above: Installation view. Opposite: Detail, Jane Hammond, *Fallen*, 2004

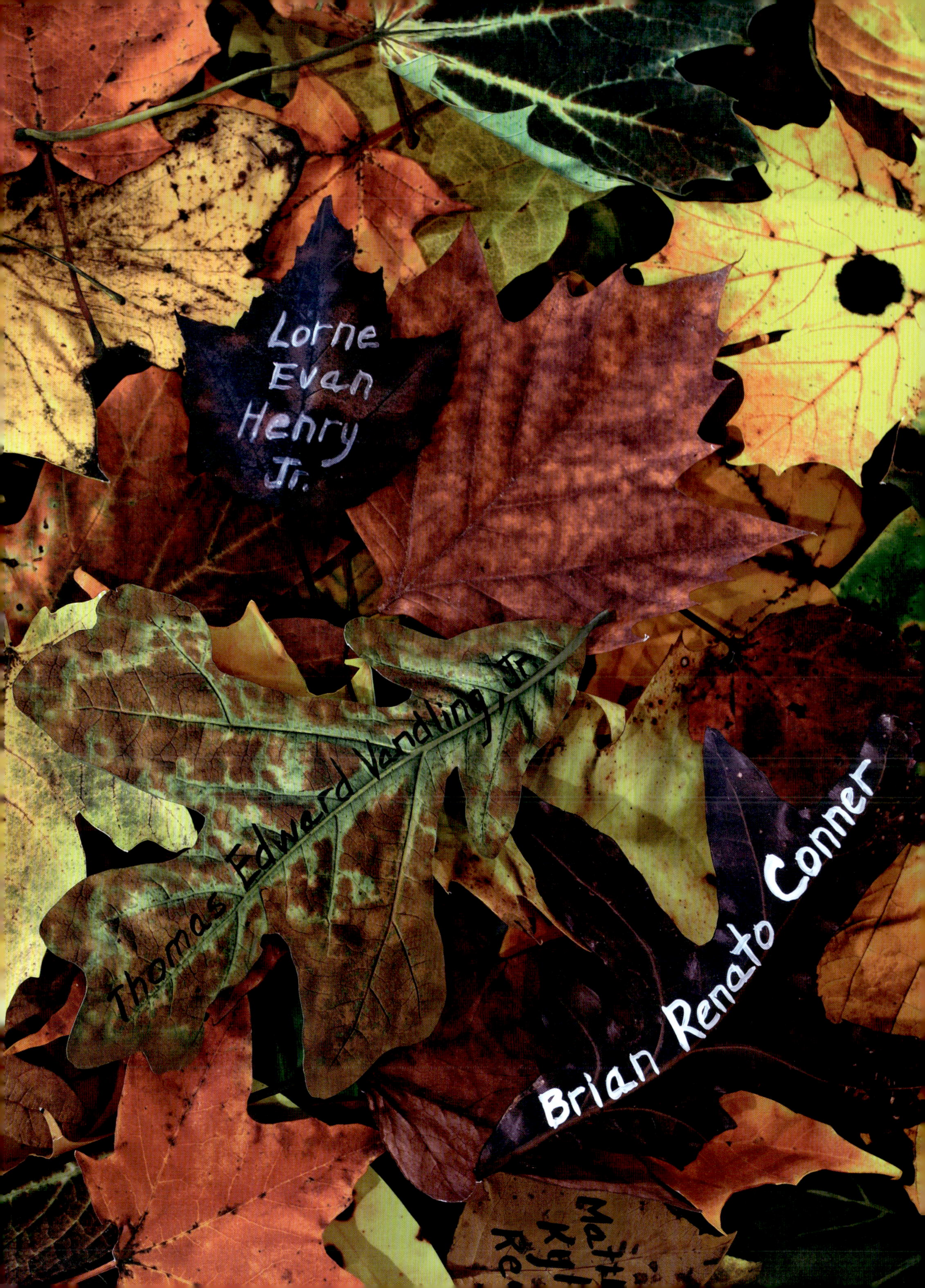
Lorne Evan Henry Jr.
Thomas Edward Vandling, Jr.
Brian Renato Conner

Jane Hammond with *Fallen*, 2004

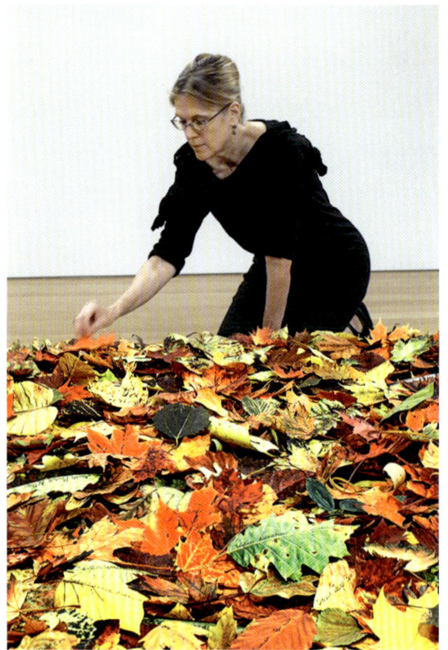

It was very special to show *Fallen* (2004) at FLAG for several reasons. The fact that it was a solo exhibition married well with the solemnity and quiet of the piece. Showing *Fallen* in New York brought it back to my home, to where the dream of it began. Although in the end, I gathered leaves in many states across the country, the first leaves came from my daily walks around the city. I am still tuned in to certain trees in the Village and remember watching and waiting for their leaves to reach peak coloration.

At FLAG, *Fallen* was the largest it had ever been, as shortly afterward the official end of the war in Iraq was announced and the troops were brought home. Though *Fallen* had been shown by five museums before it was at FLAG, it was always at or near ground level. In some way, the viewer's body can sense this groundedness. At FLAG, however, the piece was in the air, ten stories up, and was surrounded by sky—you knew this even when the blinds were drawn. There was a feeling of aeriality, as if the piece had risen. I felt this nowhere else.

On another note, *Fallen* is not an easy piece to exhibit. It comes from the Whitney with a full protocol for light levels, a full-time guard, a granular leaf tally at deinstallation. The platform must be built inside the space, and it takes me nearly a week to then install it. FLAG met the challenge with complete grace and total commitment. I felt the proportions between the piece and the room were perfect, and the presentation and entire experience of working with FLAG left nothing to be desired.

• • •

There is something about leaves in the autumn, at the zenith of their coloration, that is transcendent: they are both dematerializing and intensifying simultaneously. As their bodies become lighter, their color becomes more and more intense. I tried to gather leaves just at this moment when the chroma is so strong that it transcends the corpus of the leaf and becomes a kind of pure light. It rhymes with the idea of "the spirit," but in a way that I think is accessible and earthly. It is more Emerson than Aquinas.

One thing that interests me is how much more particular leaves have become for me—like the lives of the soldiers themselves. I see them now as such individuals. It is a kind of miracle how attention to something makes it so much more interesting.

Besides thinking about leaves, both in general and in particular, it is also useful to consider for a moment the nature of numbers. Numbers were invented for agricultural record keeping. They served a useful function of distilling the manyness of hundreds or thousands of sacks of wheat into a unitary phenomenon—a single number. Sometimes I think we have grown up so completely with the abstraction that is numbers that we forget the manyness and multitude that they actually represent. Every person whom I have heard say of *Fallen*, "Oh my God, it is so many," also knows, intellectually, what four thousand is, but there is something about seeing the number concretized that undoes a lifetime of thinking in the abstract.

It started out as something specific and concrete—the equation in my mind between lives and leaves. But, more and more, time entered into the equation. The ongoing quality of the piece was really its essential nature. It was a work of art in which the artist was not in control of when it was finished nor how large it became. I was something between an author and a witness. The work had a performative quality, but I did not write the script.

I suppose it was also performative in the sense that it was never a fixed arrangement of leaves. So far, everywhere the piece has gone, I arranged the leaves and, in a sense, "made" the piece. It's hard for me to imagine ever not doing this myself.

Three concepts that inform most of my work are collecting, collage, and collaboration. The gathering of the leaves themselves extended over nine autumns and in places as far apart as Hawaii, Texas, Vermont, and Mississippi. The marriage of each name and leaf is a kind of collage, and while I do not know how to perfectly extend the "collaboration" metaphor, the piece definitely feels bigger to me than my ideas or my craftsmanship or my authorship. It has at its heart our collectivity.

—Jane Hammond

Following pages: Installation view

Each unique handmade leaf has been inscribed by the artist

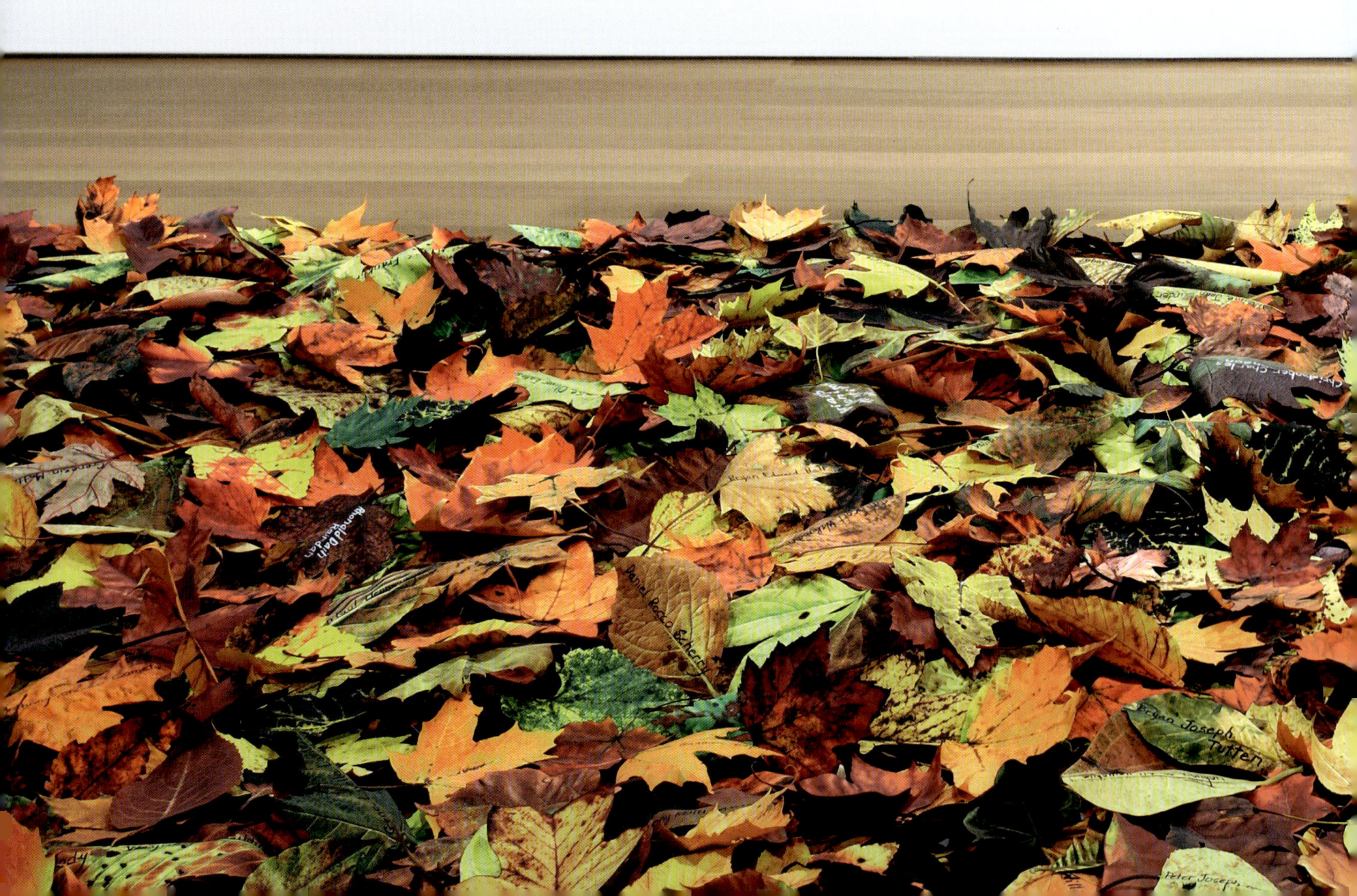

f a US soldier killed in Iraq. The exhibition begins with 4455 leaves.

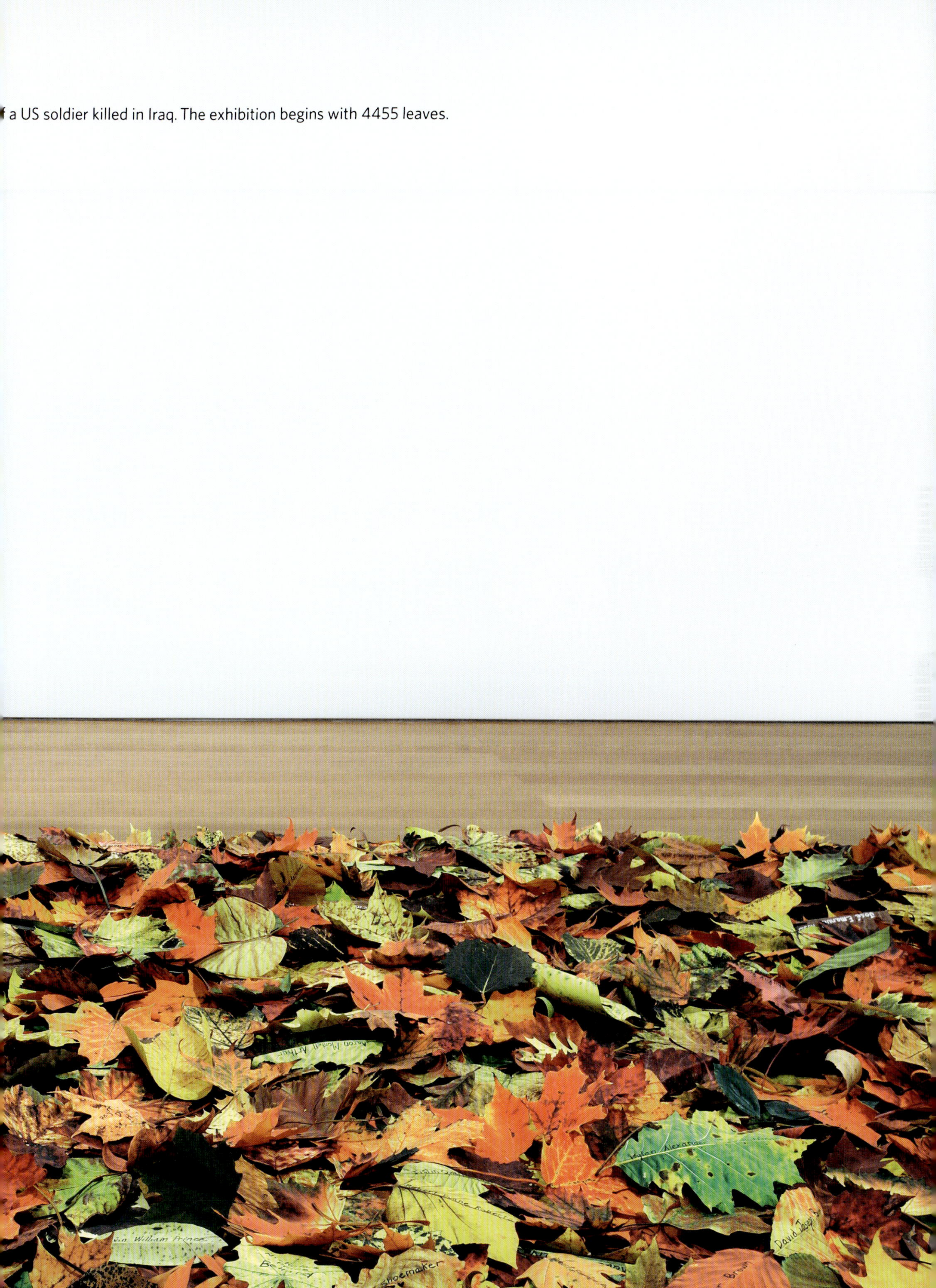

IN LIVING COLOR

January 21–May 12, 2012

Artists
assume vivid astro focus
Kristin Baker
Olaf Breuning
Dan Colen
Mark Grotjahn
Anselm Reyle
Gerhard Richter
Fred Tomaselli
Cy Twombly
Rachel Whiteread

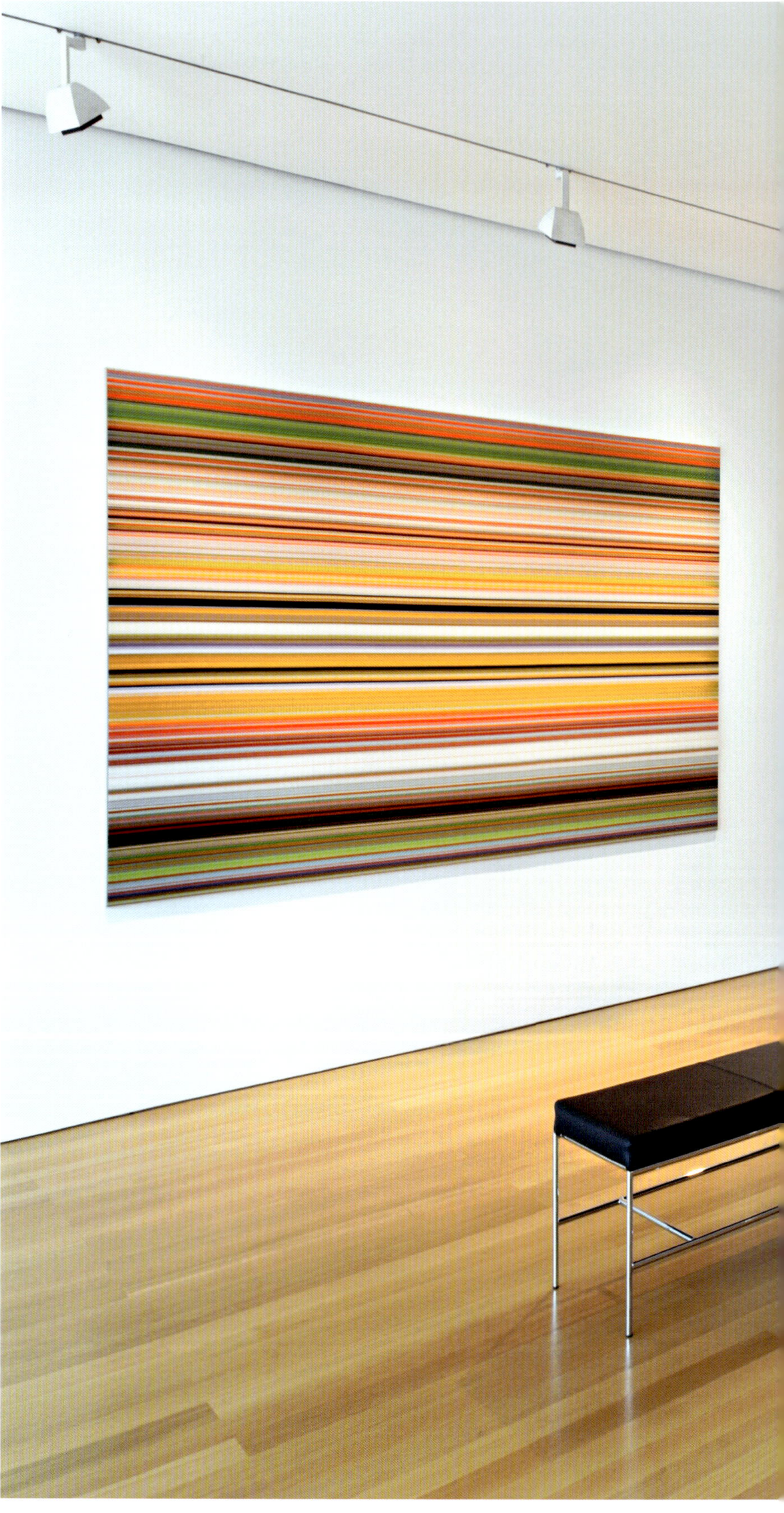

Left to right: Gerhard Richter, *Strip*, 2011; Mark Grotjahn, *Untitled (Blinded Jungle Composition BRD face 43.21)*, 2011; Cy Twombly, *Leaving Paphos Ringed with Waves (IV)*, 2009

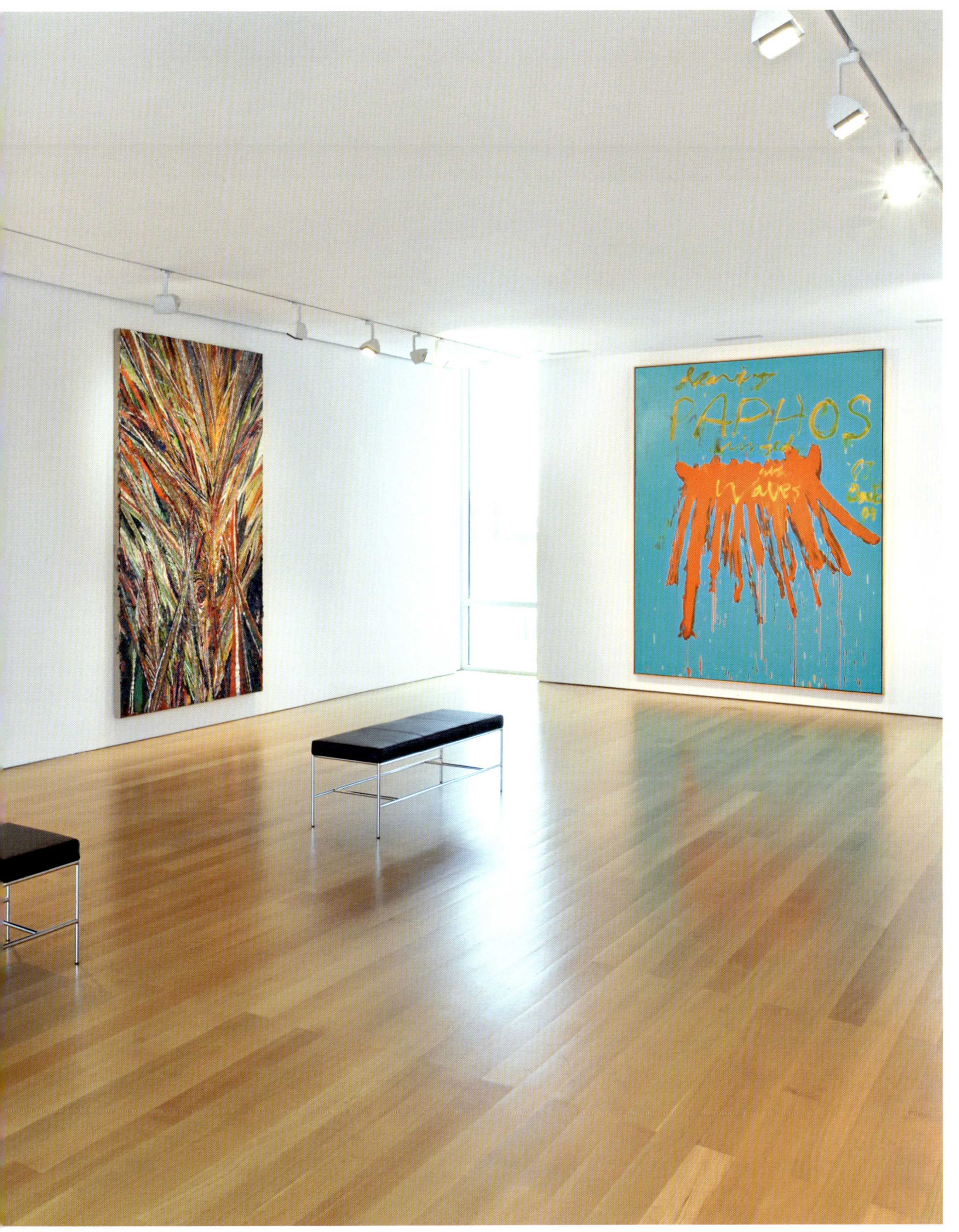
PAPHOS

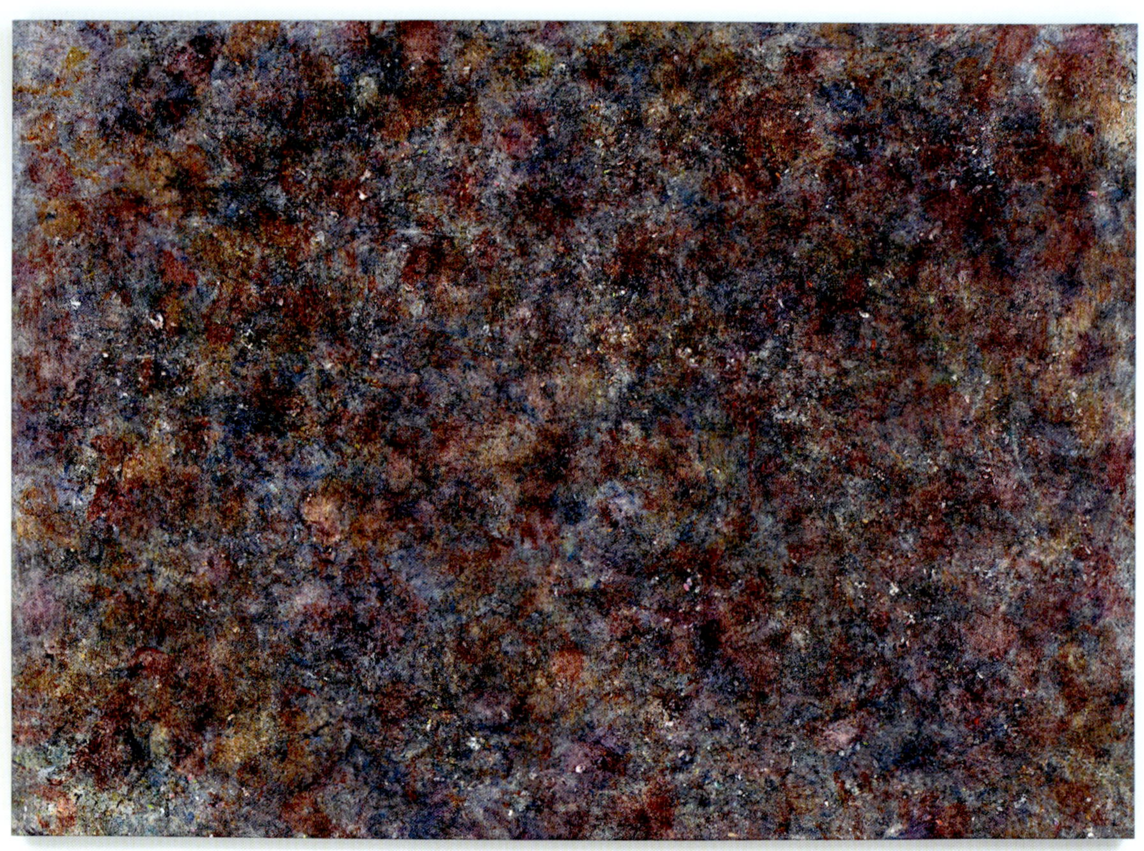

Dan Colen, *Zero for Conduct*, 2011

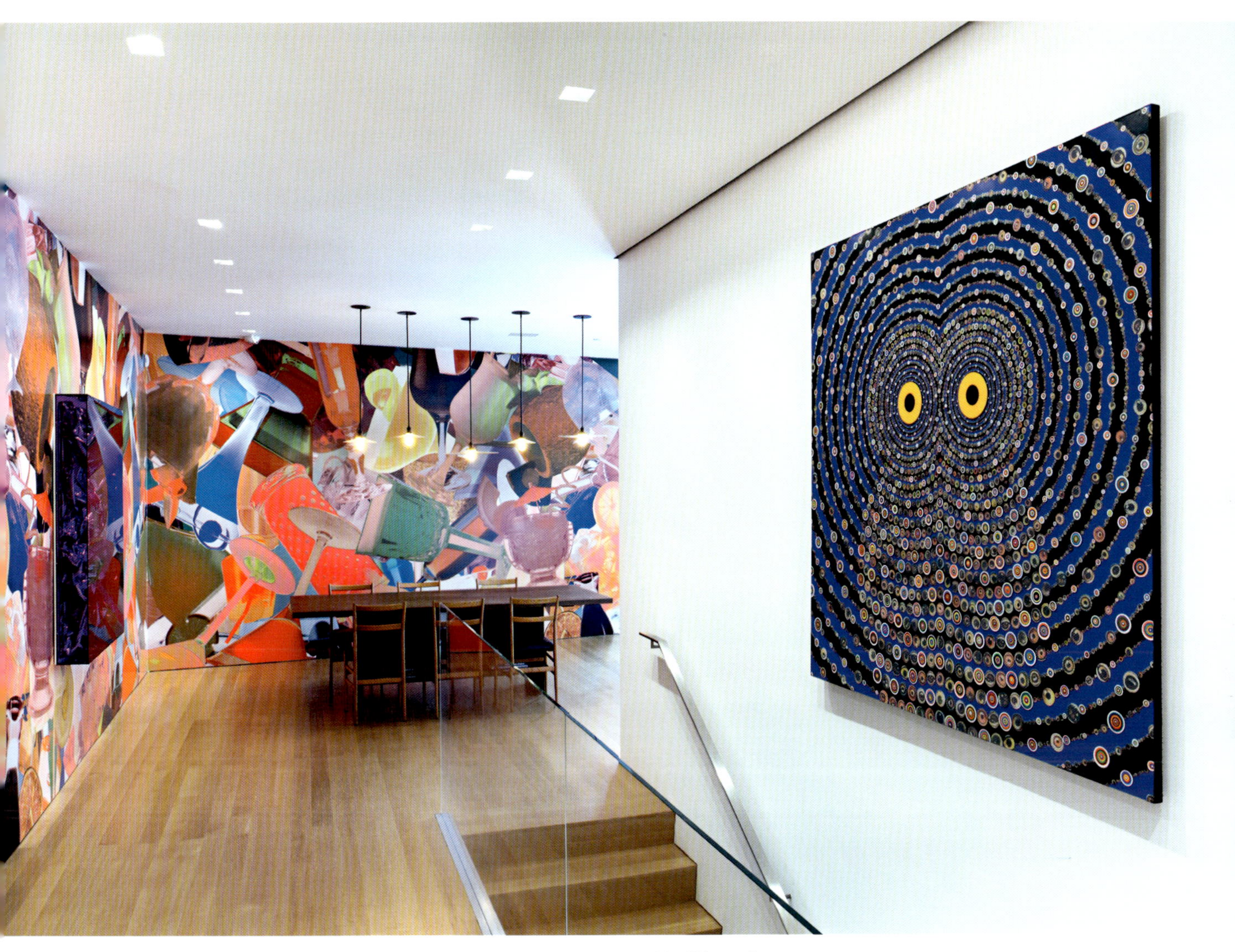

Left to right: assume vivid astro focus, *Cocktails*, 2004; Anselm Reyle, *Untitled*, 2010; Fred Tomaselli, *Night Music for Raptors–Blue*, 2011

RICHARD FORSTER

January 21–May 12, 2012

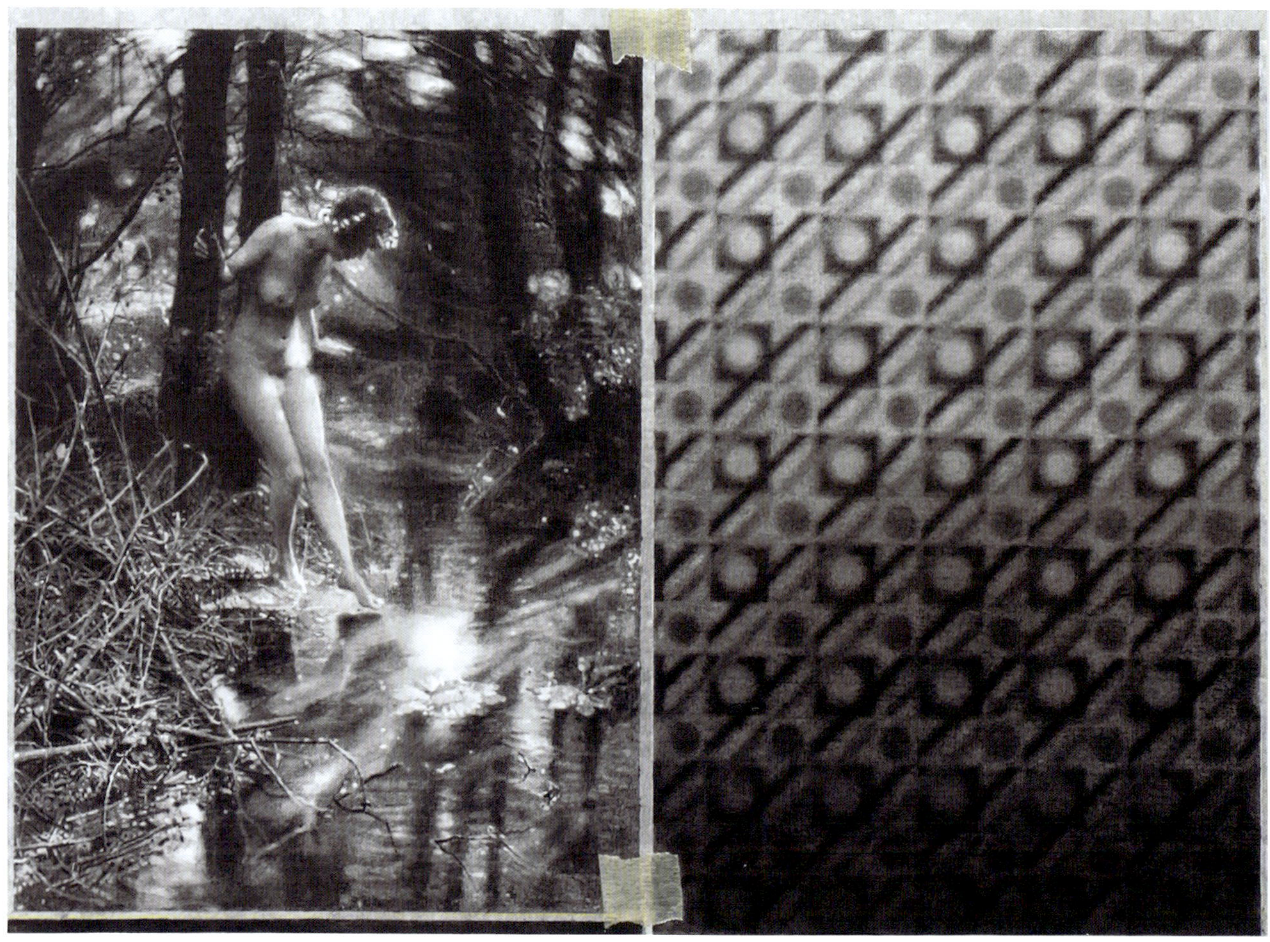

Richard Forster, *American Pastoral/Ostalgie Pattern with tape*, 2011

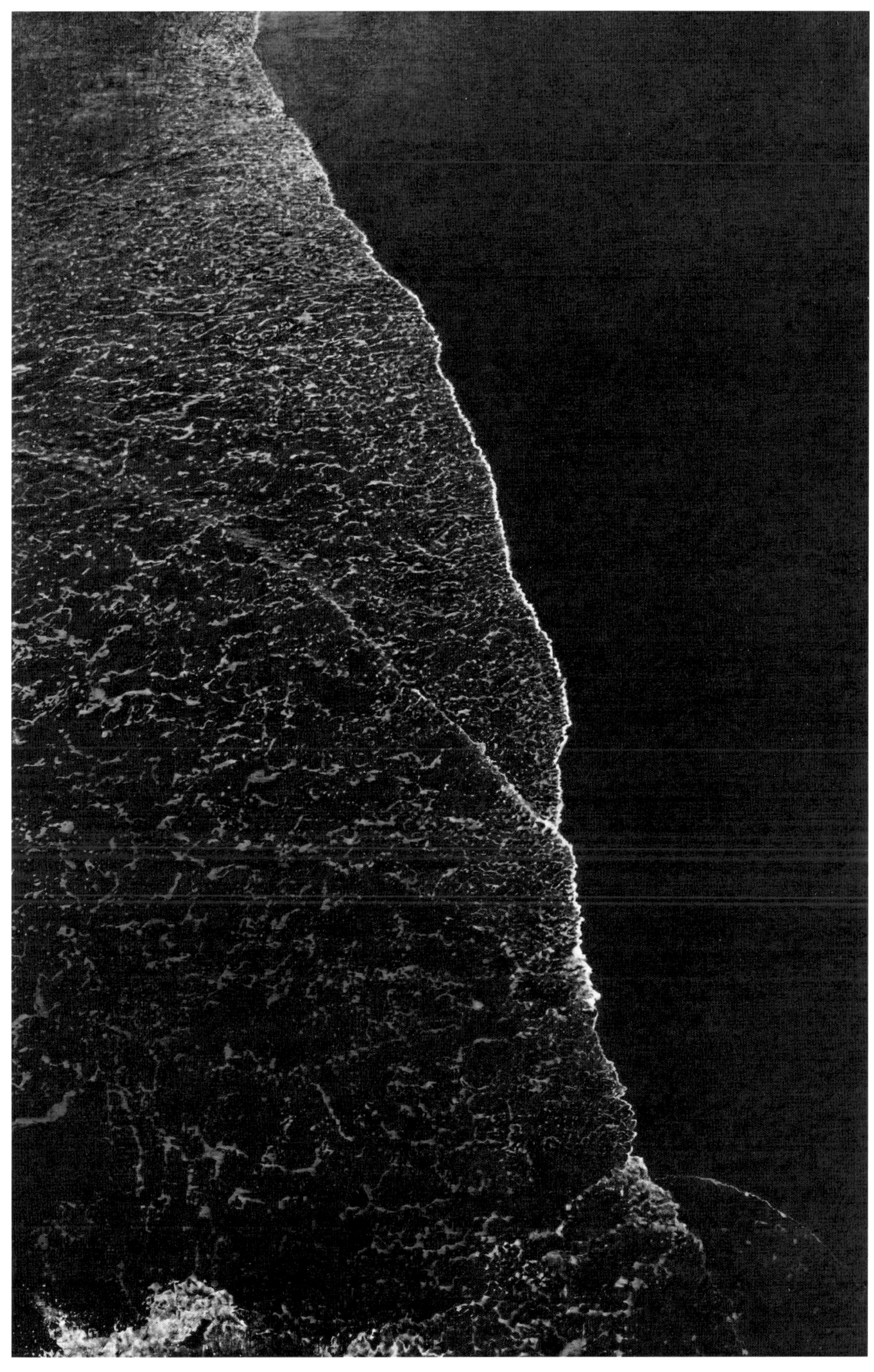

Richard Forster, *Incoming Sea's edge on fourteen consecutive occasions at random time intervals. Saltburn-by-the-Sea, Jan 5th 2010; 11.30–11.37 am*, 2011

WATCH YOUR STEP

June 7–August 24, 2012

Artists

Grimanesa Amoros
Polly Apfelbaum
Lynda Benglis
Patricia Cronin
Tara Donovan
Tom Friedman
Felix Gonzalez-Torres
Mona Hatoum
Steven and William Ladd
Wolfgang Laib
Richard Long
Joe Mangrum
Michael Phelan
Richard Serra
Kiki Smith
Matthew Stone
Julianne Swartz
Venske & Spänle
Corban Walker

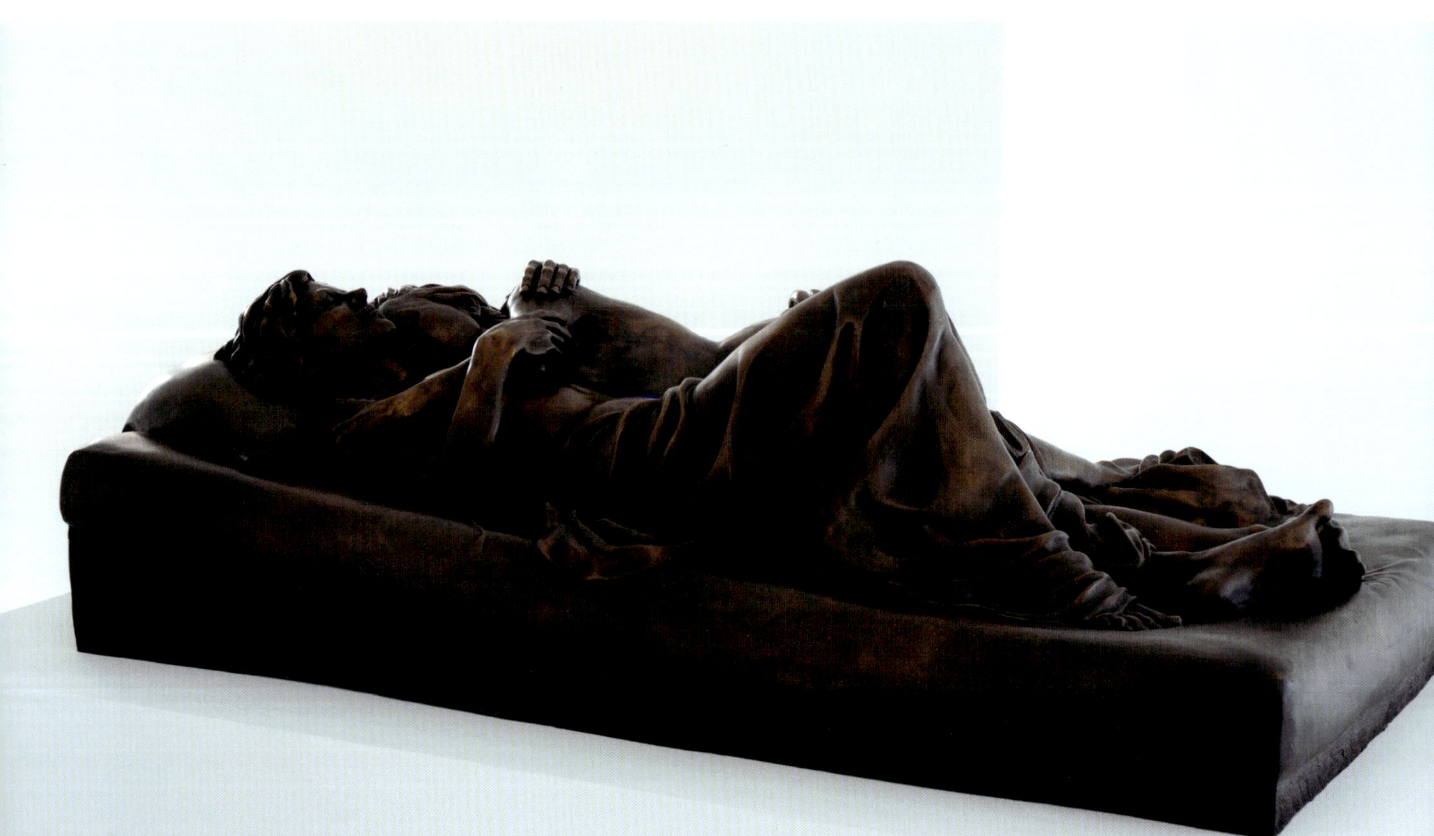

Patricia Cronin, *Memorial to a Marriage*, 2010

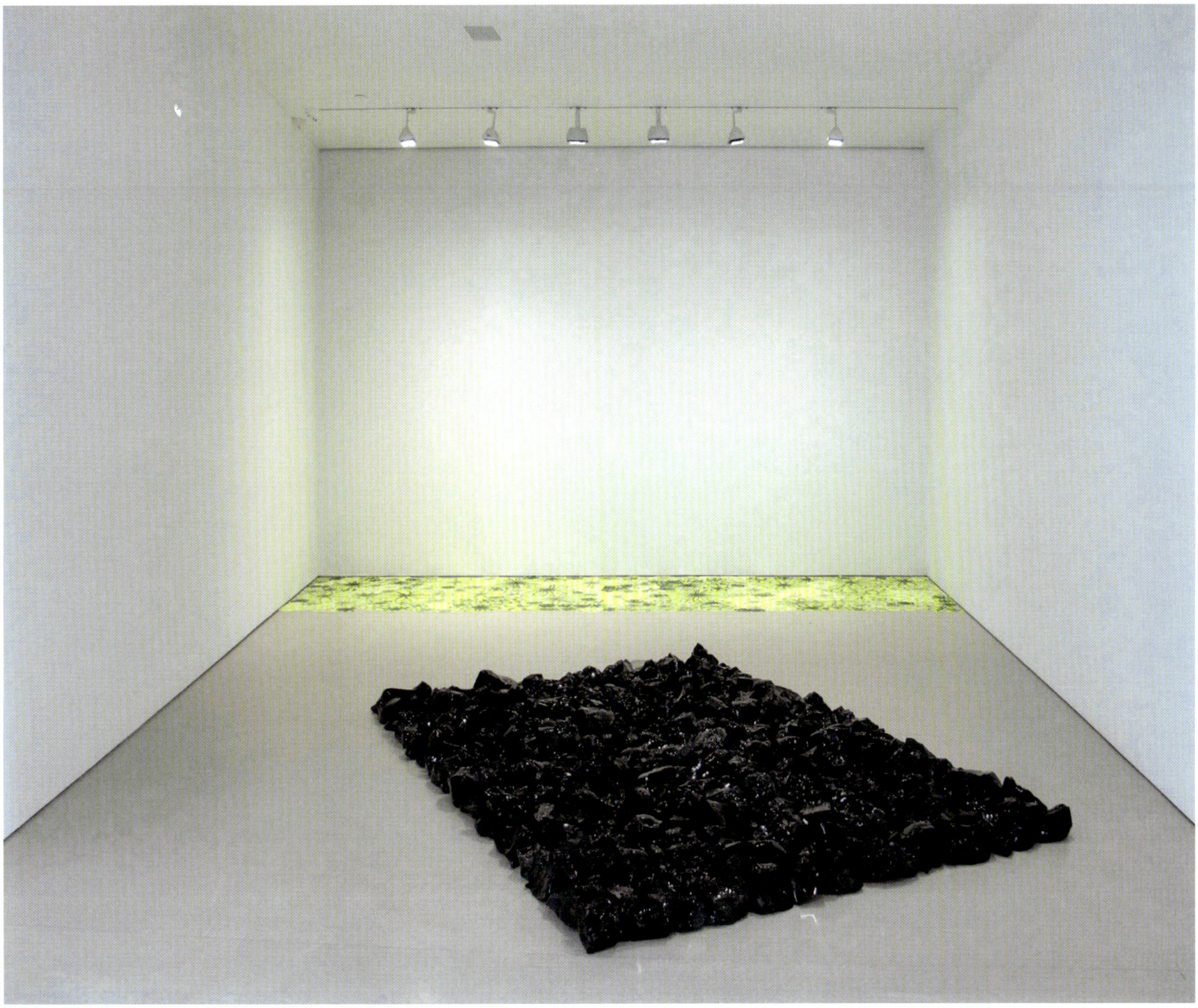

Background: Polly Apfelbaum, *Rihanna*, 2012; foreground: Michael Phelan, *Tomorrow's a new day. . . (No. 5)*, 2009–11

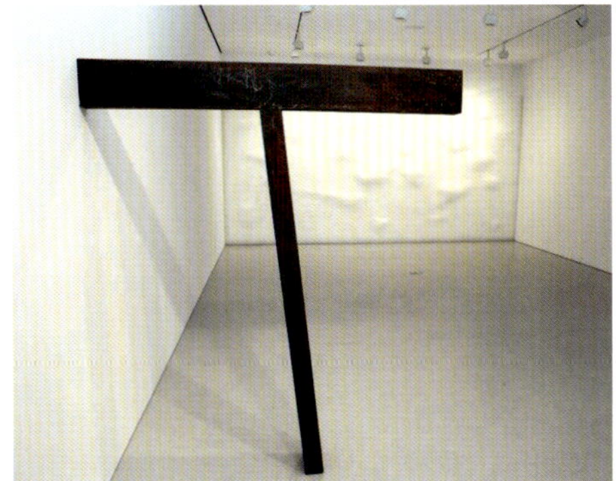

Background: Tara Donovan, *Haze*, 2005; foreground: Richard Serra, *Even Level*, 1987

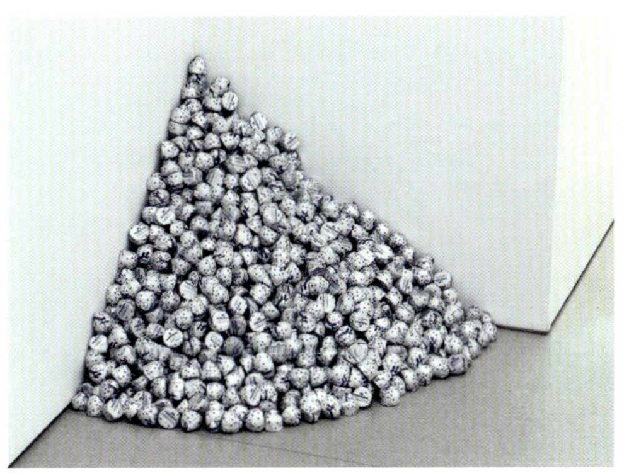

Felix Gonzalez-Torres, *"Untitled" (A Corner of Baci)*, 1990

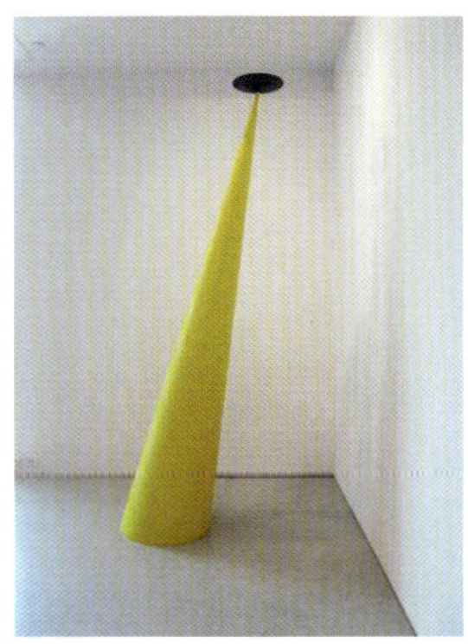

Tom Friedman, *UFO*, 2006

FUNNY.

September 21–October 27, 2012
Curated by Heidi Zuckerman

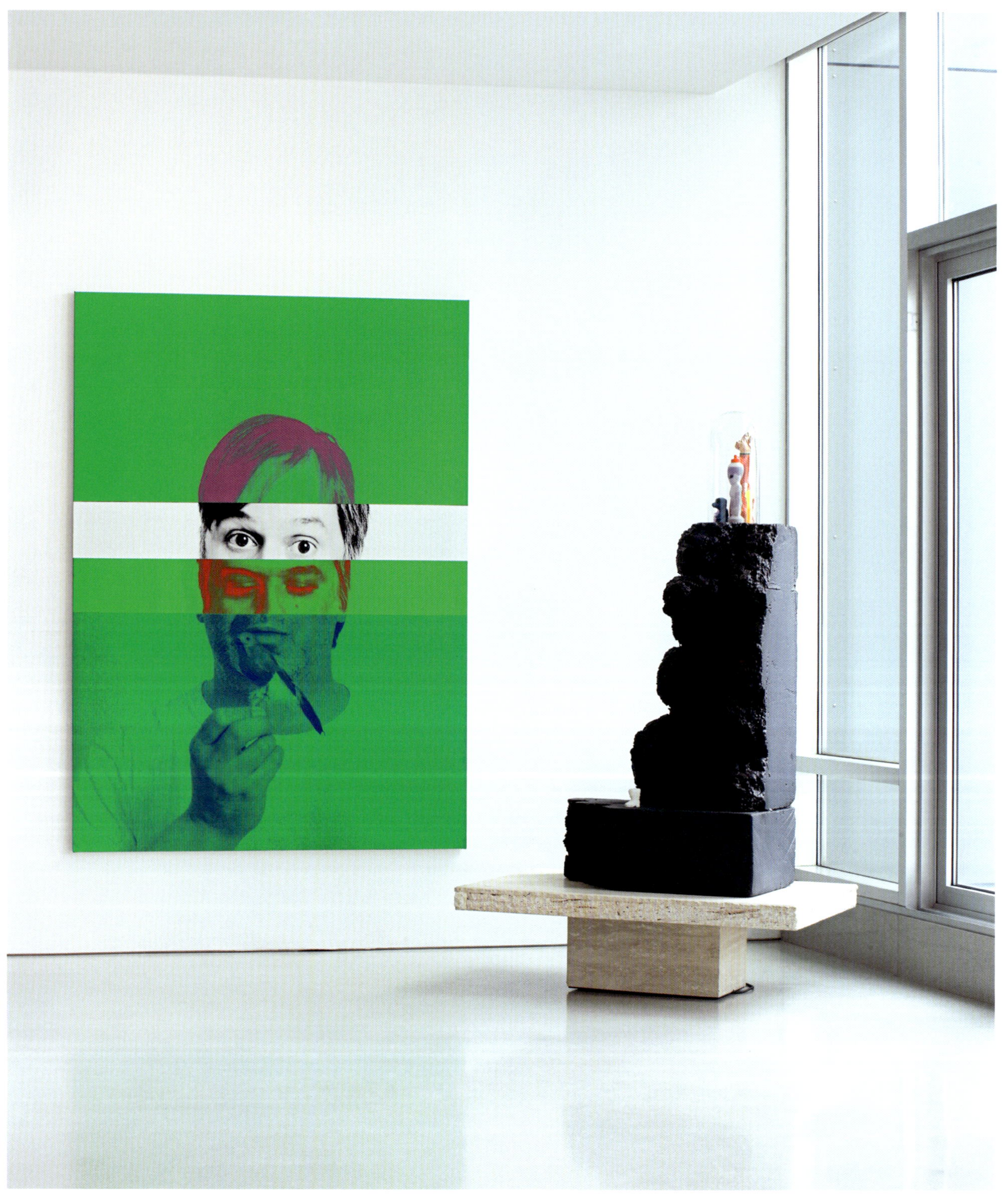

Left to right: Rob Pruitt, *Exquisite Self-Portrait: The Naturalist*, 2010; Mike Kelley, *Topo Gigio Topographical Model*, 2011

Artists
Lisa Anne Auerbach
Lutz Bacher
Darren Bader
John Bock
Maurizio Cattelan
Peter Coffin
Simon Evans
Ceal Floyer
Peter Fischli and David Weiss
Robert Gober
Joseph Grigely
Matthew Higgs
Jim Hodges
Matt Johnson
Mike Kelley
Friedrich Kunath
Hanna Liden
Sarah Lucas
Mads Lynnerup
Alix Pearlstein
Jack Pierson
Richard Prince
Rob Pruitt
Sara Greenberger Rafferty
David Shrigley
Haim Steinbach
Erwin Wurm

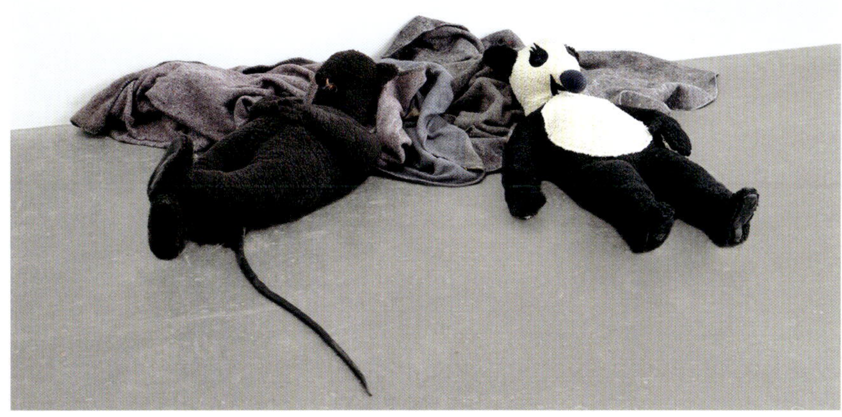

Peter Fischli and David Weiss, *Rat and Bear (Sleeping)*, 2008

When I curated the exhibition *Funny.* at The FLAG Art Foundation, I was really focused on the period that I placed after the word "funny" in the exhibition title. At the time, I intended it as a qualification, an indication that something was funny. Kind of. Mostly. I also thought a lot about the opening sentence of my essay for the exhibition catalogue: "I am constantly having to remind my husband that I am funny." After some time, I now think that the period was about space: the insertion of this punctuation as a means to allow a pause, a moment to think and collect oneself before moving forward.

Funny. included one of my favorite artworks of all time, *Rat and Bear (Sleeping)* (2008) by Peter Fischli and David Weiss, but I never got to see it included in the exhibition. The work arrived late, having come from a show at SFMOMA, and I was planning on seeing it when I returned to New York post-opening for a talk. Yet, on that day, Hurricane Sandy hit, and the show had to be closed prematurely, along with the entire building and all the exhibitions on view. Like many people, my life was permanently affected by that storm and what happened in the days immediately afterward. I found myself "stuck" in New York without power, mobile phone service, or a flight out. Time itself was suspended in a manner I had not experienced before nor have since. My interactions with others during that time had an intensity akin to an otherworldly connection. We existed there and then together in a non-chosen time warp—a long and completely unexpected pause. We stood in and experienced the space of the punctuation. It was Funny.

Today, five years later, I walked through our exhibition *Wade Guyton Peter Fischli David Weiss* (2017) at the Aspen Art Museum with someone very close to me and stopped in front of *Rat and Bear (Sleeping)*. I have spent countless hours with the work over the last few months. But today, I felt that pause as we stood in silence in the darkened gallery space, breathing alongside the sculptures. And I told him, someone I don't have to remind that I'm funny, this story.

—Heidi Zuckerman

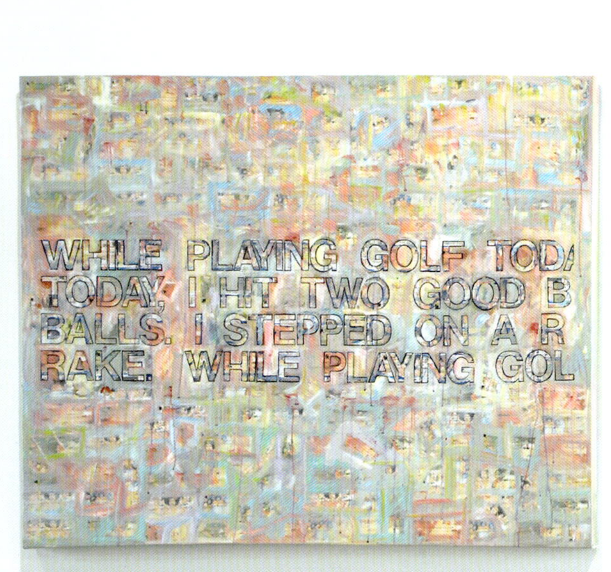

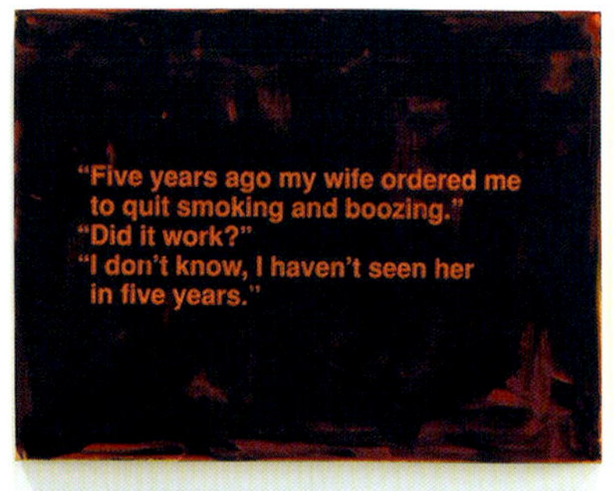

Left to right: Richard Prince, *Untitled (Joke)*, 2005; *Untitled (Five Years Ago My Wife)*, 1998

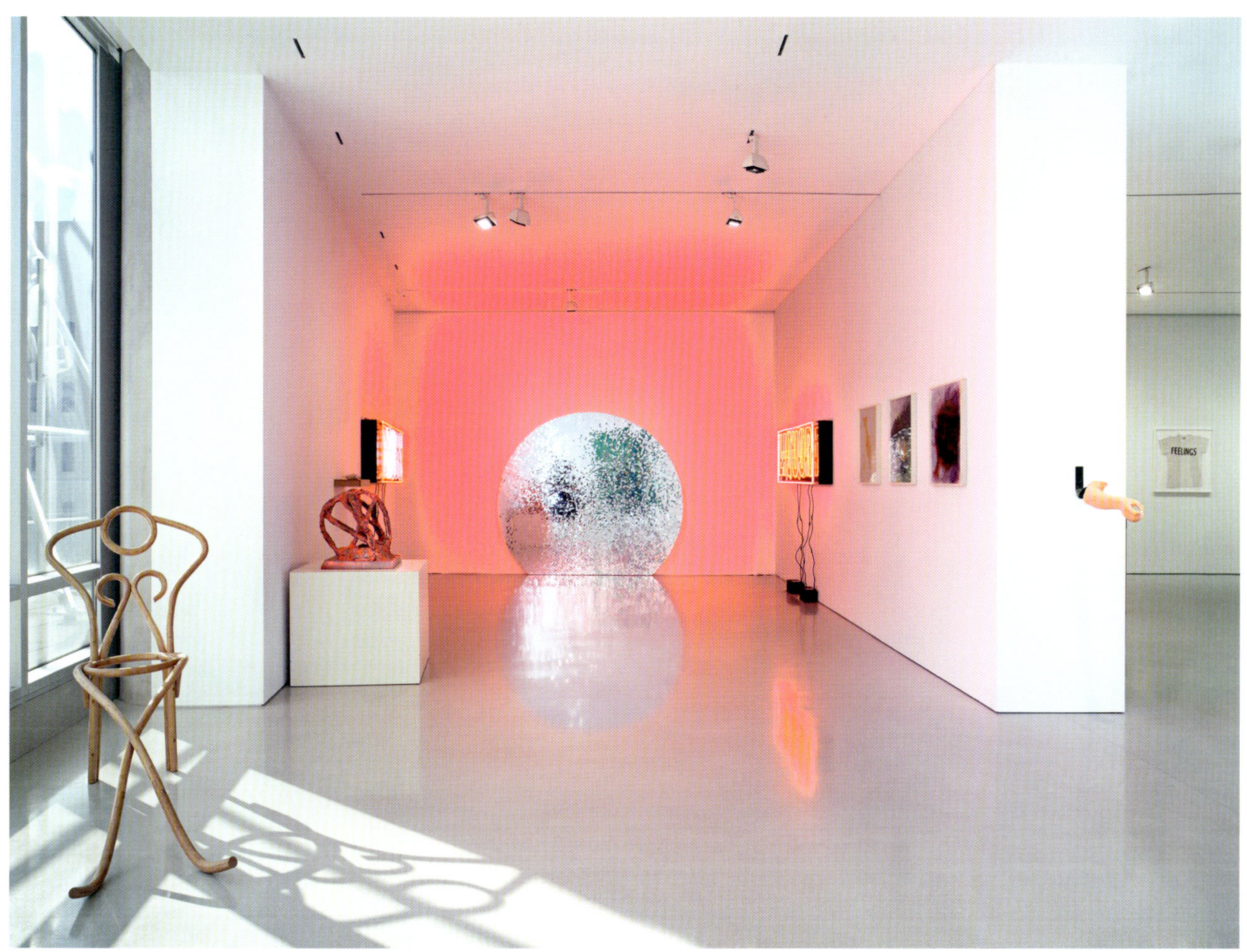

Installation view

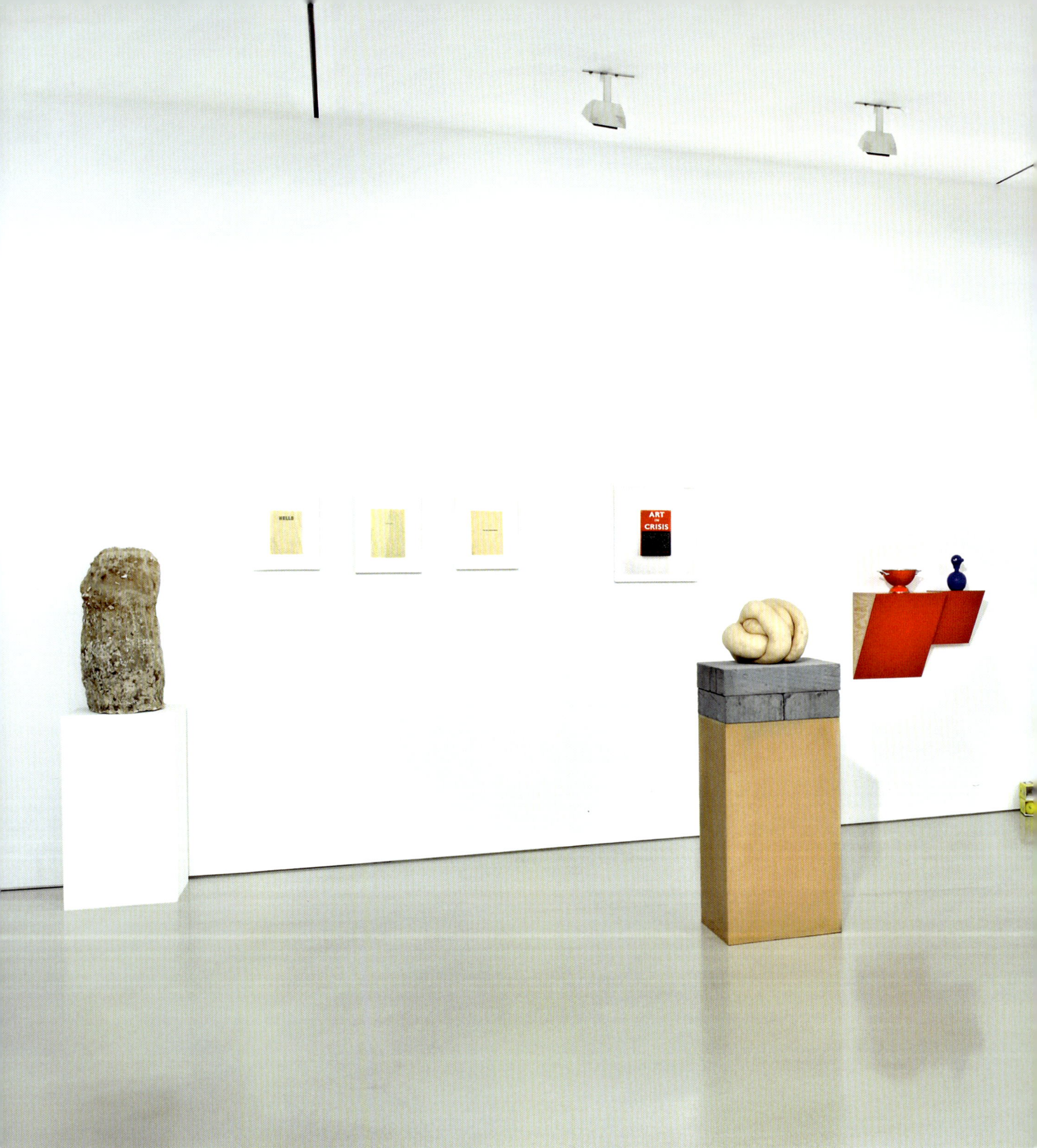

Installation view

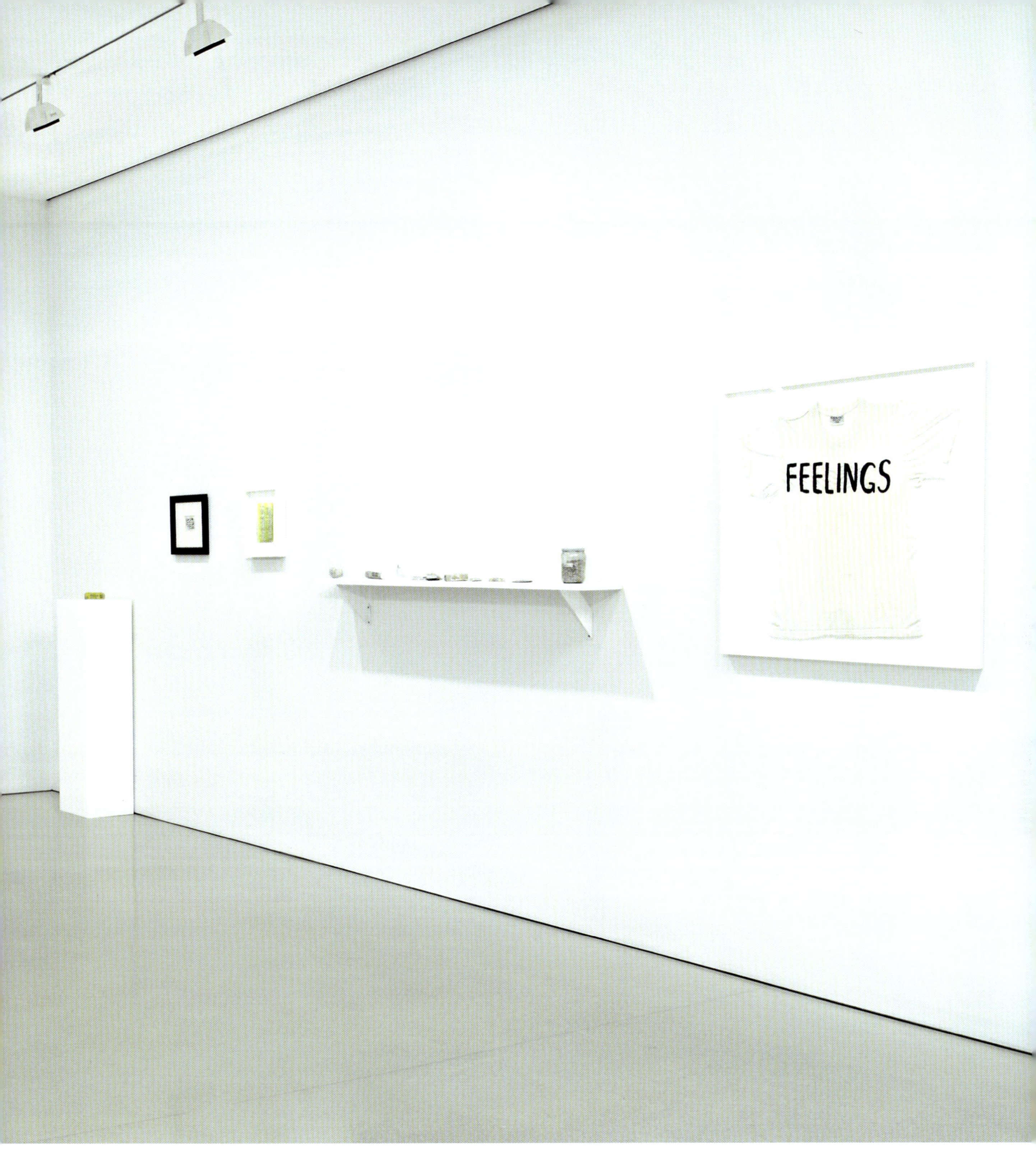
FEELINGS

LESLEY VANCE

September 21–October 27, 2012

Memories from my 2012 solo FLAG exhibition have such a presence in my mind, because more than nearly any other experience, they connect me to a specific moment in my practice and bring a sense of immediacy to each of the events during that time.

In this case, what comes to mind when I think about the FLAG show: the Manhattan views from the tenth-story windows, the Ugo Rondinone sculpture on the terrace, Shaquille O'Neal's monstrous shoe in a drawer, running into curator Gary Garrels outside on the street during installation when I was totally stuck (he figured it out!), and the colors and darknesses within my abstract paintings, which had become one with a particular trip to the Norton Simon Museum in Pasadena in 2008. During that visit, I walked from Vassily Kandinsky's *Heavy Circles* (1927) over to Francisco de Zurbarán's *Still Life with Lemons, Oranges and a Rose* (1633). Having spent a few years making small representational paintings of organic objects, I had lately become grumpy, feeling that something in my work needed to change. I had no idea how this should happen. But standing in front of that Zurbarán after the Kandinsky made it clear. It was most likely the fruit—the lemons and oranges began to spin out from the surface of the painting, seemingly freeing themselves from their forms so they could fulfill their destinies as celestial bodies. These paintings were kindred spirits. I wanted to know what would have happened if Zurbarán had continued painting beyond this point. The painting is perfect, so I'm glad he didn't, but I still wanted to know. The quest I envisioned was different from simply abstracting what was before him. So I went back to the studio to get to work.

The show at FLAG captured a very focused period, a time when I discovered and developed my painting language over the course of the years between that visit to Pasadena and the week we installed my show in New York. It contained all that intense energy. Looking back at the works in the show, my initial feeling is, *How did I make those?!* I never know how I've made a painting when I finish it.

—Lesley Vance

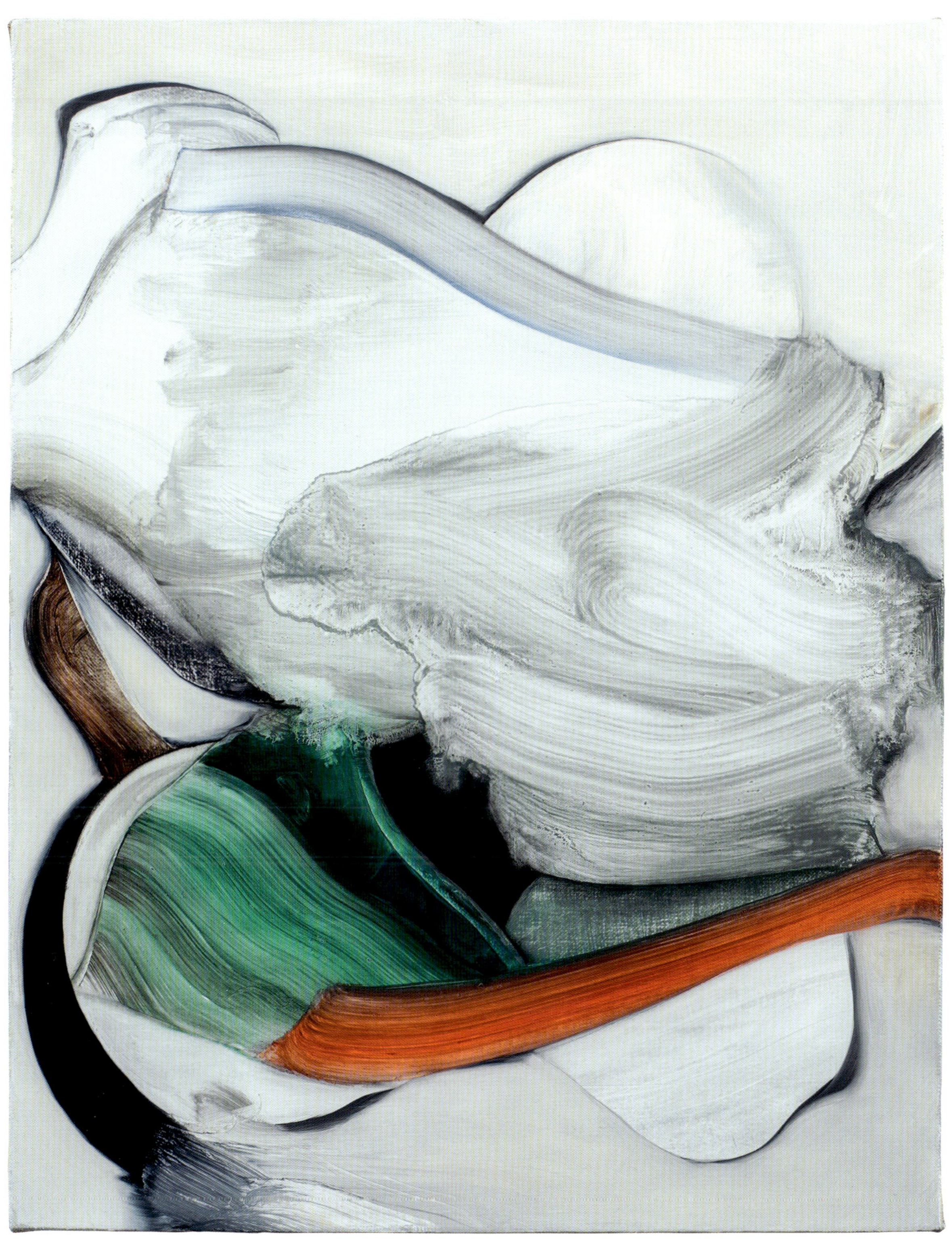

Lesley Vance, *Untitled*, 2012

TOM MOLLOY: ISSUE

February 8–May 18, 2013

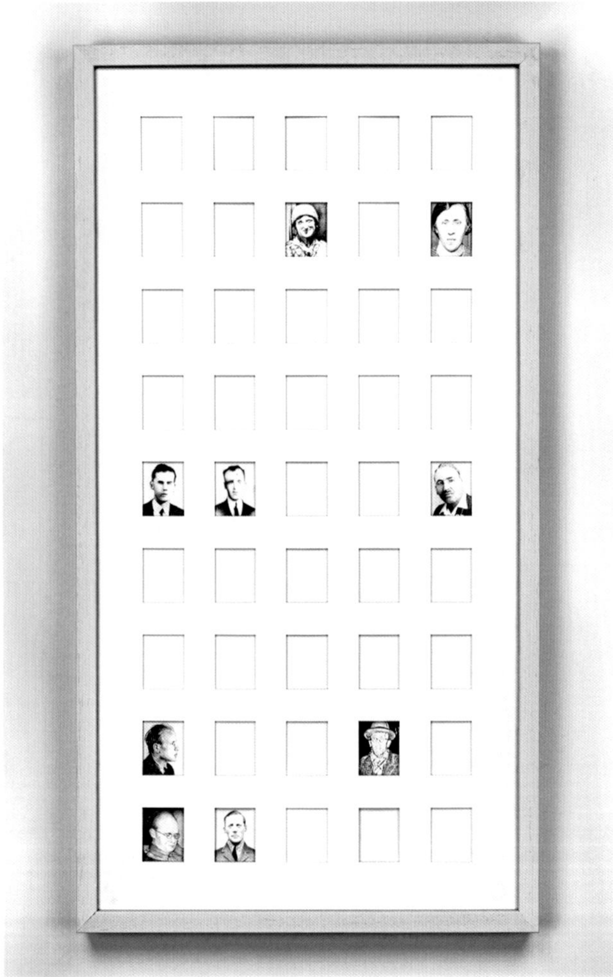

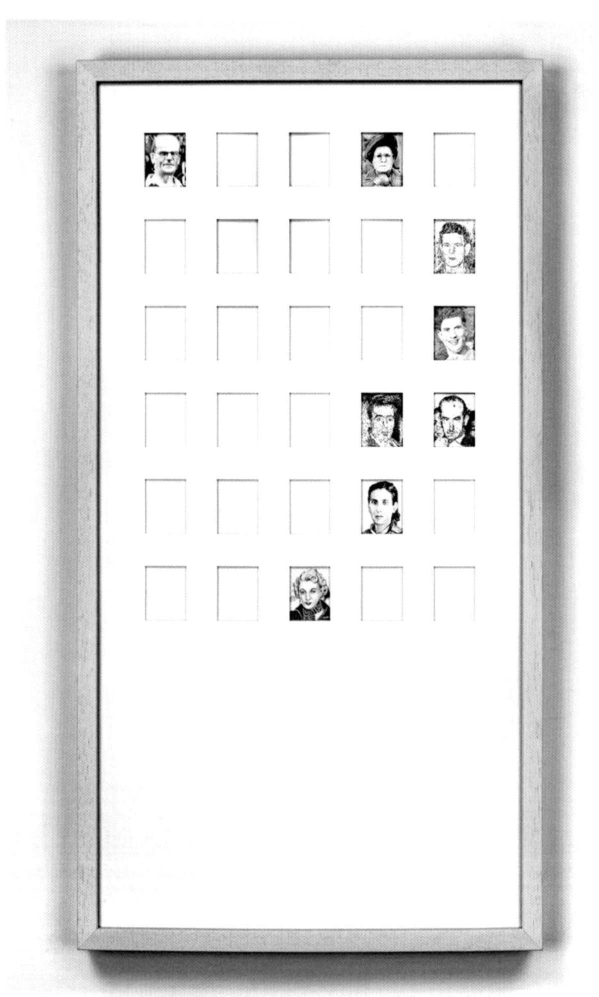

Detail, Tom Molloy, *Albert*, 2012

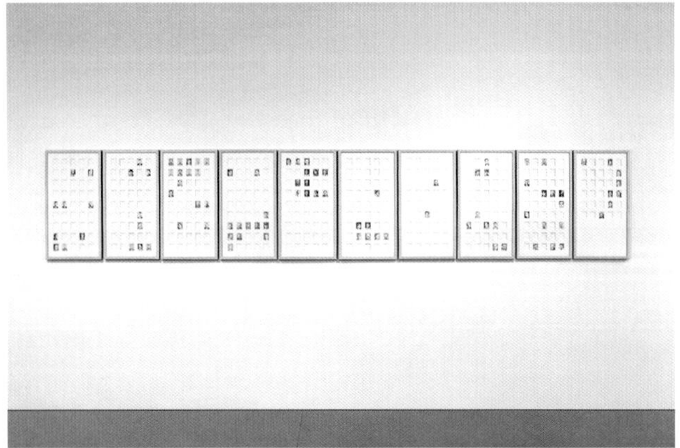

Installation view

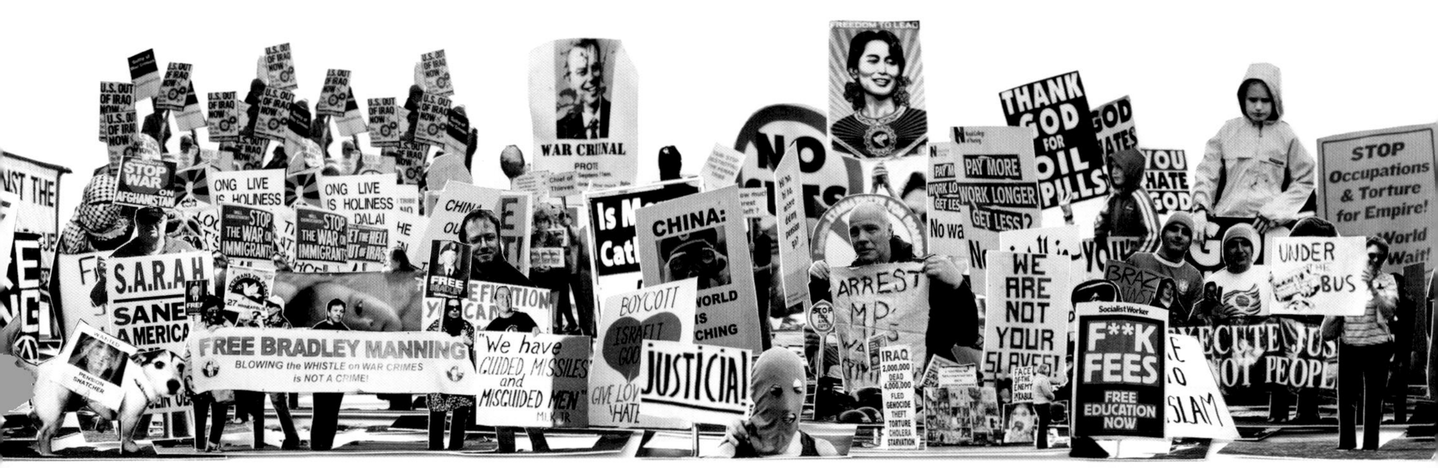

Detail, Tom Molloy, *Protest*, 2012

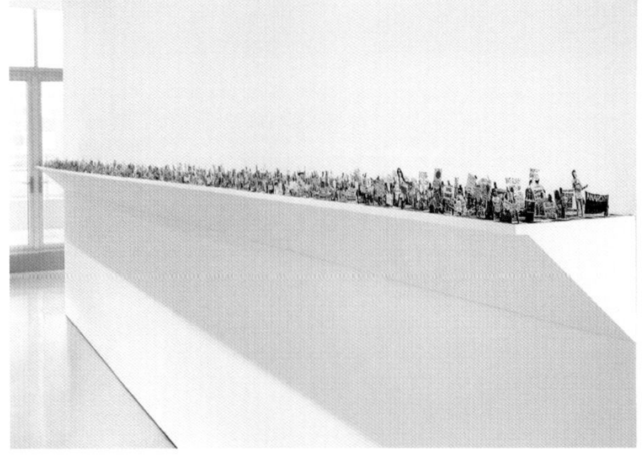

Installation view

HILARY HARKNESS

February 8–May 18, 2013

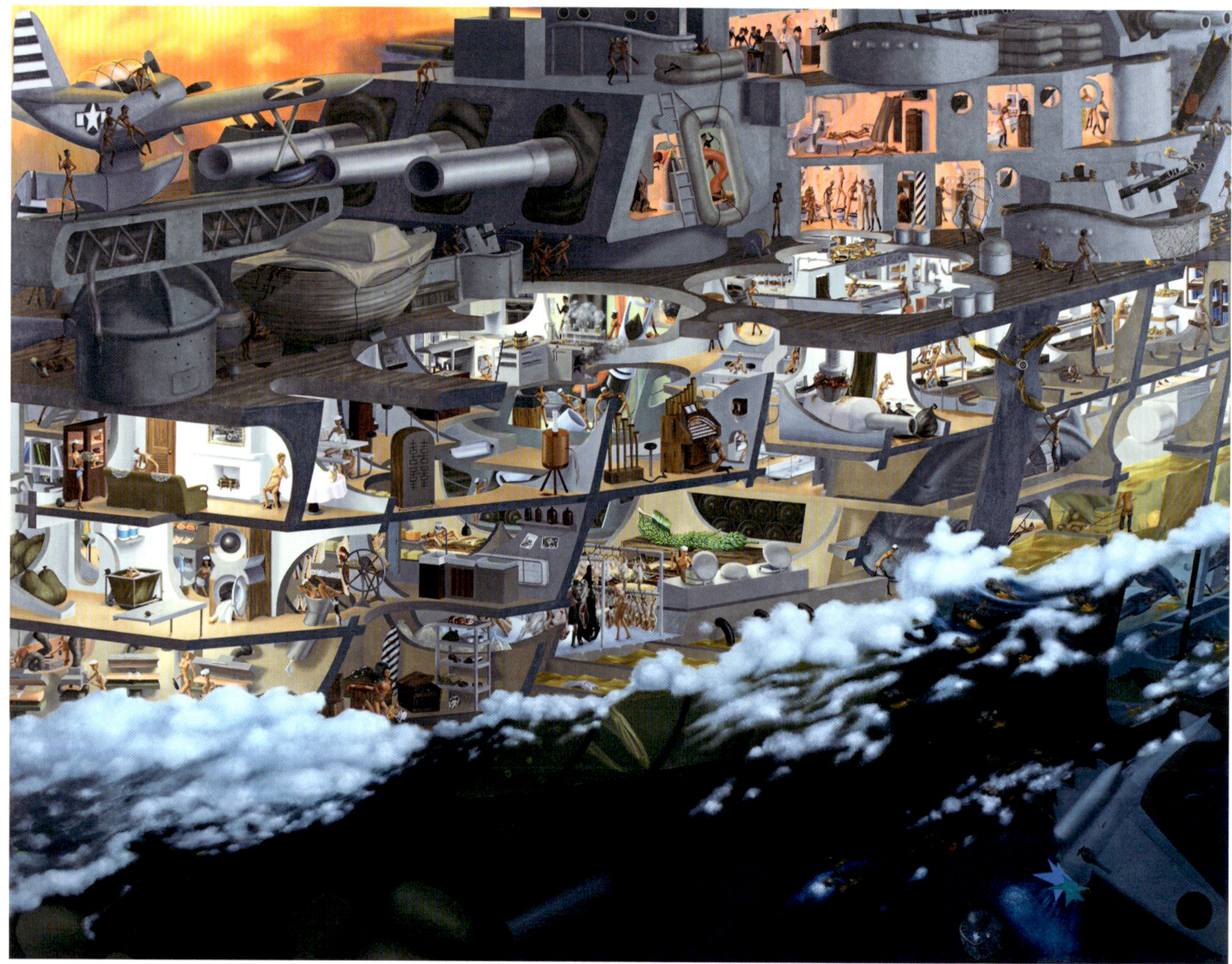

Hilary Harkness, *Fully Committed, Might Mo'*, 2007–8

Opposite: Detail, Hilary Harkness, *Fully Committed, Might Mo'*, 2007–8

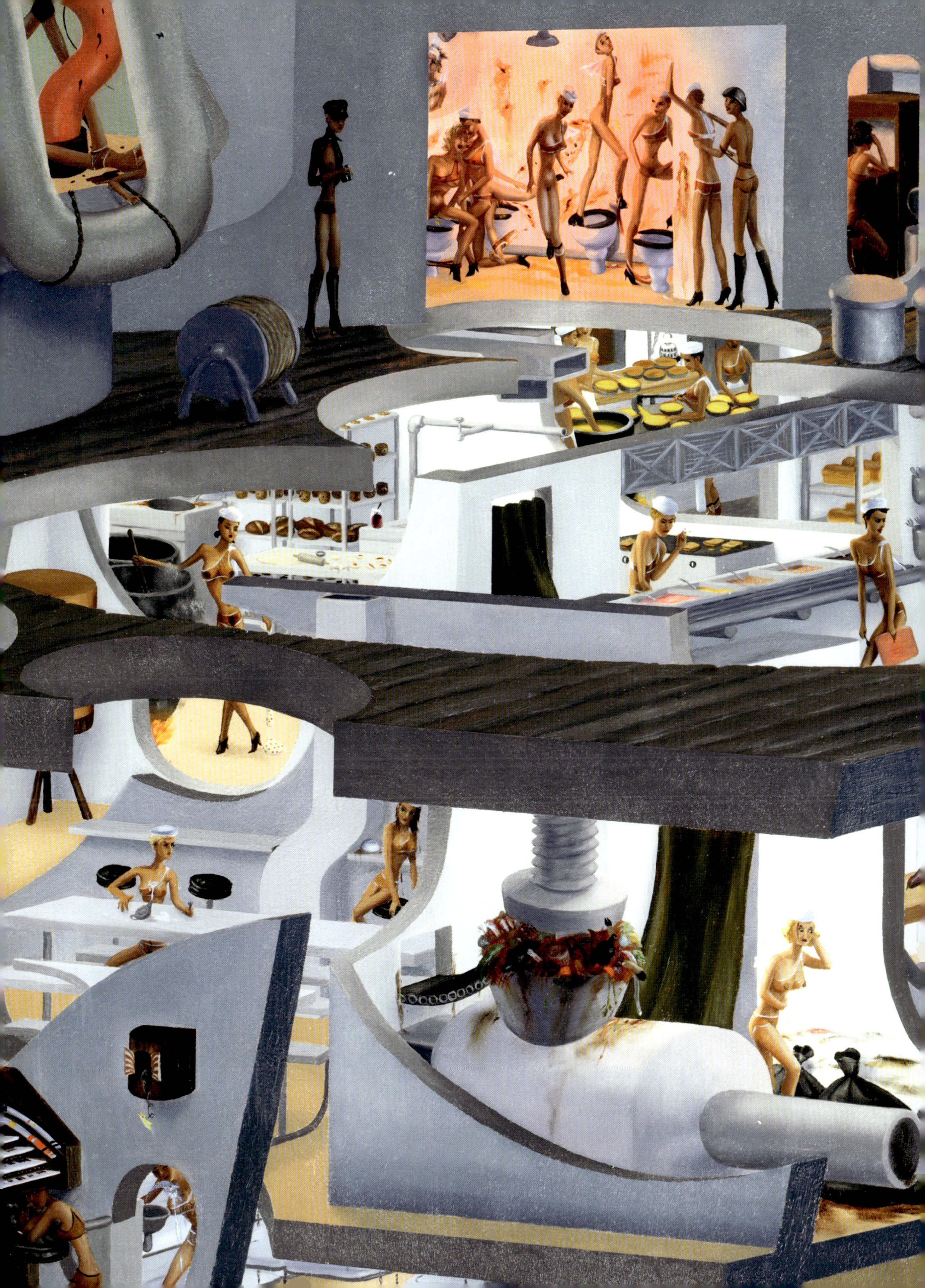

New York, 2012. Glenn Fuhrman calls and invites me to show my complete body of cross-section paintings from the past twelve years. It's an invitation I gladly accept, while breaking into a horrified sweat. The paintings were never meant to be hung together.

San Francisco, late '90s. I'm recovering from art school; from the East Coast; from feeling like there wasn't space for me as an emerging artist. I'm throwing that experience away and starting over. I run in Golden Gate Park. I rest. I read. I paint.

I look out my studio window and see auto body shops and a convenience store. There is a small movie house down the block. I reimagine these into postapocalyptic cross-sectioned street scenes where you can see everything and how it all works.

Power? Women have seized control.

Food? Pigs are being raised and slaughtered in the streets.

Reproduction? Men are chained up in the movie theater, forced to fuck pigeon carcasses for semen collection.

Science? Pigs and pigeons may or may not be successfully interbreeding with human genetic material as an aid.

But it's far from utopia.

The paintings take on a maximalist quality. More is never enough.

New York, early 2000s. Both of my U.S. military veteran grandfathers die in quick succession. I move to Chelsea and begin painting cross-sections of battleships where all of the sailors are women. I'm getting more interested in chains of command and what happens to honor and valor when boredom and other catastrophes strike. I'm still preoccupied with genetics and reproduction. Over time, I also begin exploring what happens when domesticity and commerce enter this dystopia. These are the paintings that Glenn Fuhrman will discover.

New York, 2013. FLAG, with help from my longtime art dealer Mary Boone, works swiftly to coordinate the loans of my paintings across collections and time zones. I'm grateful for the time that Glenn, Stephanie Roach, Ron Warren, the staff at FLAG, and the Mary Boone Gallery staff devoted to pulling it off.

The show opens.

I experience the collective force of over 1,200 individual characters as an explosion. I walk through the show with a sense of wonder, seeing many of my paintings for the first time in a decade. It was like another Hilary had painted them, and I marvel at her invention.

The numerous events that FLAG graciously hosts while the show is up provide me with many opportunities to give each painting a closer look. Looking brings back intimate memories from my life over the years.

Here's the detail where I fell in love.

Here's the detail where I lost a loved one.

This detail here—I can hear the music I was listening to.

New York, 2014. I'm in my studio painting *Blue Nude*, a bedroom scene with three ladies, two dogs, a decapitated head, and a Matisse painting. It's part of another body of work. Glenn reaches out again to invite me to join Ewan Gibbs in curating *Roy Lichtenstein: Nudes and Interiors* and to contribute "something Lichtenstein" of my own to the show.

I think about Lichtenstein in my work. It figures in two of my cross-section paintings, *Nervous in the Service* (2009) and *Pearl Trader* (2006), but Glenn has just shown those. I'll need to think of something else.

My trial drawings are destined for the recycling bin.

I try another tack. Less about the paintings and more about the painters. Roy and Hilary.

Roy and I both fell in love with the art of Picasso and Matisse at a young age. His painterly language grew out of a time and place where comic books, advertising, and other popular culture references were hard to ignore. Add fashion magazines, old movies, and video games to my list.

Roy's late nudes, some of which I chose to feature in the show, were painted when he was in his seventies, when he no longer had anything to prove and nothing to lose. The ease that came with this ultimate mastery is evident in the pervasive joie de vivre of these works. Lichtenstein had a freedom that is so powerful for artists—one that allows for interiority and agency, and space to play.

I turn back to the painting already nearly finished on my easel, *Blue Nude*. This will be my contribution.

New York, 2017. As FLAG celebrates its tenth anniversary, I celebrate that it has been one of the important art institutions in my career. There is space for me here—to paint the way I paint, to be the artist I am.

More is still not enough.

—Hilary Harkness

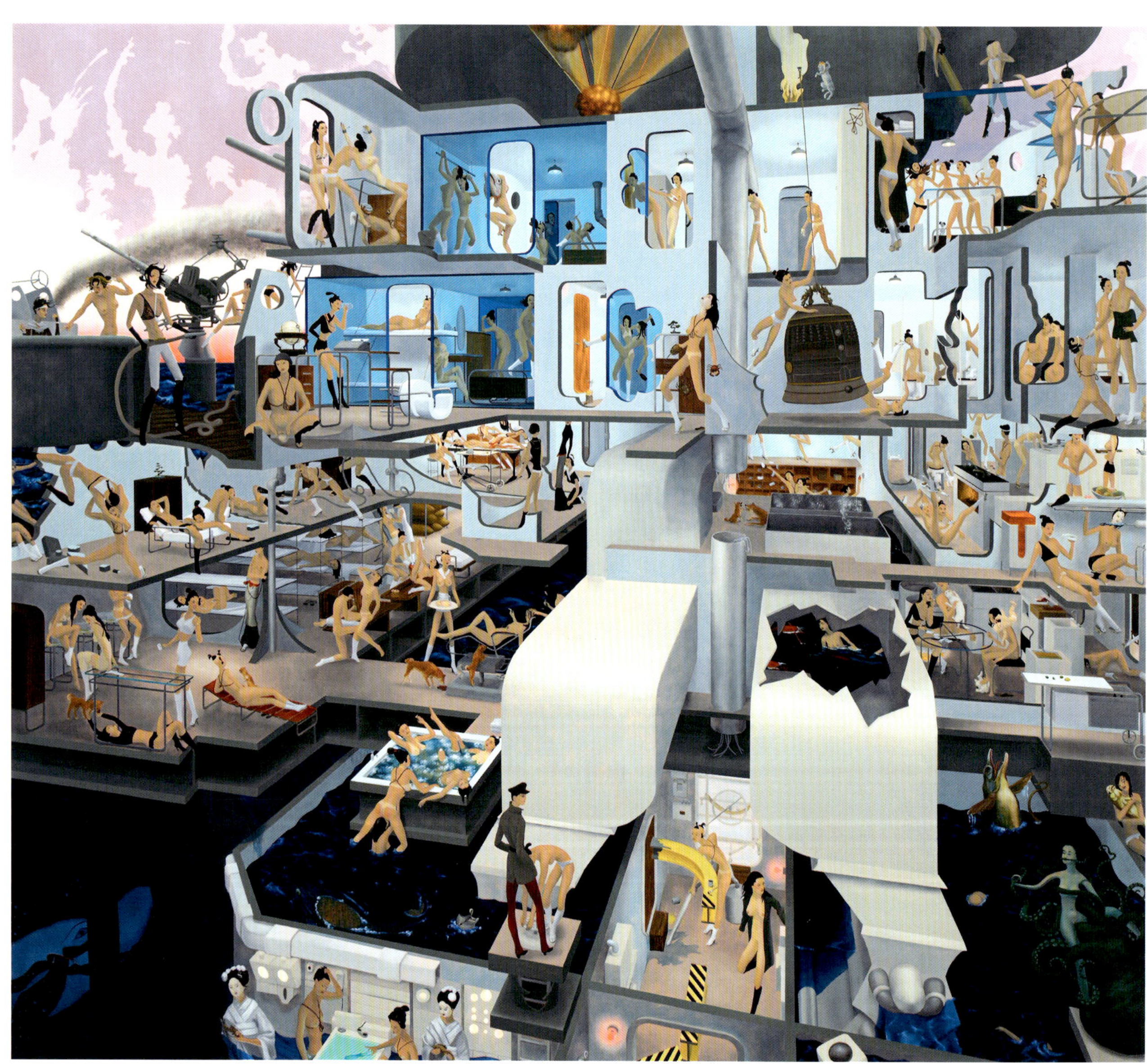

Hilary Harkness, *Red Sky in the Morning*, 2010–11

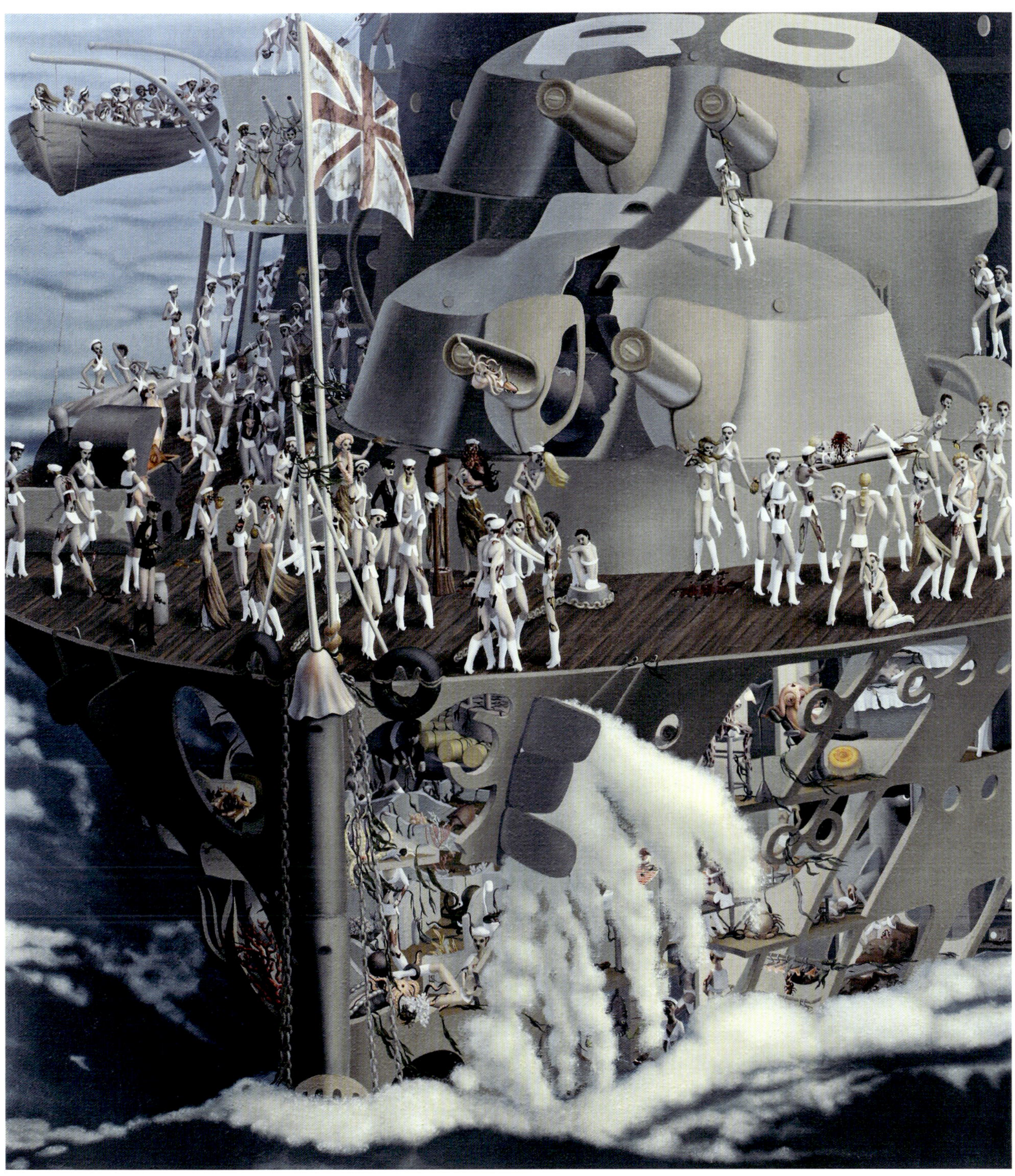

Hilary Harkness, *Crossing the Equator*, 2003

PERSONAL, POLITICAL, MYSTERIOUS

June 7–September 7, 2013

Artists

Louise Bourgeois
Mark Bradford
Jennifer Dalton
Ben Durham
Elmgreen & Dragset
Awol Erizku
Sissi Farassat
Theaster Gates
Ewan Gibbs
Robert Gober
Joseph Grigely
Nancy Grossman
David Hammons
Jim Hodges
Roni Horn
Rashid Johnson
Brian Jungen
Glenn Ligon
Donald Moffett
Tom Molloy
Jonathan Owen
Frank Selby
Robert Therrien
Mickalene Thomas

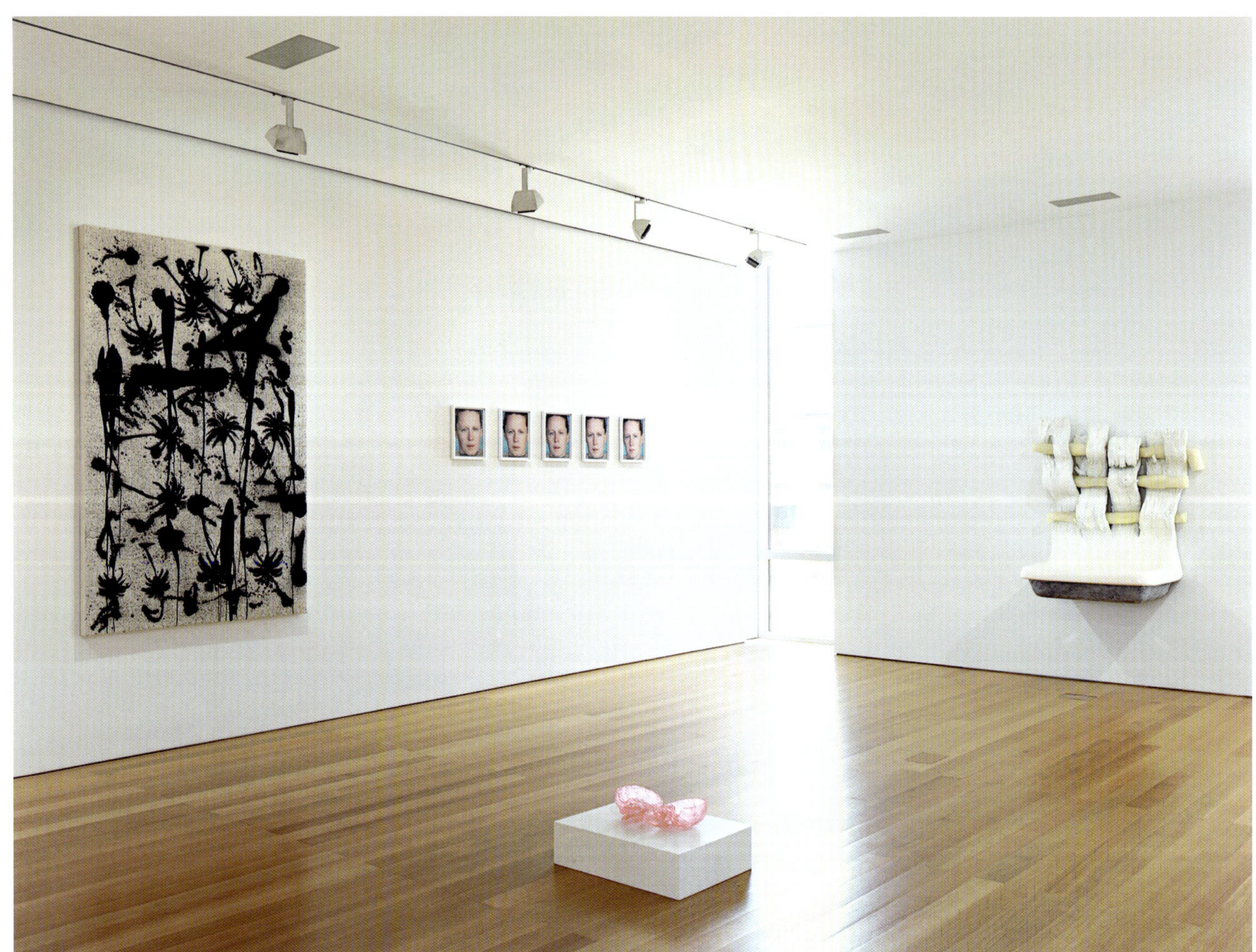

Clockwise from bottom: Jim Hodges, *picturing: my heart*, 2004; Rashid Johnson, *Grindin*, 2011; Roni Horn, *Untitled (Weather)*, 2010–11; Robert Gober, *Untitled*, 2012

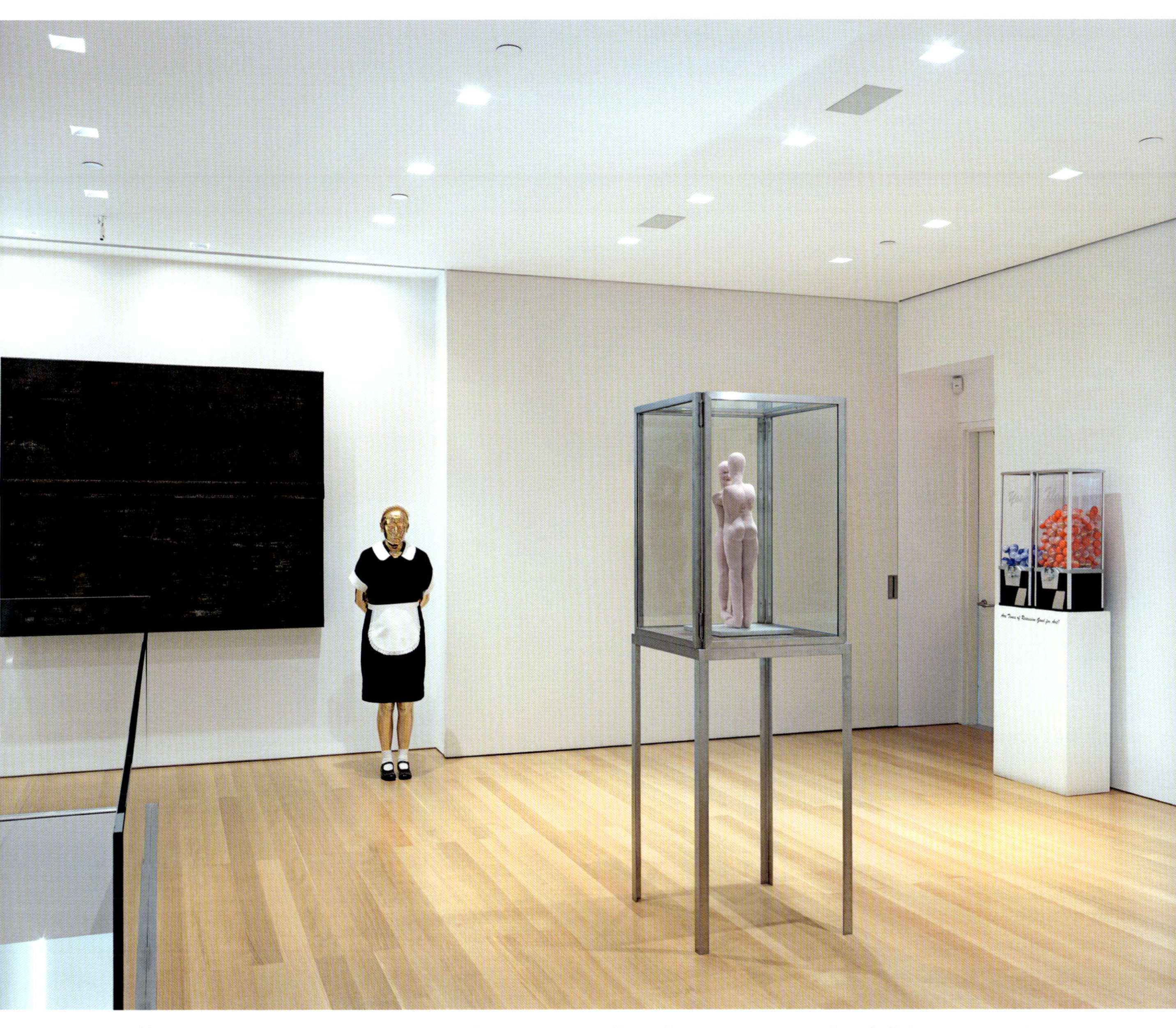

Left to right: Theaster Gates, *Horizon Bleed*, 2013; Elmgreen & Dragset, *Rosa*, 2006; Louise Bourgeois, *Couple*, 2004; Jennifer Dalton, *Are Times of Recession Good for Art?*, 2008

SOMETHING ABOUT A TREE

July 10–September 7, 2013
Curated by Linda Yablonsky

Artists
Darren Bader
Jules de Balincourt
James Brown
Bill Burns
Sarah Cain
Cynthia Daignault
Tacita Dean
Mark Dion
Mitch Epstein
Francesca Gabbiani
Cyprien Gaillard
Sally Gall
Anya Gallaccio
Robert Gober
April Gornik
Rodney Graham
Katy Grannan
George Haas
Jim Hodges
Georgie Hopton
Steven and William Ladd
Jim Lambie
Zoe Leonard
Sherrie Levine
Robert Longo
Andrew Lord
Sarah Lucas
Brendan Lynch
Goshka Macuga
Sylvia Plimack Mangold
Mirabelle Marden
Tony Matelli
Rory McEwen
Peter Nadin
Richard Nonas
Giuseppe Penone
Jessica Rath
Charles Ray
Tim Rollins and K.O.S.
Ugo Rondinone
Peter Schlesinger
Jennifer Steinkamp
John Stezaker
Michael Stipe
William Stone
Yuken Teruya
Oscar Tuazon
Rob Wynne
Amir Zaki

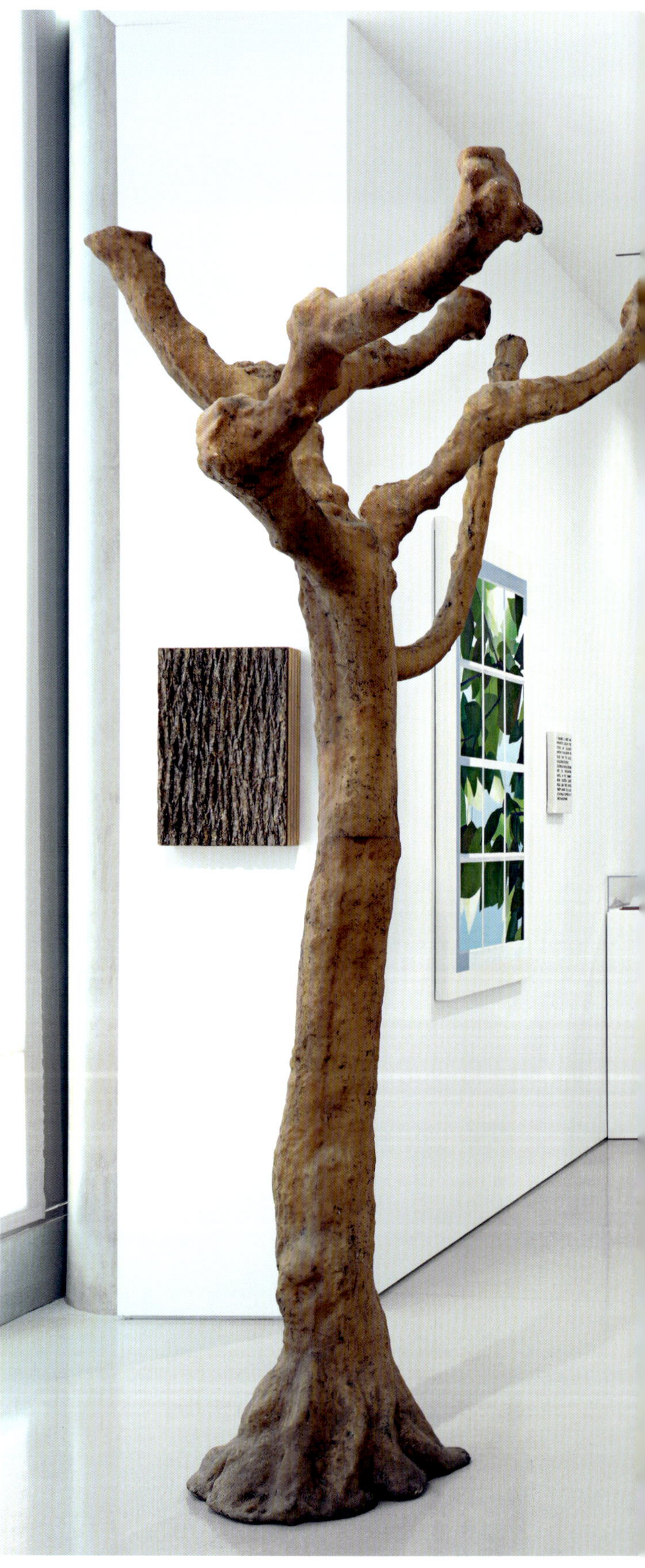

Installation view

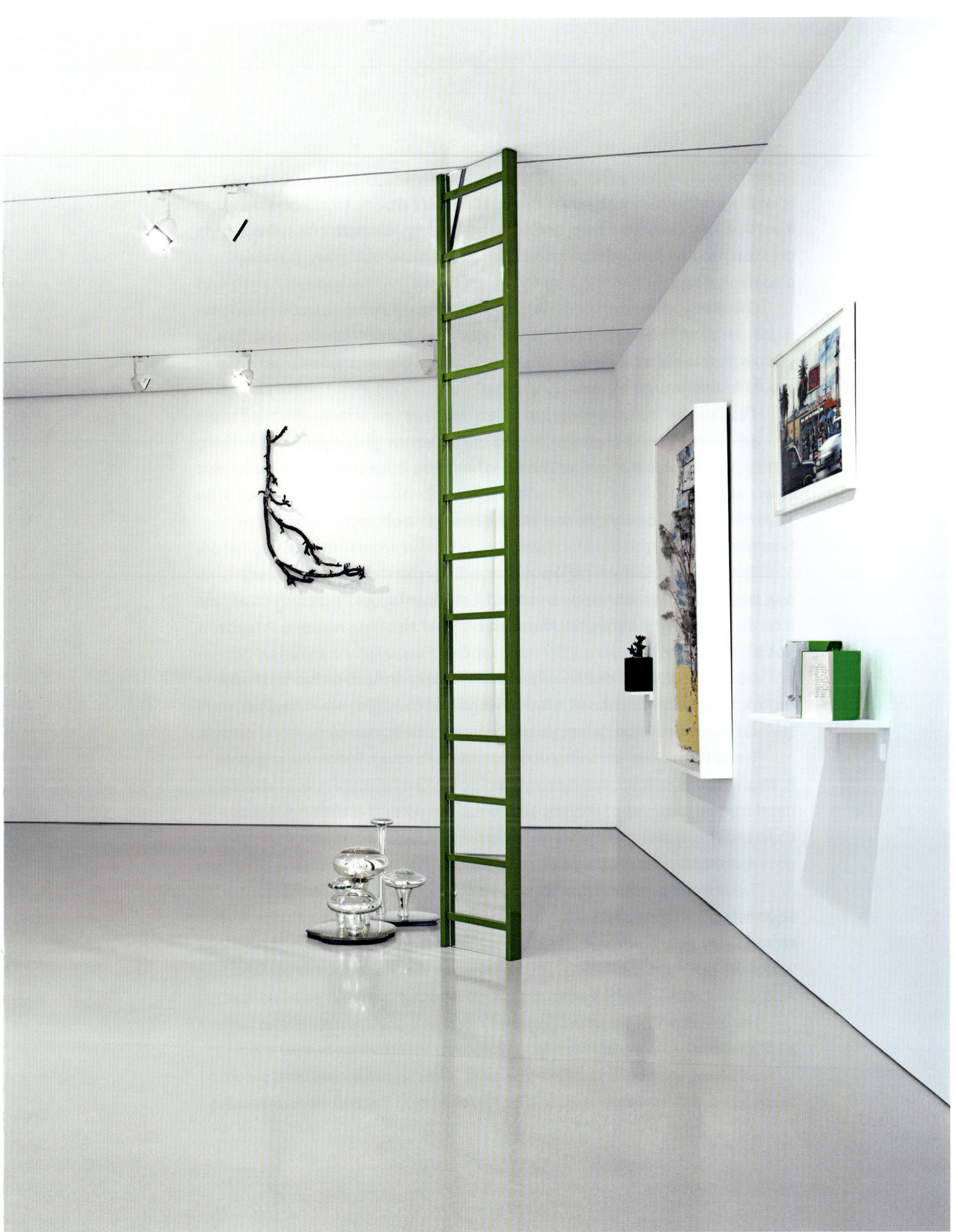

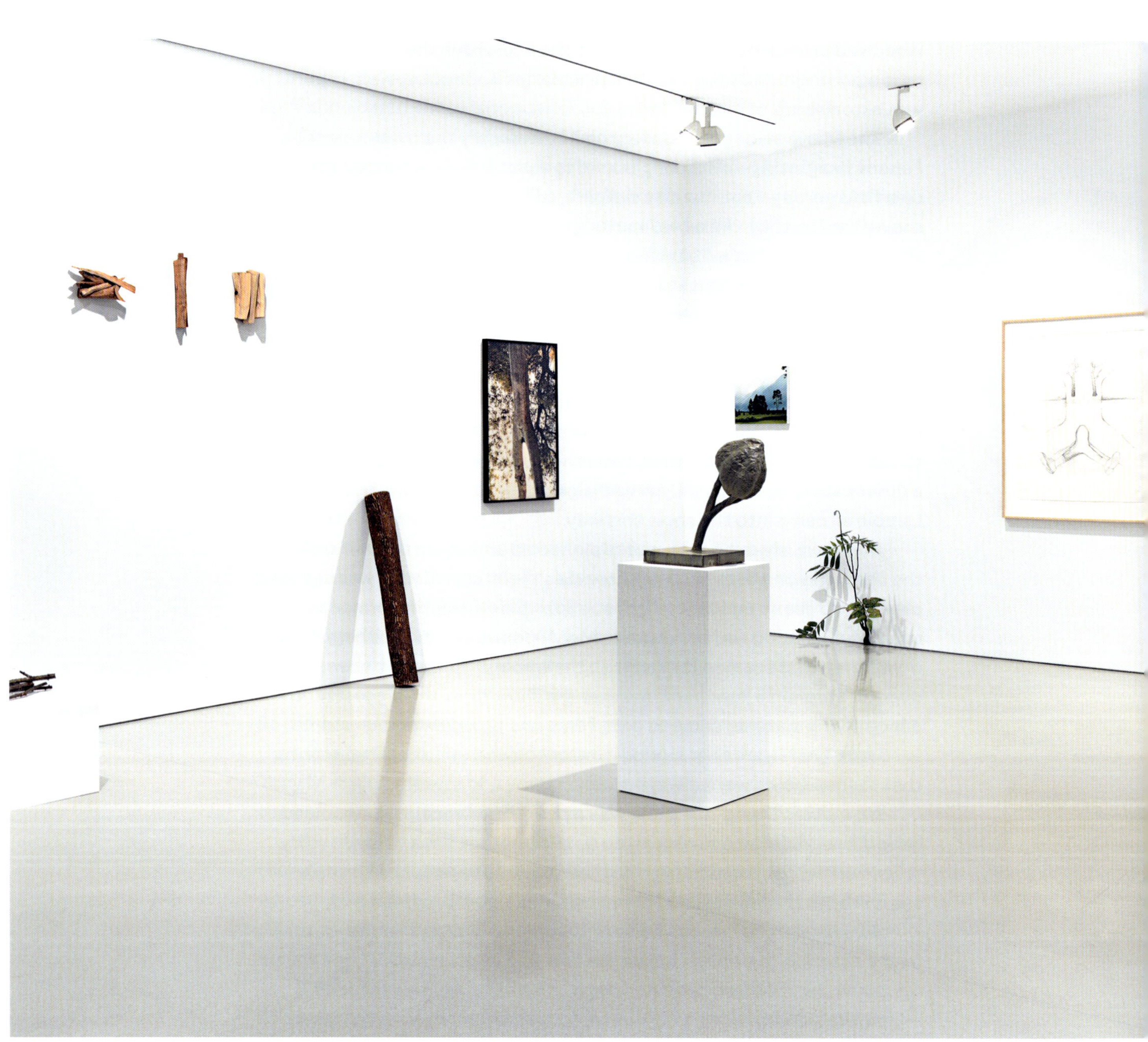

Installation view

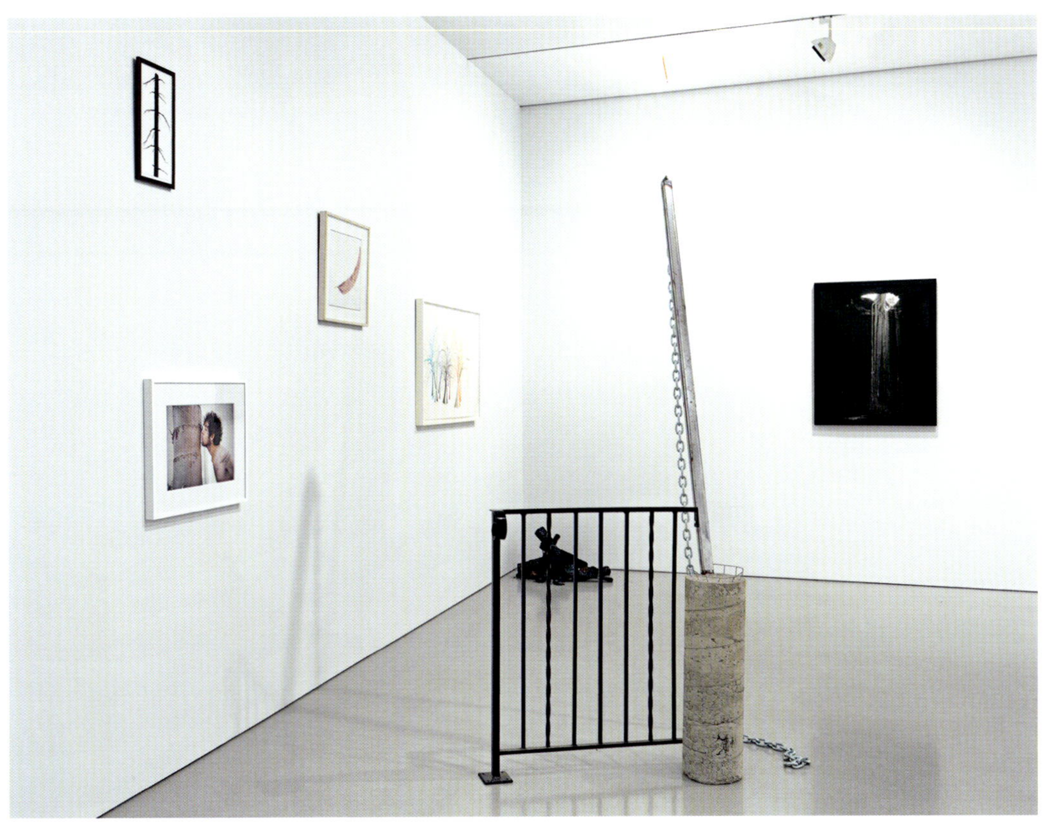

Installation view

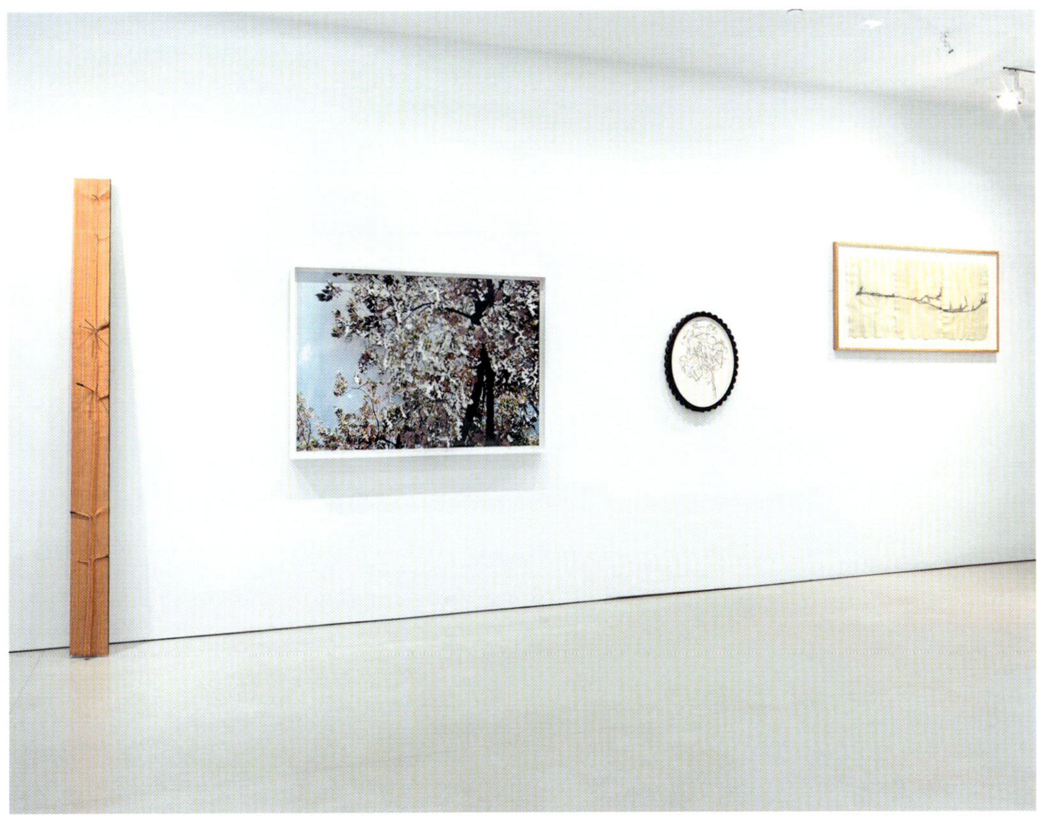

Left to right: Giuseppe Penone, *Albero di 15 rami*, 1977; Jim Hodges, *London II (pink and blue)*, 2006–9; Georgie Hopton, *A Windy Day*, 2012; Andrew Lord, *apple bough, Wootton*, 2009

FLAG'S 5TH ANNIVERSARY GROUP EXHIBITION

October 5–December 14, 2013

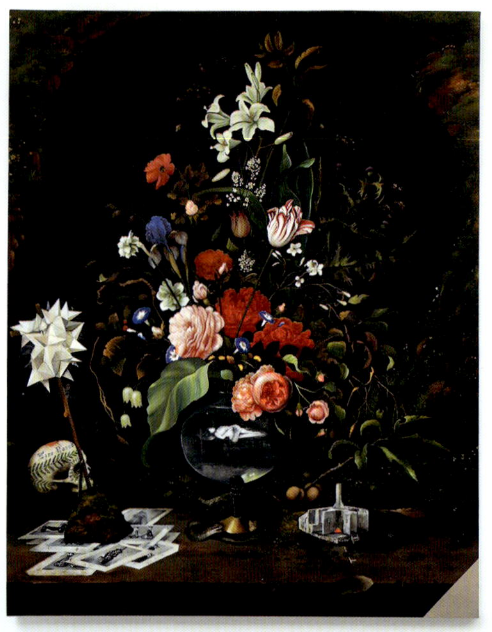

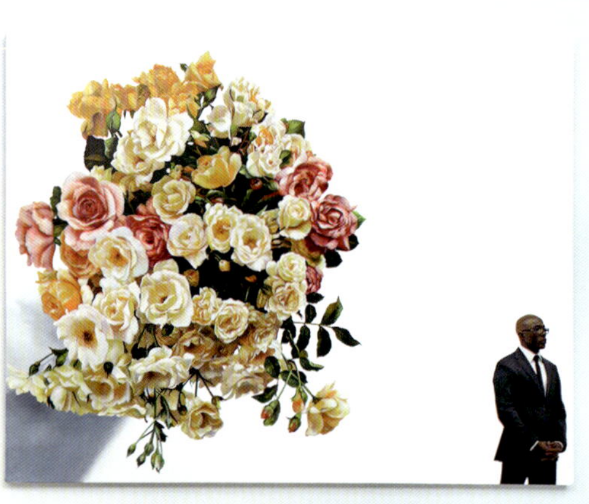

Left to right: Ged Quinn, *Ghosts and Benedictions*, 2012; Marc Dennis, *The Mythology of the Readymade*, 2013

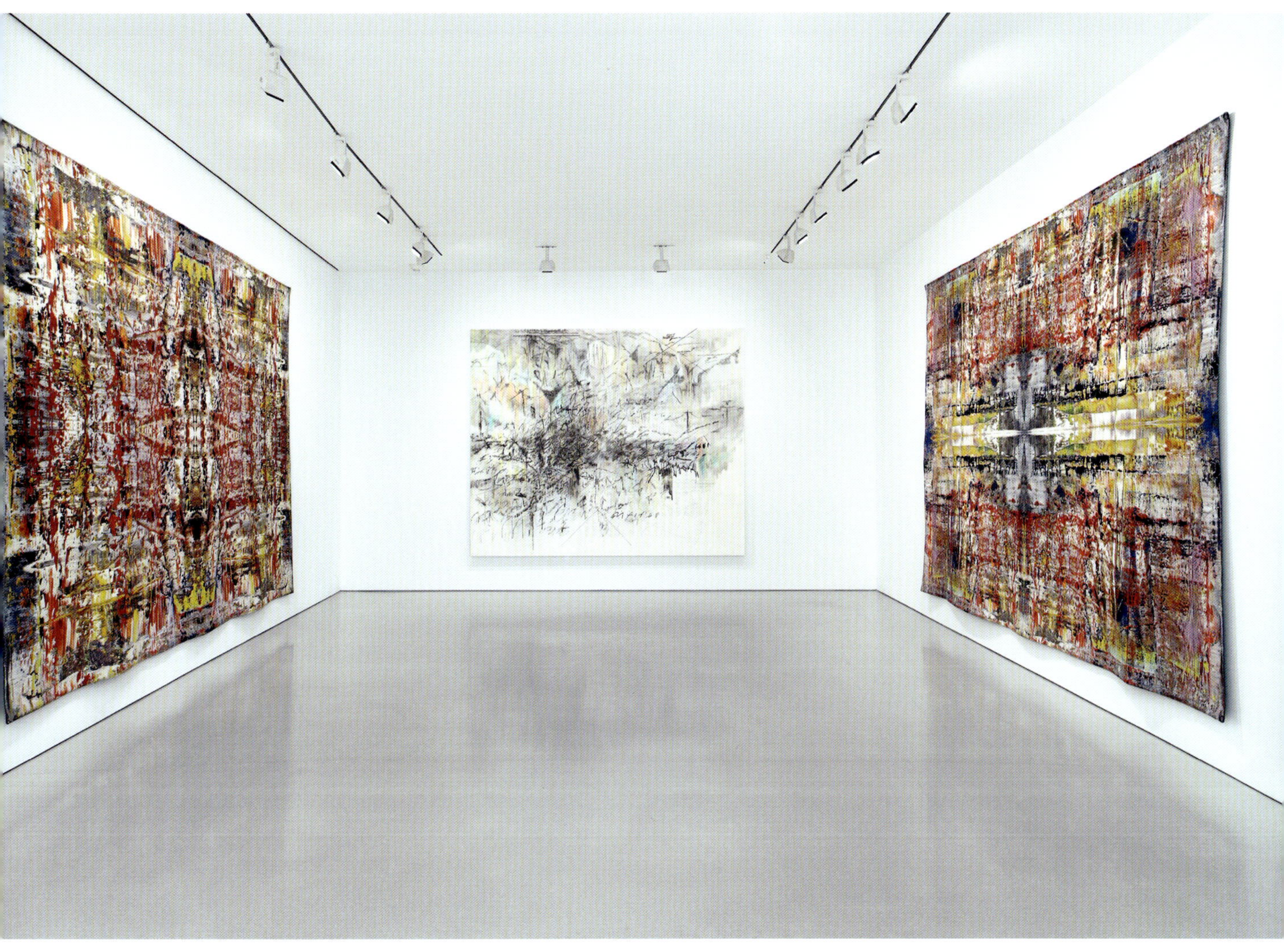

Left to right: Gerhard Richter, *YUSUF*, 2009; Julie Mehretu, *Fever graph (algorithm for serendipity)*, 2013; Gerhard Richter, *MUSA*, 2009

Artists

Cecily Brown
Marc Dennis
Ellen Gallagher
Jane Hammond
Nir Hod
Jim Hodges
Wayne Lawrence
Josephine Meckseper
Julie Mehretu
Chris Ofili
Ged Quinn
Charles Ray
Gerhard Richter
Jeff Sonhouse
Mathew Weir

IMAGES OF VENUS FROM WAYNE LAWRENCE'S ORCHARD BEACH: THE BRONX RIVIERA

October 5–December 14, 2013
Curated by Awol Erizku

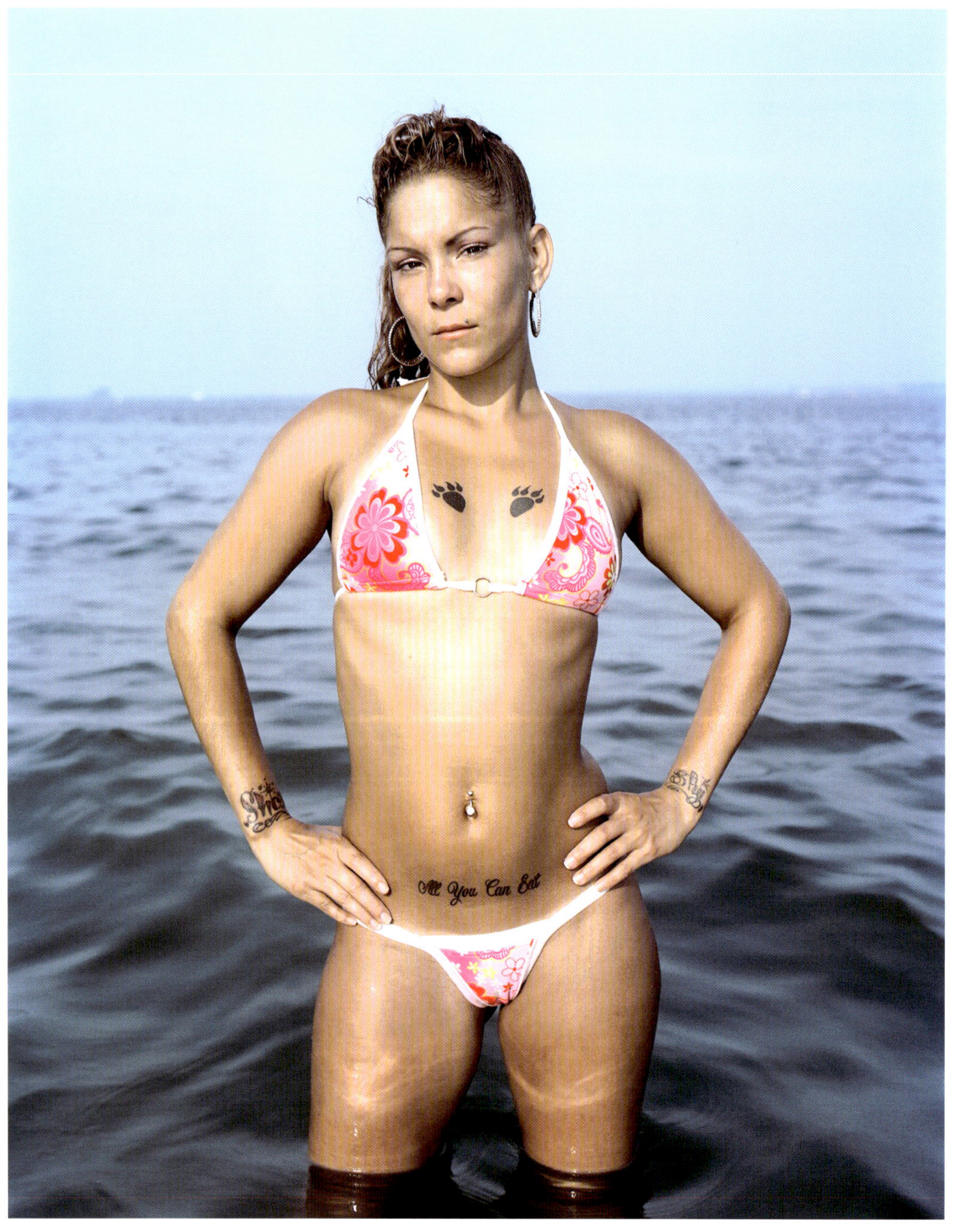

Wayne Lawrence, *Yari*, 2011

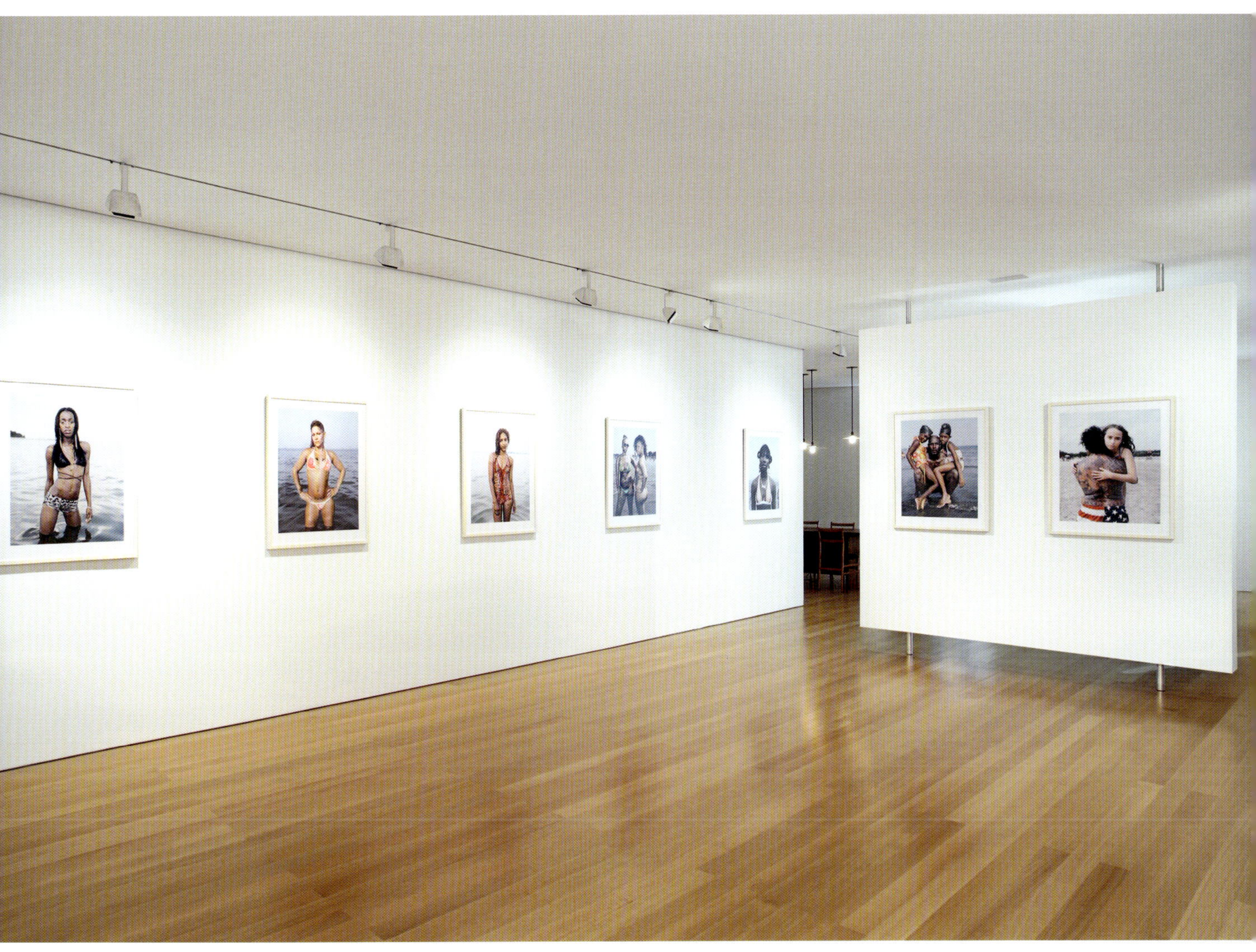

Installation view

RICHARD PATTERSON: I'M WALKING HERE!

February 8–May 17, 2014
Curated by Toby Kamps

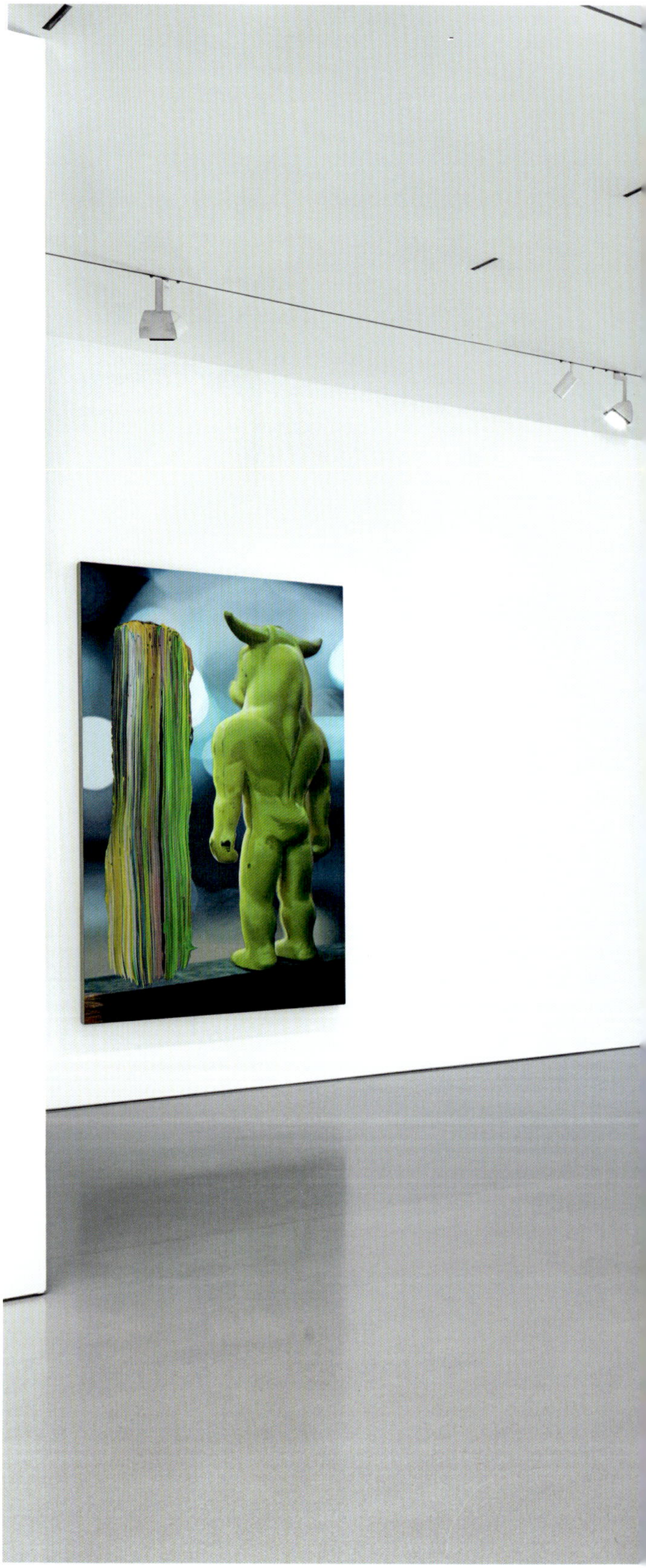

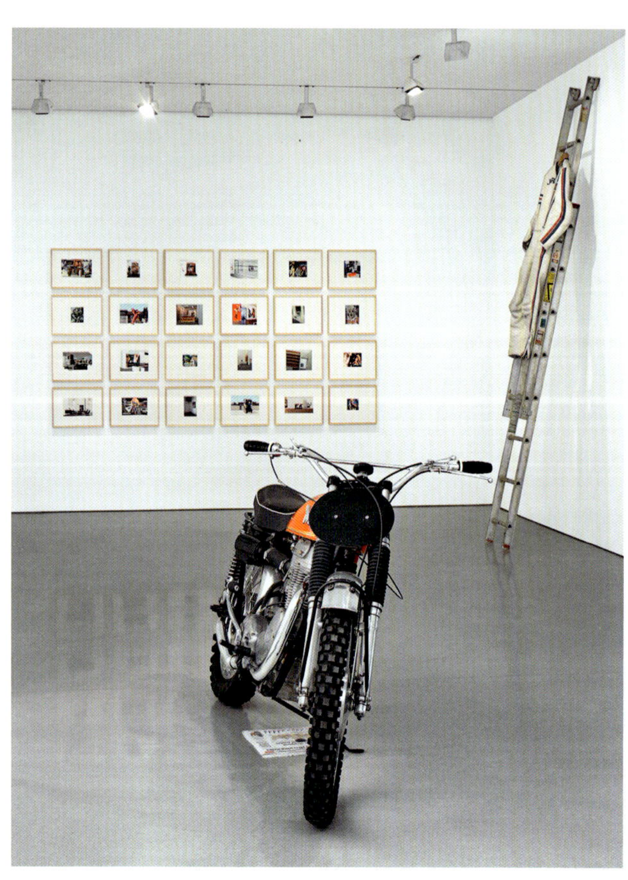

Clockwise from front: Richard Patterson, *Matchless Typhoon*, 2014; *24 Studies*, 2005–14; and *Bartholomew Fair*, 2009

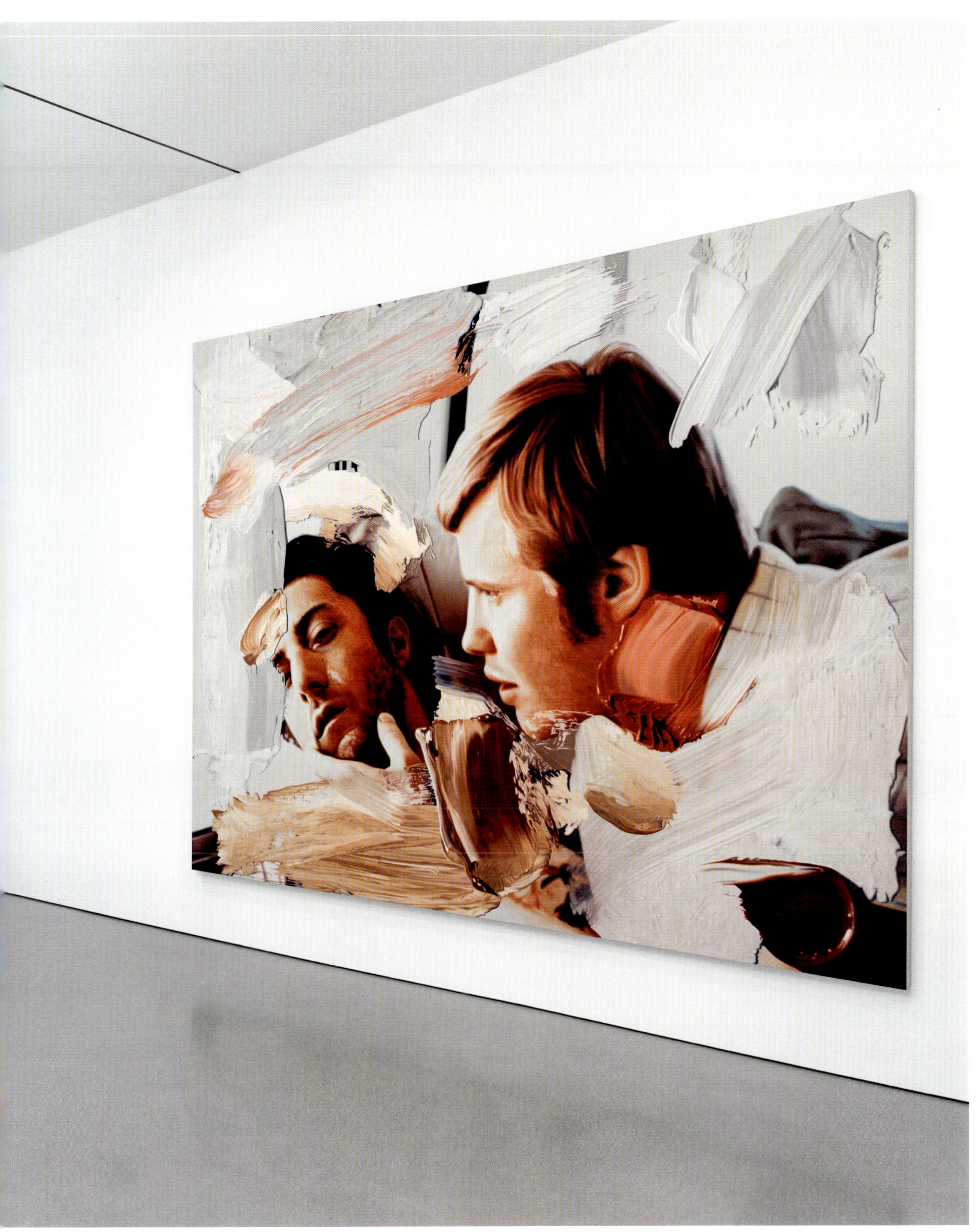

Left to right: Richard Patterson, *Young Minotaur*, 1997; and *The Kennington Years*, 2001

There's an old music hall song from the early 1900s by Harry Champion. It's sung from the point of view of a tramp, who sleeps rough in Trafalgar Square, but it's delivered in the grandiose manner of a Mayfair toff, as if bedding down for the night is like moving from one luxury hotel to the next.

Chorus:
I live in Trafalgar Square
With four lions to guard me
Fountains and statues all over the place
And the "Metropole" staring me right in the face
I'll own it's a trifle draughty
But I look at it this way you see
If it's good enough for Nelson
It's quite good enough for me

Shortly after 9/11, my wife and I moved from London to New York City, where we stayed a few years before moving on to America. Both New York and Dallas seemed to me lacking in stone lions. Meanwhile, the sense of place and belonging gradually crept up on me as a defining subject. Making paintings became as much a form of accommodation as expression.

I'd painted Dallas Cowboys cheerleaders a bit when I was in Waterloo, London, and then a bit more in New York as my imaginary personal lions—partly as cyphers for muses, but partly as complete strangers (we didn't really have the culture of cheerleaders in Britain), since studio life is quite a solitary affair. Painting them was in lieu of living personal cheerleaders messing up the studio with their asterisk-worthy pompoms and tiny shorts, which these days are not really considered acceptable studio wear.

In considering a show for FLAG, my good friend Toby Kamps, then curator at the Menil Collection in Houston, was asked to curate a cross-section of work, including elements from my studio: studies and starting points that might round things out, which was a first for me. Previously, I'd tried to keep shows baggage-free and as enigmatic as possible. Toby felt the interstitial stuff was a dimension worth divulging, and so I now had the opportunity to exhibit some of my models and maquettes. Which meant that I almost included a slightly Christian

Marclay-esque film I'd made. But it possibly lacked credible "interstitiality" and family-friendliness, so we omitted it.

Perhaps most importantly for me, I got to show some of my own personal touchstones, which took the form of altered small plastic figures that I'd painted onto and then later used as my own dark muses. The resulting paintings constituted my first New York show in 1999. For FLAG, I presented them in actuality for the first time and made for them a model retro-modernist pavilion, as if to demonstrate that they might well have been full-scale sculptures as well as paintings. More than this, though, I wanted people to see the tiny figures as I'd originally seen them—as the "blow-ups" and kernels of thought for later things. I didn't consider this personal model museum to be art; I considered it "thought." I set the model at child's eye level—not for children, but so that adults had to alter their position to look at it clearly, like something out of *Gulliver's Travels*.

To add to my golem-like figures—to give a sense of scale—I'd bought some tiny hand-painted architectural lead figures that seemed to belong to a bygone era. These were to be "art world people," the public, the people who go to galleries. I could only get four of the six I wanted. The person who made them in small batches had stopped making them; I wondered if he/she had died, and the figures' non-availability added extra pathos and unintended stories.

The lead figures were like characters from Edward Hopper paintings and with a distinctly 1940s feel. One that was no longer available was "The Business Man," a back-catalogue figure rushing and clutching a newspaper and an attaché case. He could have been David Zwirner, but The Business Man is no more.

Another figure had a pale blue short-sleeved shirt, a bald head, and a bit of a paunch. I decided he was "The Critic"—a sort of amalgam of Dave Hickey and Jerry Saltz, with Dave's belly and Jerry's Buñuel-like inability to leave the New York gallery space. "The Critic" stands next to the sculpture *If* (1999).

Then there's the hobo walking across the back of my model museum with his bindle stick, indifferent to the whole shebang in front, which is a grotesque-absurd sculpture-idea of a posturing self-exposing male figure

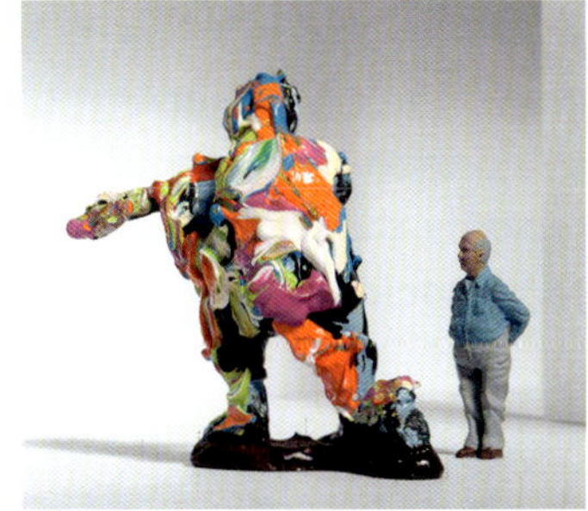

Richard Patterson, *If*, 1999

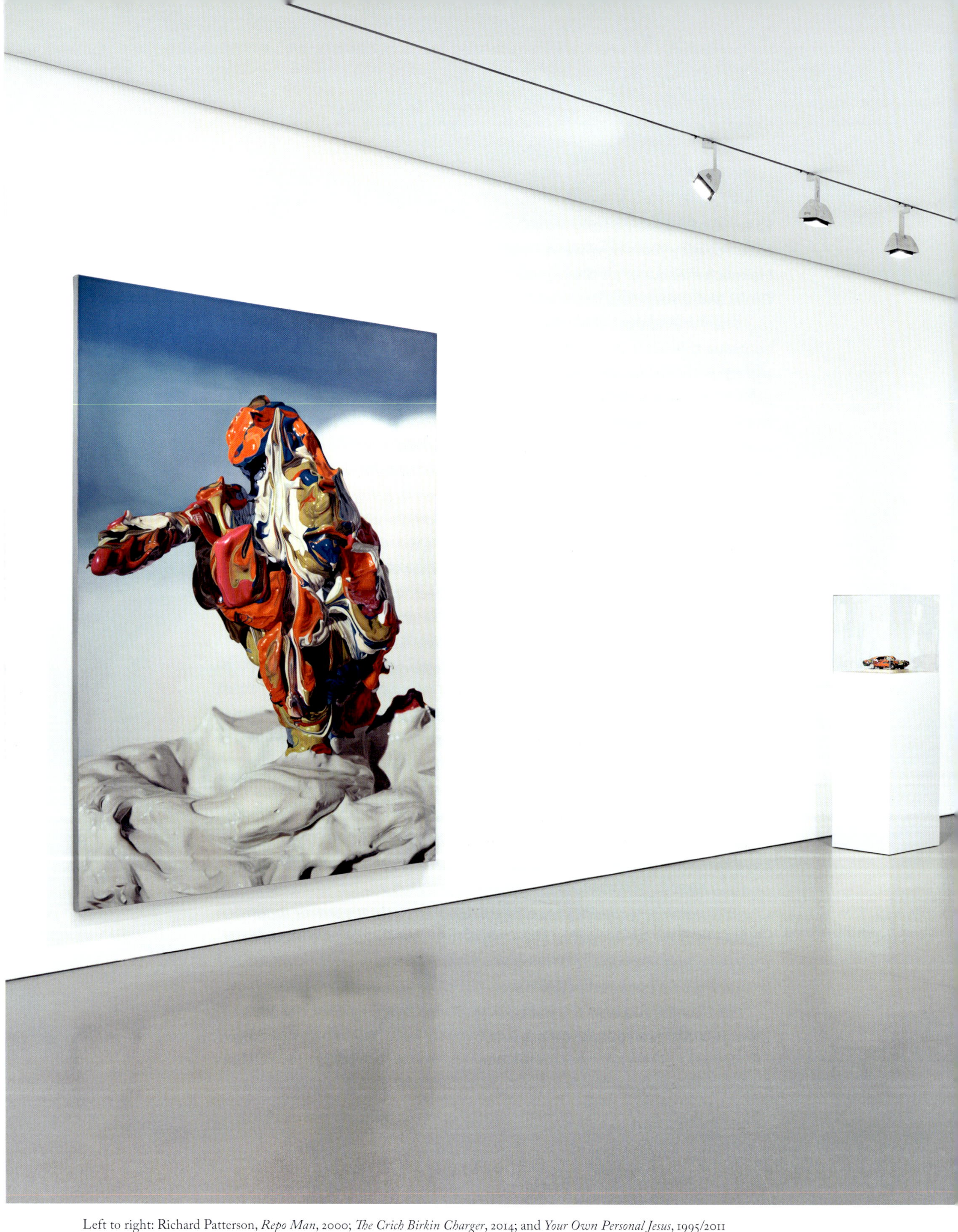

Left to right: Richard Patterson, *Repo Man*, 2000; *The Crich Birkin Charger*, 2014; and *Your Own Personal Jesus*, 1995/2011

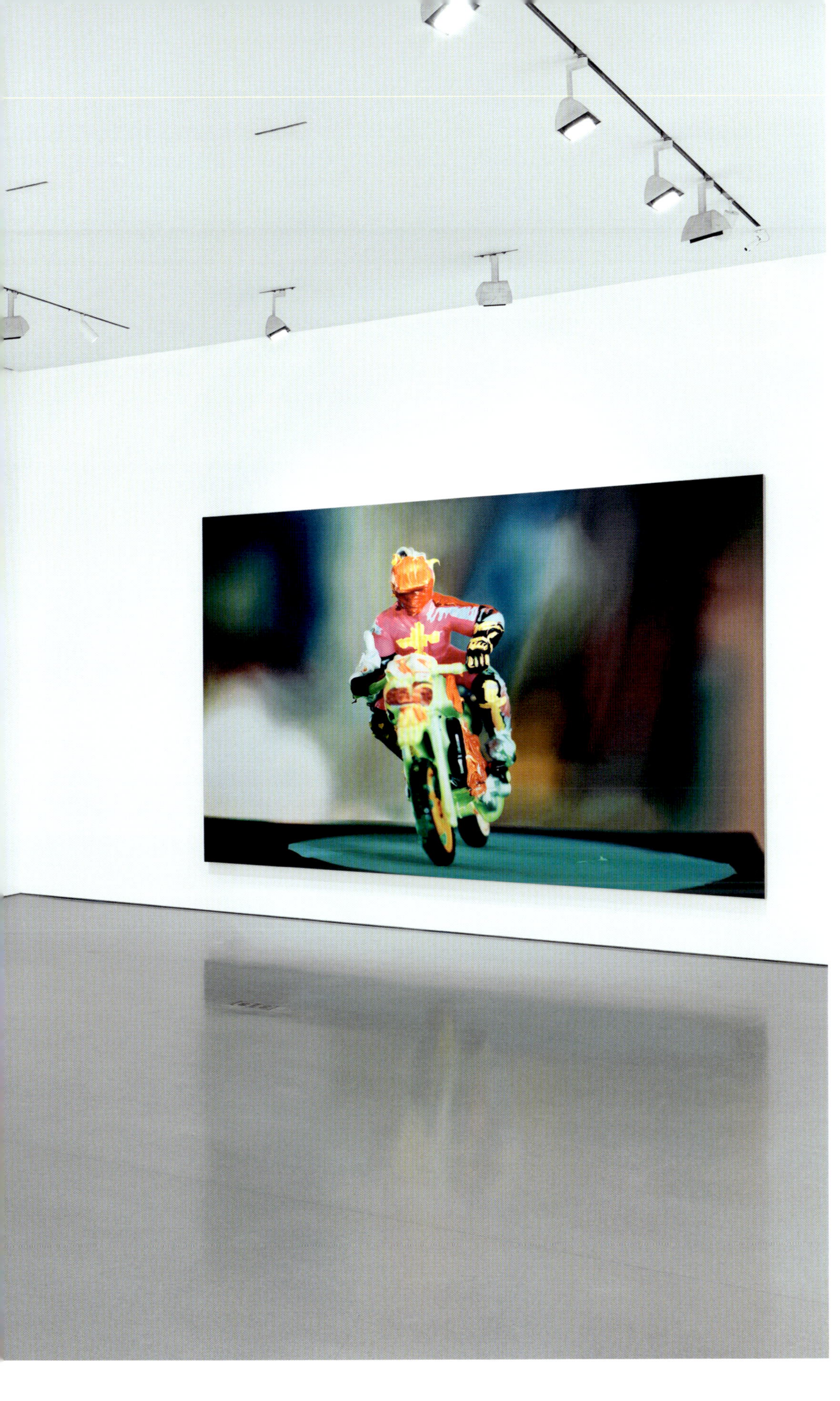

ROY LICHTENSTEIN: NUDES AND INTERIORS

February 8–May 17, 2014
Curated by Hilary Harkness and Ewan Gibbs

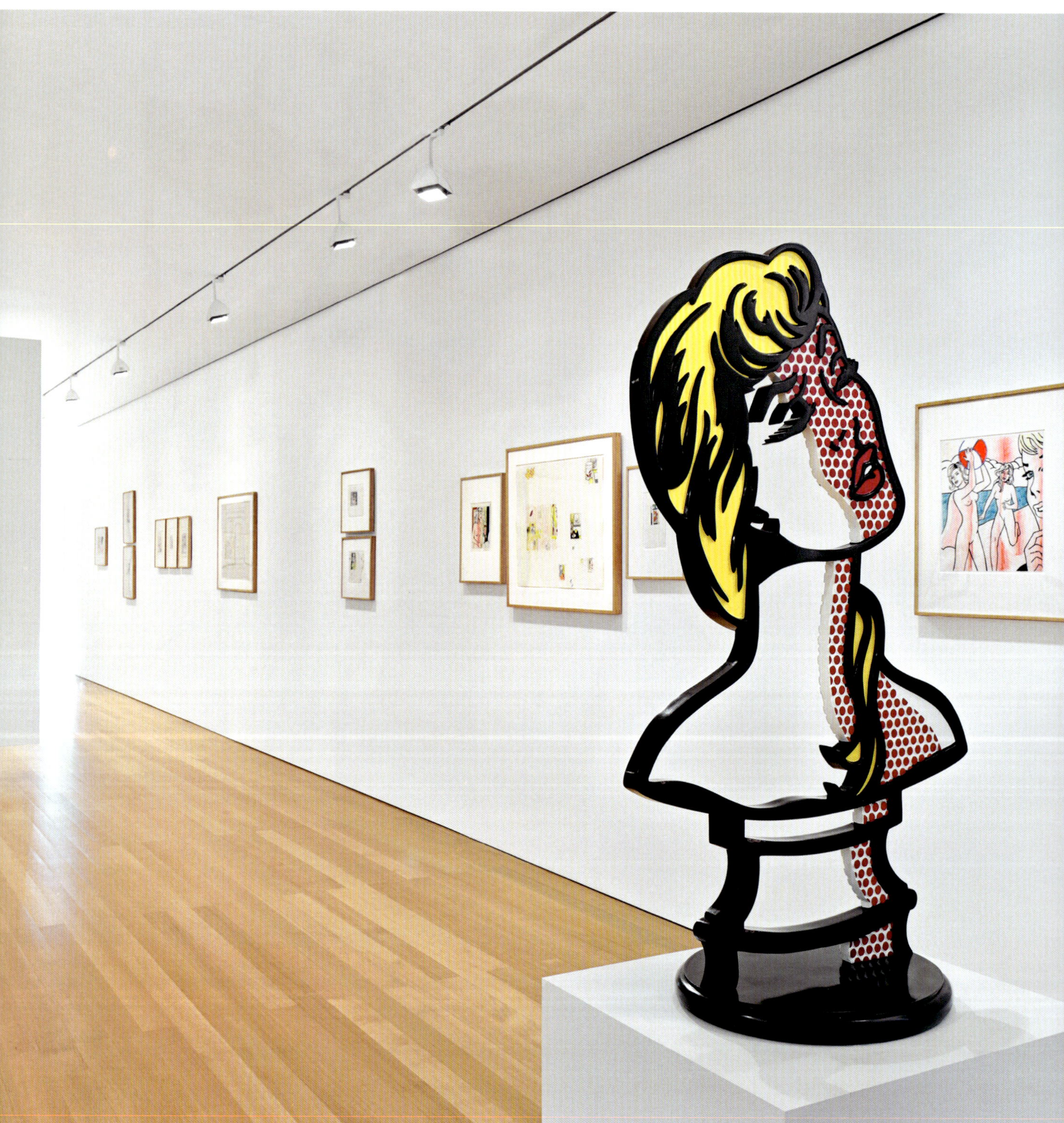

Installation view

FLAG was founded on family values to such an extent that Glenn named the foundation using the initials of the nuclear unit he grew up with.

Over the last few years, Glenn and his wife, Amanda, have also started their own family, which with three delightful children now outnumbers the original Fuhrman four.

The FLAG family has also increased exponentially over the last decade, exhibiting more than four hundred artists whose names represent every letter of the alphabet except X and whose studios are spread across the globe.

FLAG Fosters Learning And Growth and embraces the world of art, from emerging talent to established practitioners, all-stars, and legends across many disciplines.

FLAG is Glenn's baby, and just as children tend to take on the characteristics and interests of their parents, the works you will see and have seen at FLAG more often than not reflect Glenn's tastes and preoccupations.

As offspring grow up and venture out, though, they are hopefully inspired and challenged by the people they come into contact with, be they teachers, mentors, or the extended family.

FLAG has positively encouraged outside influence. Its breadth and depth have been expanded by an ever-growing cast of curators, artists, curating artists, and even a curating NBA Hall of Famer.

While Glenn gets on with his day job, which keeps FLAG flying, the hard work and forward momentum behind the scenes has been driven by Stephanie Roach, who has been an ever-present champion of FLAG, and Risa Daniels and Jonathan Rider, among others, who work tirelessly to make FLAG the best it can be.

Many parents strive to keep their offspring on the straight and narrow, but not Glenn where FLAG is concerned; he has positively encouraged FLAG away from the straitlaced and narrow-minded.

I feel very fortunate to count myself part of the FLAG family and very much look forward to seeing what kind of teenager FLAG will become in time.

— Ewan Gibbs

Following pages: Installation view

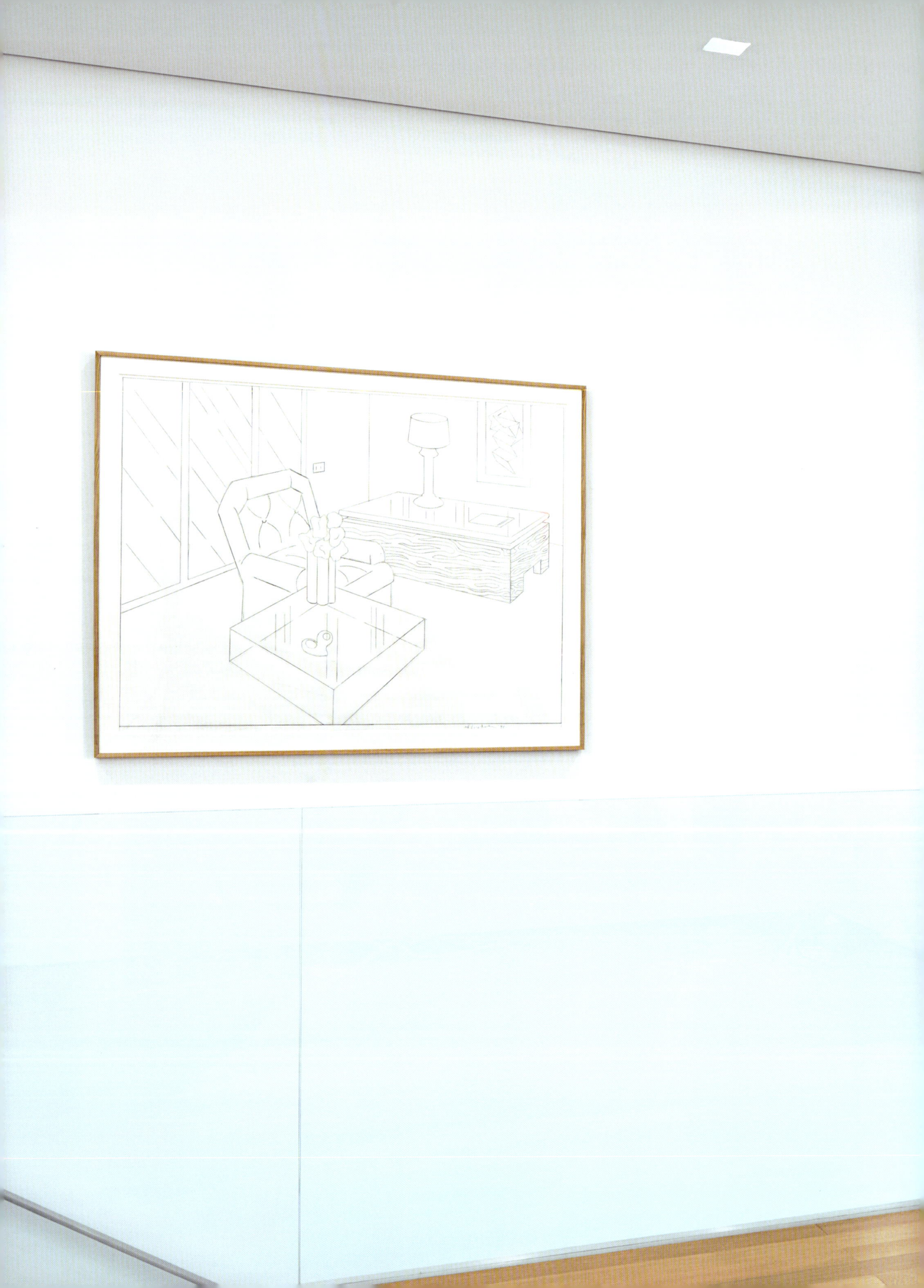

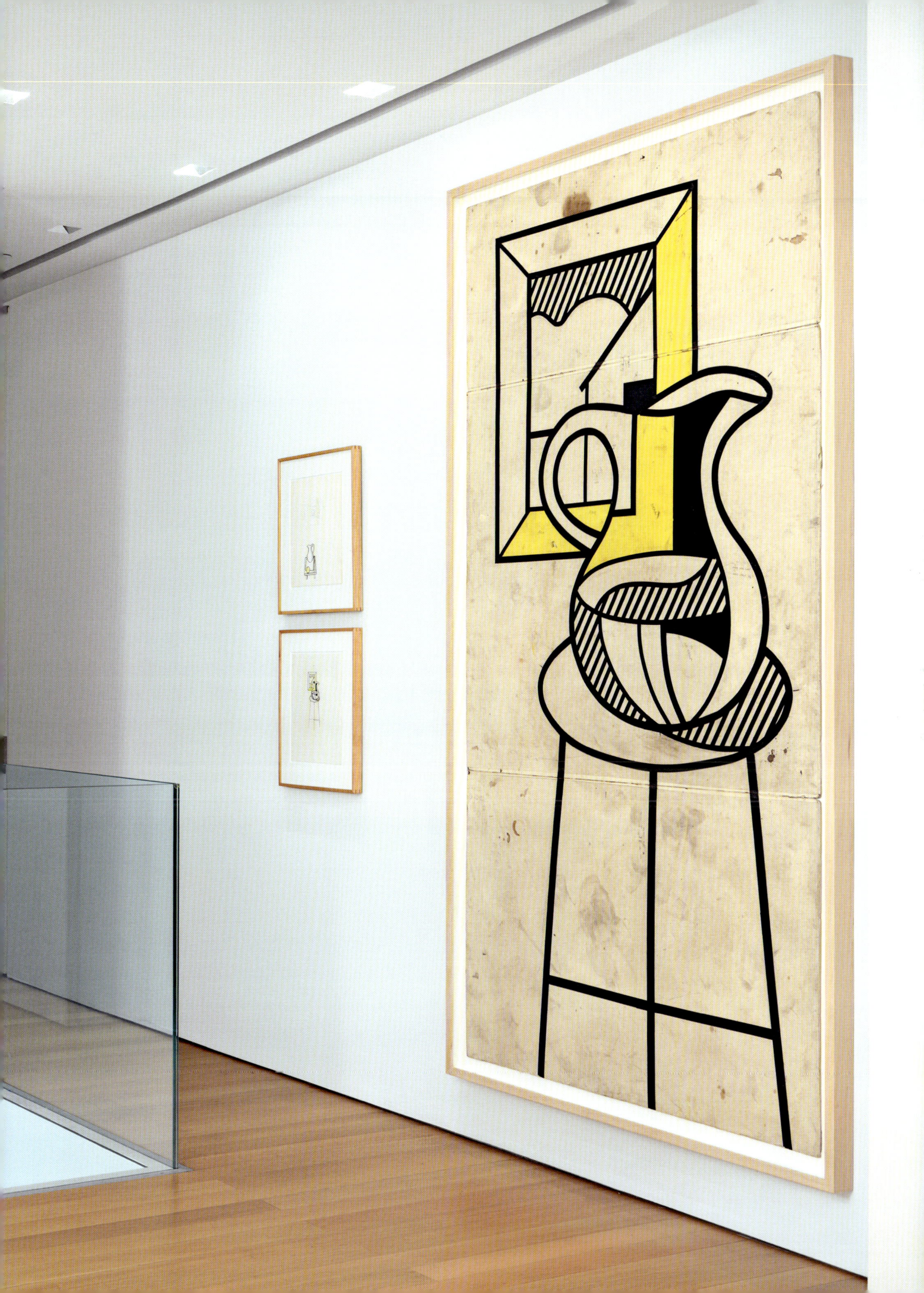

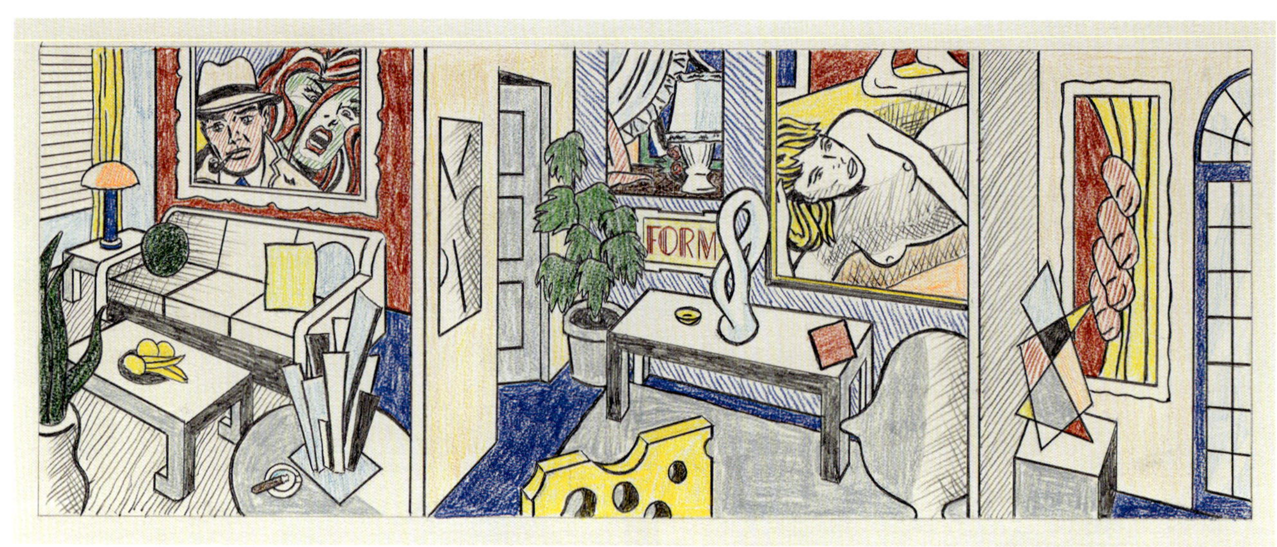

Roy Lichtenstein, *Drawing for Large Interior with Three Reflections*, 1993

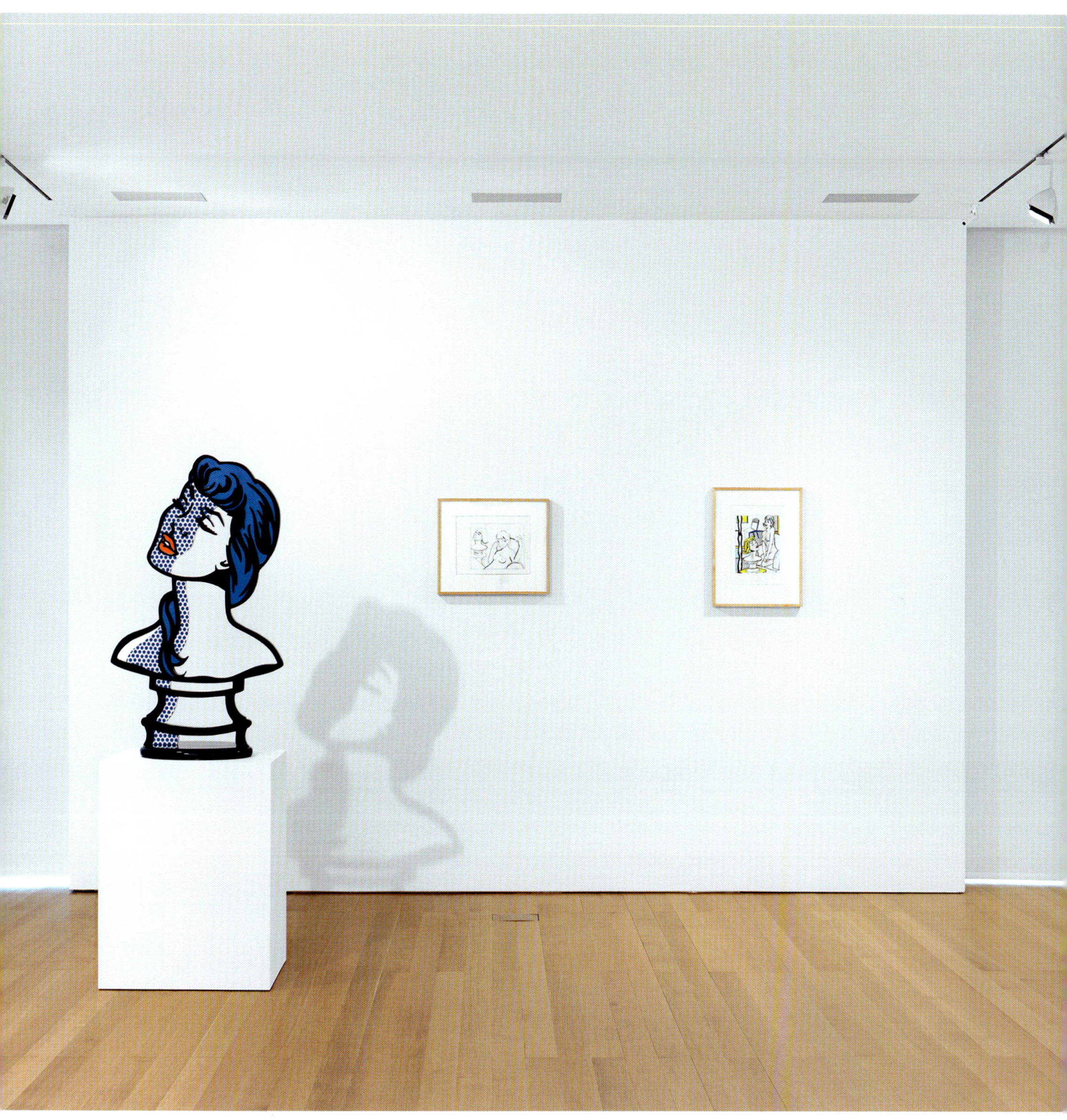

Left to right: Roy Lichtenstein, *Woman: Sunlight, Moonlight*, 1996; *Sketch for Nude with Bust*, 1995; and *Drawing for Nude with Bust*, 1995

DEEP END: YALE MFA PHOTOGRAPHY THESIS EXHIBITION

June 5–18, 2014
Curated by Roe Ethridge

Artists
Erin Desmond
Awol Erizku
Genevieve Gaignard
Hannah Hummel
Fumikazu Ishino
Casey McGonagle
Tyler Moore
Hannah Price
Billie Stultz
Evan Whale

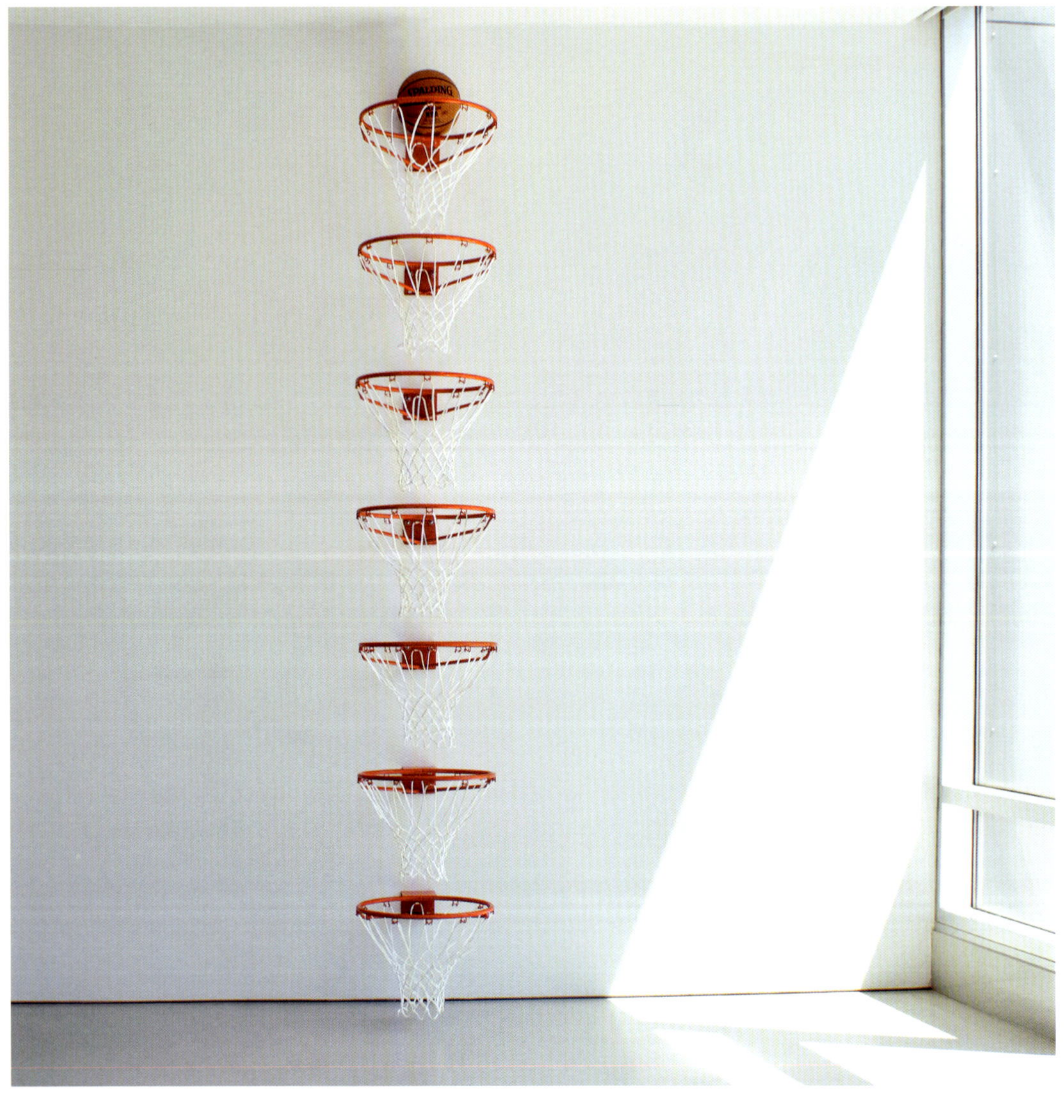

Awol Erizku, *Oh, what a feeling, fuck it, I want a Billion*, 2014

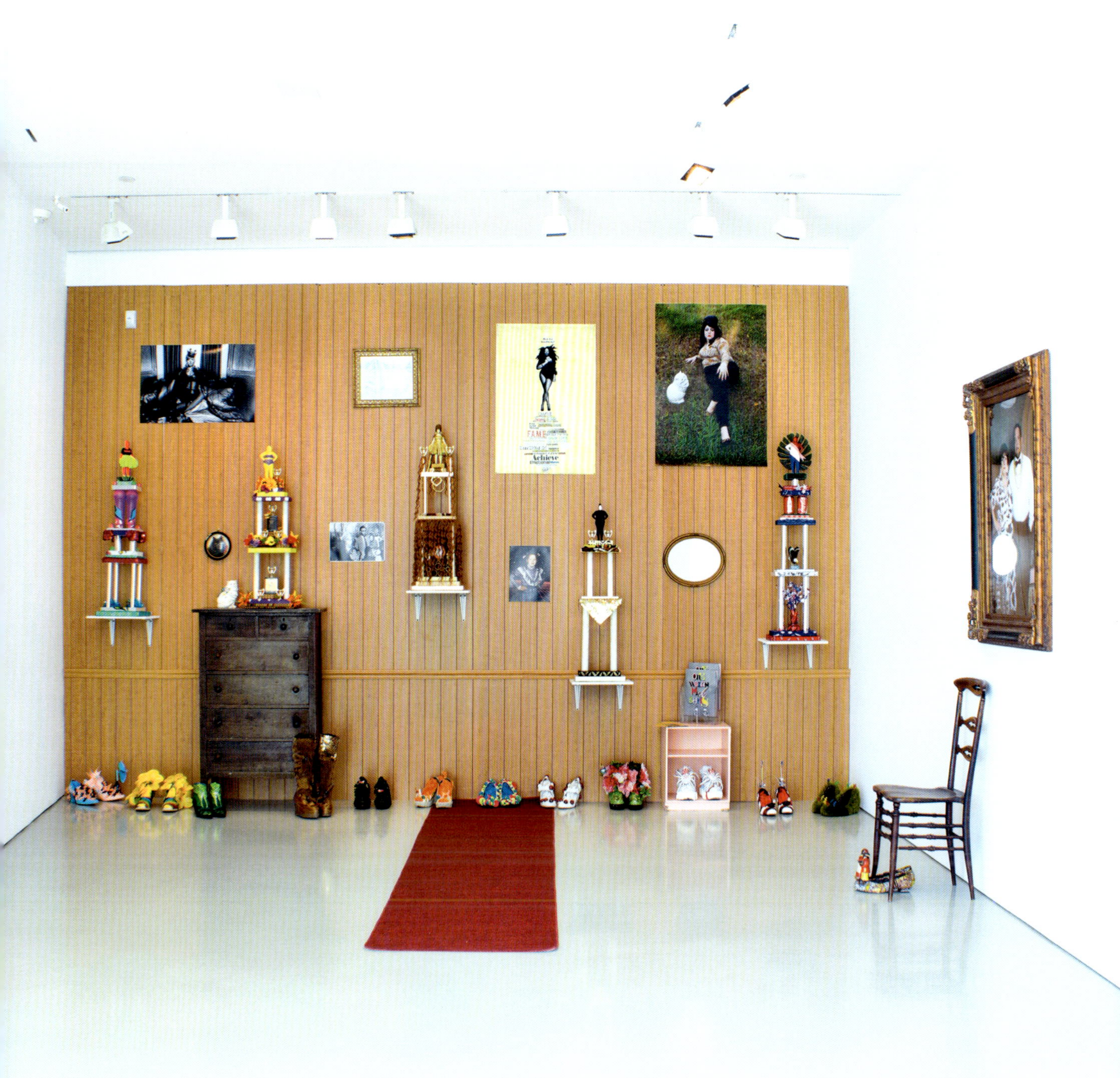

Installation view

EAST SIDE TO THE WEST SIDE

June 26–August 15, 2014
Curated by Brennan & Griffin, James Fuentes, and Rachel Uffner

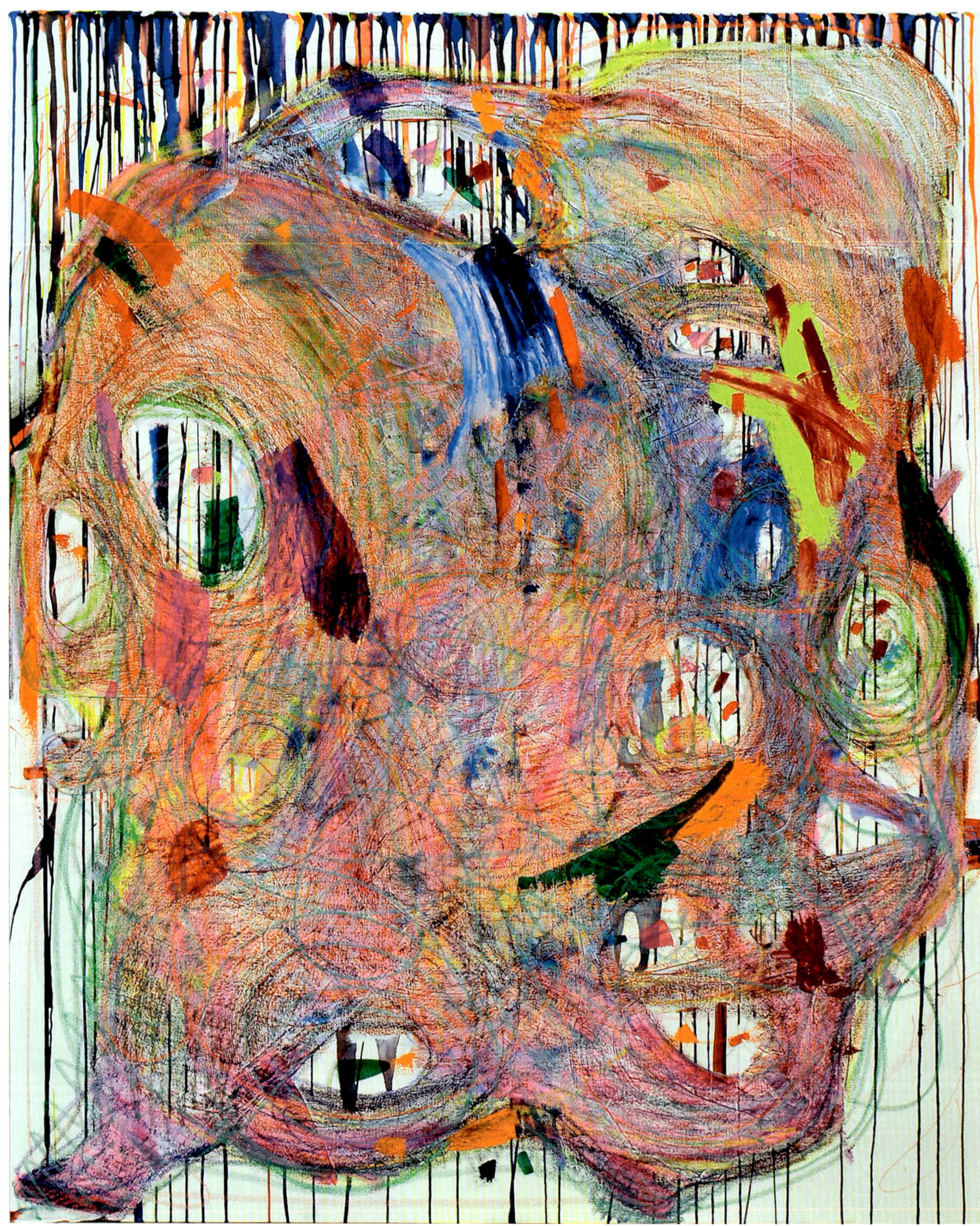

Joanne Greenbaum, *Untitled*, 2013

Artists
Bianca Beck
Joanne Greenbaum
Heather Guertin
Hilary Harnischfeger
Naotaka Hiro
Anya Kielar
Dave McDermott
Sam Moyer
Sara Greenberger Rafferty
Benjamin Senior
Michele Tocca

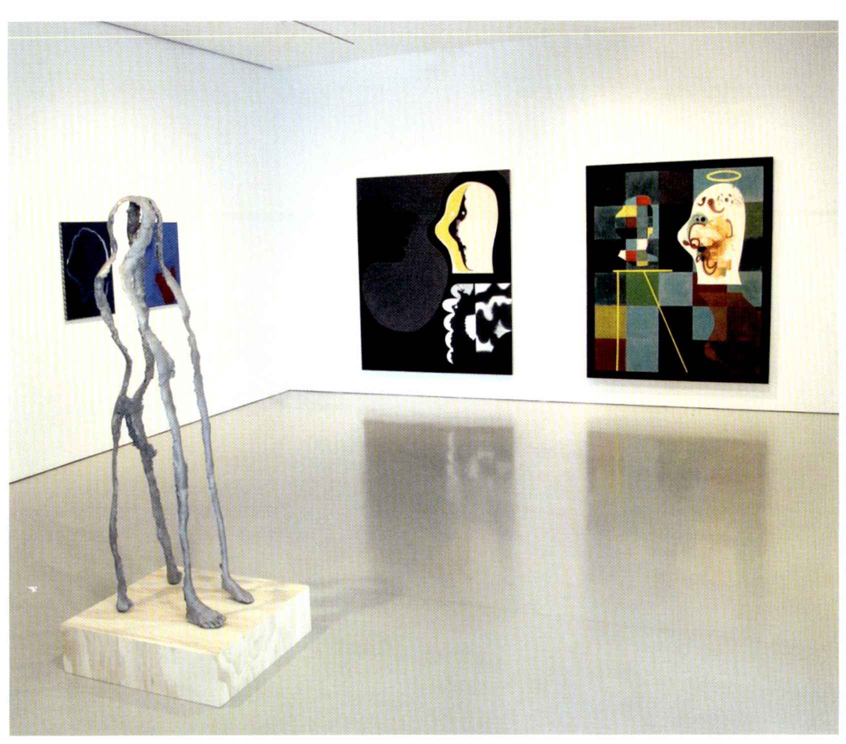

Clockwise from front: Naotaka Hiro, *Four-Legged (Toe to Heel)*, 2014; Heather Guertin, *Pete in Everyone*, 2012; and *Untitled (Kas)*, 2012; Dave McDermott, *Tschüg*, 2014; and *Requesting Resurrection for an Octopus at Garbet*, 2014

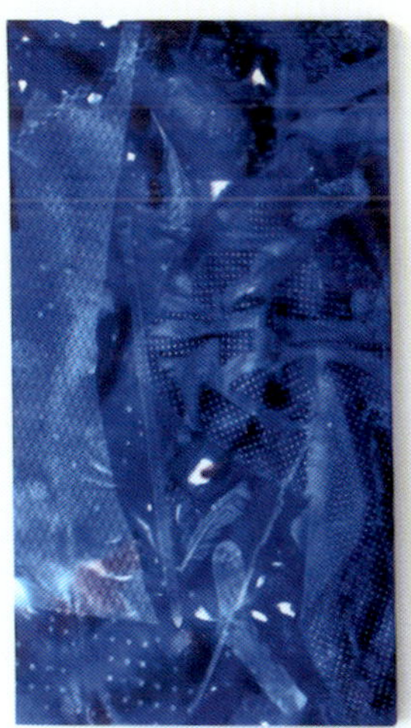

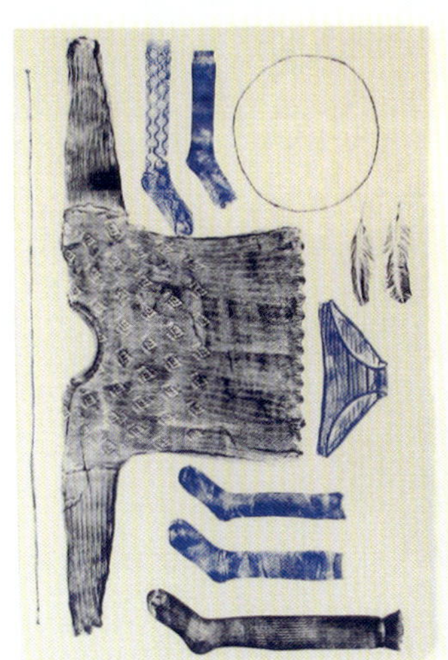

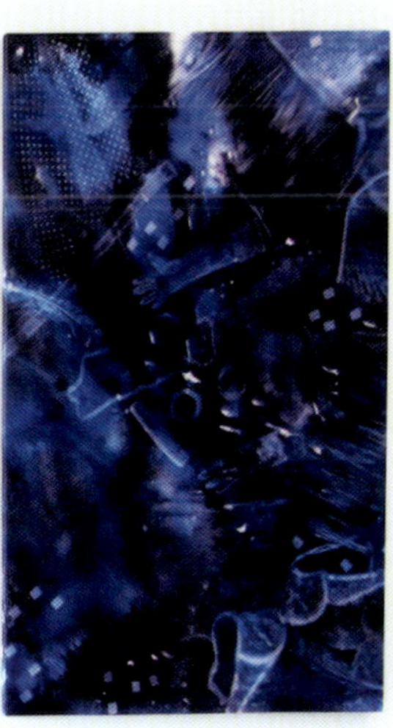

Left to right: Anya Kielar, *Feather*, 2013; *Sweater*, 2013; and *Accessories*, 2013

ROY LICHTENSTEIN: INTIMATE SCULPTURES

June 26, 2014–January 31, 2015

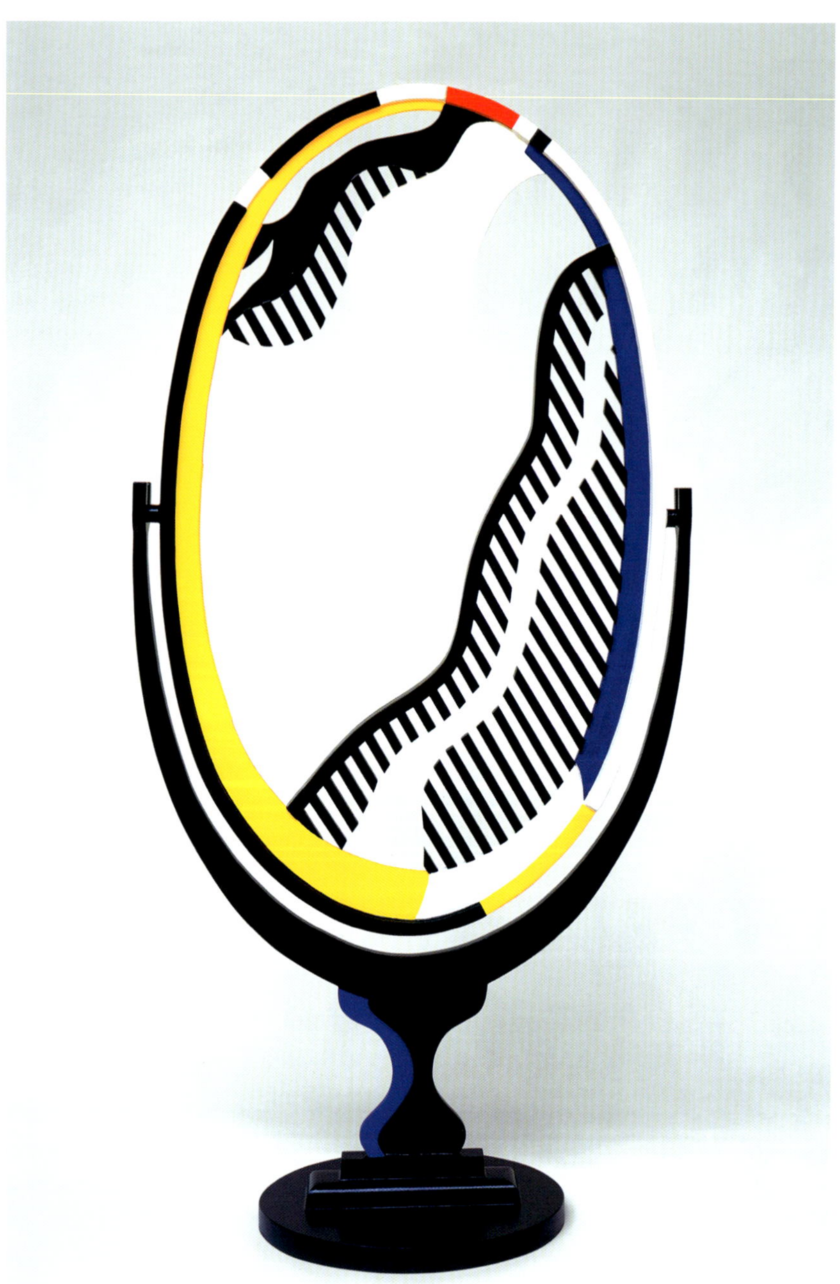

Roy Lichtenstein, *Mirror II*, 1977

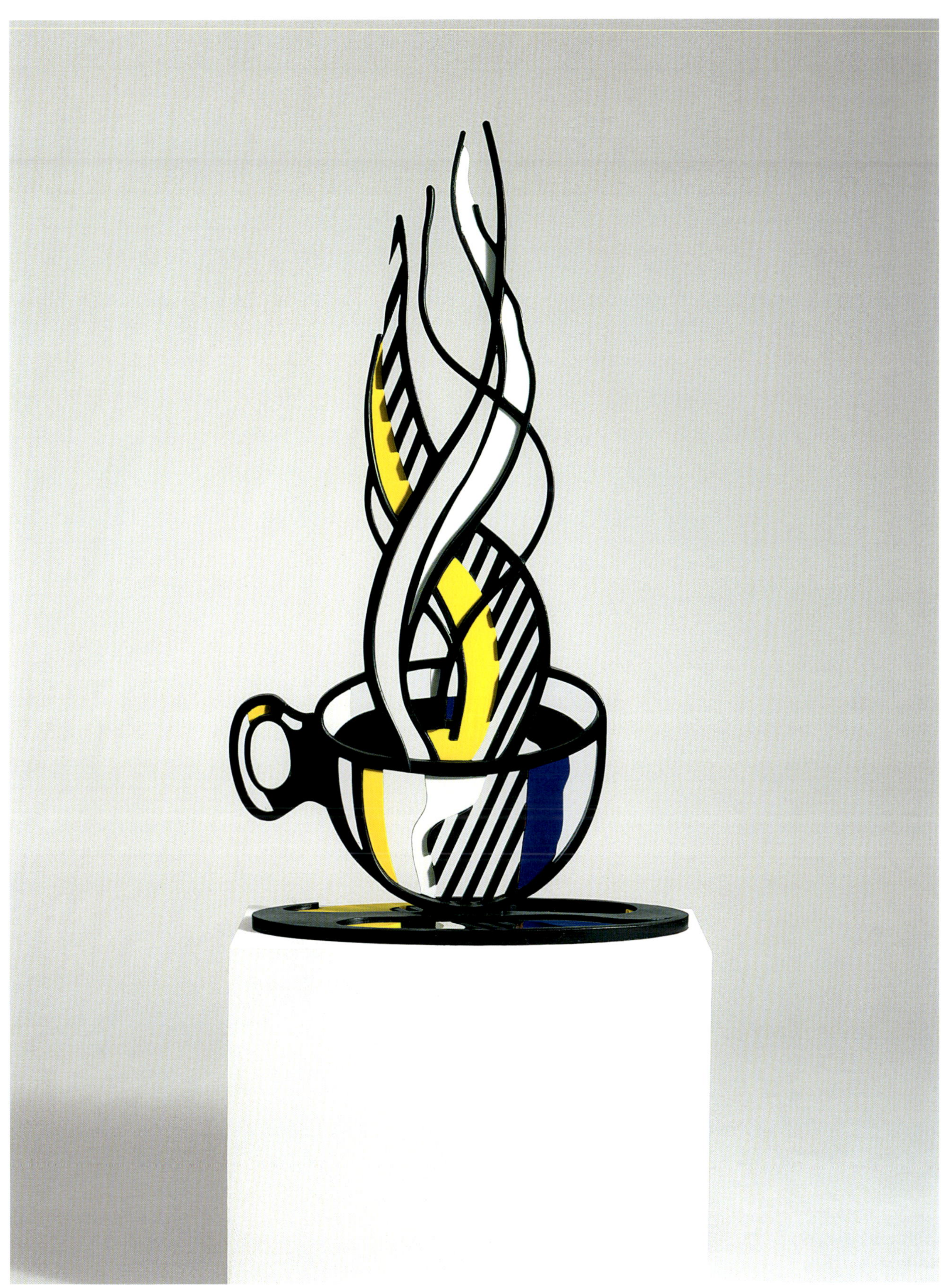

Roy Lichtenstein, *Cup and Saucer II*, 1977

SHAQ LOVES PEOPLE

at EXPO CHICAGO
September 18–21, 2014
Curated by Shaquille O'Neal

Artists
Kamrooz Aram
Tau Battice
Dawoud Bey
Mark Bradford
Marc Dennis
Jamie Diamond
Ben Durham
Awol Erizku
Hossein Fatemi
Genevieve Gaignard
Ellen Gallagher
Ewan Gibbs
Bruce Gilden
Nir Hod
Cary Kwok
Wayne Lawrence
Mary Ellen Mark
Ron Mueck
Jeff Muhs
J.D. 'Okhai Ojeikere
Carlos Rolón/Dzine
Ferdinando Scianna
Martin Schoeller
David Seymour
Cindy Sherman
Malick Sidibé
Jim Torok
Mark Wagner
Corban Walker
Kehinde Wiley

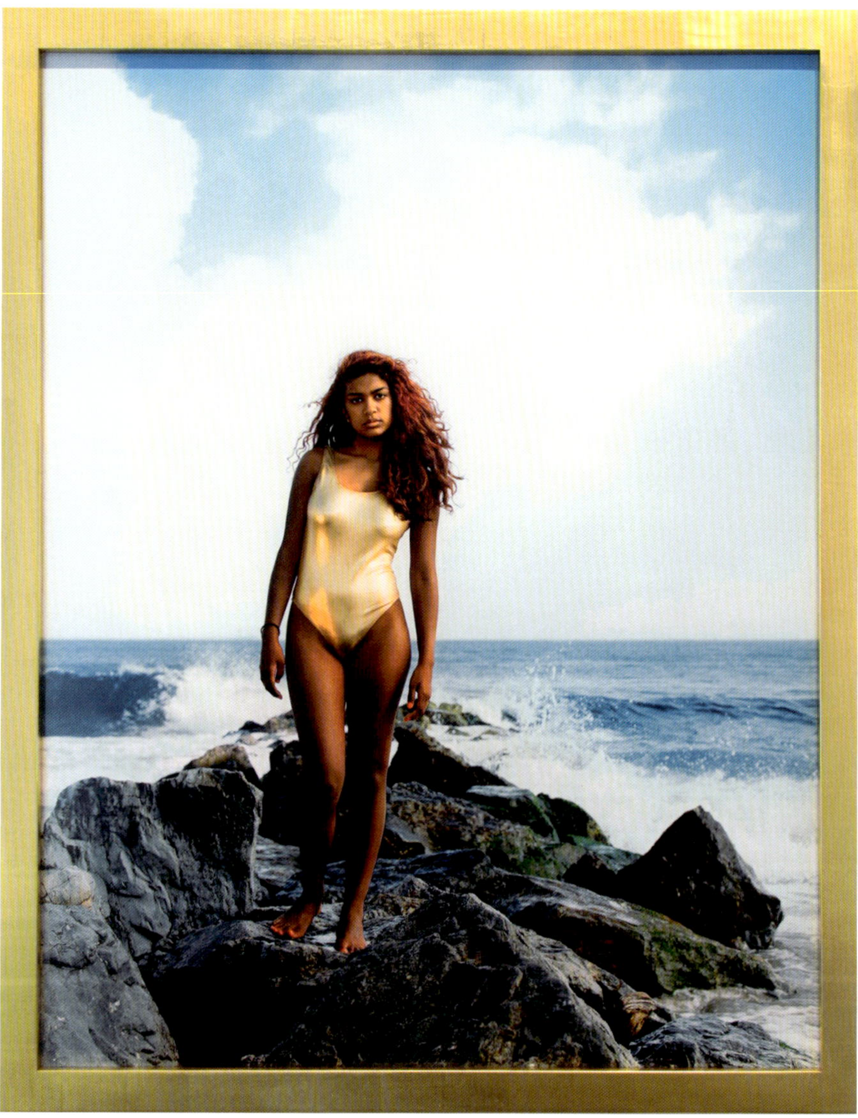

Awol Erizku, *Teen Venus*, 2013

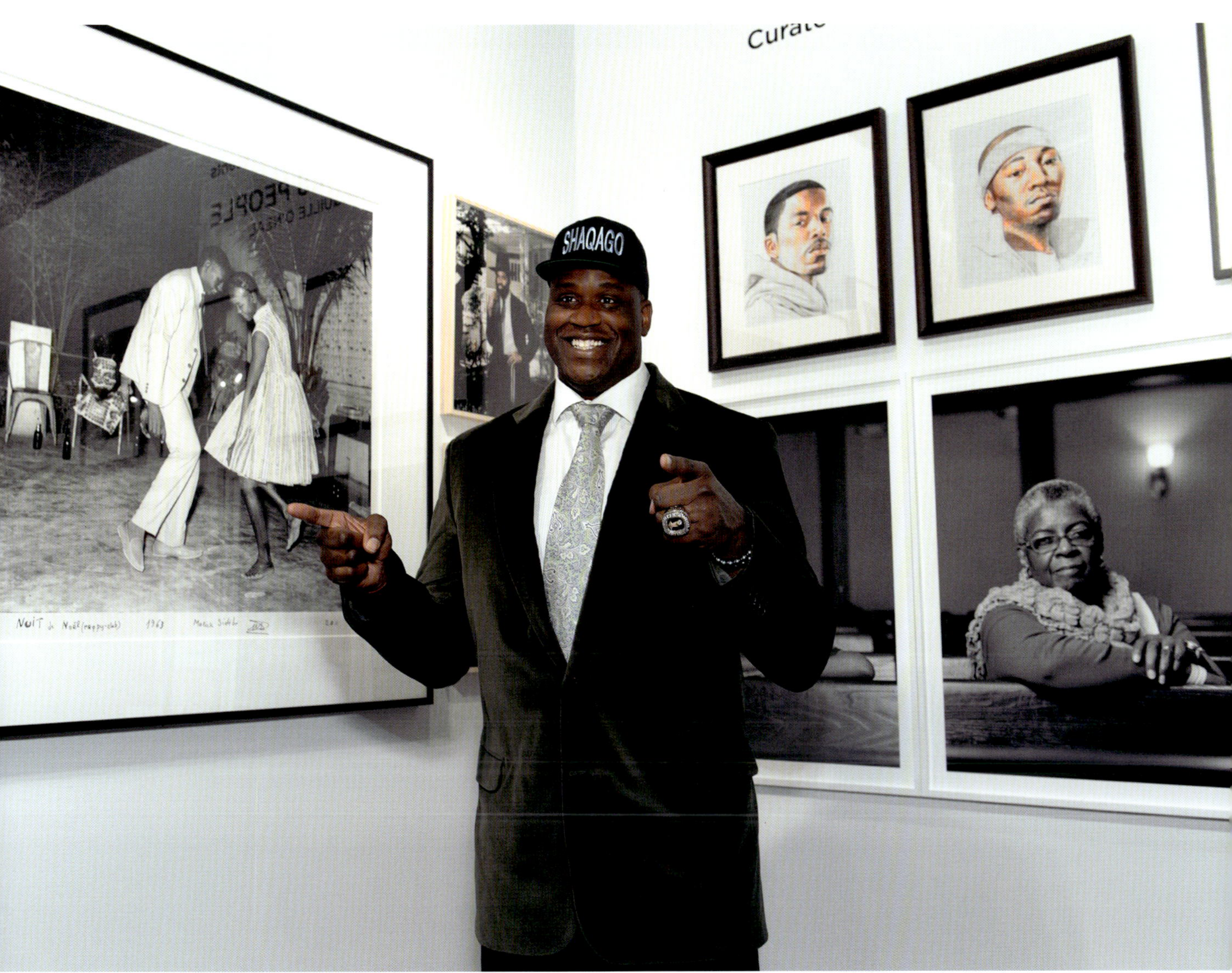

Shaquille O'Neal at EXPO CHICAGO installation

DISTURBING INNOCENCE

October 25, 2014–January 31, 2015
Curated by Eric Fischl

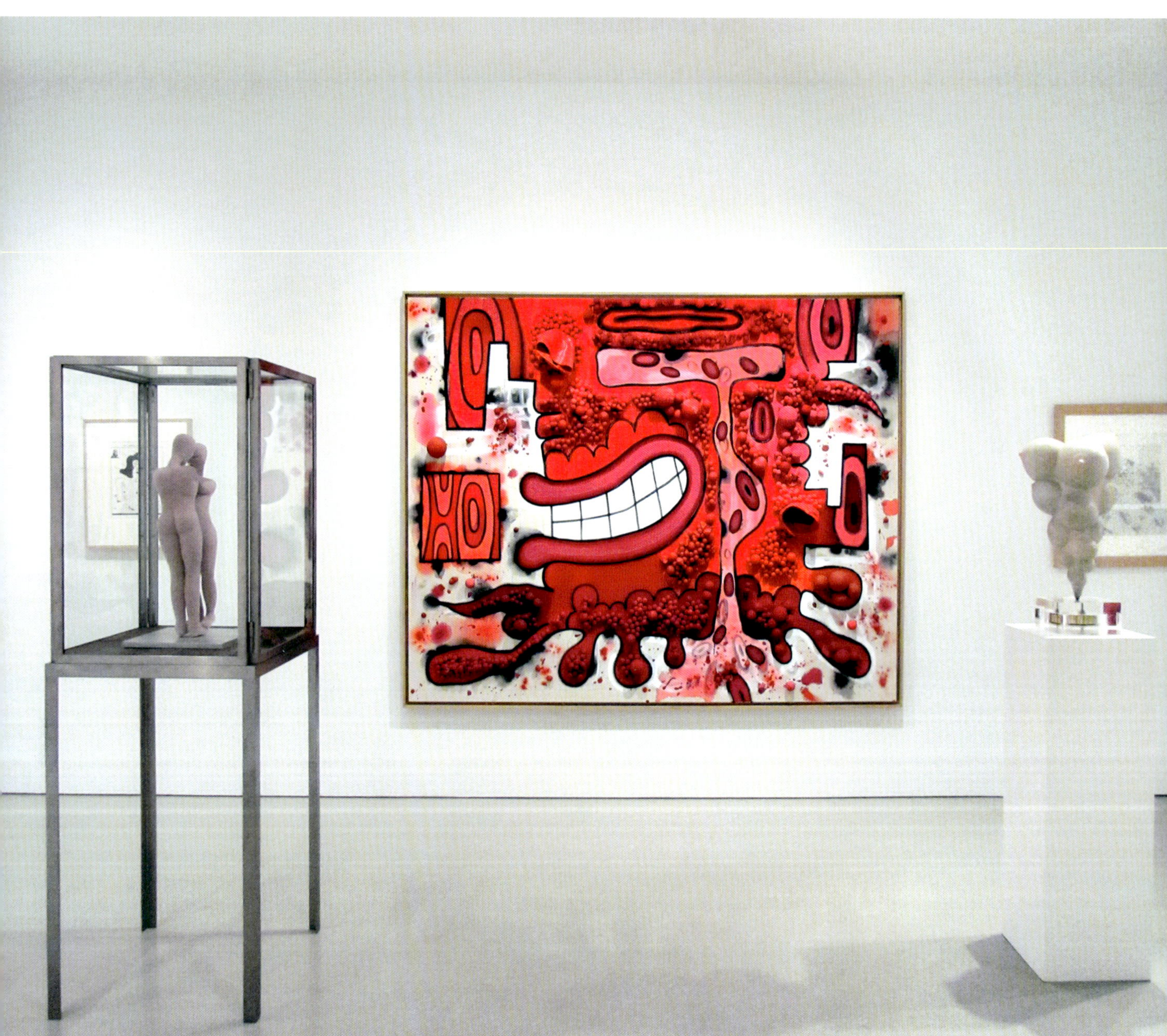

Clockwise from left: Louise Bourgeois, *Couple*, 2004; Carroll Dunham, *Red Studies Itself*, 1994; Hans Bellmer, *La toupie*, 1938/1968

The FLAG Art Foundation approached me and, in a most casual way, offered that if I ever wanted to curate a show for them, they'd be willing.

So offhand and nonchalant, my reply sounded like that of a slacker: "Sure."

Shortly thereafter, I suggested we do a show about artists who play with dolls. For me, this fairly recent phenomenon of faux innocence in the arts was disturbing: Why now? Why dolls?

The title, *Disturbing Innocence*, appeared almost simultaneously with those questions, and that is the show I proposed.

The good people at FLAG said, "Sure."

Why can't all of life be that easy?

The memories come flooding back as I write this. I can't tell you how agreeable and rewarding an experience it was for me to work with a team of professionals who are so smart and competent and generous that the shape and depth of the show I had so casually proposed took on profound and unexpected significance in pursuit of answers. The wish list of artists and artworks, with few and understandable exceptions, was realized. I did not hear a single "no." I was never made to feel like I was asking too much from the FLAG team or that what I was asking for was entirely out of their reach. What I always heard was, "We'll try." And they did, with great success.

The show did not answer my questions but rather expanded them deeper into the soft tissue of the psychological and emotional imperatives that are an inseparable part of the transition from childhood to adulthood, along with all its confusion and its scars.

I can't sing enough praises for the good work and generosity of Glenn Fuhrman and his remarkable staff—Stephanie Roach, Risa Daniels, and Jonathan Rider. By providing space for artists and curators to do projects outside of the rigid and crippling bureaucracy of mainstream museums or the solely commercial concerns of galleries, FLAG has opened up opportunities for reimagining, reconfiguring, and reasserting art's essential purpose: to connect deeply and meaningfully as a society and a culture.

Happy tenth anniversary, FLAG!

—Eric Fischl

Artists

Morton Bartlett
Vanessa Beecroft
Hans Bellmer
Amy Bennett
Louise Bourgeois
James Casebere
Jake & Dinos Chapman
Bonnie Collura
George Condo
Will Cotton
Gregory Crewdson
James Croak
Chris Cunningham
Henry Darger
E.V. Day
Peter Drake
Carroll Dunham
Inka Essenhigh
Eric Fischl
Alberto Giacometti
Steve Gianakos
Ralph Gibson
Robert Gober
Martin Gutierrez
Hilary Harkness
Andrew Huang
Mike Kelley
Elizabeth King and Richard Kizu-Blair
Charles LeDray
David Levinthal
Roy Lichtenstein
Sarah Lucas
Loretta Lux
Walter Martin & Paloma Muñoz
Paul McCarthy
Ralph Eugene Meatyard
Malcolm Morley
Jim Nutt
Tony Oursler
Alexandra Penney
Ellen Phelan
Richard Prince
Aura Rosenberg
Jennifer Rubell
Gideon Rubin
David Salle
Claudette Schreuders
Cindy Sherman
Laurie Simmons
Wolfgang Stoerchle
Helen Verhoeven
John Waters
John Wesley
Lucy Winton
Ivan Witenstein
Dare Wright
Lisa Yuskavage

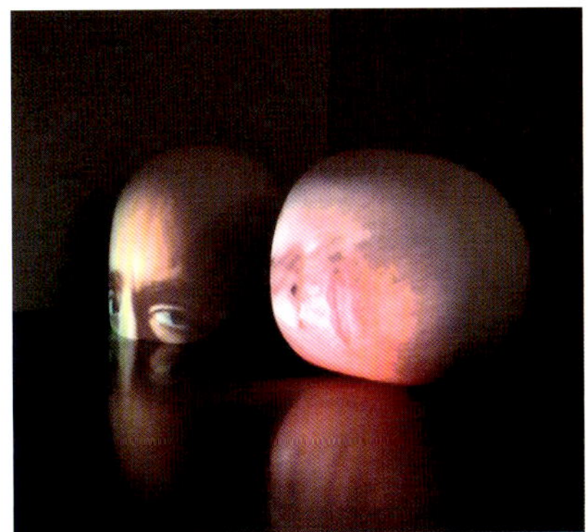

Tony Oursler, *Half (Brain)*, 1998

A SECRET AFFAIR: SELECTIONS FROM THE FUHRMAN FAMILY COLLECTION

February 21–May 16, 2015
Curated by Louis Grachos

Artists
Matthew Barney
Louise Bourgeois
Maurizio Cattelan
Katharina Fritsch
Robert Gober
Felix Gonzalez-Torres
Subodh Gupta
David Hammons
Jim Hodges
Anish Kapoor
Jim Lambie
Ron Mueck
Juan Muñoz
Marc Quinn
Charles Ray
Thomas Schütte
Yinka Shonibare MBE
Kiki Smith
Gillian Wearing

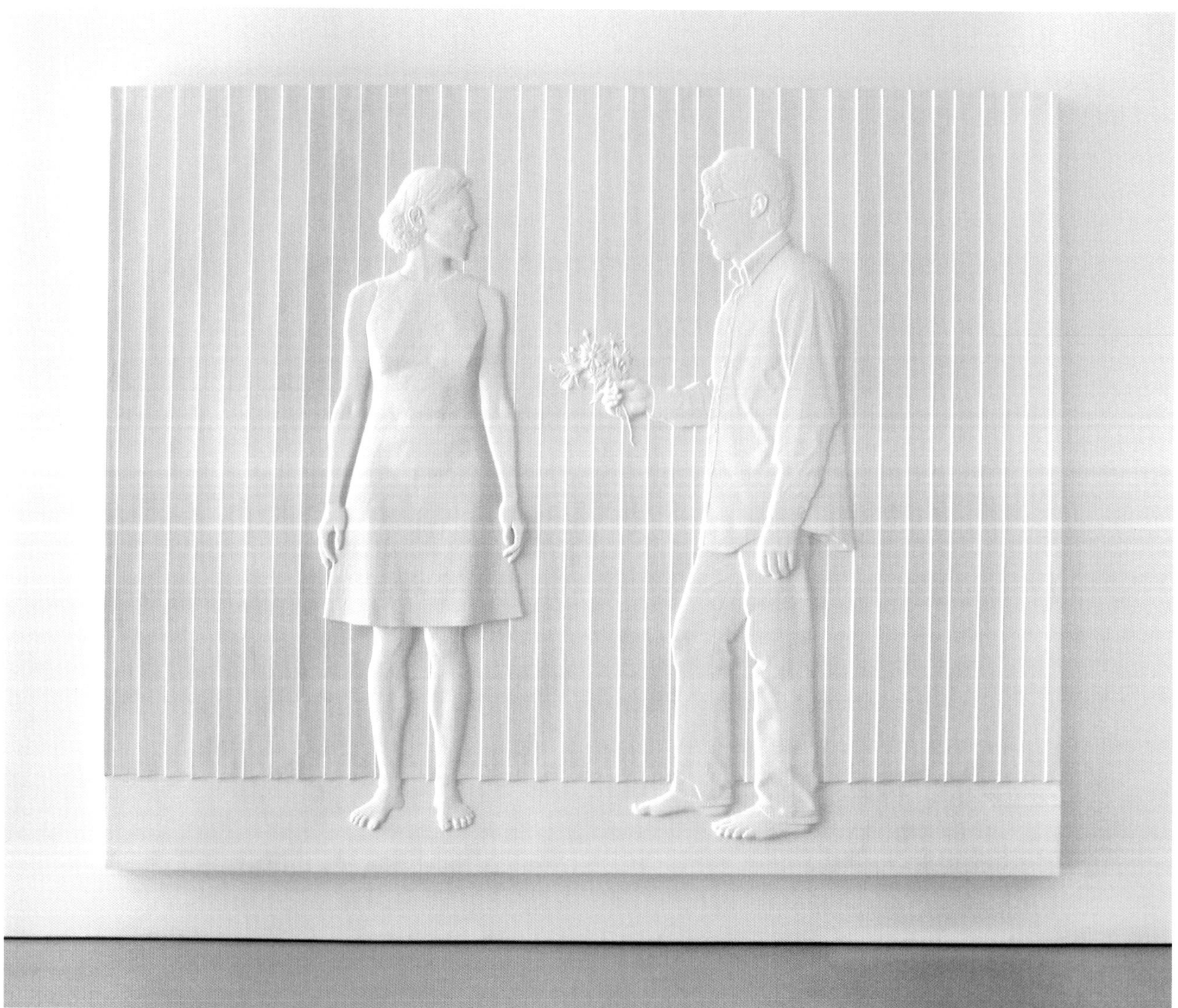

Charles Ray, *Light from the Left*, 2007

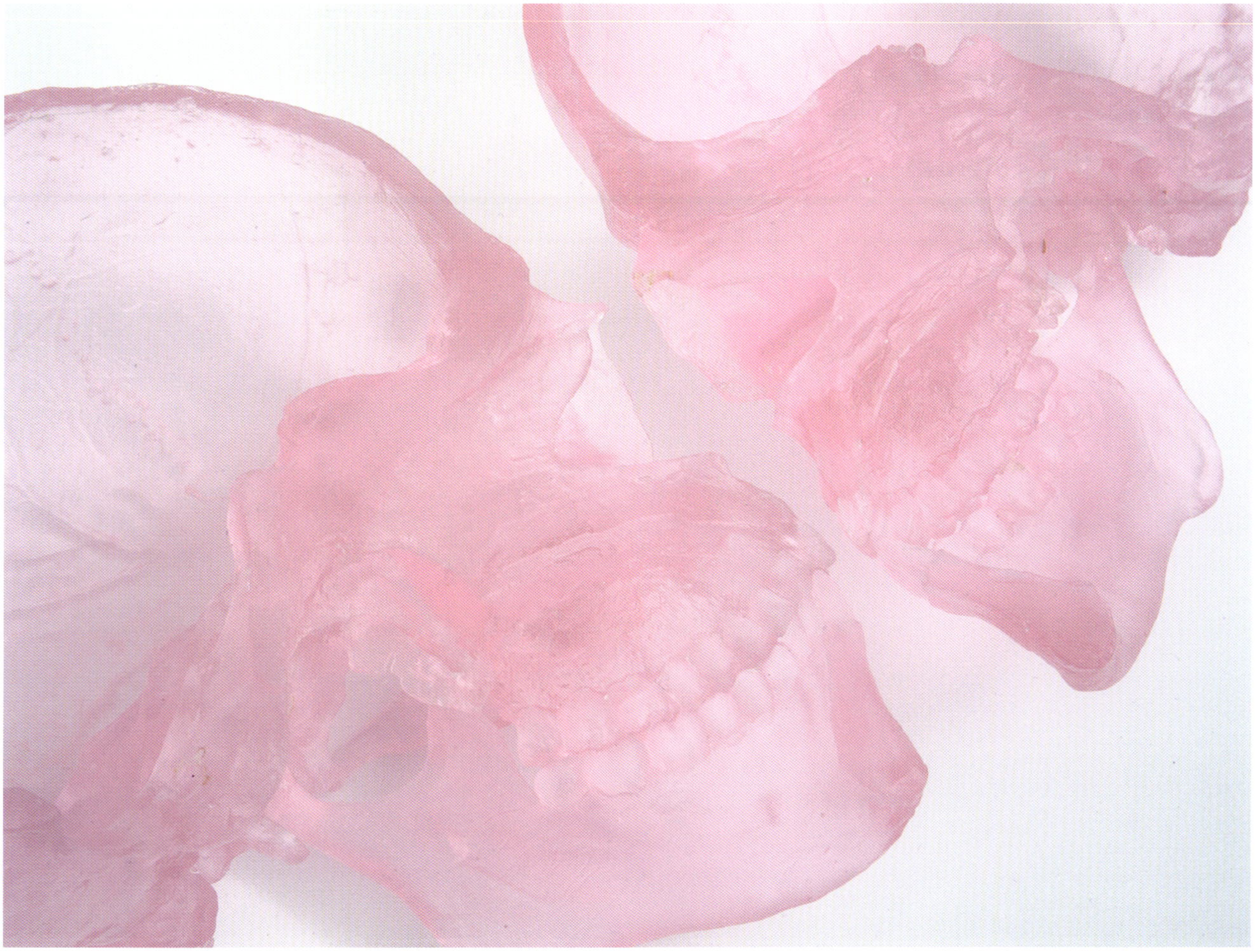

Detail, Jim Hodges, *picturing: my heart*, 2004

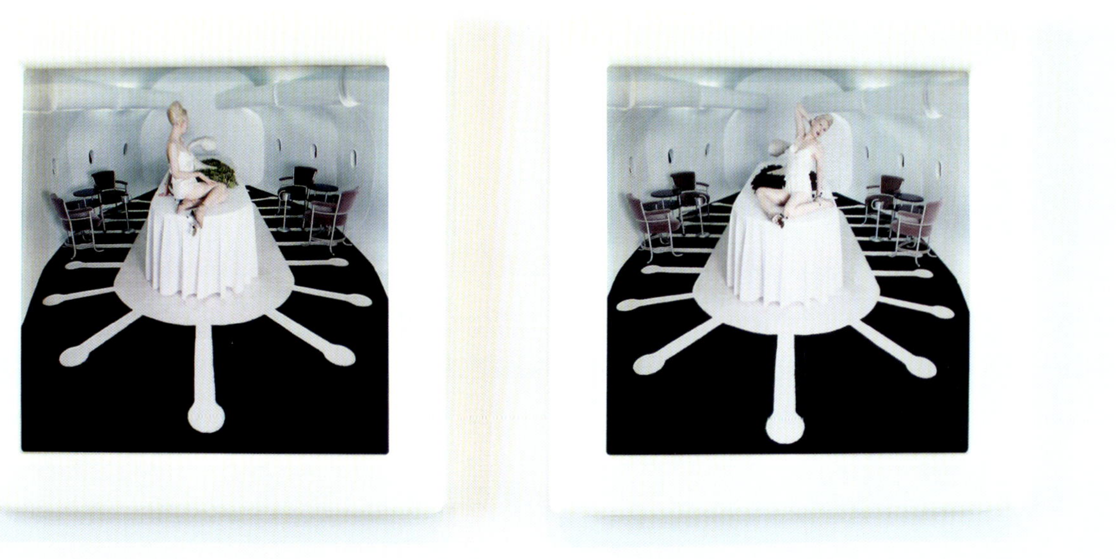

Matthew Barney, *Cremaster 1: Goodyear Lounge*, 1995

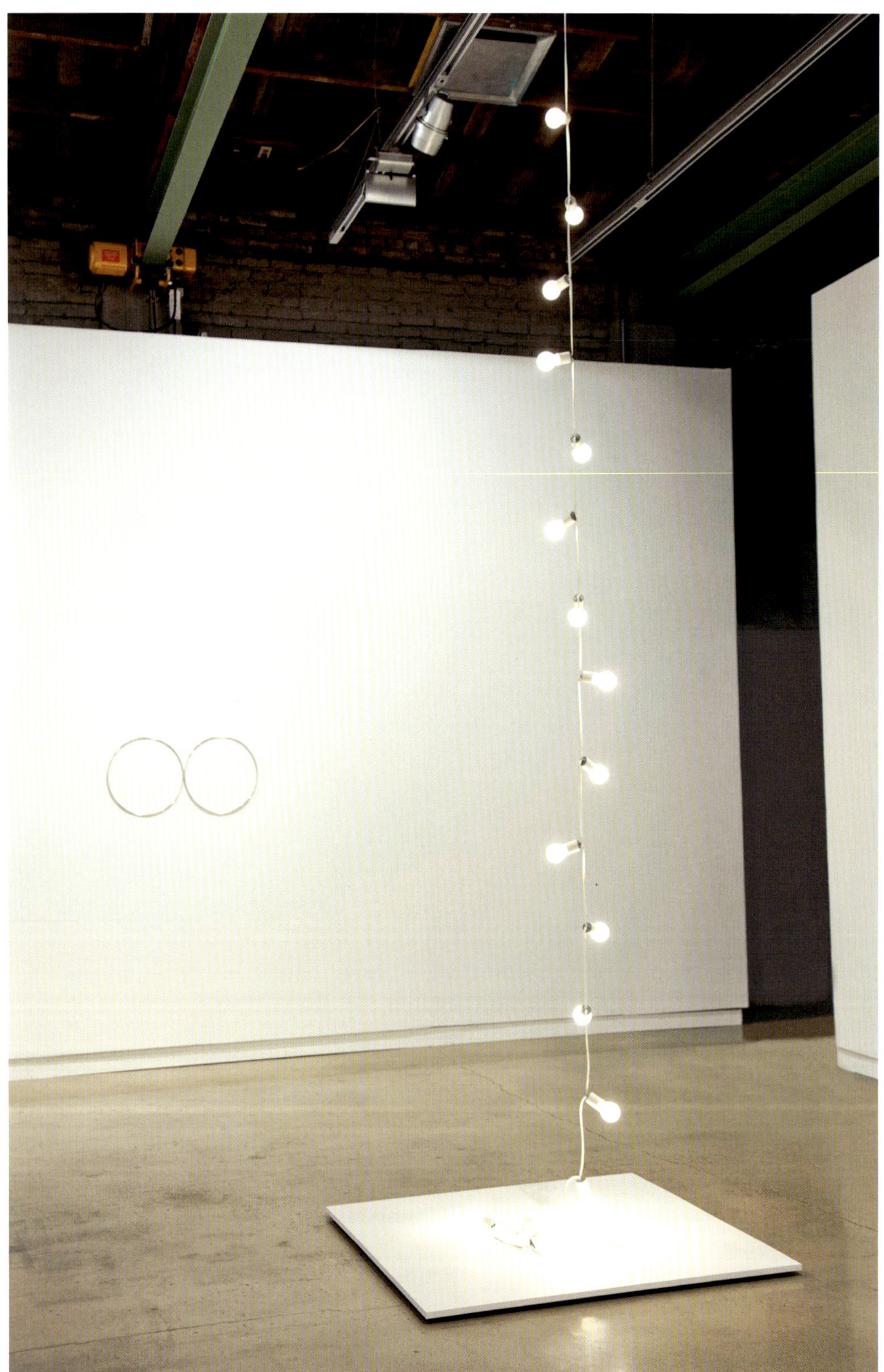

Installation view at The Contemporary Austin, Austin, TX, 2014. Left to right: Felix Gonzalez-Torres, *"Untitled"*, 1995; and *"Untitled"*, 1992

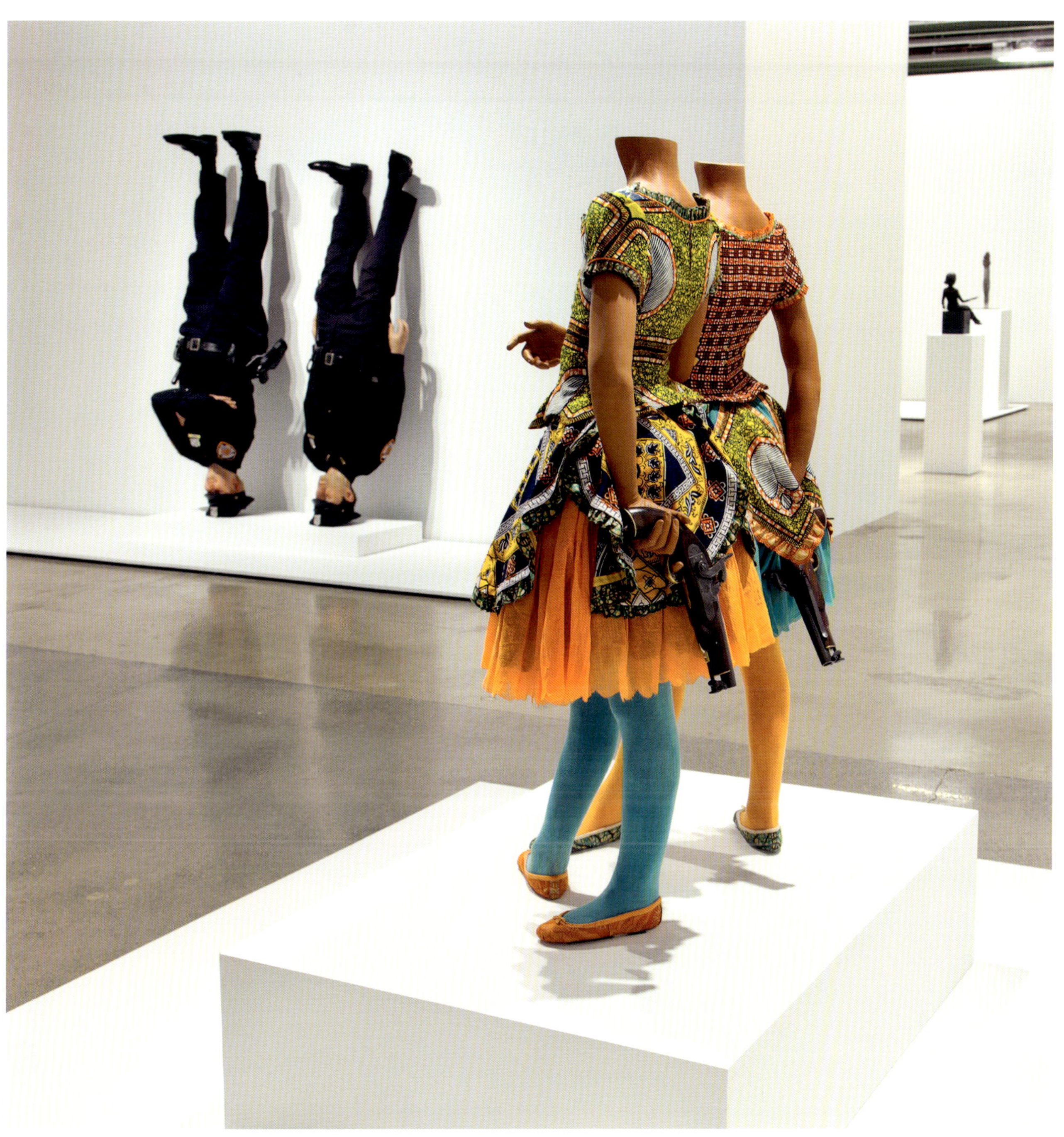

Installation view at The Contemporary Austin, Austin, TX, 2014. Left to right: Maurizio Cattelan, *Frank and Jamie*, 2002; Yinka Shonibare MBE, *Girl Girl Ballerina*, 2007

SPACE BETWEEN

June 3–August 14, 2015
Curated by Louis Grachos and Stephanie Roach

Ellsworth Kelly, *Blue Relief over Green*, 2004

Over the past fifteen years, the art world has witnessed the establishment of a growing number of private contemporary art foundations, not just in the Unites States, but all across the globe. Seeking to share with the public the vision of a private collector, these foundations have carved out a unique space for themselves nestled between the gallery world and traditional museum culture. The physical exhibition space and the programmatic structure of these foundations form exciting new platforms for the introduction of divergent curatorial ideas; they are an artistic laboratory of sorts. Unrestrained by the typical time and resource constraints of more traditional institutions, these foundations allow for innovative exhibitions. They give a voice to emerging artists and unexplored curatorial concepts while operating with the integrity and best practices of the museum world.

One of the finest examples of such foundations is The FLAG Art Foundation. Since its founding by patron Glenn Fuhrman ten years ago, FLAG has provided an opportunity for curators to showcase critical exhibitions that might not have fit the bill in a traditional gallery space or museum. FLAG has become a dedicated platform for scholarship and publications with fresh curatorial perspectives. It is, without a doubt, an integral part of the cultural fabric of both New York and the greater contemporary art landscape. For me, it has become an important destination on each of my visits to the city.

I have been fortunate to work with Glenn and FLAG on several occasions. My first experience, in 2009, was hosting an important touring exhibition organized by FLAG, *WALL ROCKETS: Contemporary Artists and Ed Ruscha*, curated by Lisa Dennison, at the Albright-Knox Art Gallery in Buffalo. The exhibition included works by a significant group of artists who, in some shape or form, were influenced by Ruscha: friends of the artist (John Goode, Dennis Hopper); artists who also work with language (John Baldessari, Barbara Kruger, Keith Tyson); those with a similar sense of humor (Tom Sachs, Joseph Grigely and Amy Vogel); other modern-day surrealists (Robert Therrien, Aya Uekawa, Charles Ray); and those who share a fascination with the unique landscape of Los Angeles (Florian Maier-Aichen, Thomas Scheibitz, Mark Bradford). The close proximity of works provided valuable insight into the impact Ruscha has had on these artists. We were

Artists
Sadie Benning
Douglas Coupland
Sarah Crowner
Svenja Deininger
Tony DeLap
Thomas Demand
Olafur Eliasson
Liam Gillick
Mark Grotjahn
Andreas Gursky
Jim Hodges
Roni Horn
Wyatt Kahn
Ellsworth Kelly
Agnes Martin
Kaz Oshiro
R. H. Quaytman
Julia Rommel
Sérgio Sister
Blair Thurman
Rebecca Ward
Rachel Whiteread

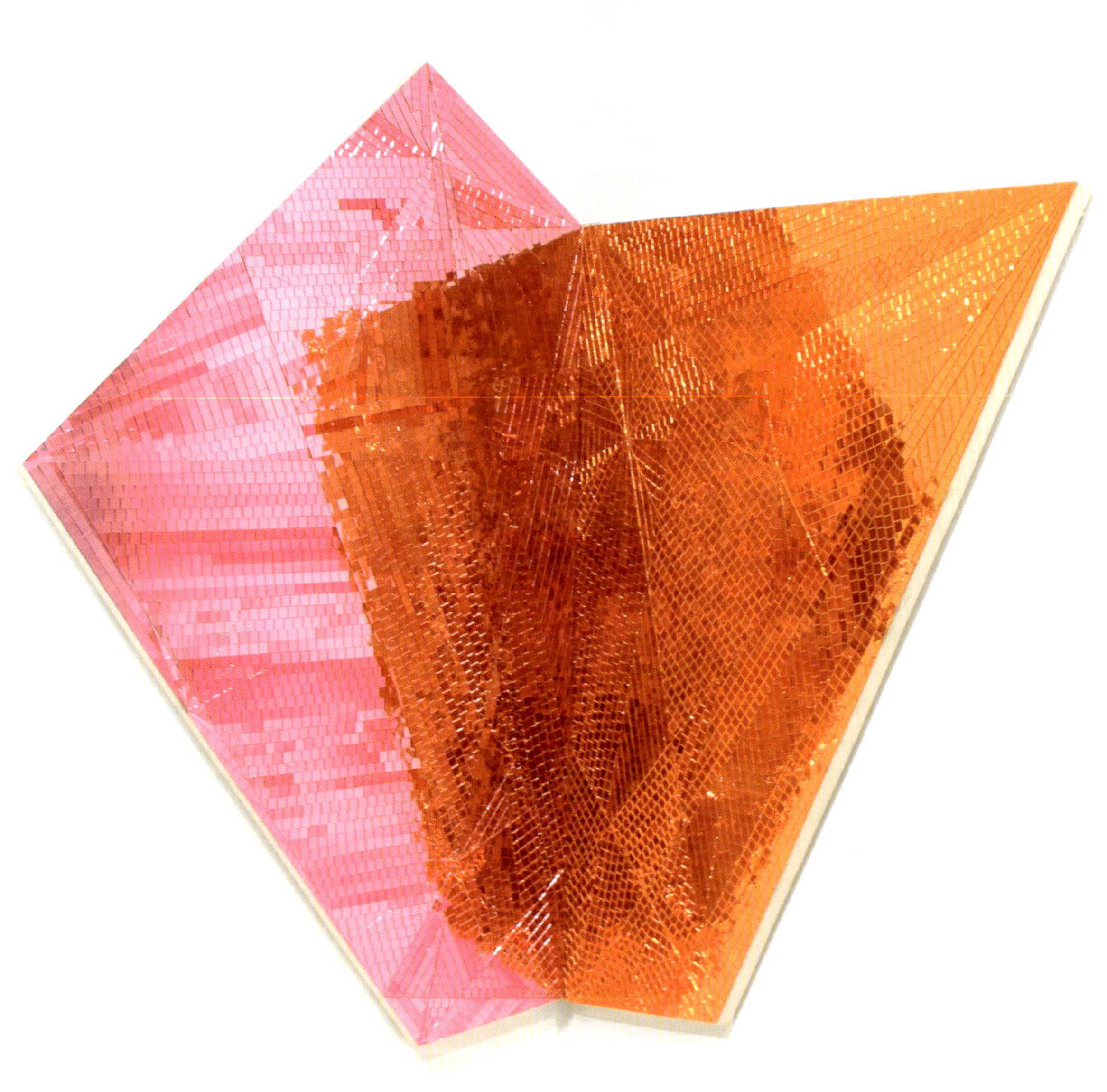

Jim Hodges, *Toward Great Becoming (orange/pink)*, 2014

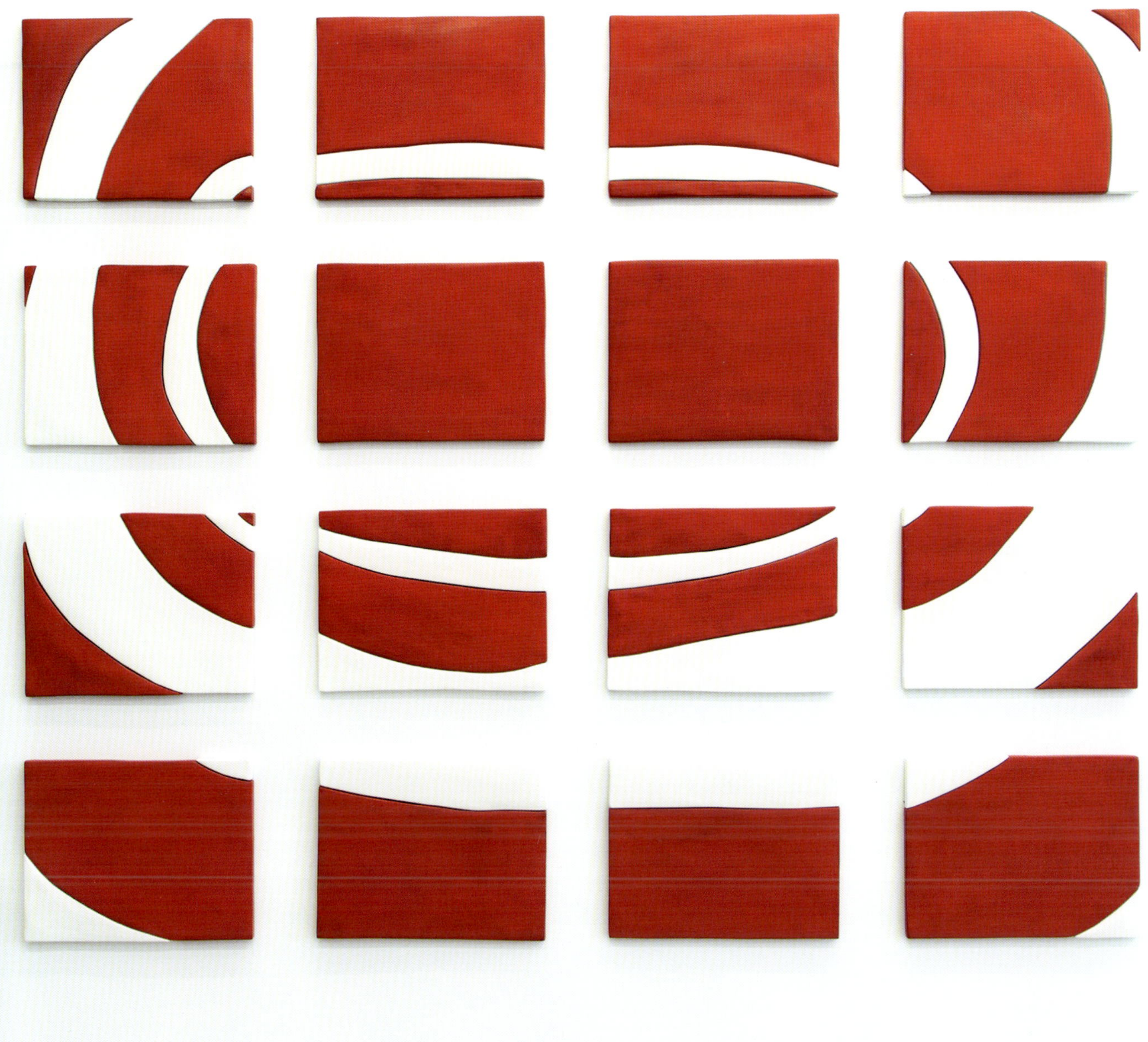

Sadie Benning, *Red and White Painting*, 2013

AWOL ERIZKU: NEW FLOWER | IMAGES OF THE RECLINING VENUS

September 17–December 12, 2015

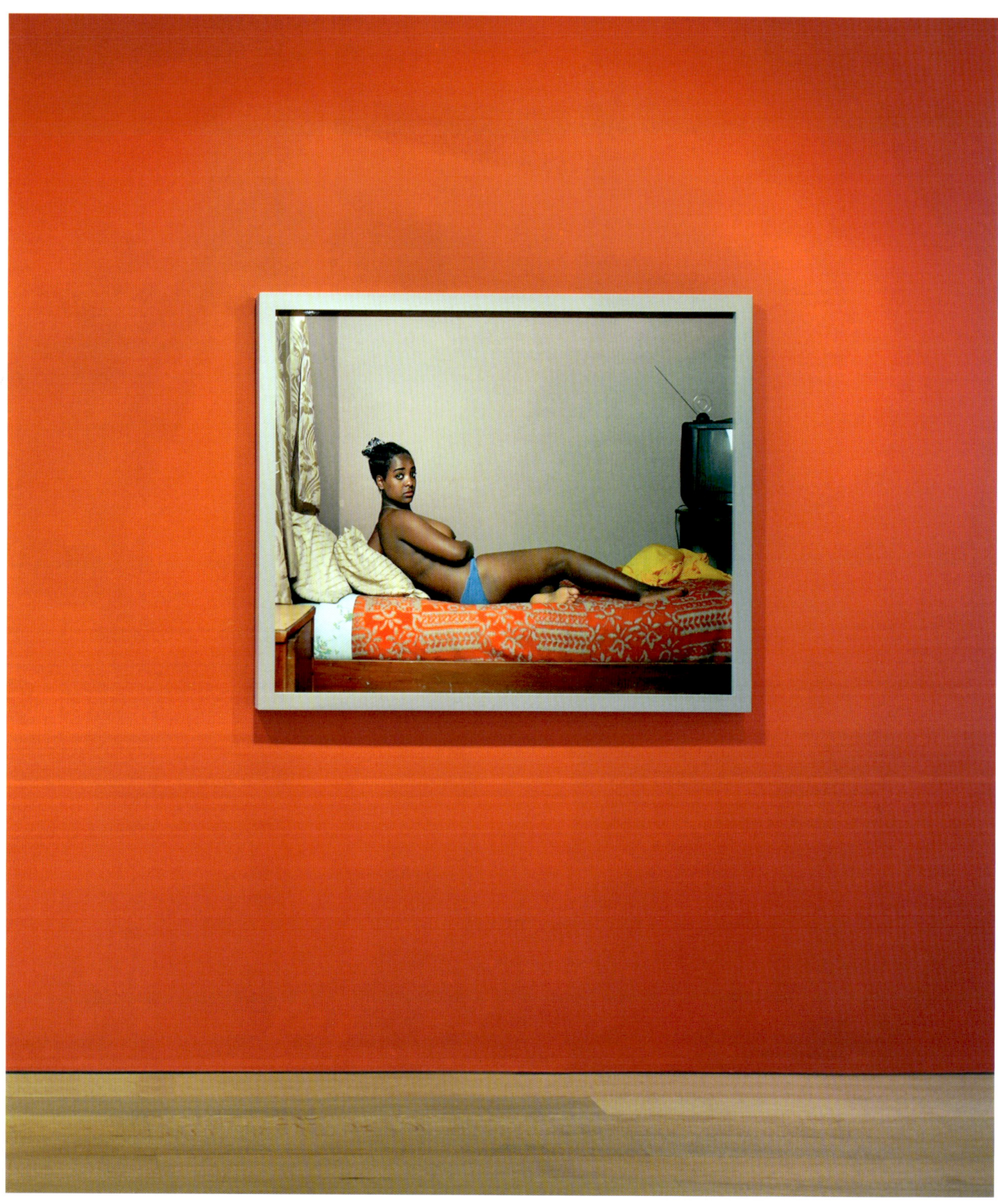

Awol Erizku, *Aziza*, 2013

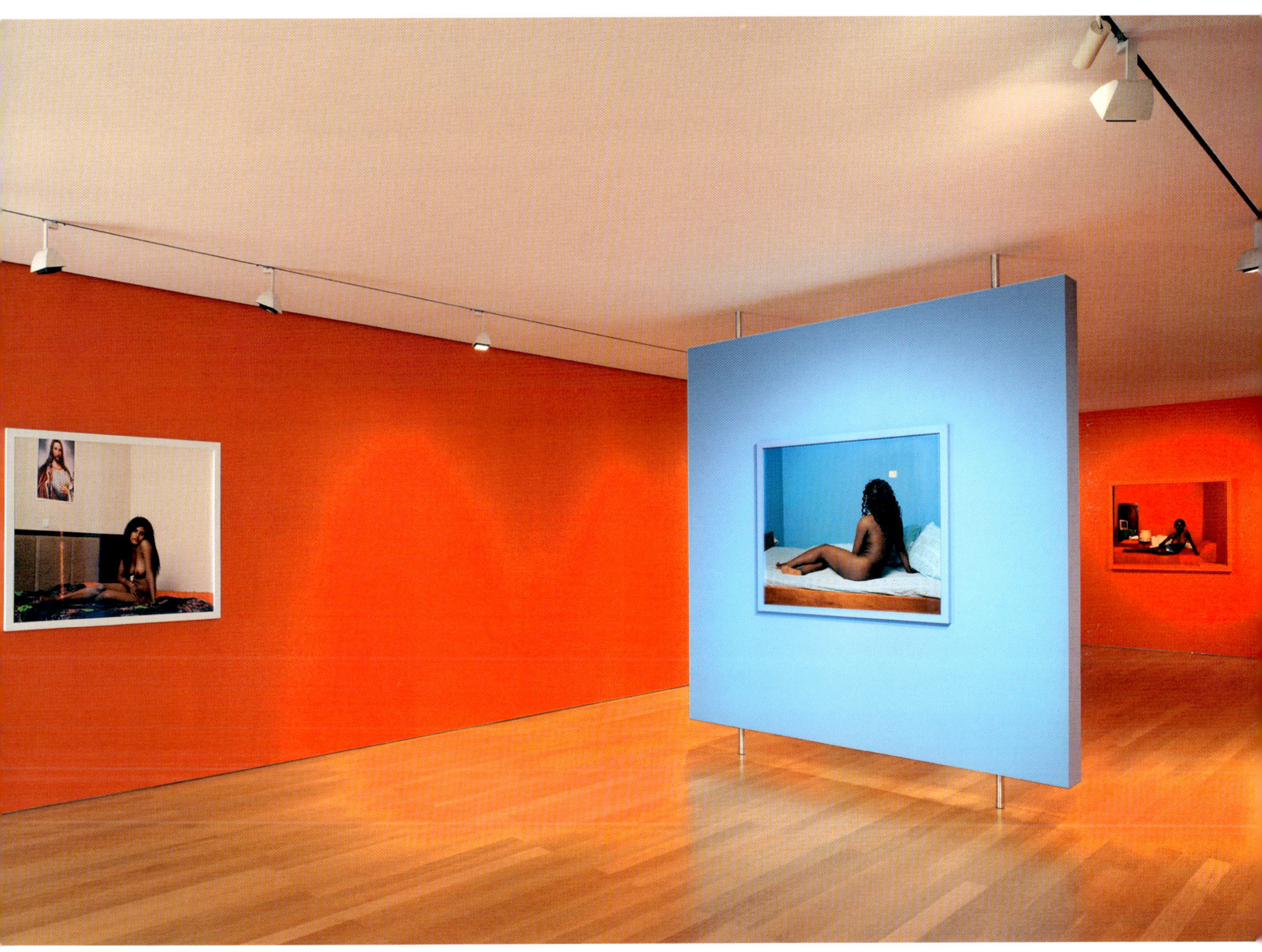

Installation view

Legend has it that in 2011, Glenn Fuhrman was attending an evening auction at Phillips auction house. At the time, it was in the same building as Milk Studios, where I was interning in the digital department—cleaning equipment that just came back from a shoot or prepping laptops, lenses, and digital backs for a new job going out. In a last-minute decision, I entered two of my popular images at the time to the annual Milk Underground show, which featured upward of sixty artists that year. It was last-minute because I hesitated to submit work to another group show that focused only on photography at a time when *Girl with a Bamboo Earring* (2009) was how most people saw my work and viewed me as an artist.

I was only twenty-two and I hadn't made the body of work that I wanted to make to let people see everything that my work encompasses today. I was fresh out of art school at The Cooper Union and looking to make a name in the art world, much like anyone at that age in my position.

Early one morning as I was preparing to head to work, I got a phone call from Glenn, who apparently had been calling everyone from that Milk Underground show roster in search of "Awol." I was skeptical at the time because of how nice he was and I'm always the last to Google people, so I asked my friend Lauren Kelly how legit this Glenn Fuhrman really was, and her response was, "Do you not know who Glenn is? He's a BIG DEAL." It was then that I figured it was time to research who he was, and I found out about his work and, more importantly, The FLAG Art Foundation, which had just closed the exhibition curated by Shaquille O'Neal.

Glenn was interested in including *Girl with a Bamboo Earring* in an upcoming exhibition, which would become my debut art world group show, with the likes of Richard Prince, Roe Ethridge, and Kehinde Wiley. Needless to say, I was curious as to where I fit in and how. *Art²* (2011) was crucial on so many levels for me starting out. It showed me that I could hang with my idols and hold court, but it also got me a studio visit from two gallerists who were at the show for their artist, and this led to my first Chelsea gallery in New York.

As the years went by, my bond with Glenn, as well as with the others at FLAG—Stephanie Roach, Jon Rider, and Risa Daniels—got tighter, and they became my second family in a lot of ways. I would always stop by FLAG to catch up and ask them what shows to see while I was in Chelsea. This routine became important for me once I was at Yale getting my MFA and would come back for weekends with a short time to see the shows that mattered most.

I've had the great pleasure of curating an exhibition for FLAG and had my last New York exhibition, *New Flower | Images of the Reclining Venus* (2015), premiere there as well. Because of the nature of the photographs and the subject matter I was presenting, the exhibition had to be held in what I considered a safe space for art and artists, a place outside the art market and away from dealers who would ask to show the work in a way that focused only on making a sale, which wasn't of much interest to me at the time. It was very important that this particular exhibition wasn't seen through that lens, and FLAG allowed me to not only paint the walls but also to really create an experience that was true to my practice exactly as I had envisioned when I was making the images in Ethiopia.

By having the show at FLAG, I felt I was allowing these sensitive images to be seen in the context that best protected their dignity, which was very important to me. FLAG to me is a space of neutrality in Chelsea, a space with no agenda other than presenting exhibitions that challenge the status quo without any hype or fluff.

I'm grateful to have had the tremendous support of Glenn and the great team at FLAG early in my career. My curatorial and artistic practices have been pushed further as a result of the opportunities they've provided me in the eight or so years I've known about the foundation. I can't wait to see what the next ten, twenty, and thirty years of FLAG will bring to the larger art community, not only in New York but also around the world.

—Awol Erizku

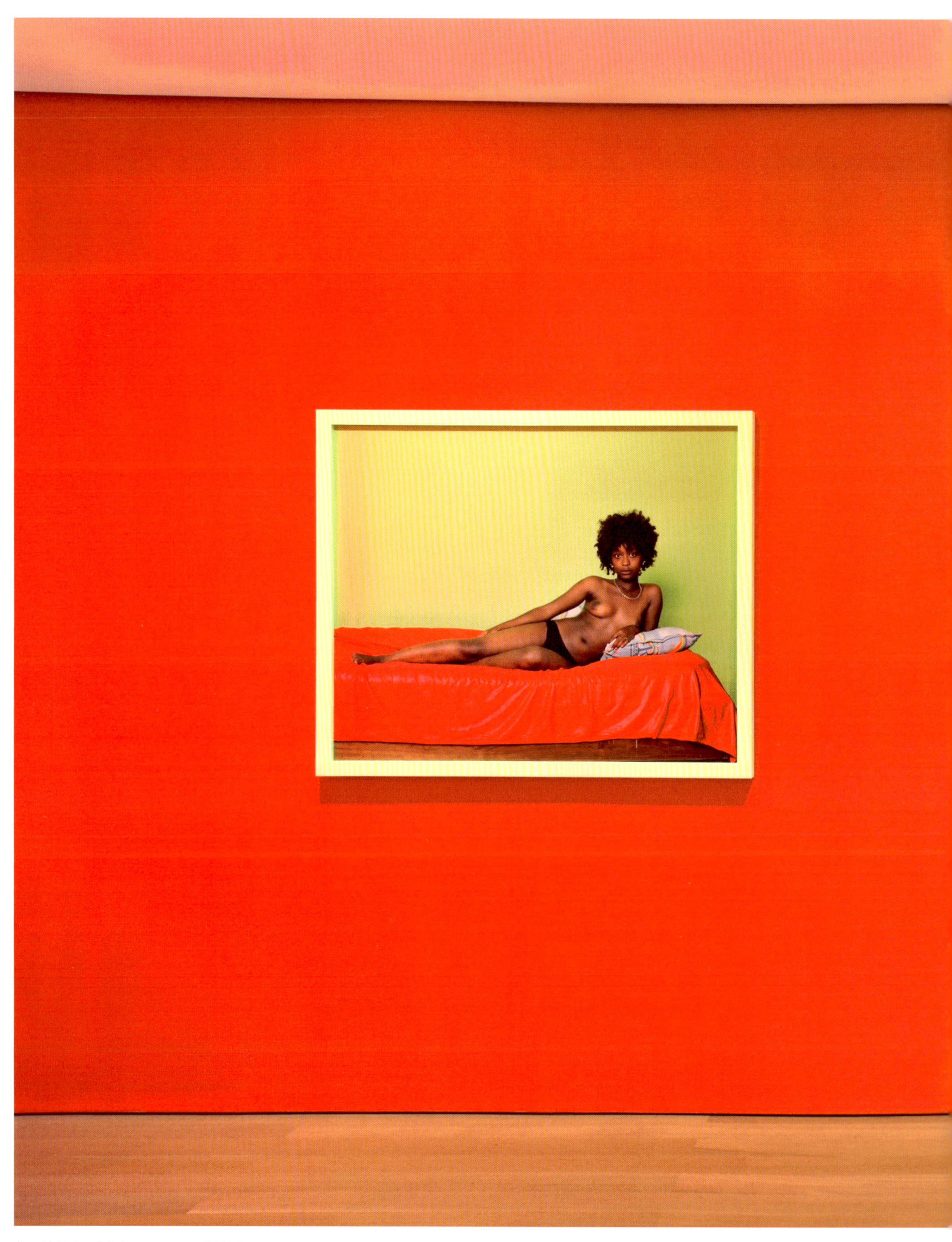

Awol Erizku, *Meskerem*, 2013; and *Nigist*, 2013

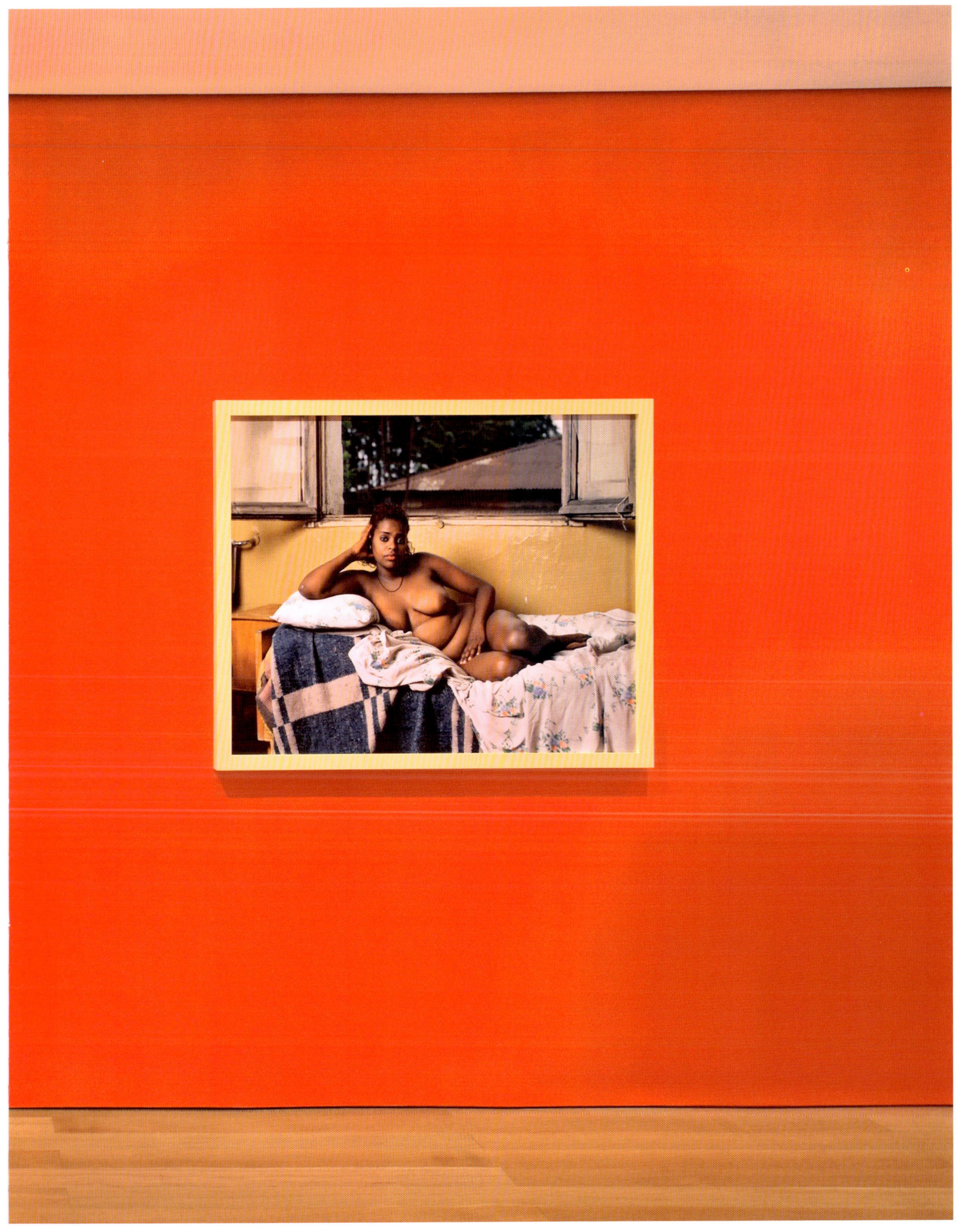

CECILY BROWN, JEFF KOONS, CHARLES RAY

January 20–May 14, 2016

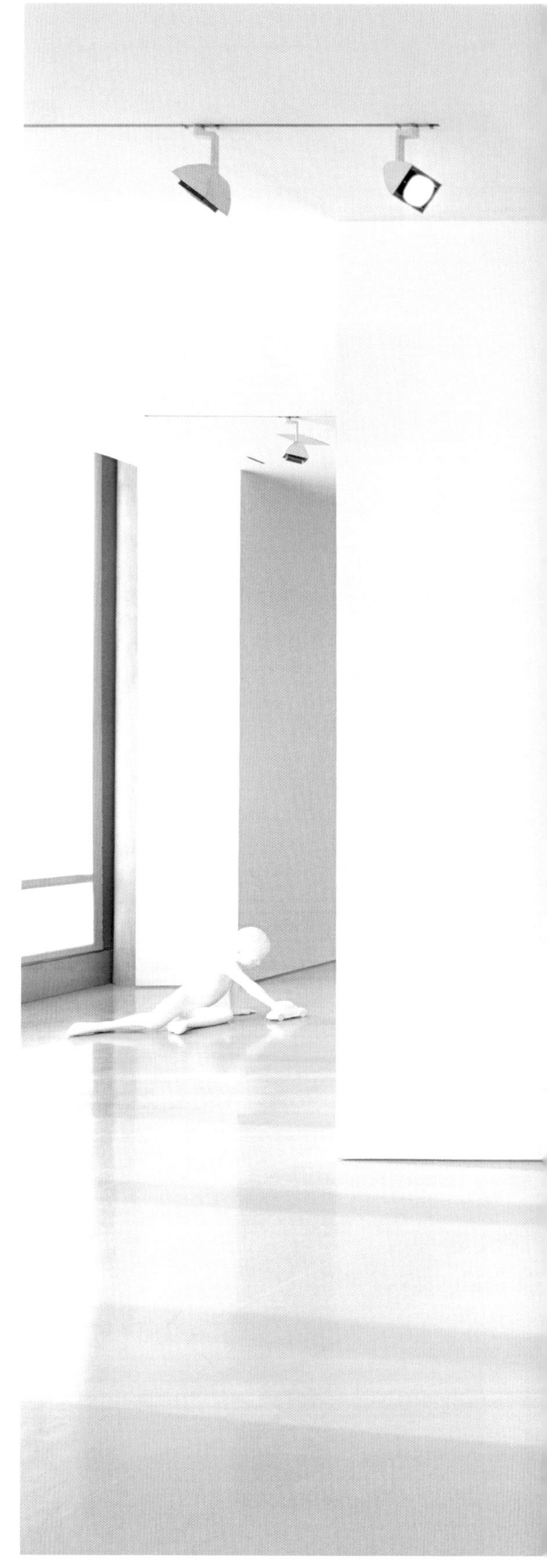

Left to right: Charles Ray, *The New Beatle*, 2006; Jeff Koons, *Cat on a Clothesline (Red)*, 1994–2001

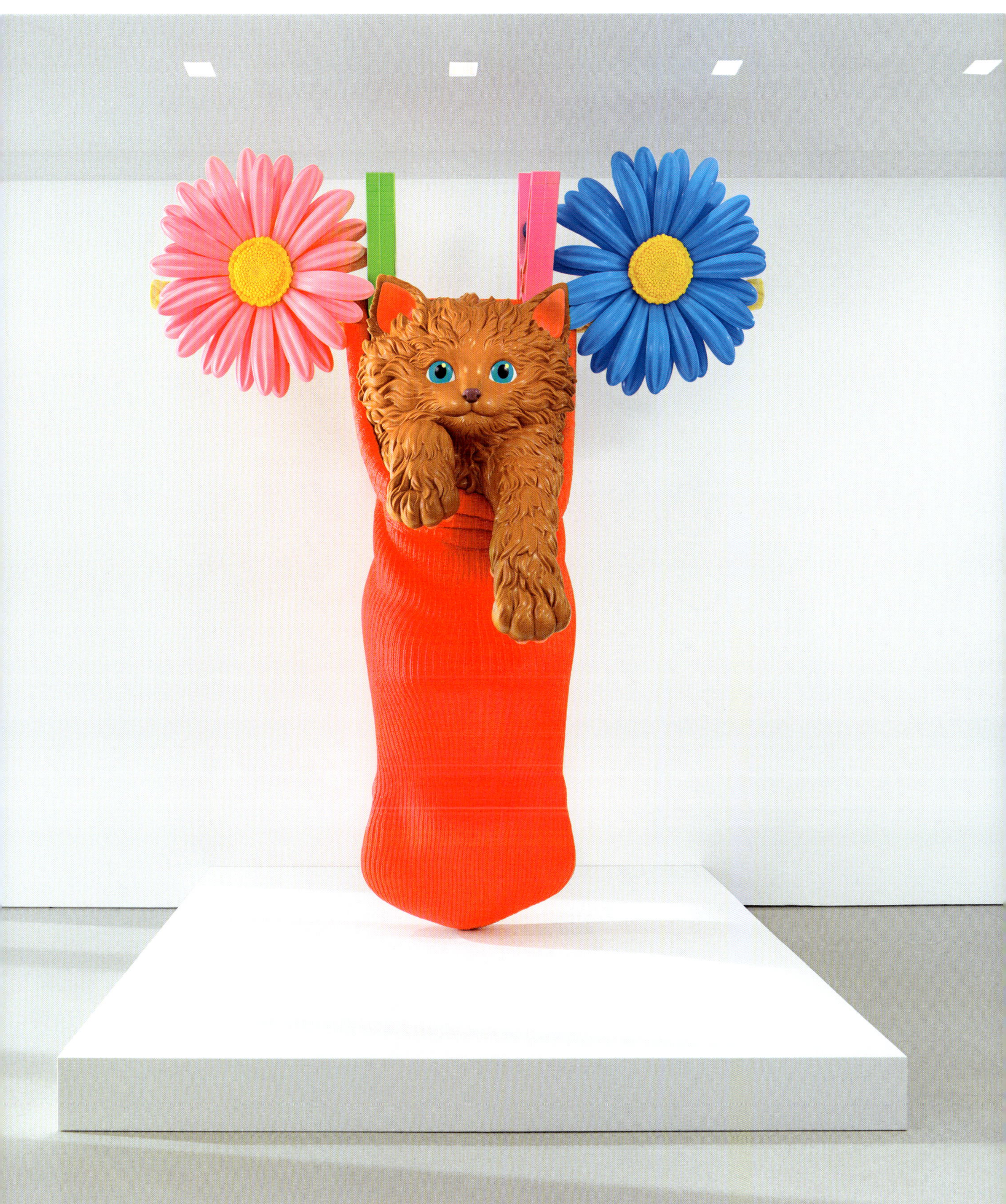

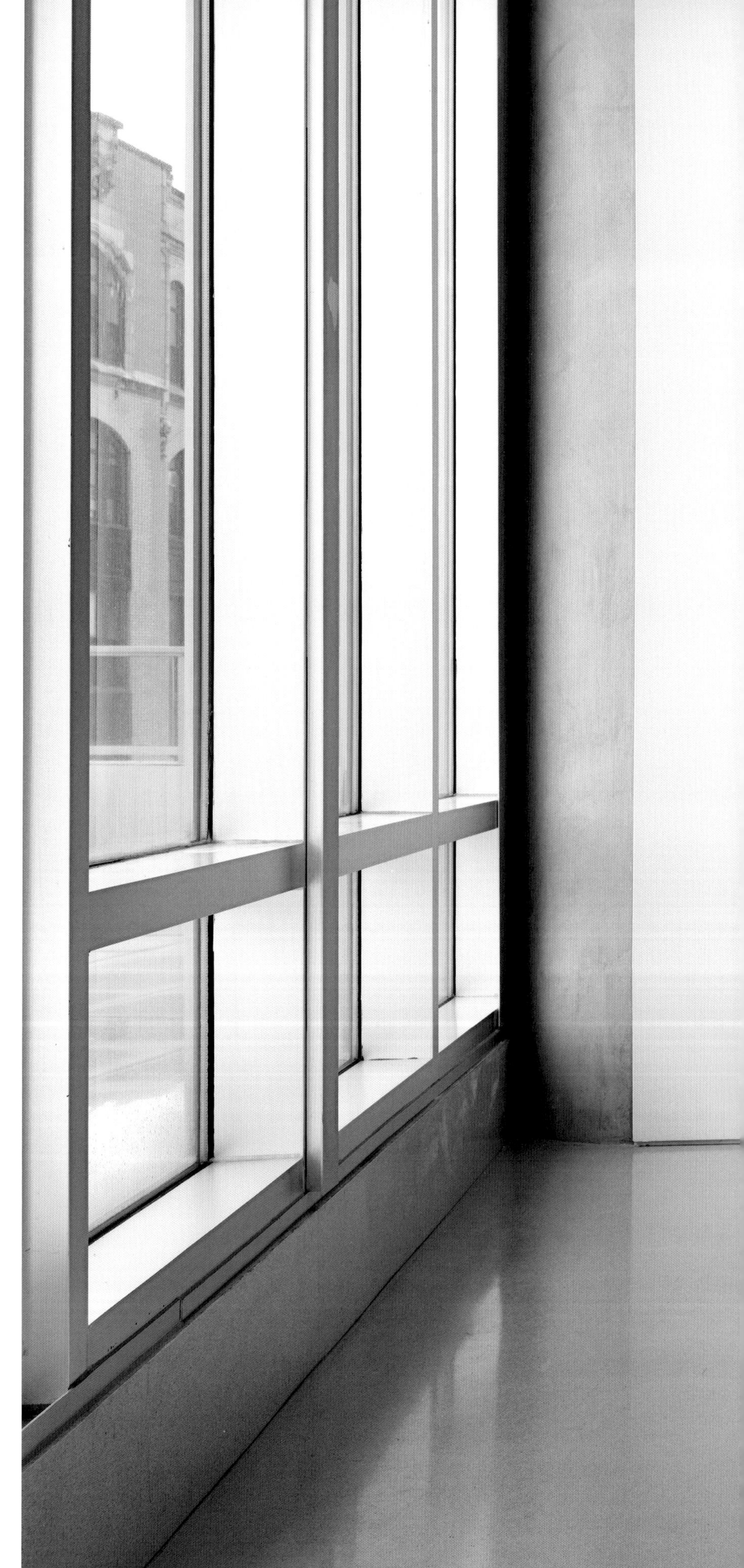

Left to right: Charles Ray, *The New Beatle*, 2006; Jeff Koons, *Sling Hook*, 2007–09

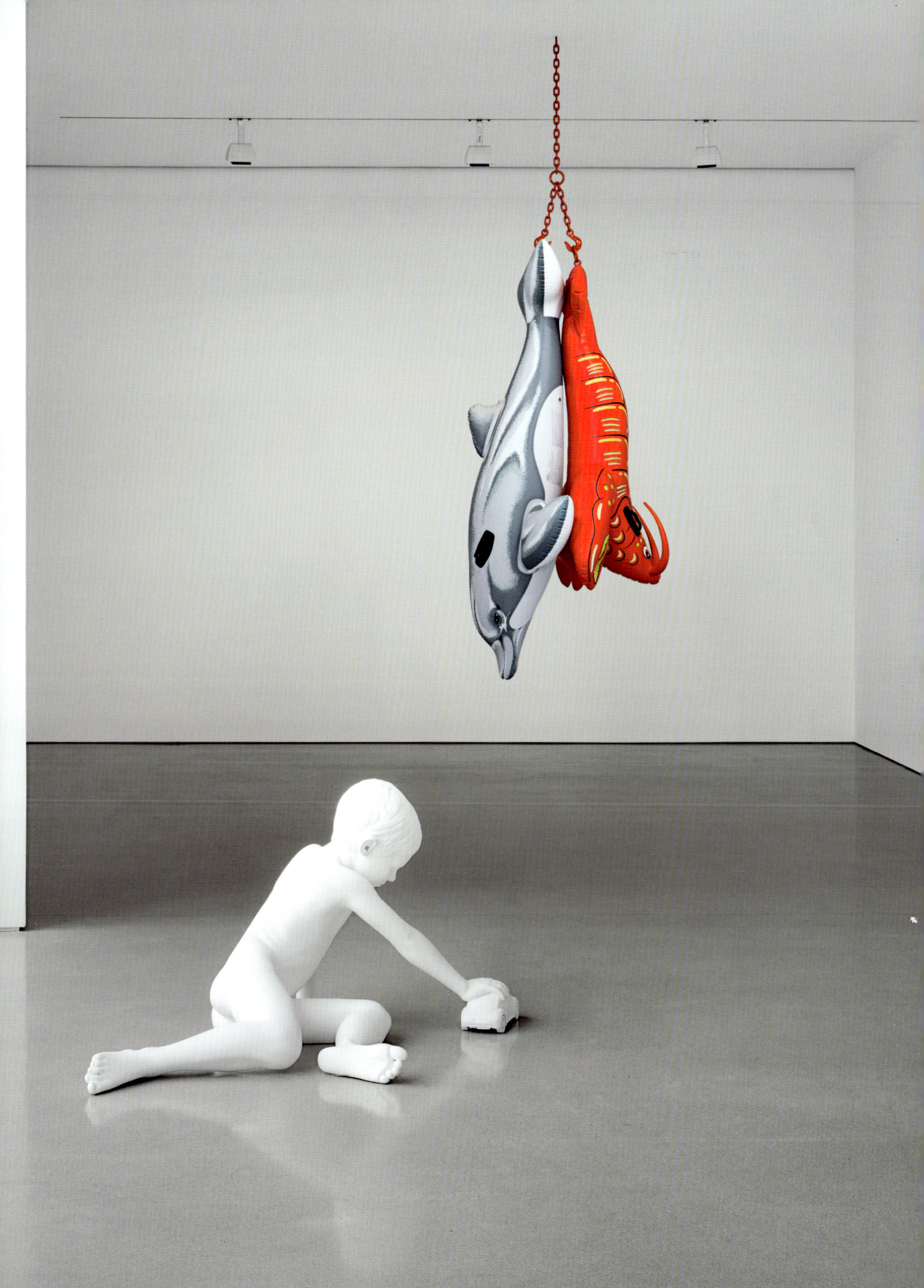

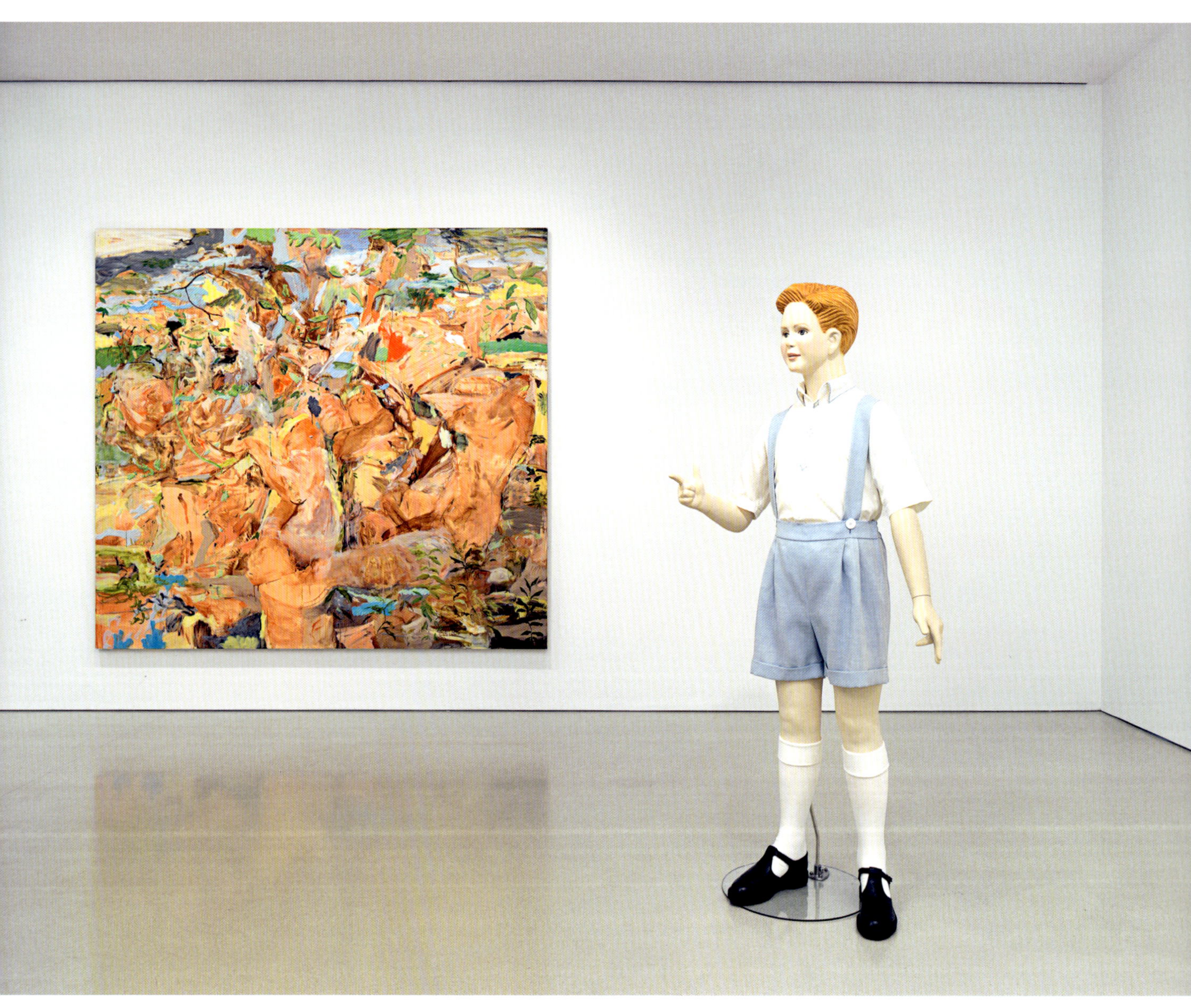

Left to right: Cecily Brown, *Figures in a Landscape I*, 2001; Charles Ray, *Boy*, 1992

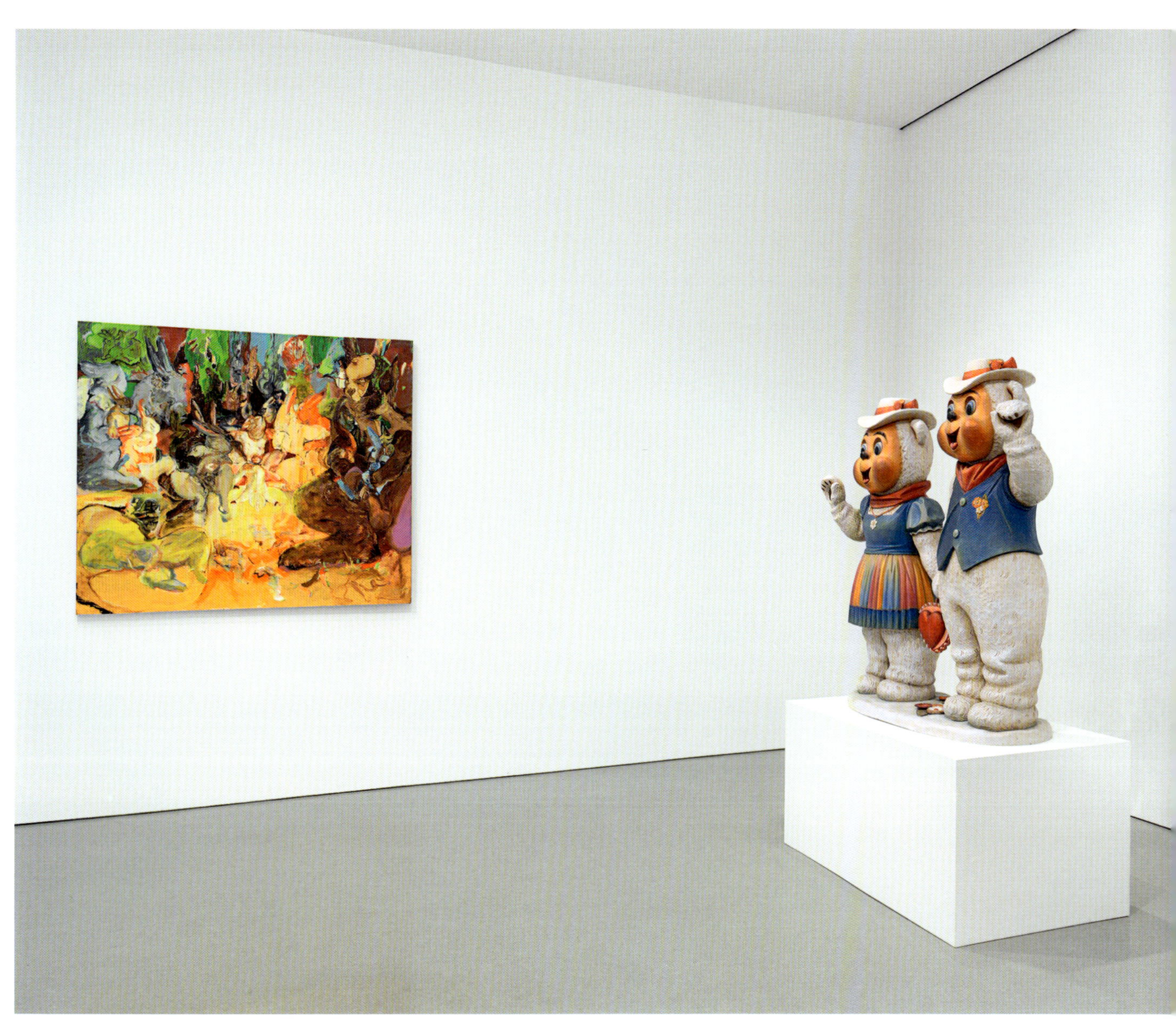

Left to right: Cecily Brown, *Untitled*, 1996; Jeff Koons, *Winter Bears*, 1988

BETTY TOMPKINS: WOMEN WORDS, PHRASES, AND STORIES

January 20–May 14, 2016

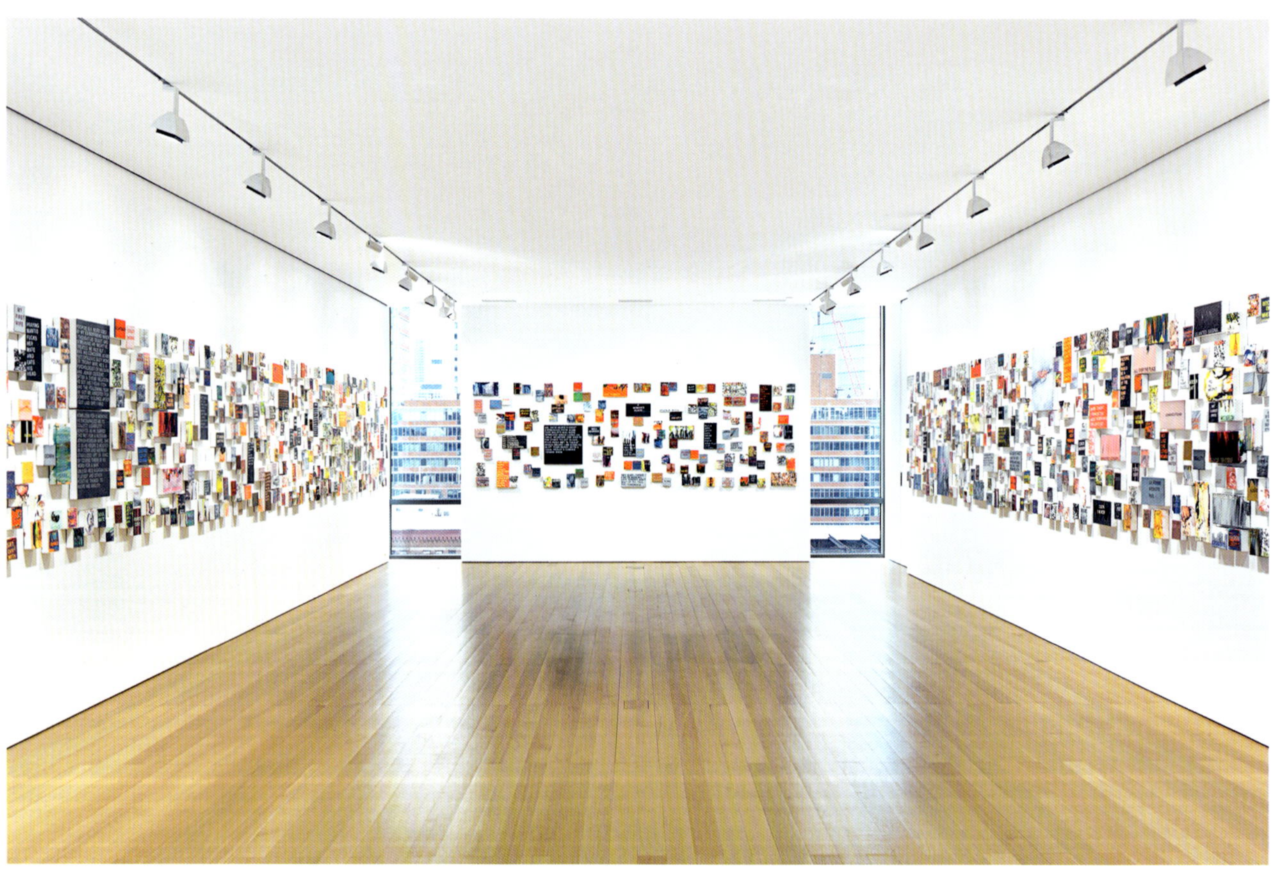

Installation view

Opposite: Installation view

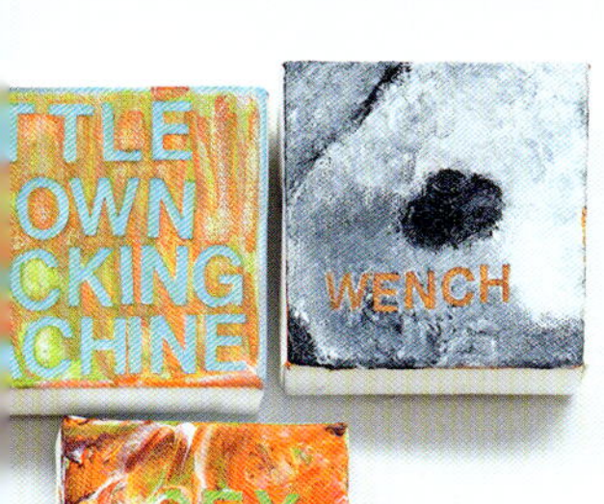
TLE
OWN
CKING
CHINE
WENCH
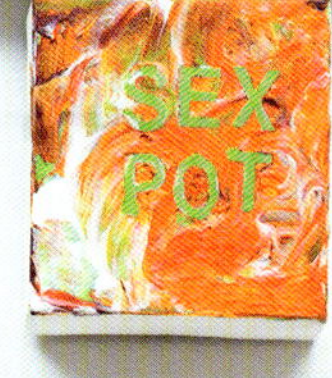
SEX
POT
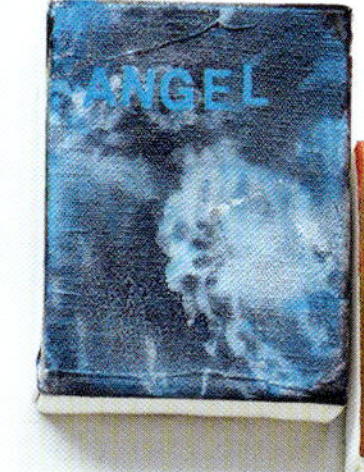
ANGEL
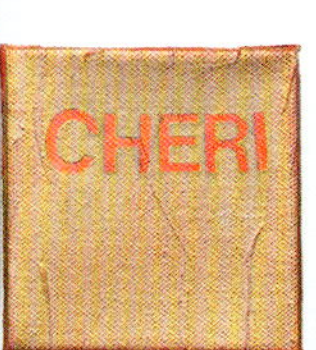
CHERI
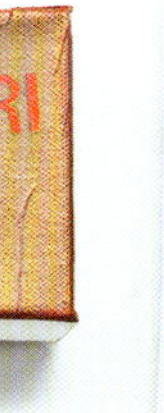
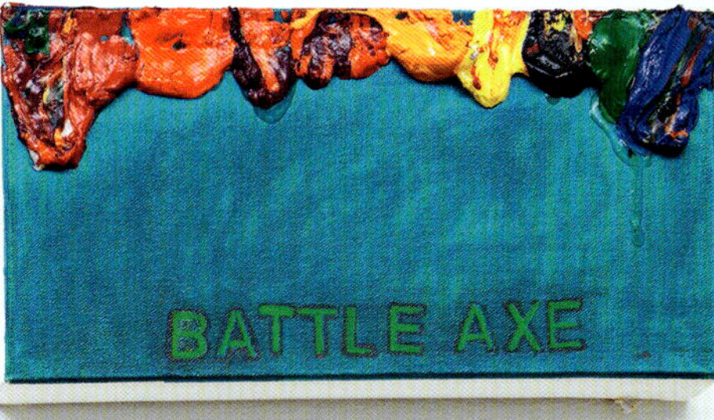
BATTLE AXE

CRAZY BITCH

SHIT
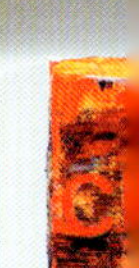
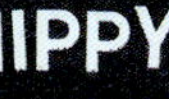
IPPY
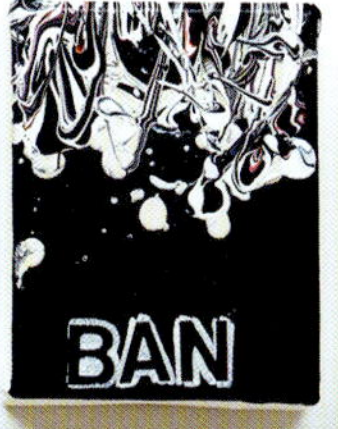
BAN
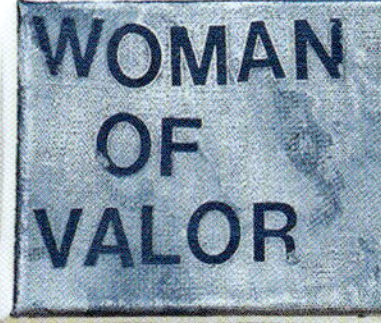
WOMAN
OF
VALOR
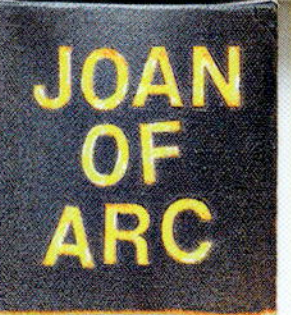
JOAN
OF
ARC
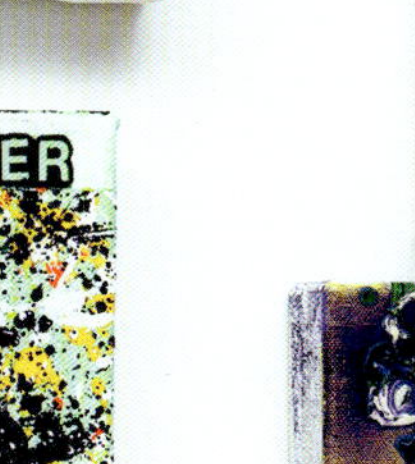
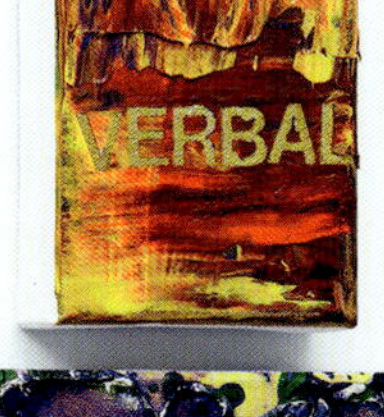
VERBAL
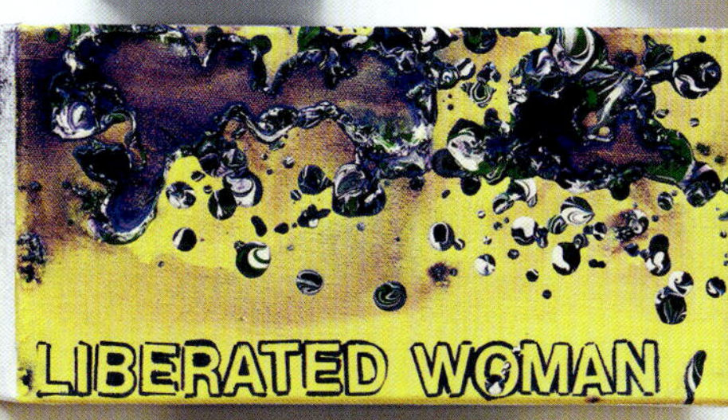
LIBERATED WOMAN
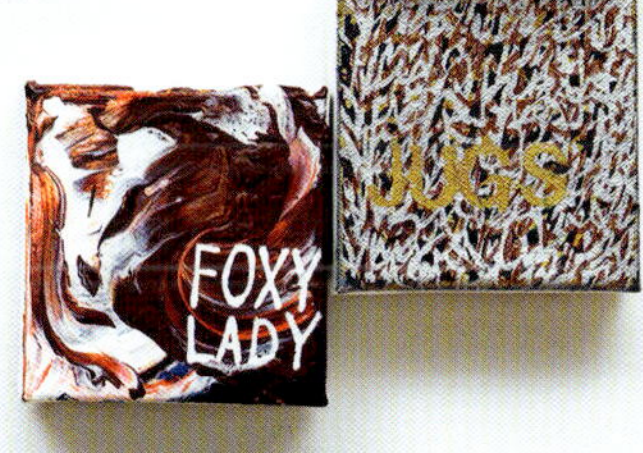
FOXY
LADY
JUGS
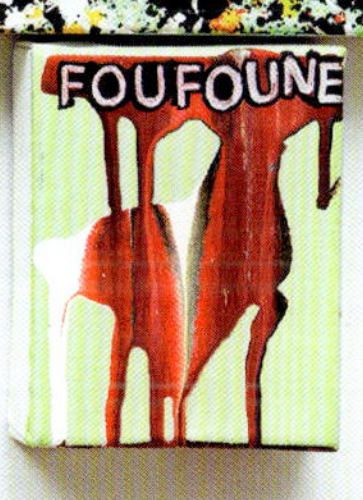
FOUFOUNE
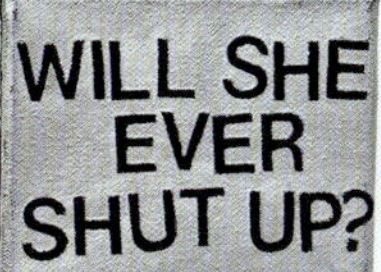
WILL SHE
EVER
SHUT UP?
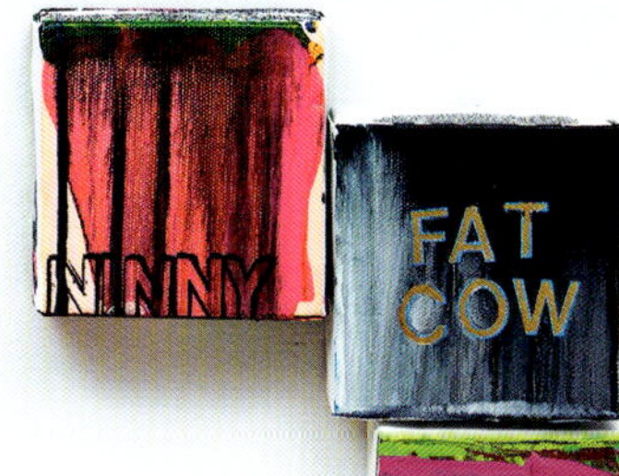
NINNY
FAT
COW
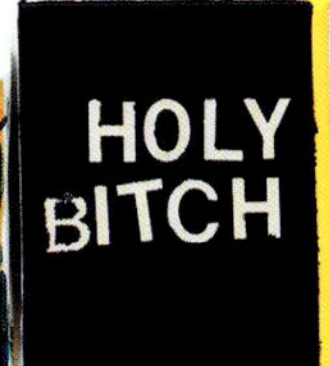
HOLY
BITCH

OLD
MAID
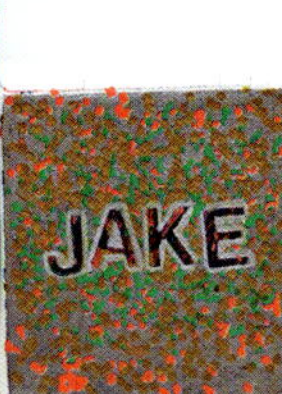
JAKE
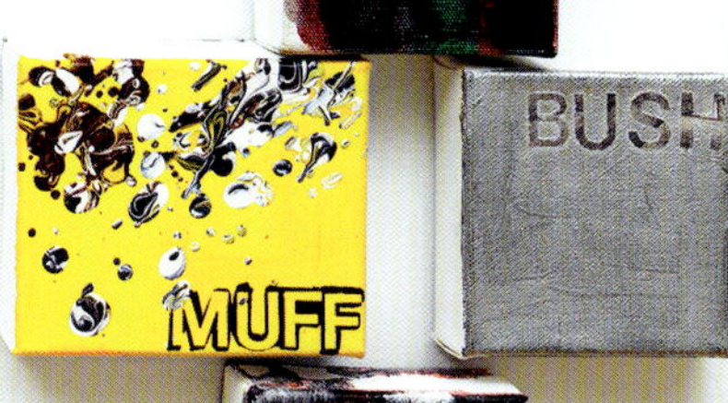
LHOOQ
MUFF
BUSH
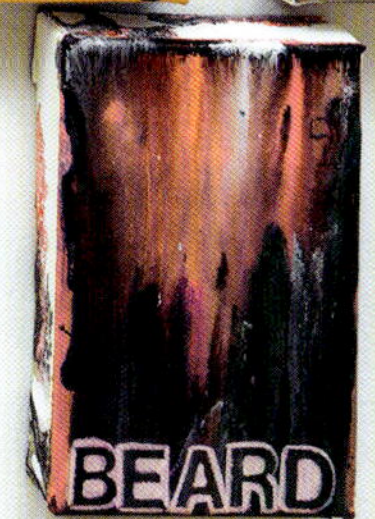
BEARD
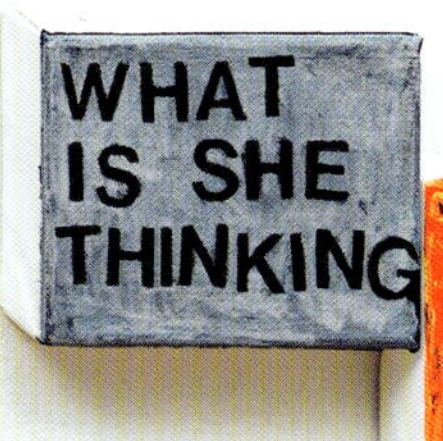
WHAT
IS SHE
THINKING
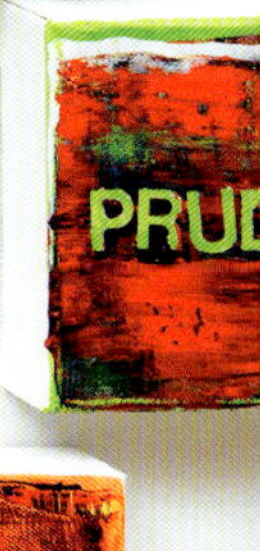
PRUD

KUT

SUMMER SCHOOL

June 9–July 29, 2016

Artists

John Baldessari
Gina Beavers
Dan Colen
Will Cotton
Jennifer Dalton
Tara Donovan
Awol Erizku
Tom Friedman
Genevieve Gaignard
Felix Gonzalez-Torres
Mark Grotjahn
Alex Israel
Steven and William Ladd
Tony Matelli
Marilyn Minter
Vik Muniz
Charles Ray
Tim Rollins and K.O.S.
Ugo Rondinone
Robert Therrien
Tom Sachs

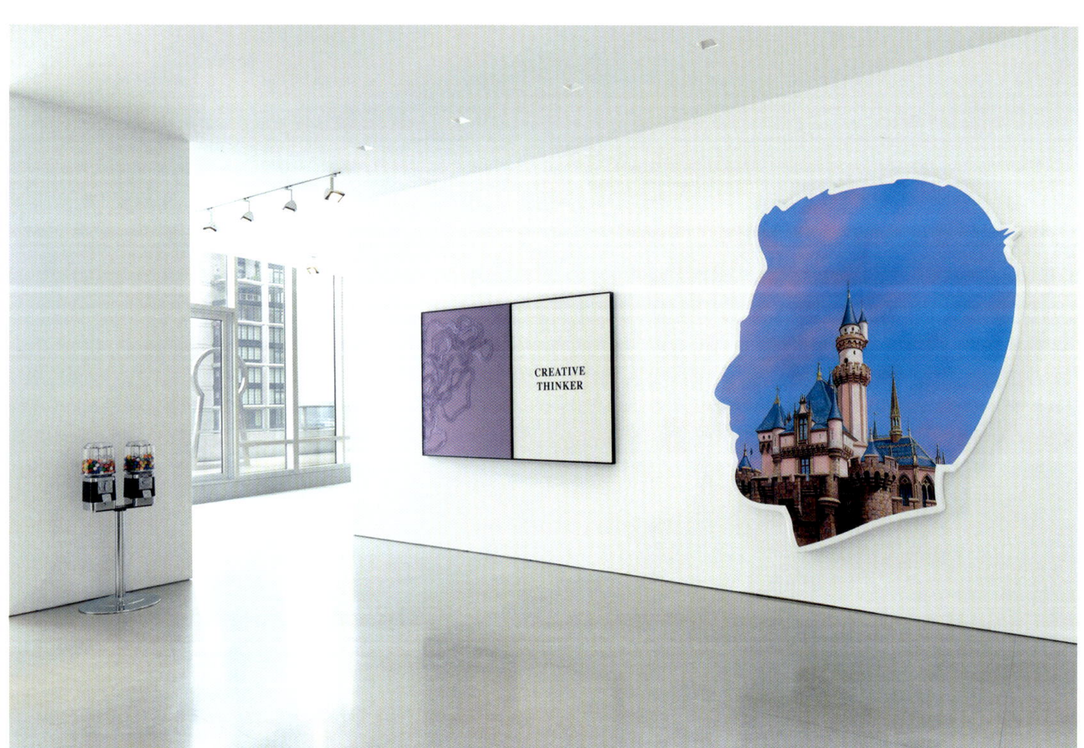

Left to right: Jennifer Dalton, *Decision Analysis*, 2014; John Baldessari, *Prima Facie (Fifth State): Creative Thinker*, 2007; Alex Israel, *Self Portrait (Disneyland)*, 2015

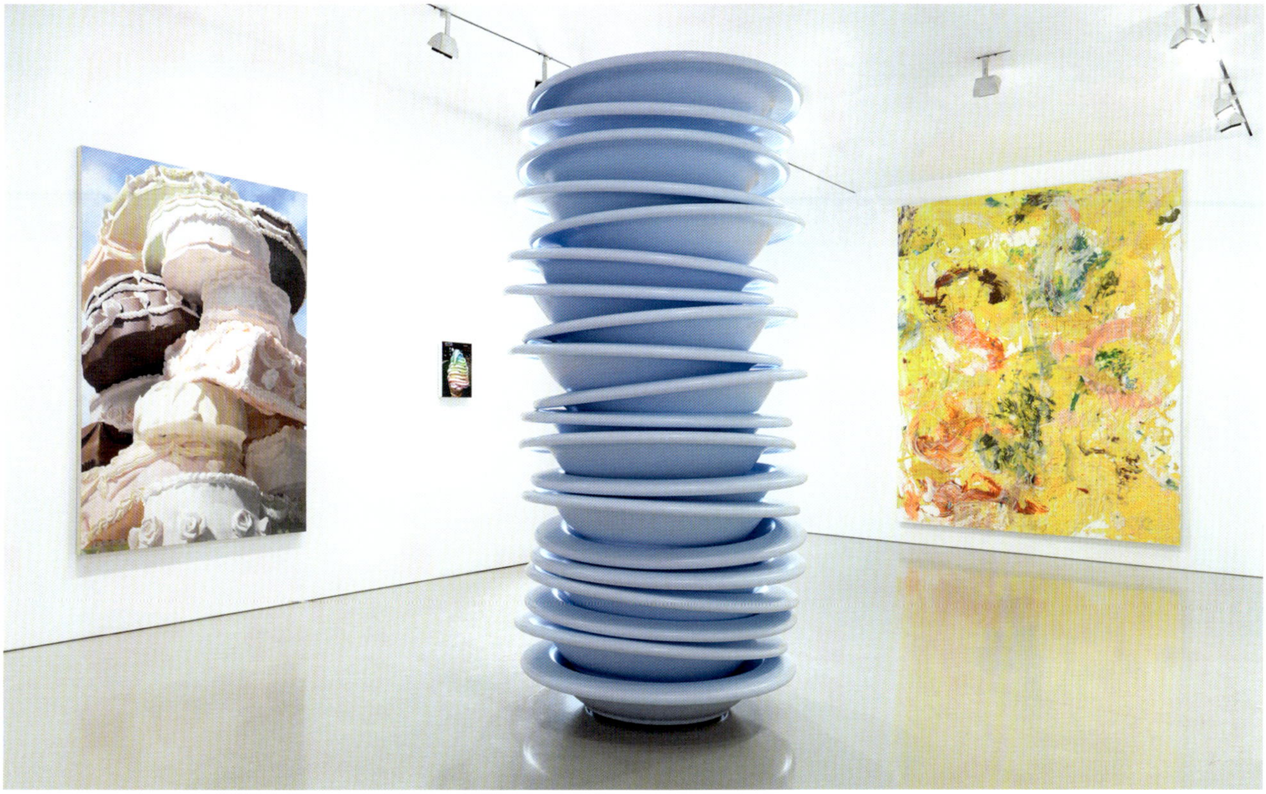

Left to right: Will Cotton, *Wedding Cake*, 2009; Gina Beavers, *The Life I Deserve (Ice Cream)*, 2016; Robert Therrien, *No Title (Stacked Plates)*, 2006; Dan Colen, *Pennies from Heaven*, 2015

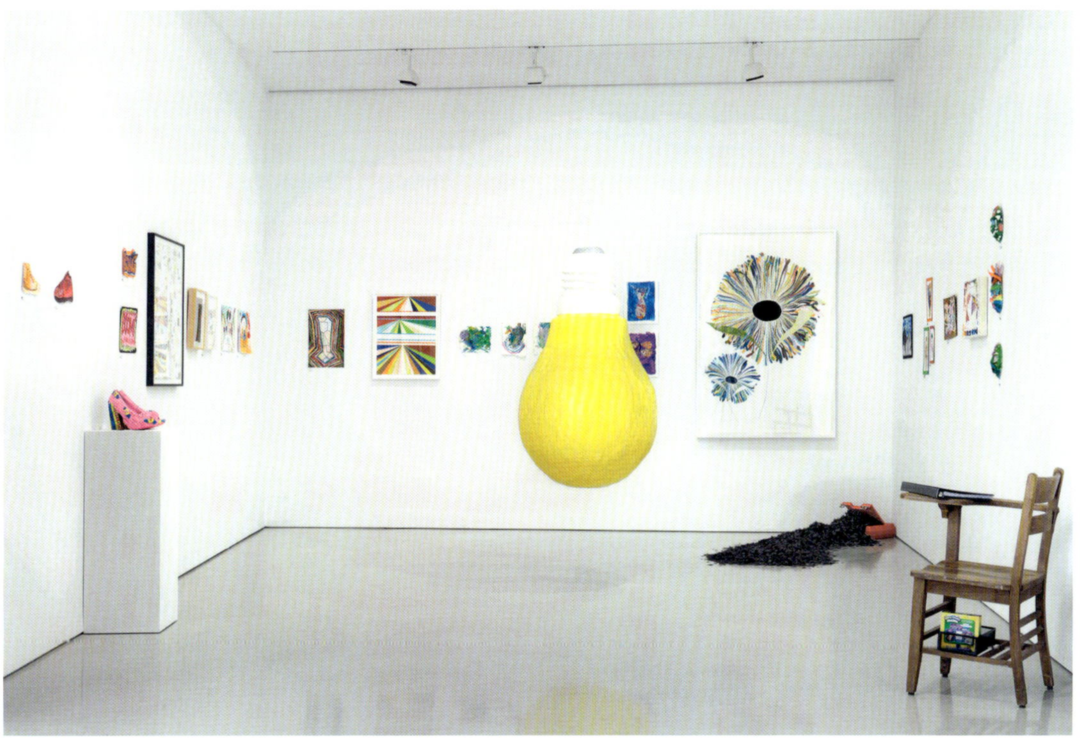

Installation view

PATRICIA CRONIN: SHRINE FOR GIRLS, NEW YORK

June 9–July 29, 2016

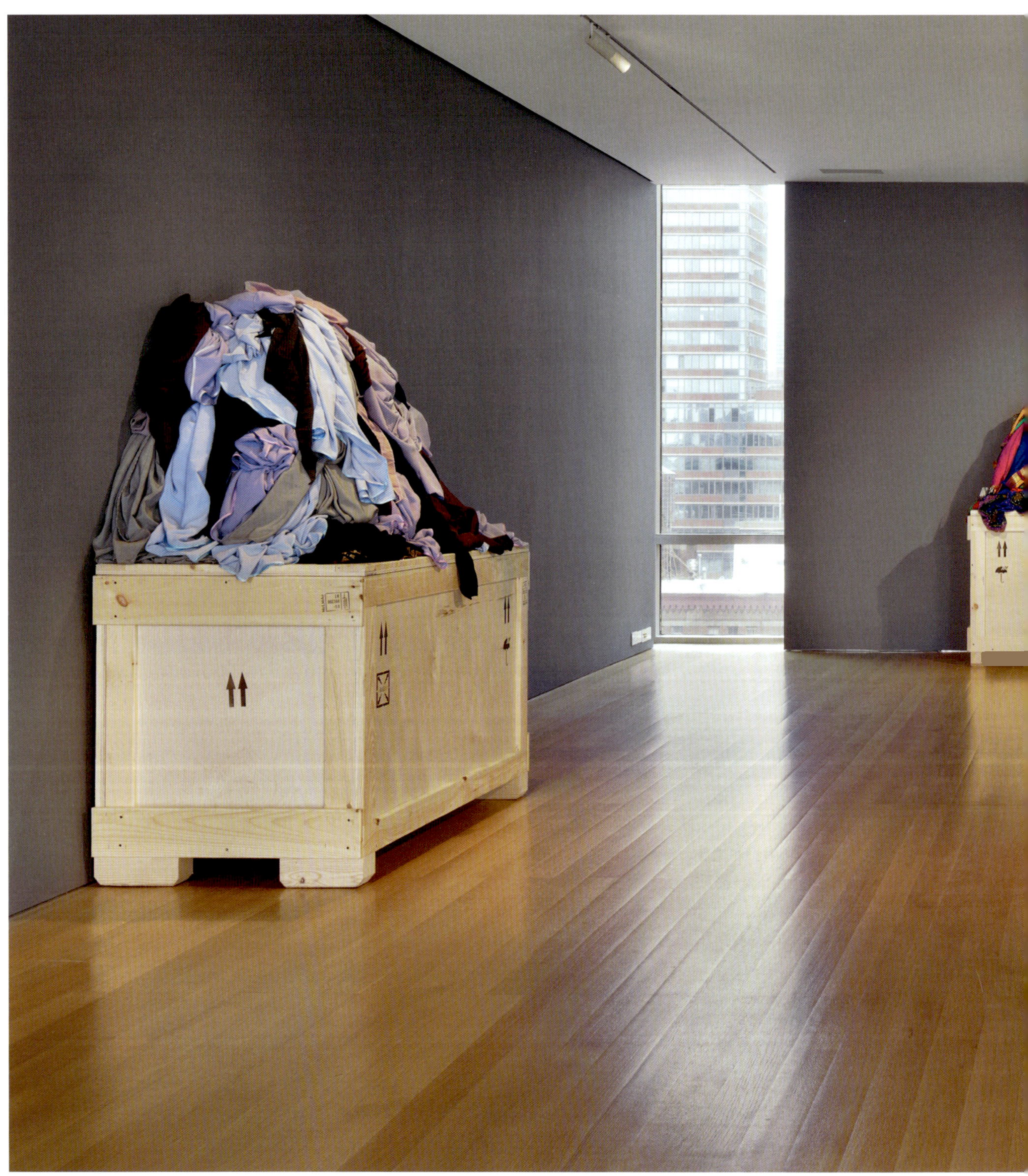

Left to right: Patricia Cronin, *Shrine for Girls (Chibok)*, 2015; *Shrine for Girls (Uttar Pradesh)*, 2015; and *Shrine for Girls (United Kingdom)*, 2015

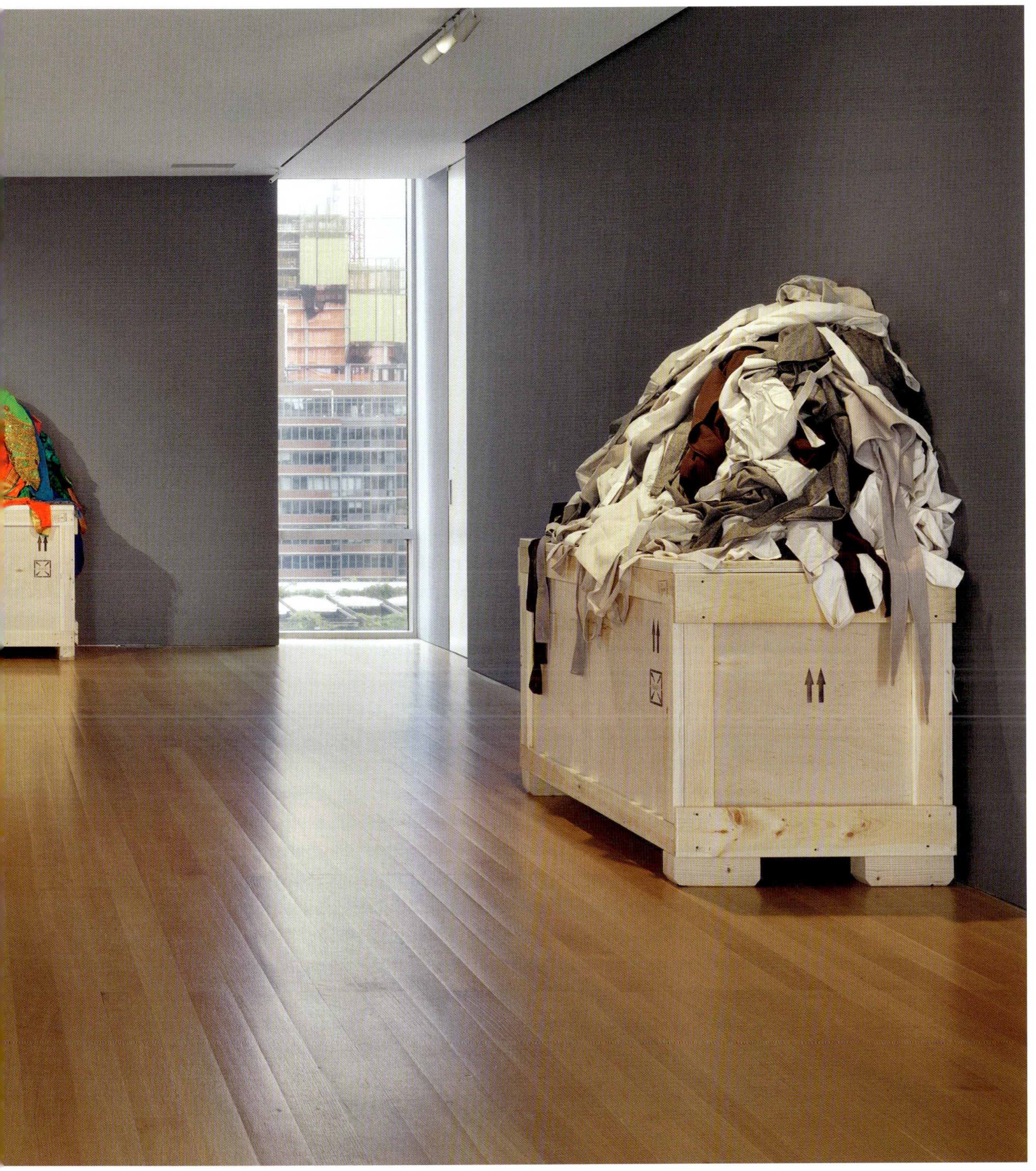

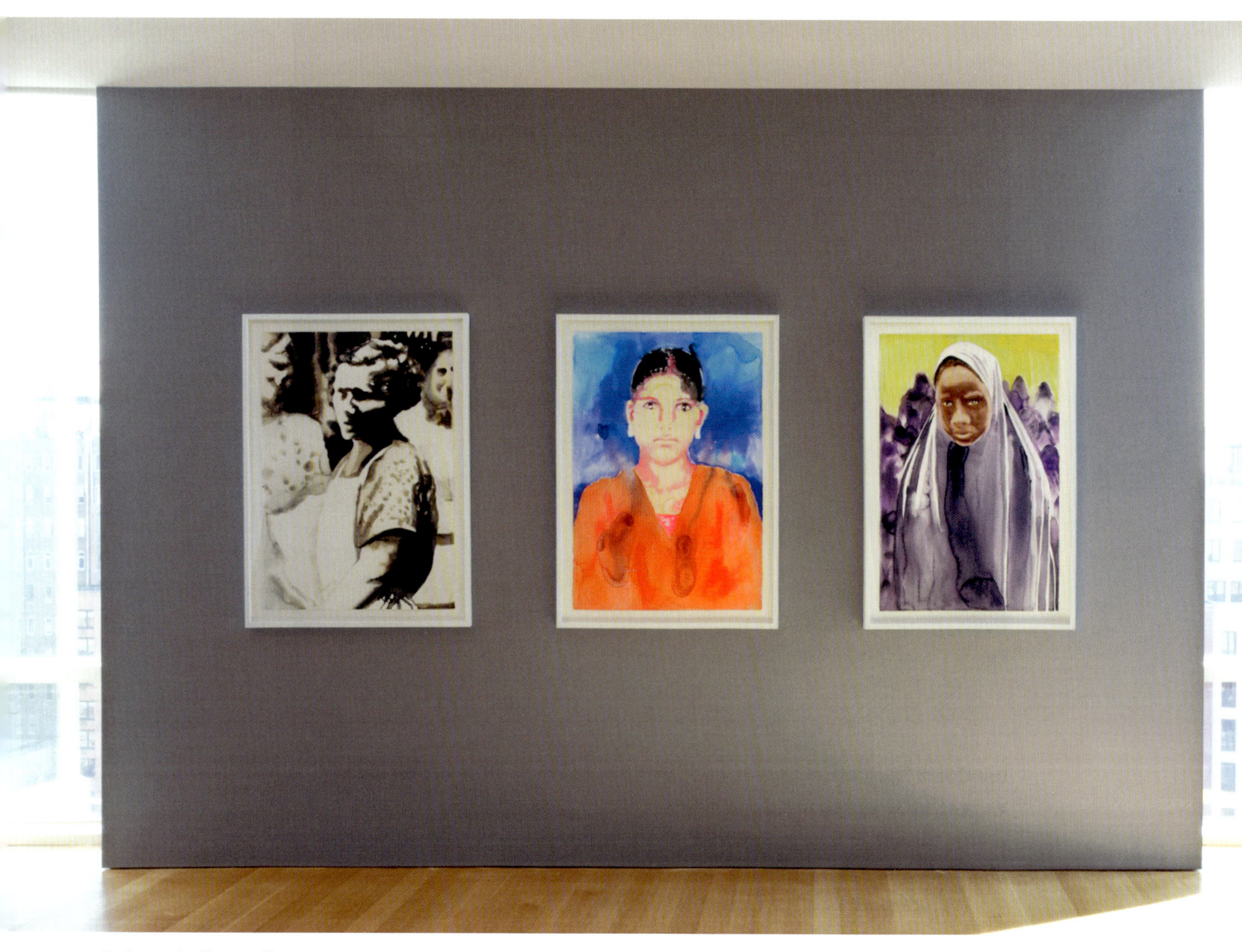

Left to right: Patricia Cronin, *Magdalene Laundry Girl*, 2016; *Pushpa*, 2016; and *Chibok Student*, 2016

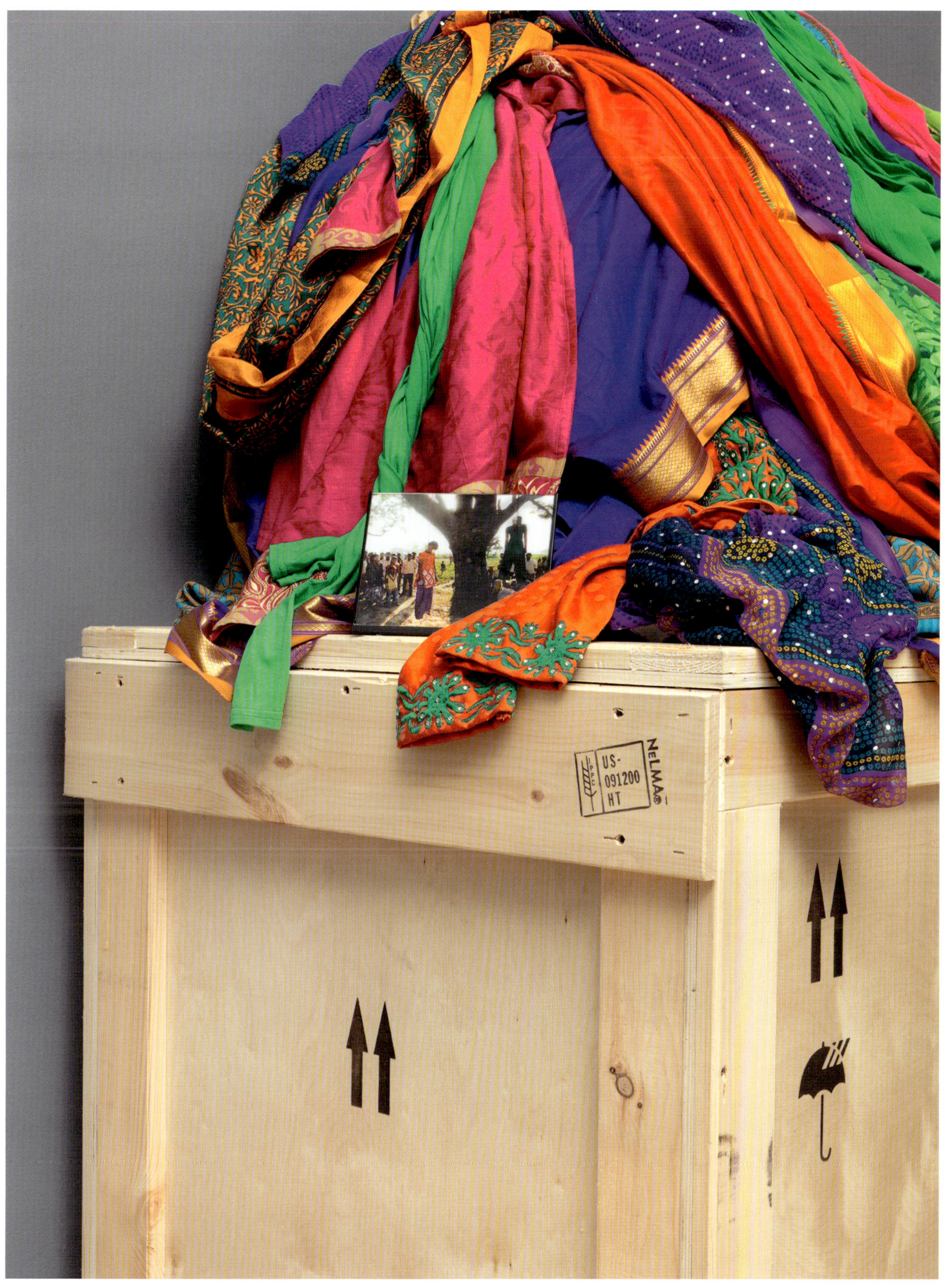

Detail, Patricia Cronin, *Shrine for Girls (Uttar Pradesh)*, 2015

ELMGREEN & DRAGSET: CHANGING SUBJECTS

October 1–December 17, 2016

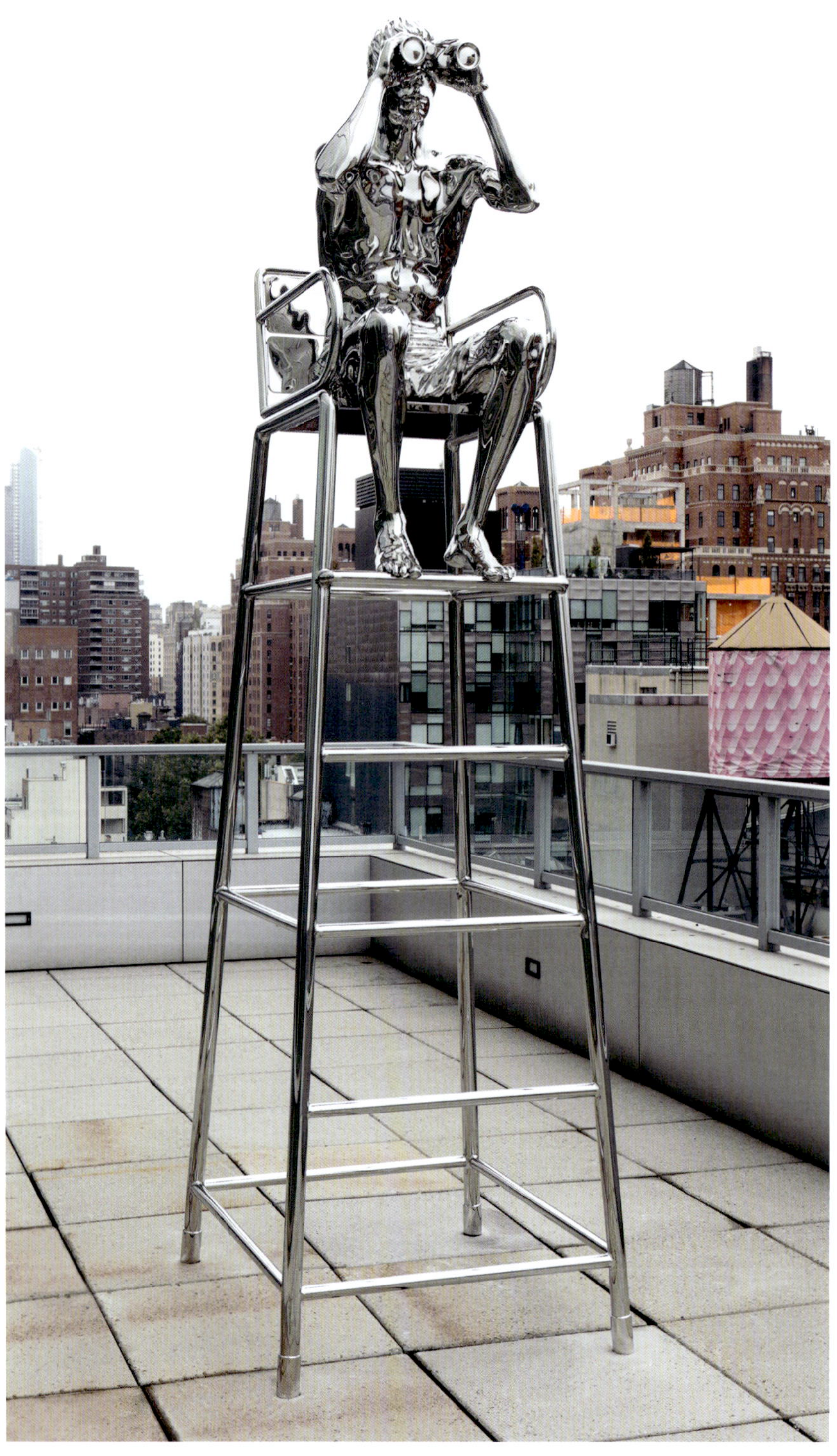

Elmgreen & Dragset, *Watching*, 2016

Watching

You are an action. A verb
Present past future
Are . . . were . . . will . . . be
Watching

Cast in the image of creators
Who had no idea
Who you are
What you will be

Like chameleons polished to perfection
Mirroring images of our . . . selves
Changing the subject
Changing
Your blood count
Now
And again

Mute in the noise
From the streets and sorrows
Like an echo without sound
Observing
Every move you make
Every step you take
Motionless

And no there is no cure
For your fear
Then
Or when it will hit you again
Hardly dressed in your skin
To protect you from what you want
Me to desire

You are a proverb
Spoken in silence
Decades of Stigma
And chemical reactions
As other bodies around you decayed

Reactions to what
Was . . . is . . . will . . . be
Watching
While your brain
Is driving you crazy

—Elmgreen & Dragset

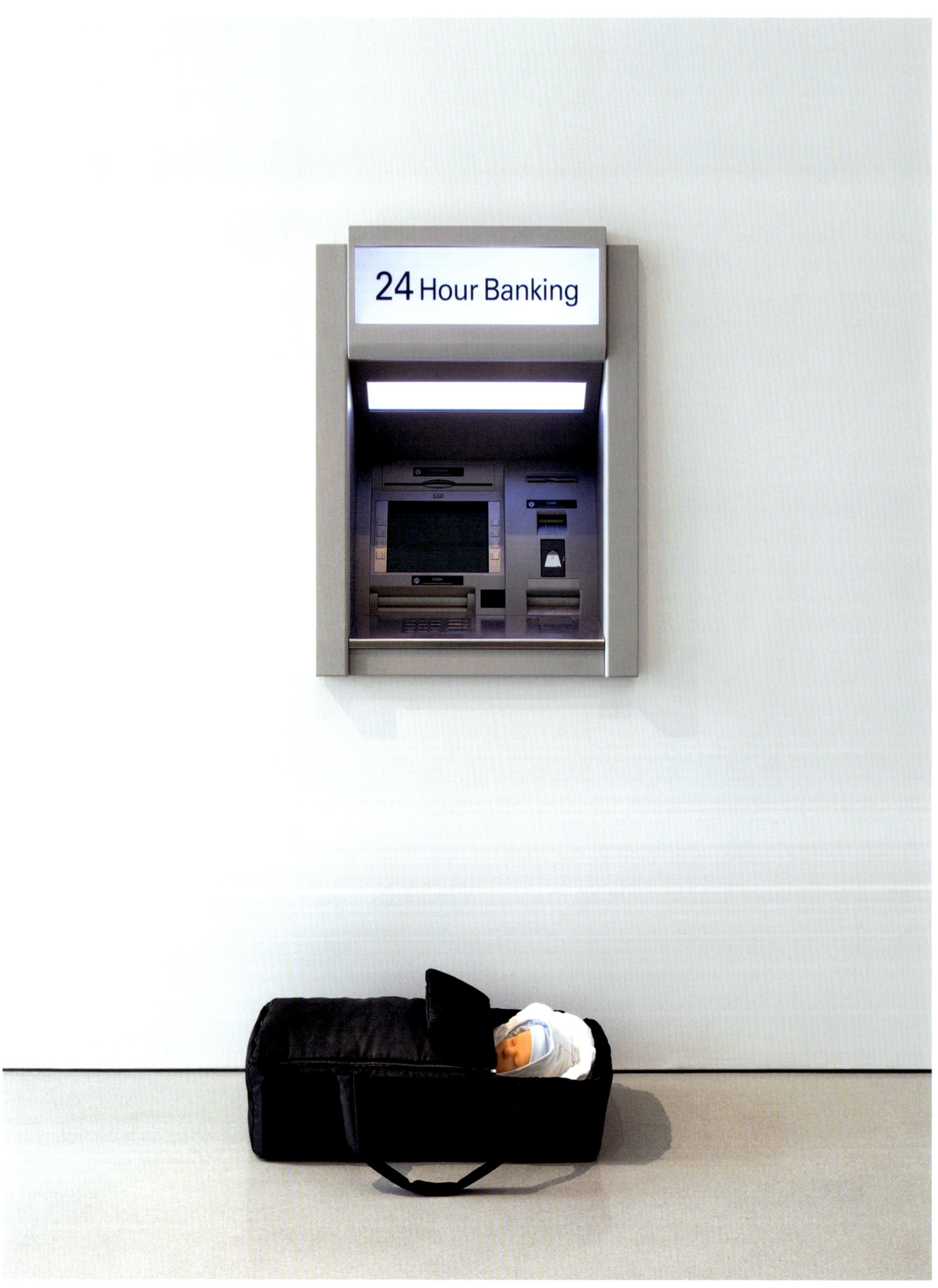

Elmgreen & Dragset, *Modern Moses*, 2006

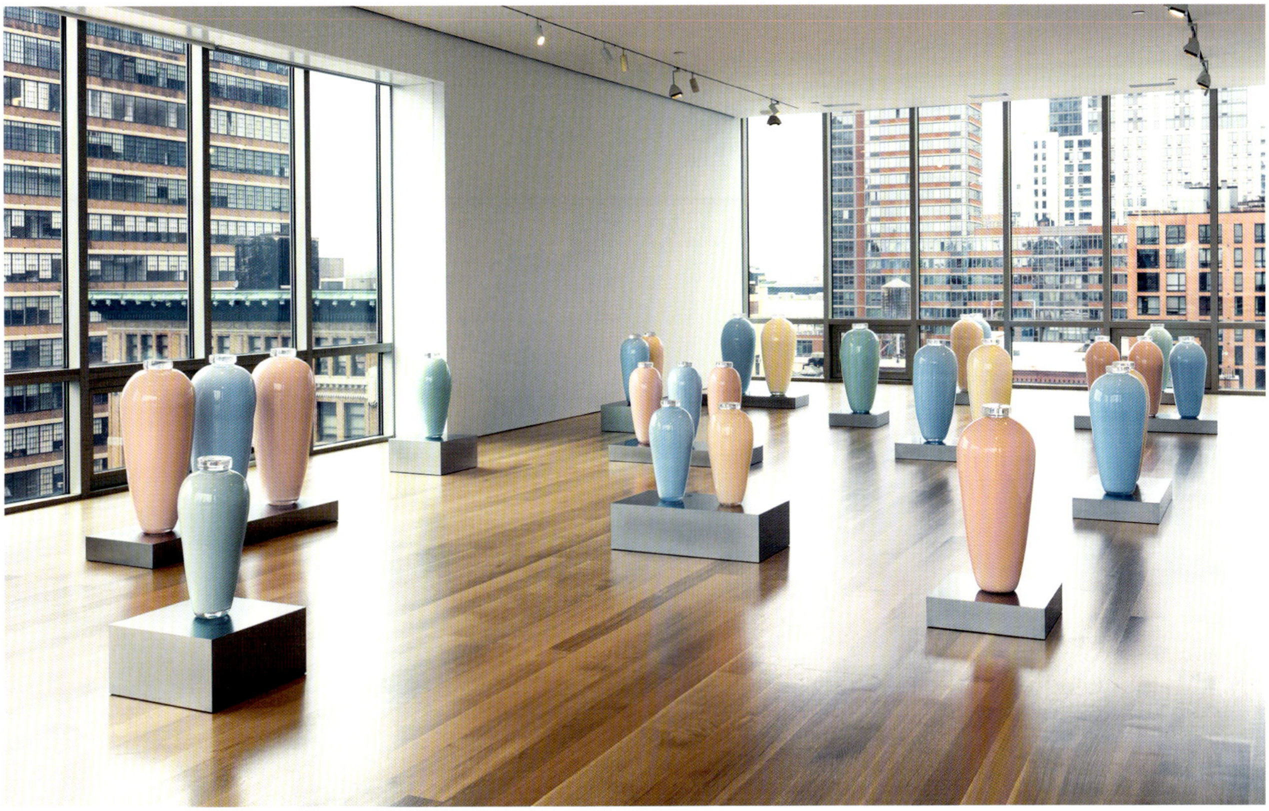

Installation view

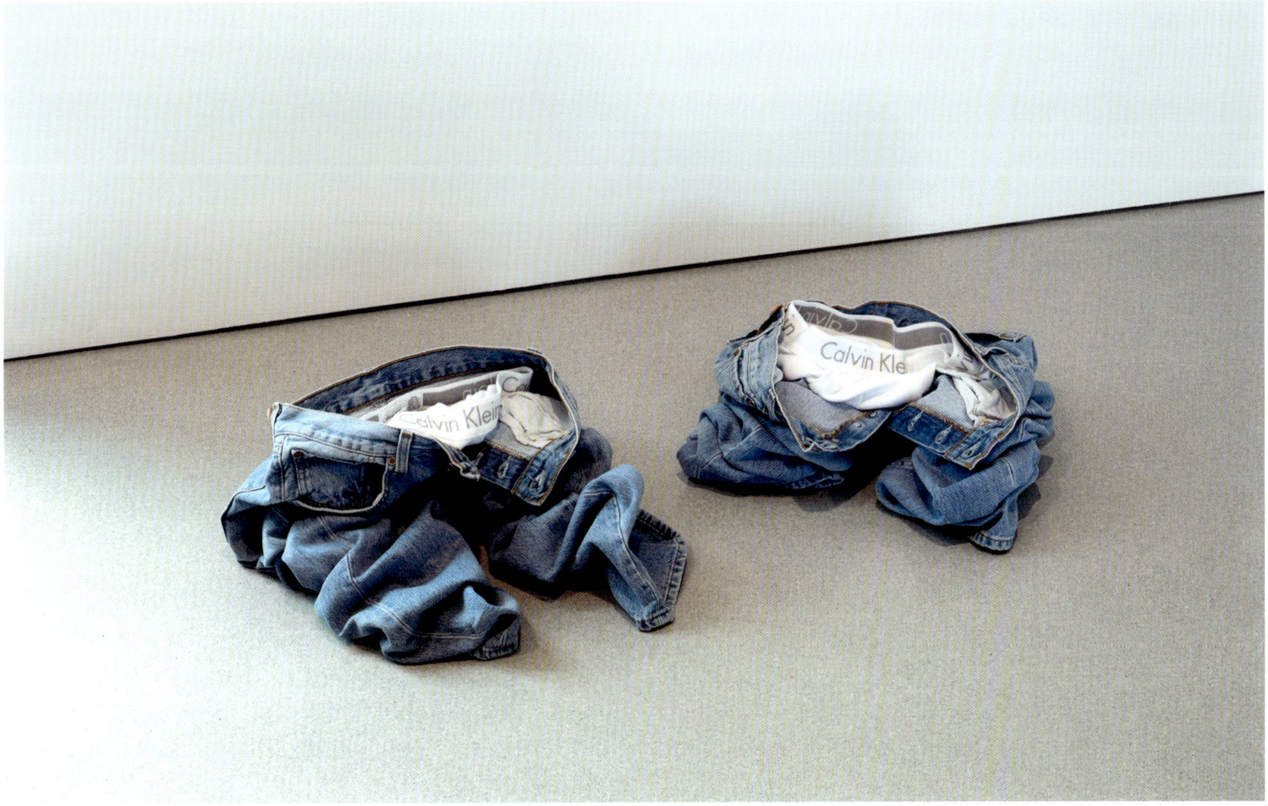

Elmgreen & Dragset, *Powerless Structure, Fig. 19*, 1998

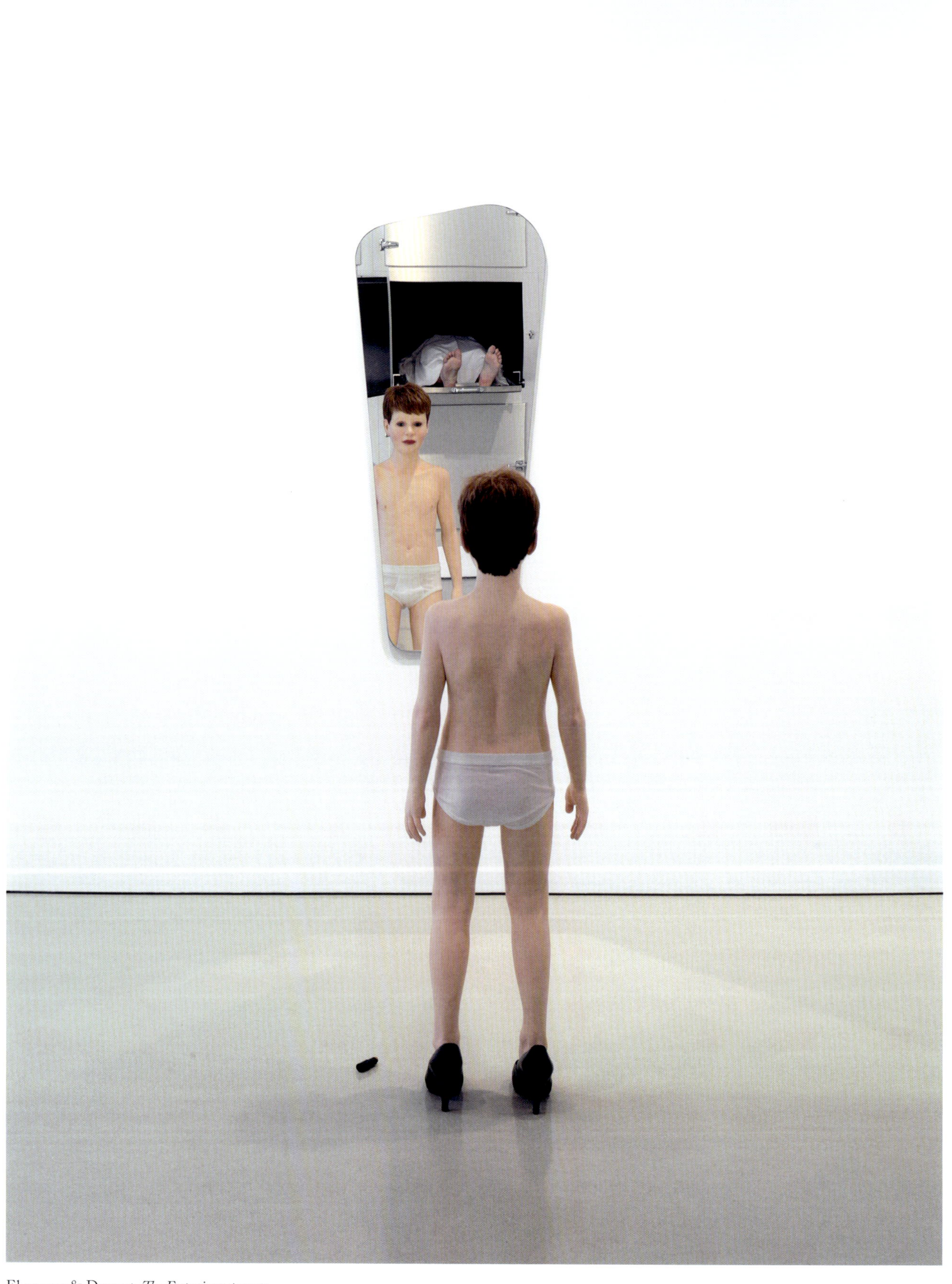

Elmgreen & Dragset, *The Experiment*, 2012

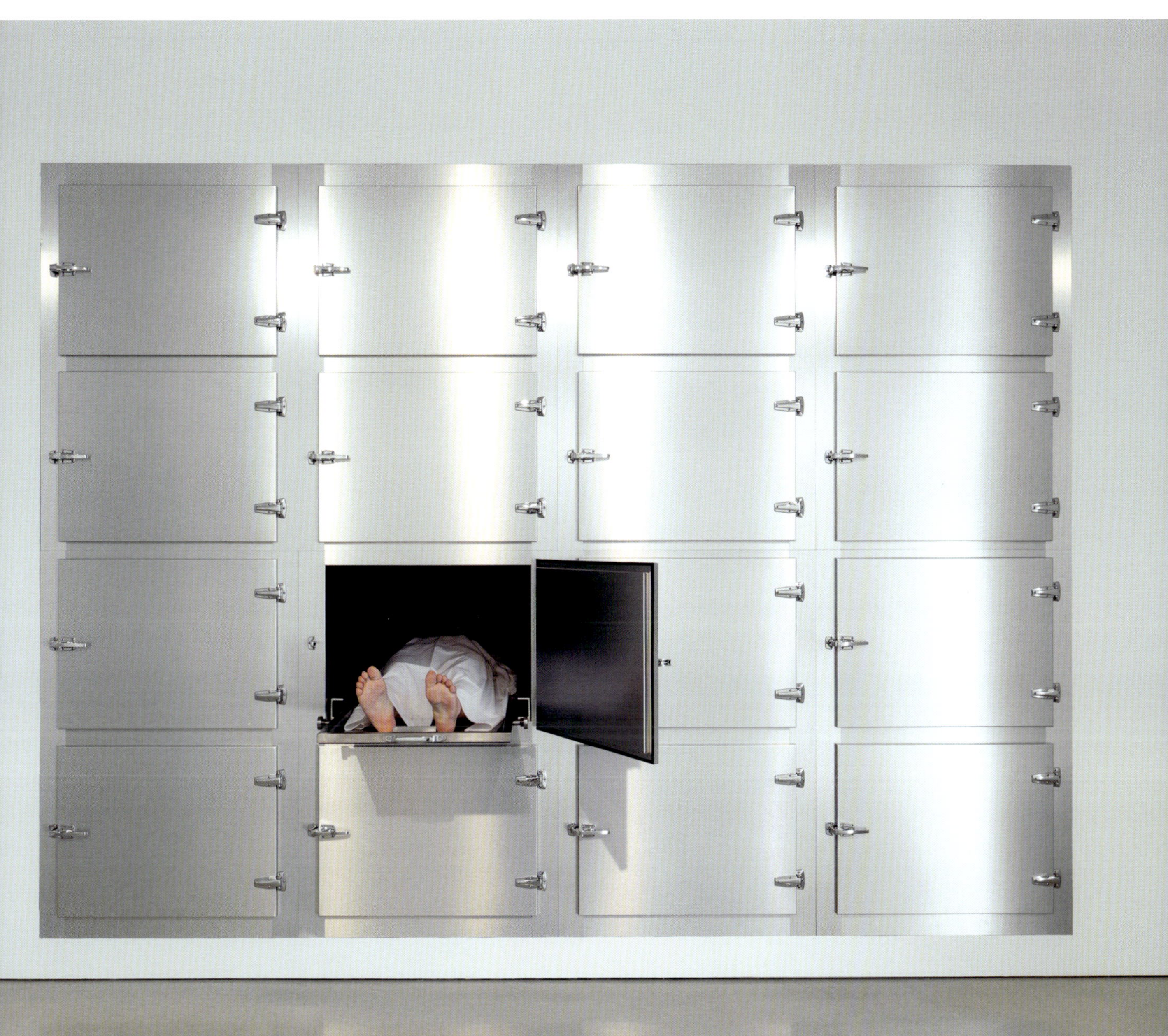

Elmgreen & Dragset, *Untitled*, 2011

ETEL ADNAN | GERHARD RICHTER

January 19–May 13, 2017

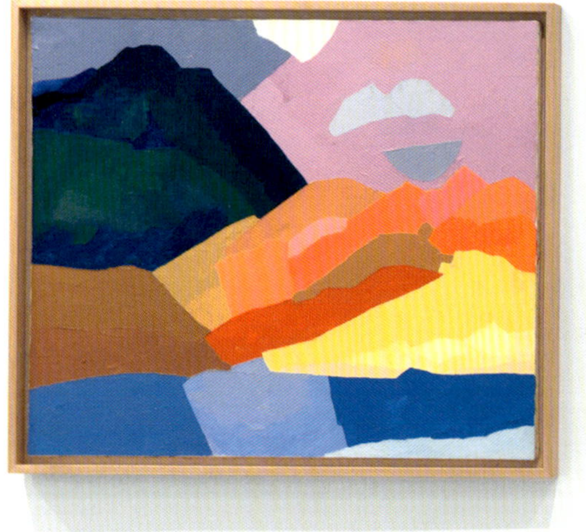

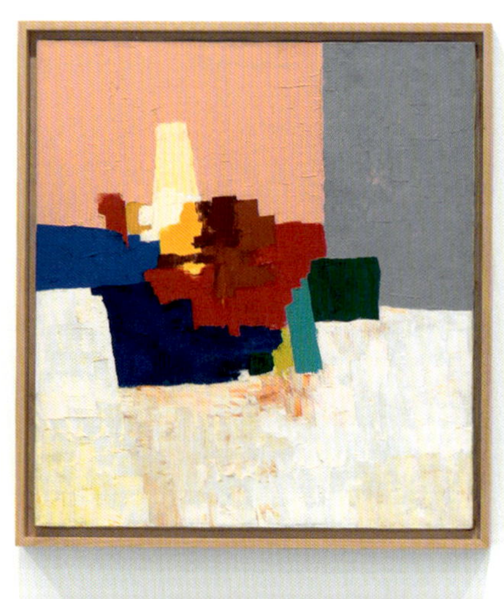

Left to right: Etel Adnan, *Sans titre*, 1983; and *Sans titre*, 1968; Gerhard Richter, *Abstract Painting (744-1)*, 1991

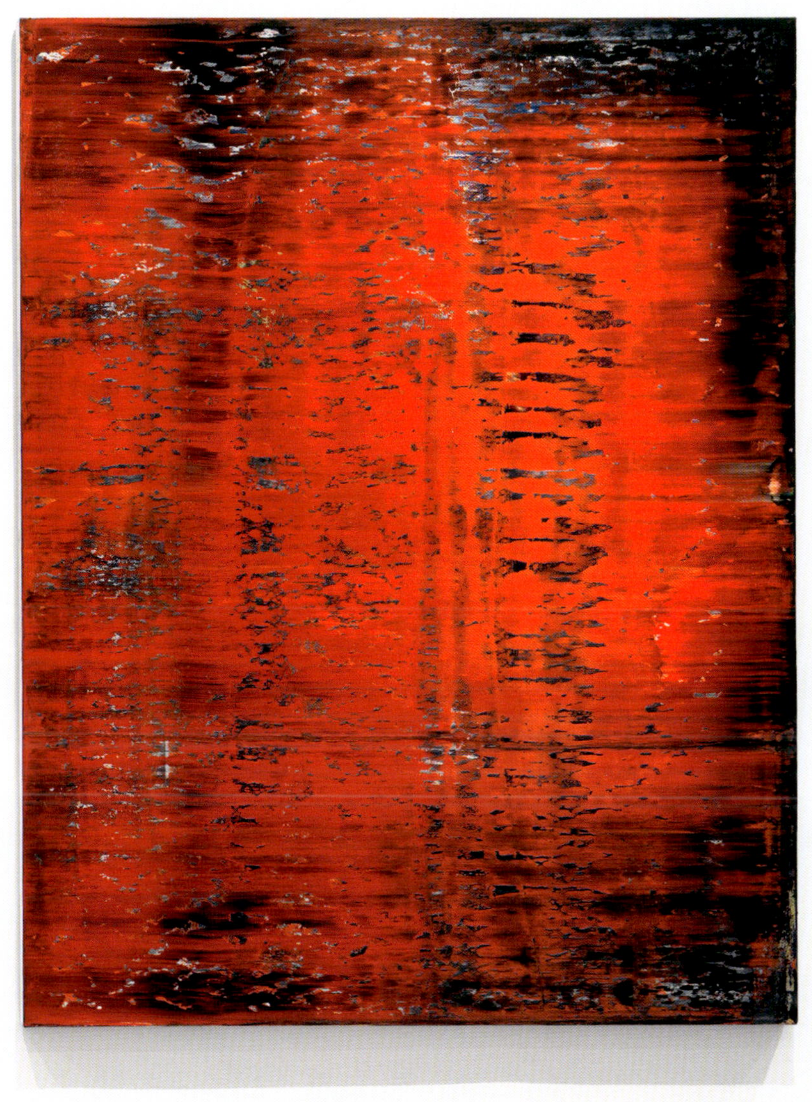

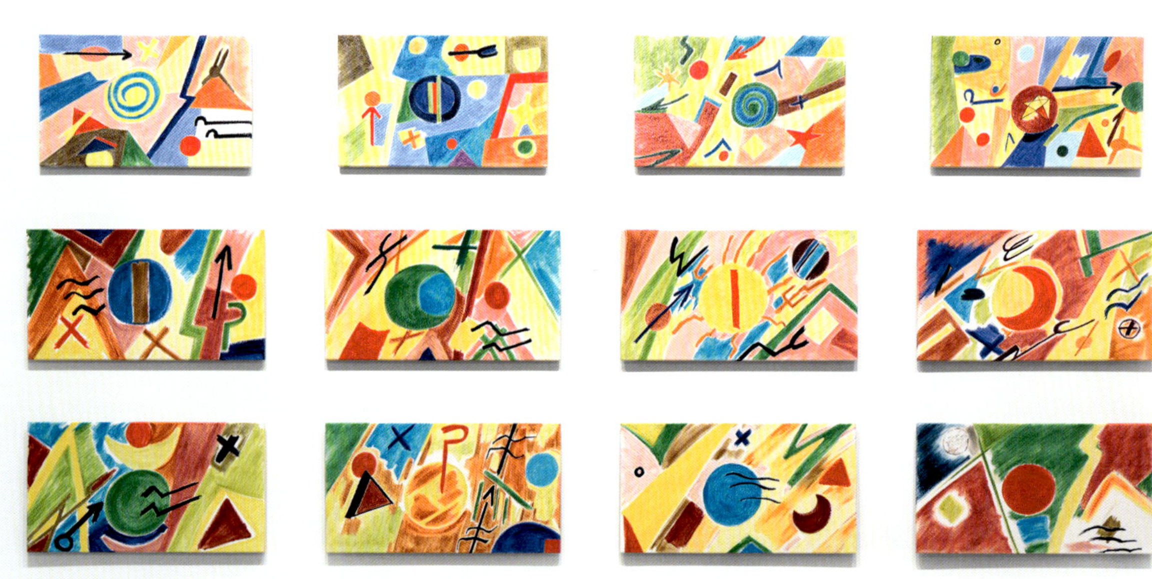

Etel Adnan, *Le Soleil amoureux de la Lune*, 2014

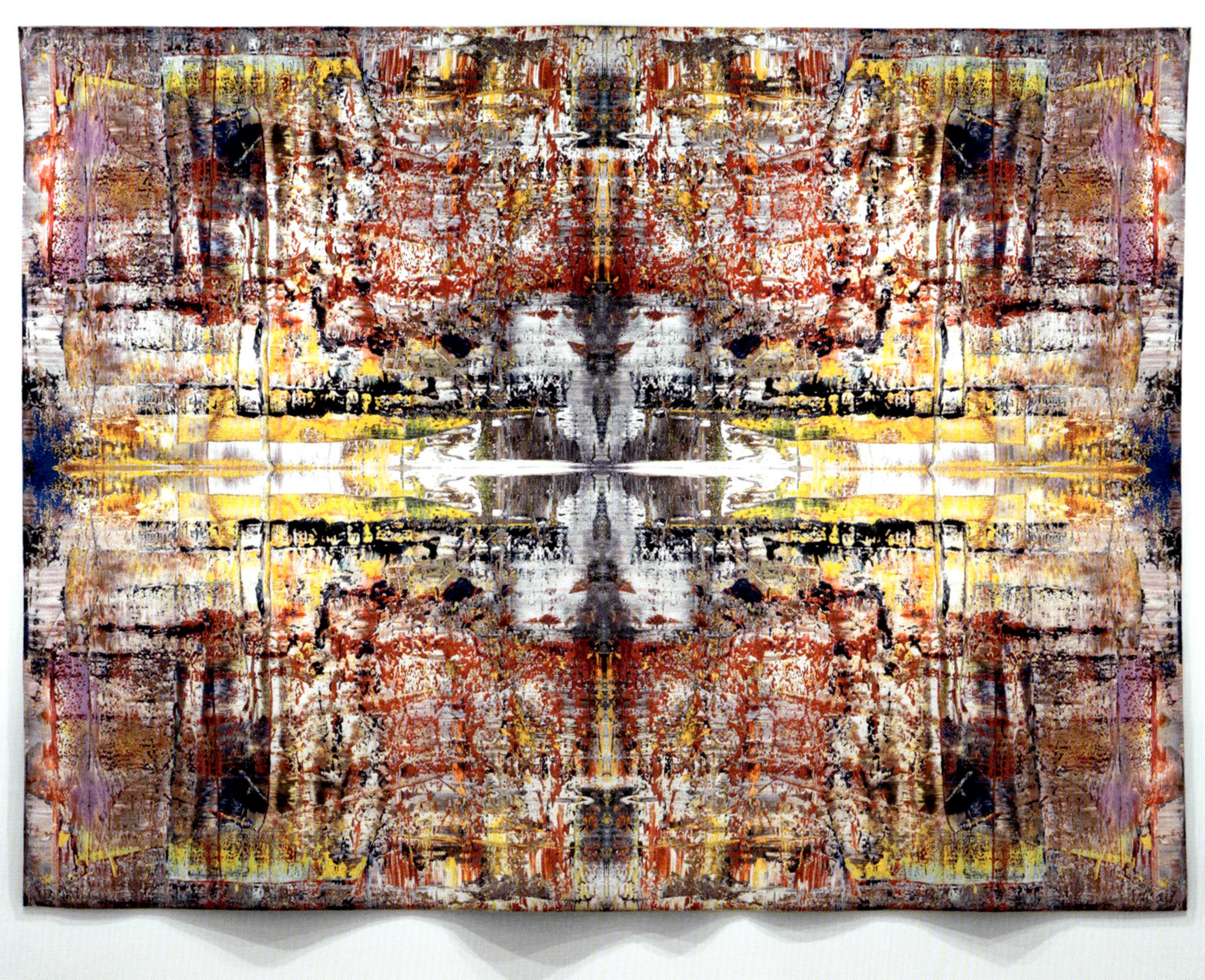

Gerhard Richter, *MUSA*, 2009

CYNTHIA DAIGNAULT: THERE IS NOTHING I COULD SAY THAT I HAVEN'T THOUGHT BEFORE

January 19–May 13, 2017

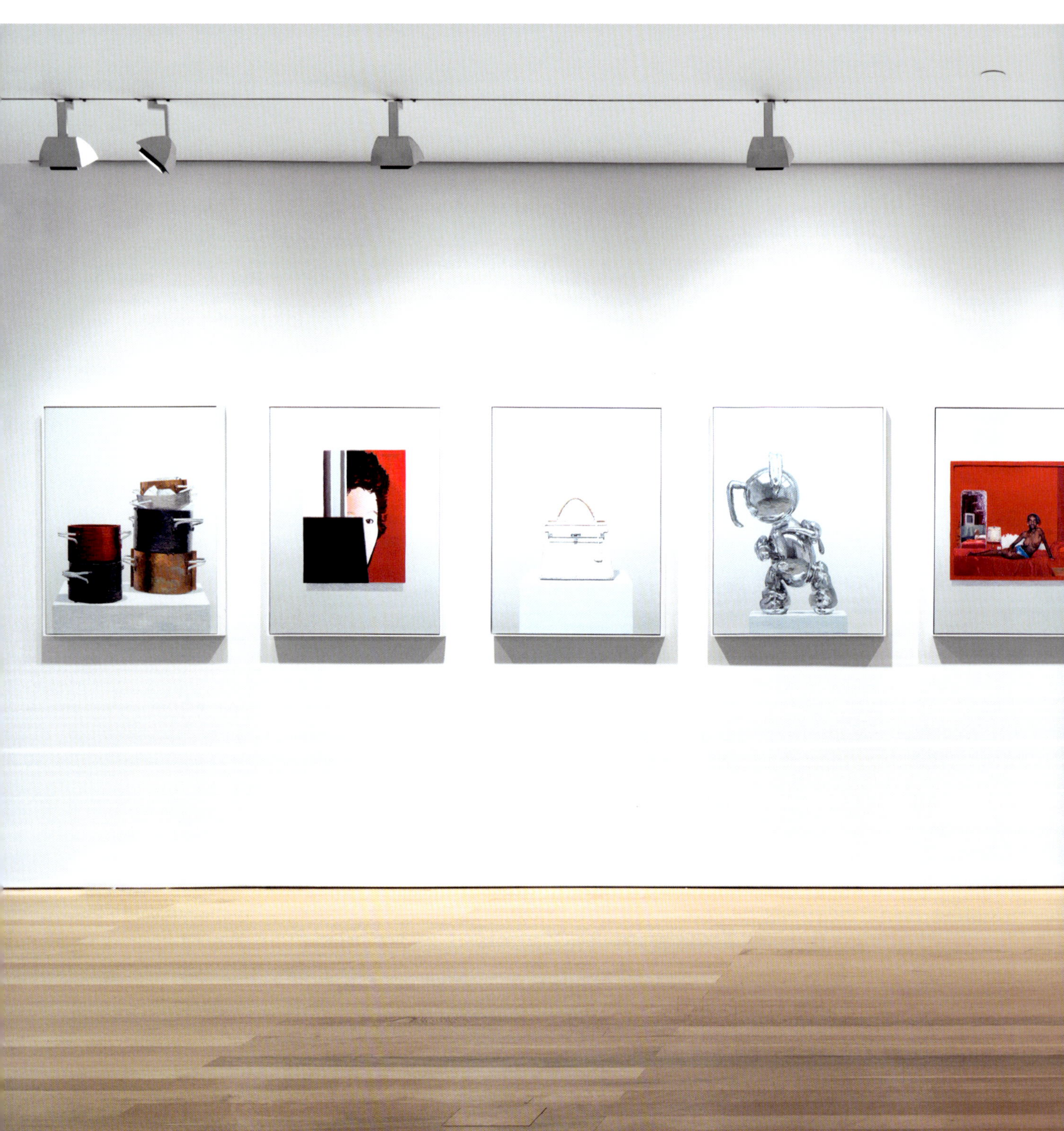

Installation view

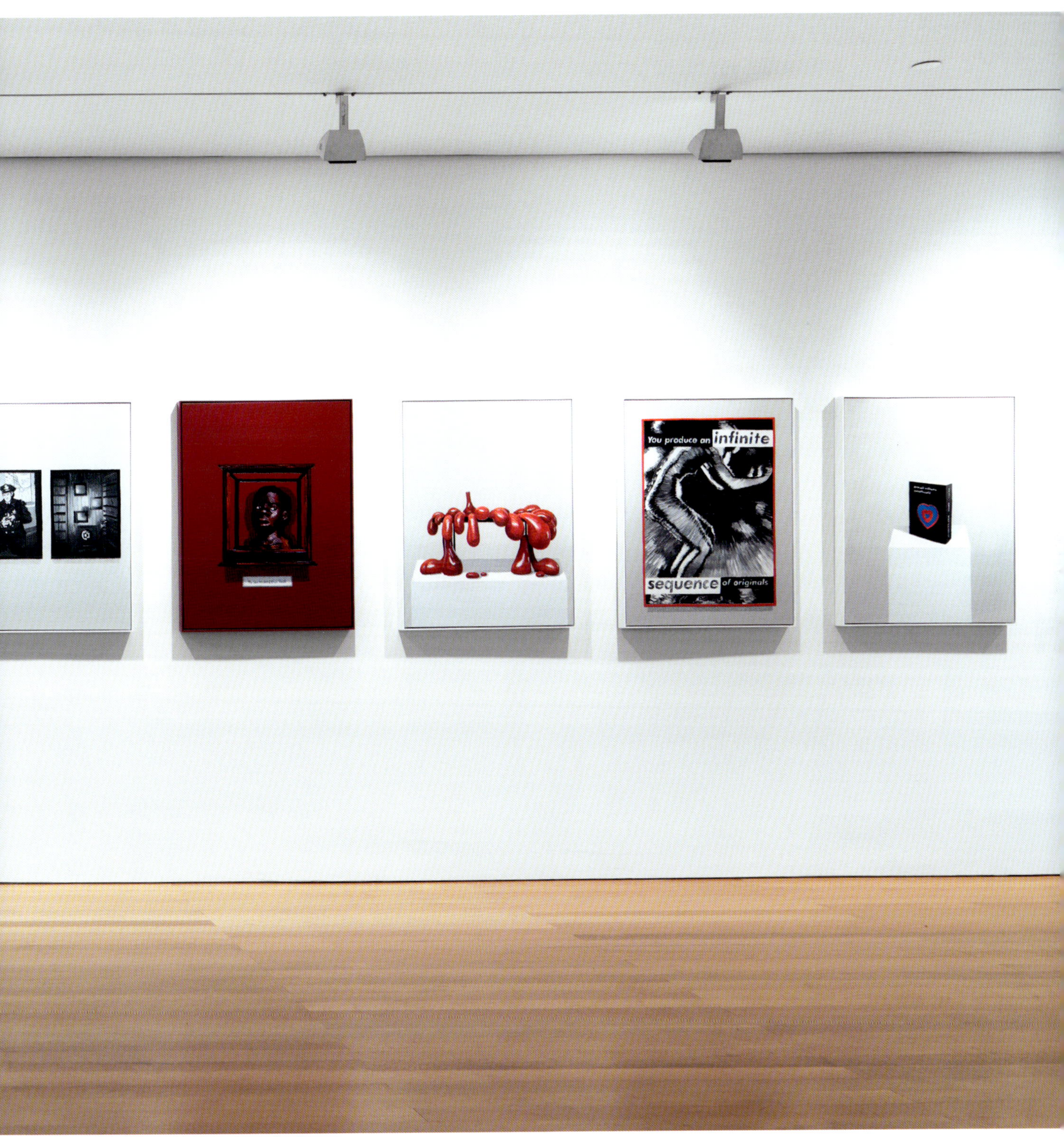
You produce an infinite
sequence of originals

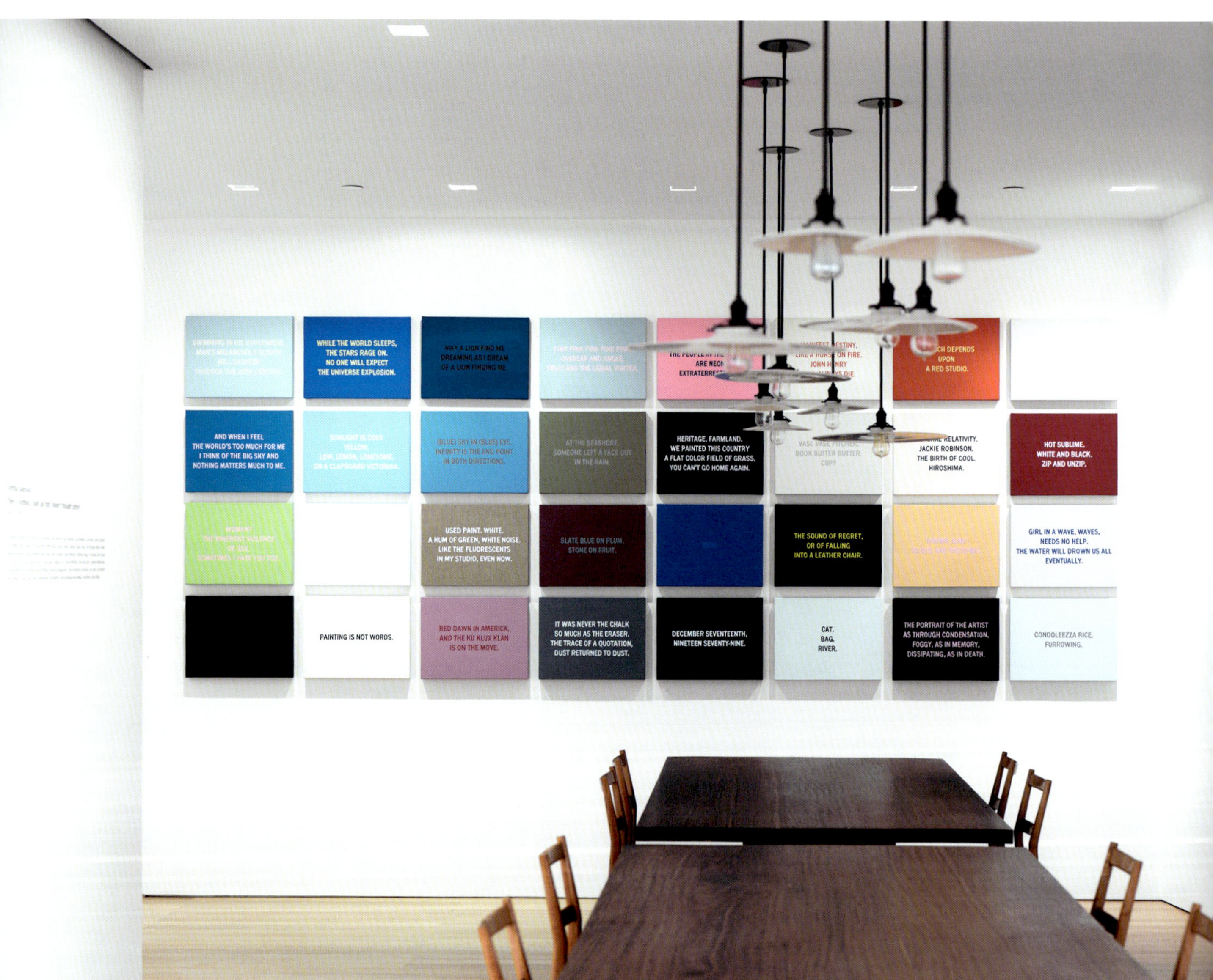

Installation view, Cynthia Daignault, *MoMA*, 2017

Every show I make is site-specific. I consider the architecture, history, and meaning of a space before deciding what to paint. When planning my exhibition for FLAG, I wanted the show to engage with the greater significance of collecting and collection. In a sense, each public and private collection is a portrait gallery of the artists exhibited, a collection of their identities and ideas. For my show, I chose to highlight this idea that a collection is a hive-mind by creating my own metaphorical portrait gallery.

Specifically, I decided to curate a group show inside my solo show, making a standard group exhibition the subject for a series of representational paintings. To do this, I invited the collaboration of thirty-six artists. I selected a wide and diverse set of artists, whose work relates to the themes of the exhibition (curation, collection, appropriation, and copying). I asked each of them to select a work of theirs for the show, telling them up front that I would be exhibiting a painted copy of the work rather than the object itself. The selections were wholly theirs. Each artist sent me a JPEG of his or her work, and I made paintings from these files. My paintings then became the exhibition—a group show inside a solo show, paintings as virtual stand-ins for the artists and the works they represent.

We are individuals at the same time that we are part of a community, and I wanted the show to reflect that binary slippage. The exhibition is both a group show and a solo show, the works are both portraits and still-lifes, the project is both collaborative and entirely mine. At the core, there is an act of appropriation in each work, but I wanted to recast appropriation as collaboration. To me, all appropriation is an exchange in which we bind ourselves to another. We're social creatures. We inevitably infect each other with our values and our ideas, and I love that.

Further, I wanted this work to engage with how we look at art today—virtually—and to remanifest those transient gestures, like a cell phone photo, or an Instagram feed, or a blog post, into tangible objects, paintings that will move forward in time. As a time capsule of artists and the objects that constitute art making today, the works themselves will go forward, not only as objects that reflect my own artistic ideas and values, but also as documents of the community, the zeitgeist, and the broader moment in time.

—Cynthia Daignault

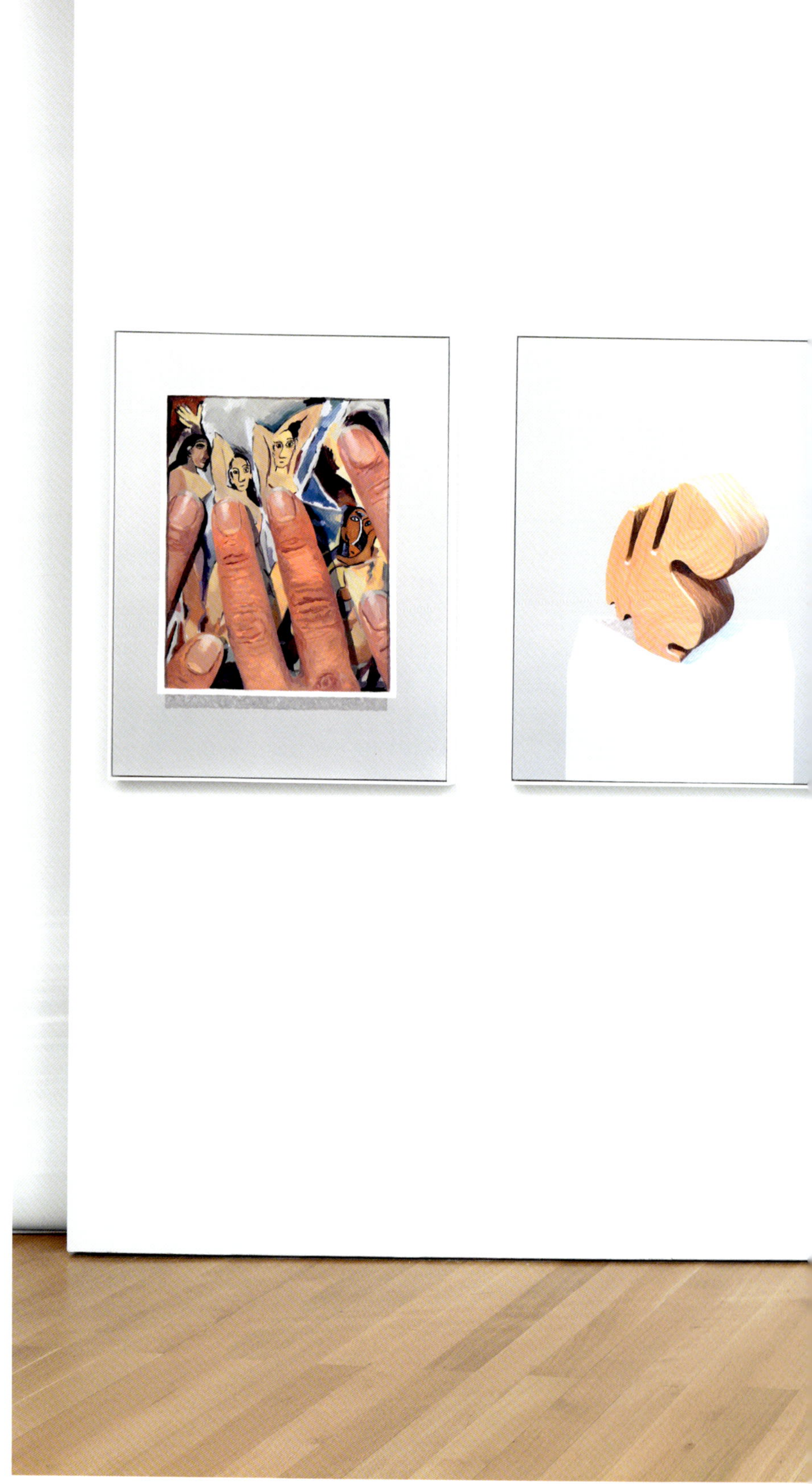

Installation view

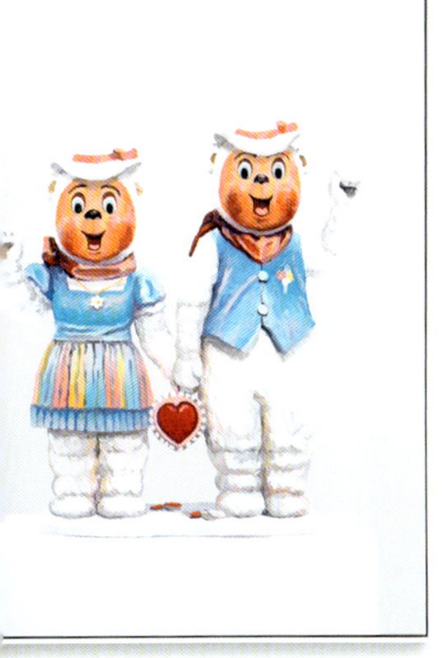

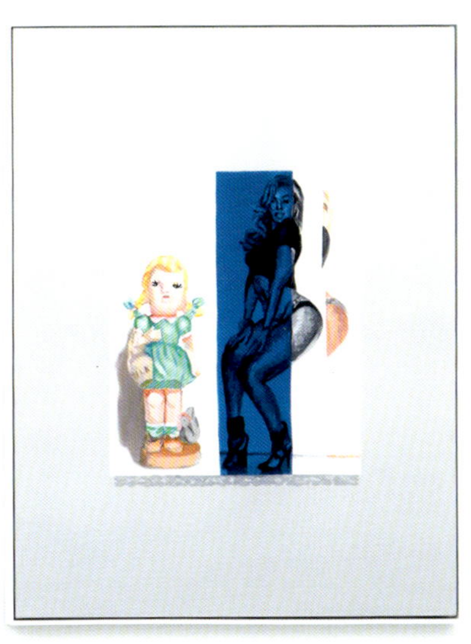

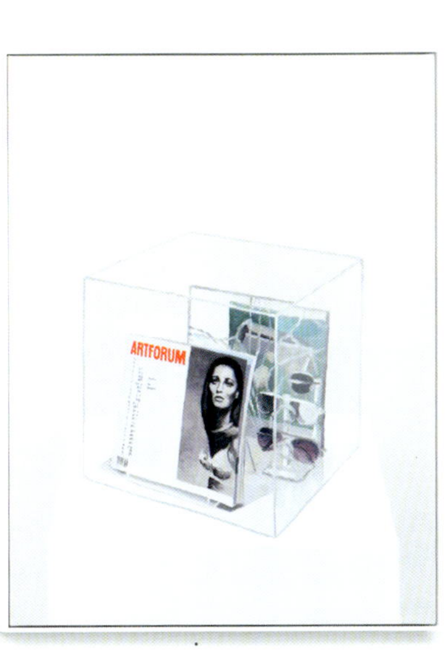
ARTFORUM

REBECCA WARD

June 1–August 11, 2017

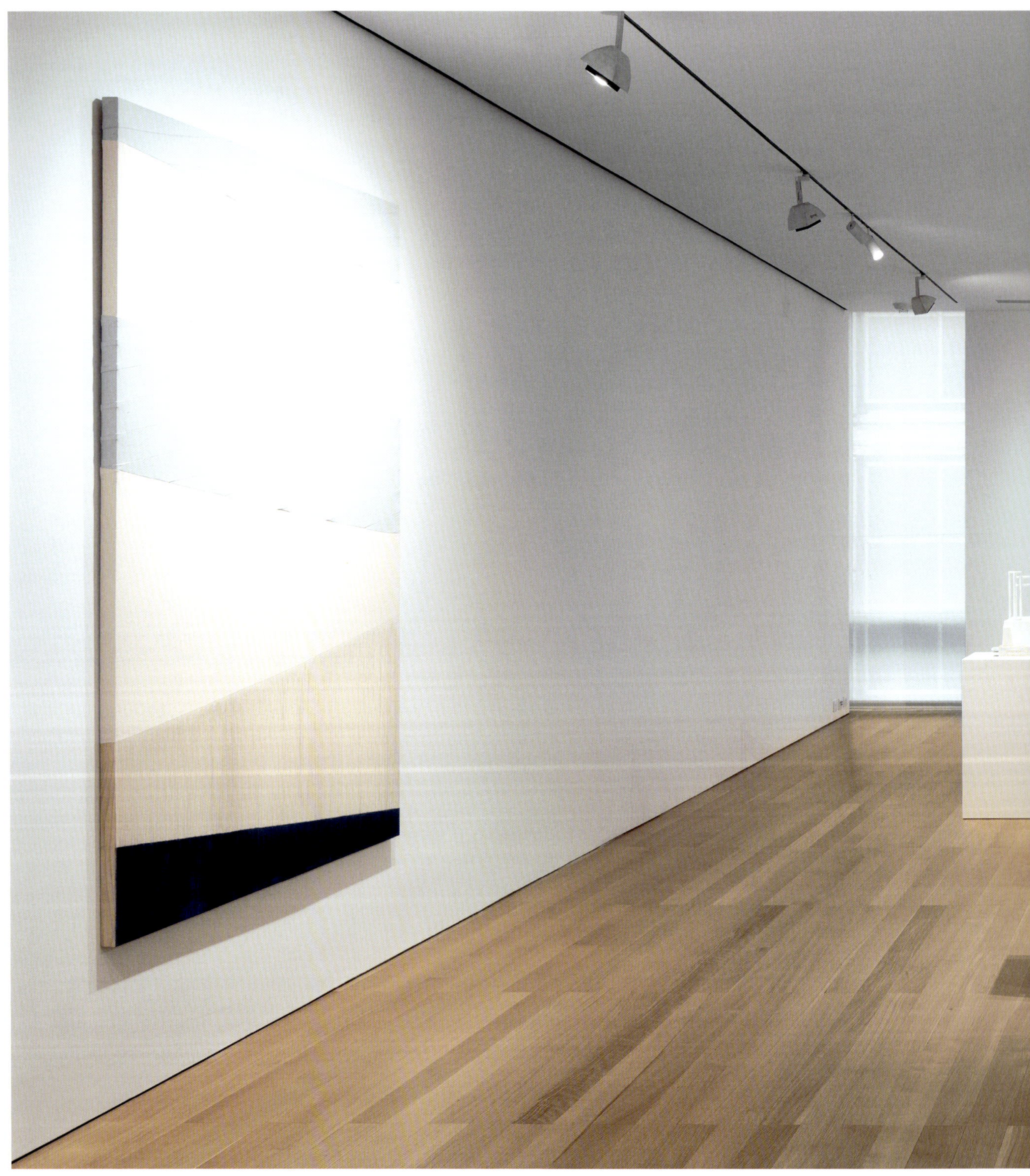

Installation view

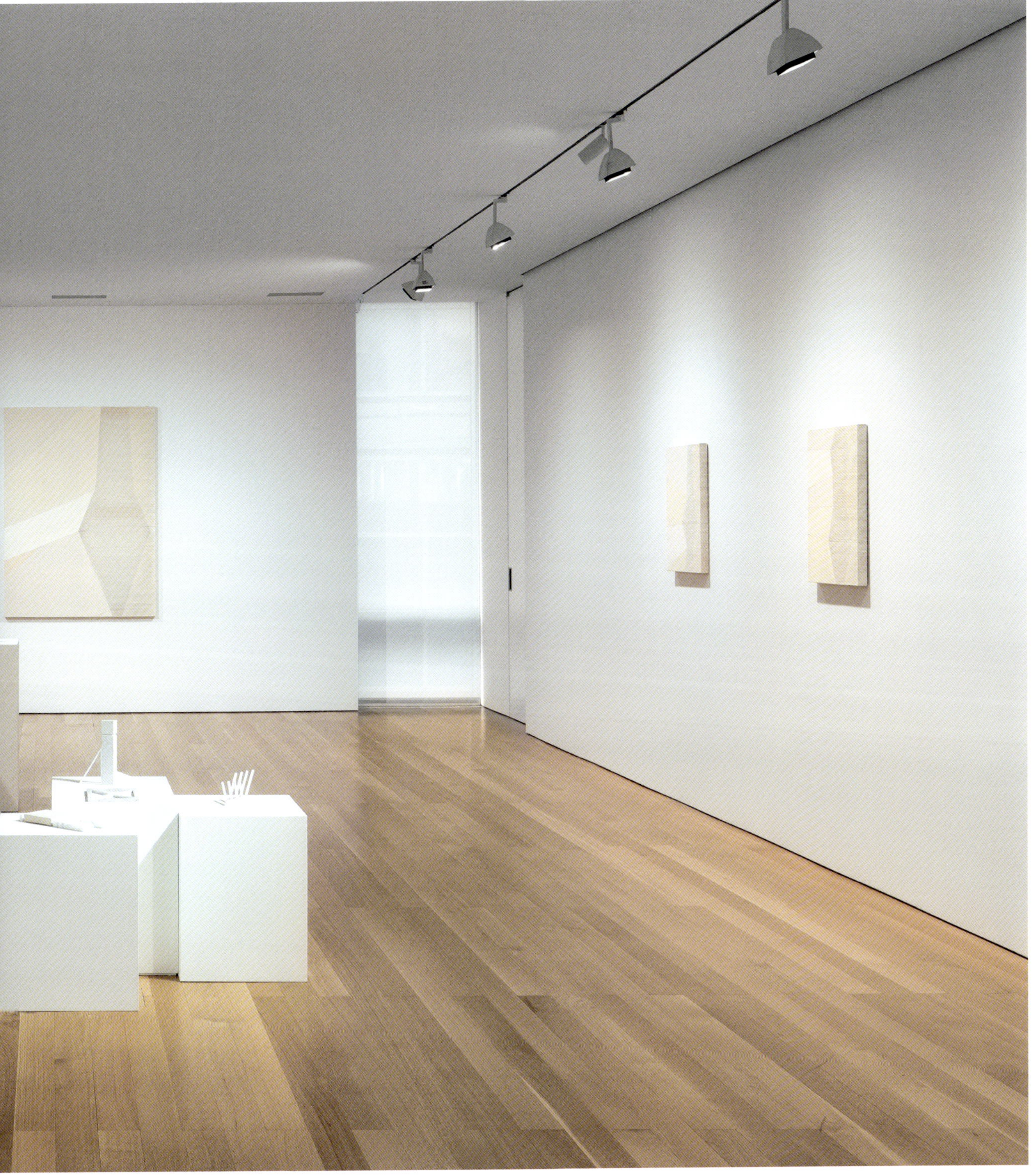

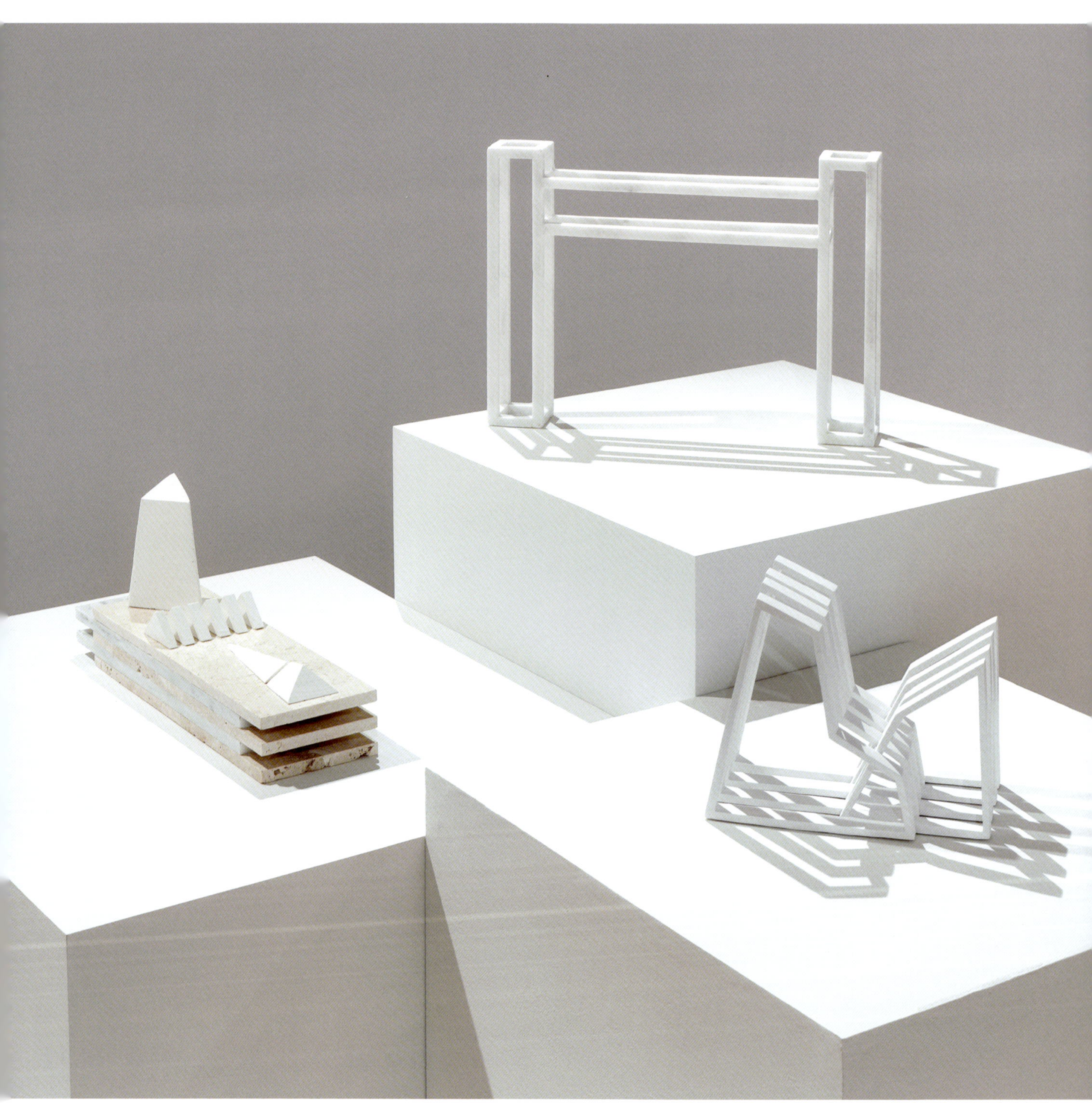

Clockwise from left: Rebecca Ward, *permission structures*, 2016; *futurologist*, 2017; and *attachment theory*, 2017

Beauty has long been central to my practice, and I see beauty as a state of being rather than a state of appearance. I see it as equilibrium and balance that stand in opposition to all the negativity and struggle we are constantly faced with. The laborious process of obtaining balance is often wrought with strife, and I think the result, minimal and pristine, is also political.

After the 2016 election, like many people I was left feeling broken and simultaneously empowered to respond through my work. I struggled with how to make something that is about both resistance and beauty. These FLAG works emerged from that intersection, as I was imagining ancient architectural forms and future dystopian ones. I wanted to use present and past architecture as a way to speak about power. It's an important time to talk about where power structures lie, and architecture is certainly capable of both disrupting hierarchies and establishing power. Making sculptures on a small scale and having a total perspective shift over them felt like a good way to exercise my own power.

When creating any work, I think about how to make its form lighter than it actually is. I want the work to feel weightless, at least in a psychological way, because life is quite heavy on its own. Several of the thread works in the show were based on the shape of a vase. I wanted to use the vase because it has such a rich role in history, much of it connected to femininity through function and form. Those works are created by unweaving, unraveling, and deconstructing fabric. Then it's all restretched and restitched one thread at a time. It looks like a solid form, but it's really a precarious situation: If you take a pair of scissors to even one string, all of the tension would be lost. Several of the sculptures were also made of the most fragile stuff imaginable—cast plaster, which is extremely brittle and vulnerable. Ultimately, the show was a reflection of the moment it was created in. It was a response to something quite precarious, holding the tension of an uncertain future.

—Rebecca Ward

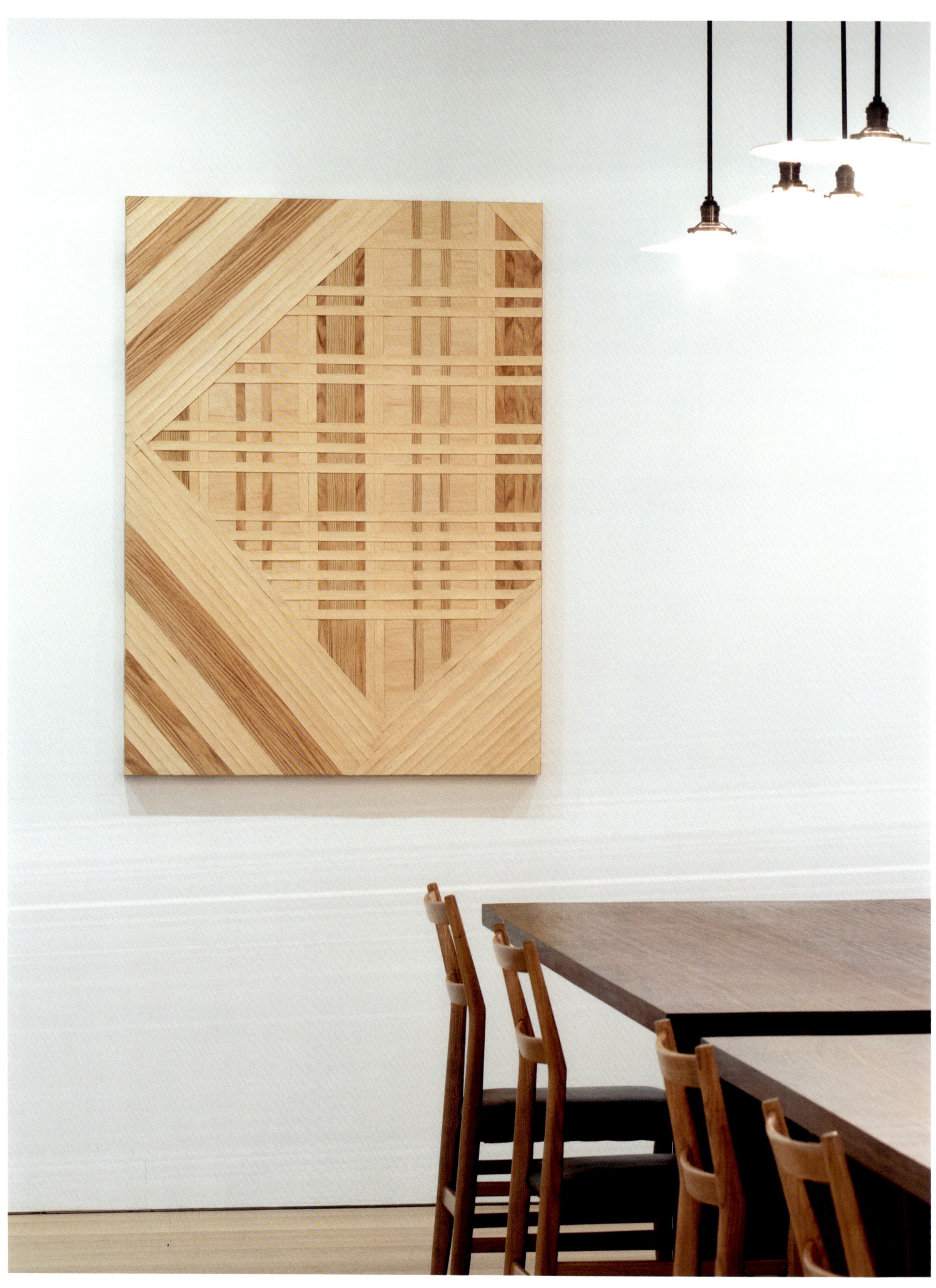

Rebecca Ward, *ideology*, 2017

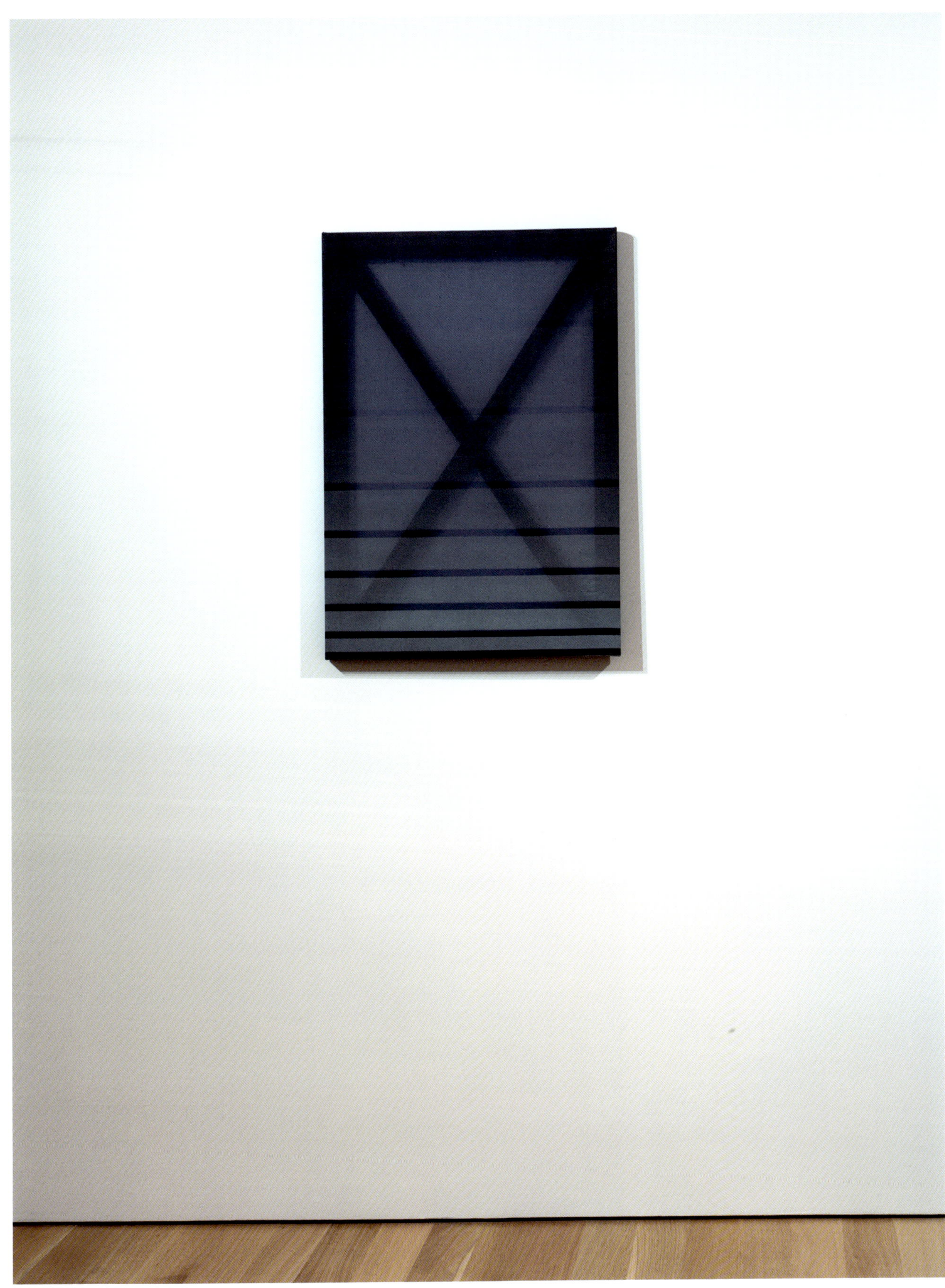

Rebecca Ward, *X (grey and navy)*, 2017

THE TIMES

June 1–August 11, 2017

Artists

Becca Albee
Doug Ashford
Luke Butler
Anthony Campuzano
Suzanne Caporael
Nancy Chunn
Mike Cockrill
David Colman
Jennifer Dalton
NiiLartey De Osu
Anne Deleporte
Mark DeMuro
Richard Dupont
Elise Engler
Laura Fields
Avram Finkelstein
Joy Garnett
Skye Gilkerson
Robert Gober
Felix Gonzalez-Torres
Gran Fury
Group Material
Matthew Hansel
Rachel Harrison
Lubaina Himid
Theresa Himmer
David Hines
Becky Howland
On Kawara
Ellsworth Kelly
Larrell Kitt
Agnieszka Kurant
Stephen Lack
Steven and William Ladd
Justen Ladda
Sean Landers
Paul Laster
Leigh Ledare
Elissa Levy
Tora López
Jason Bailer Losh
Dashiell Manley
Walter Martin & Paloma Muñoz
Stefana McClure
Dave McKenzie
Tom Molloy
Maynard Monrow
Aliza Nisenbaum
Lorraine O'Grady
Billy Pacak
Alexandra Penney
PLAYLAB, INC.
William Powhida
Richard Prince
Dominic Quintana
Beth Reisman
Hunter Reynolds
Bruce Richards
Guy Richards Smit
Carlos Rolón/Dzine
Randall Rosenthal
Donna Ruff
Michael Scoggins
Lauren Seiden
Paul Sietsema
Adam Simon
Ken Solomon
Ruby Sky Stiler
Linda Stillman
Sarah Sze
Yuken Teruya
Rirkrit Tiravanija
Fred Tomaselli
Jim Torok
Panos Tsagaris
Phoebe Washburn
Evan Whale
Carmen Winant
Andrew Witkin
Yes Men
Mark Zawatski
Angela Pulido Zorro
and more

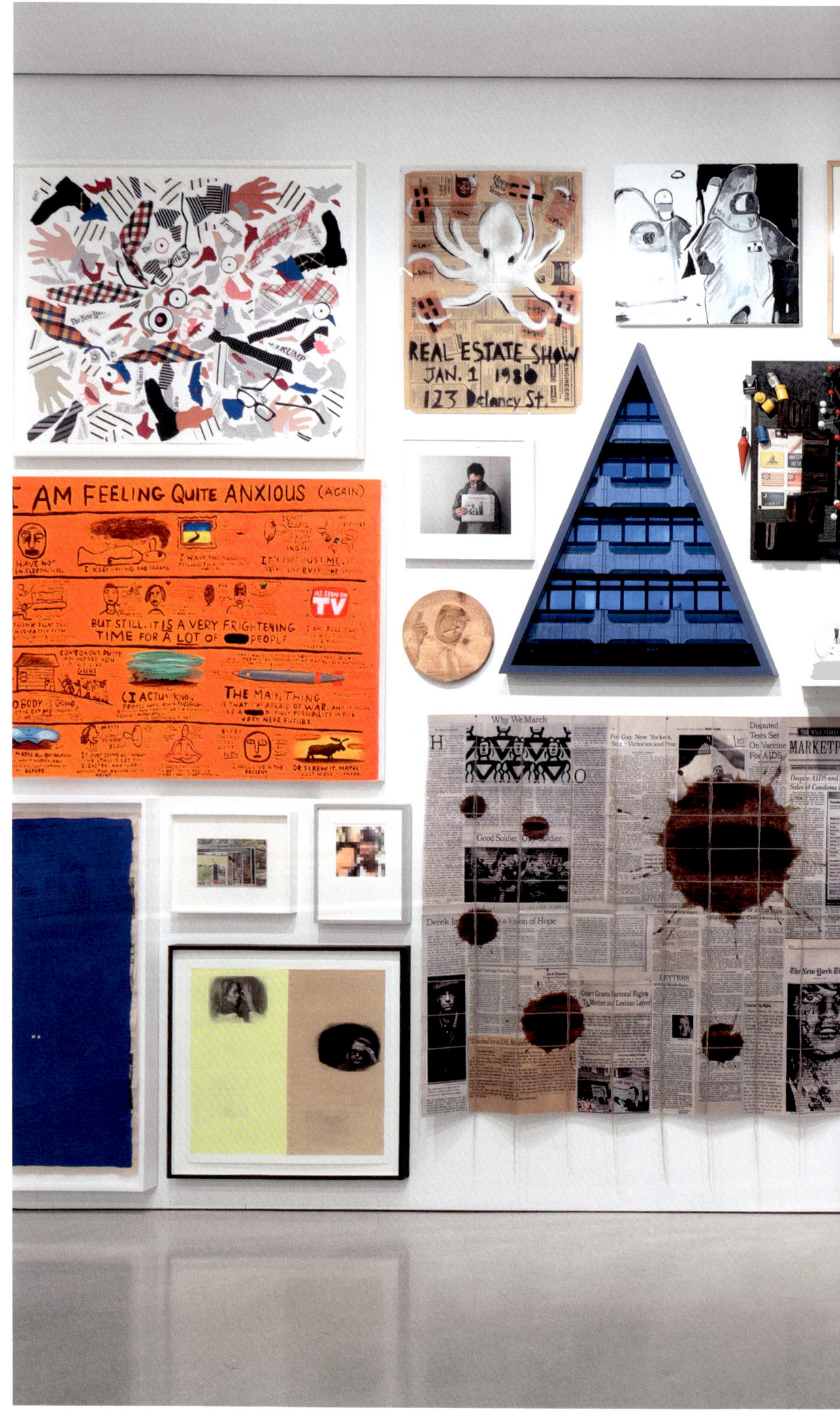

Installation view

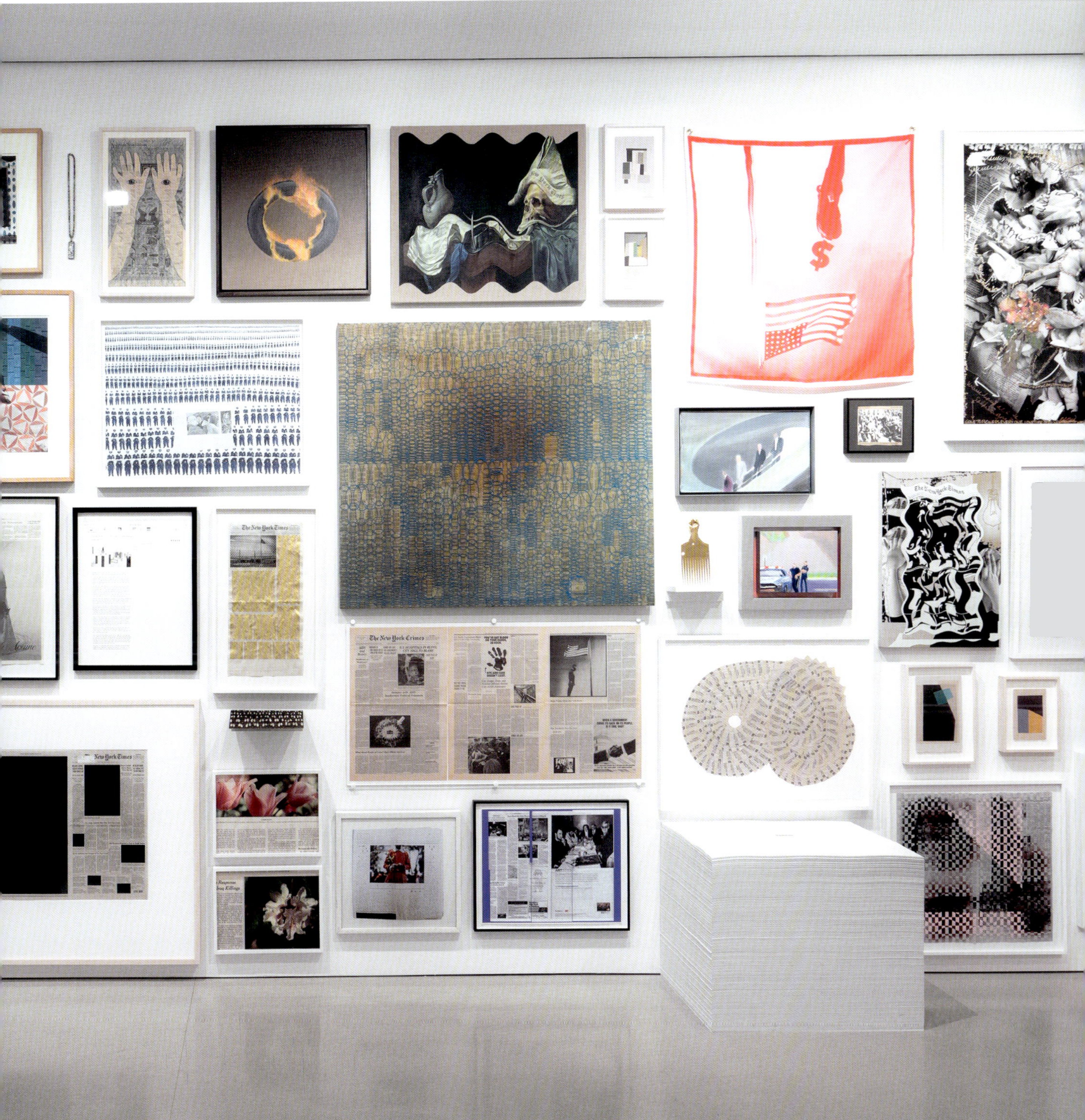

ASHLEY BICKERTON

September 23–December 16, 2017

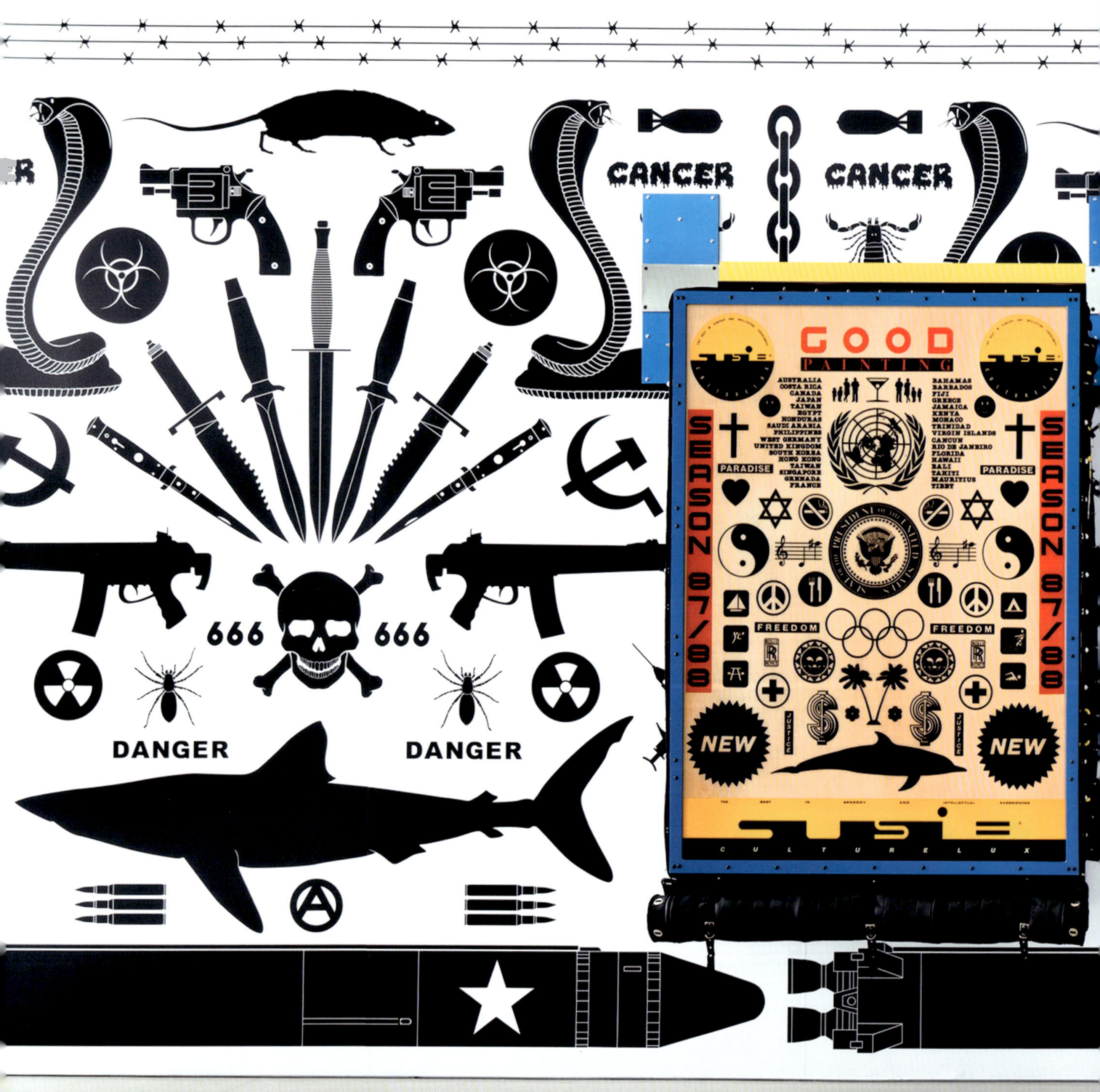

Background: Ashley Bickerton, *Bad Wall*, 2017;
foreground: Ashley Bickerton, *Good Painting*, 1988

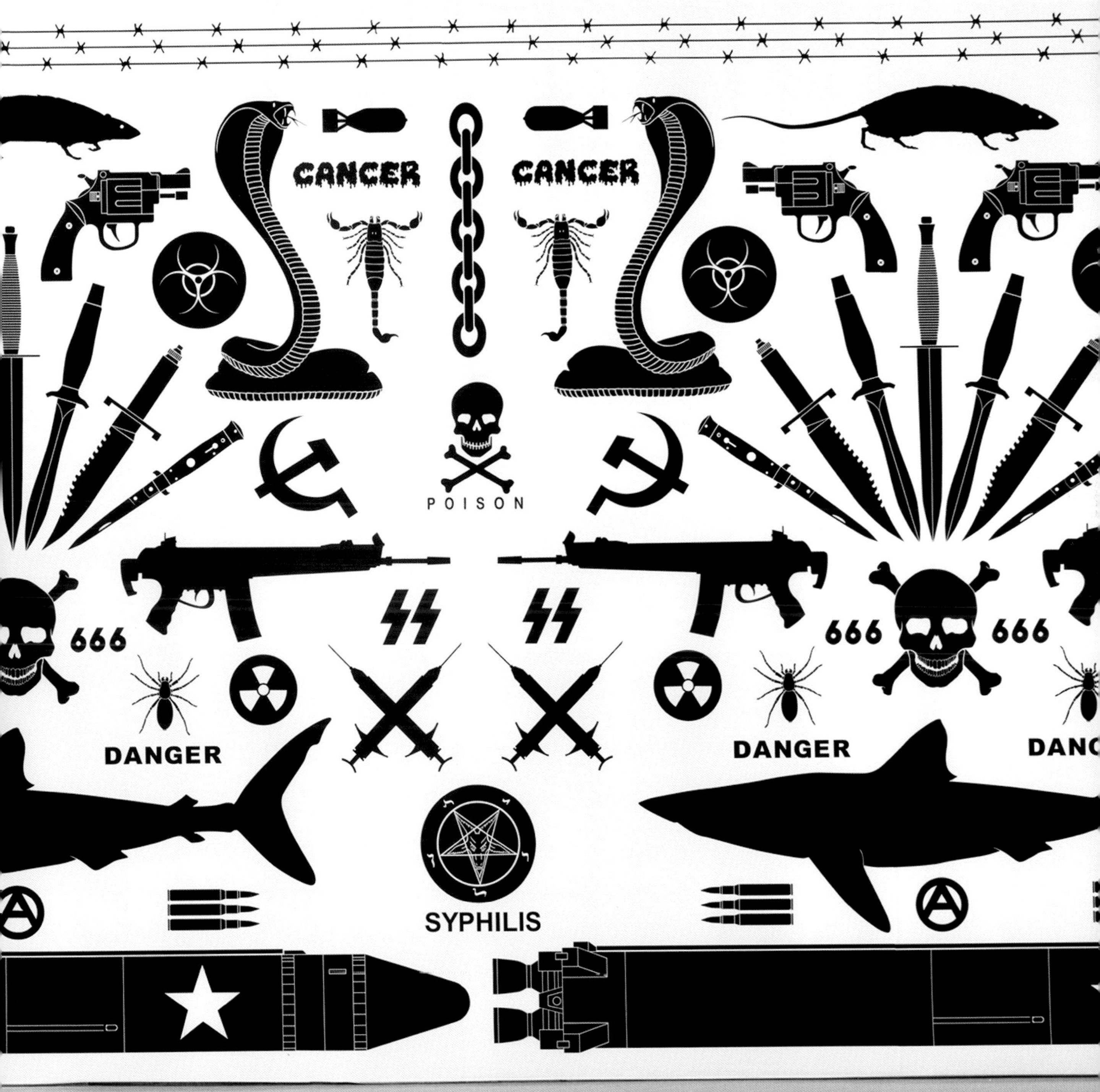

Something strange happened when I installed my show at The FLAG Art Foundation. It's what I had wanted to happen—maybe for many, many years—but when I saw it taking shape before my eyes, it was nevertheless an oddly curious experience.

We have to shoot back a couple of decades to put it all in proper context. It appeared, maybe more to others than to myself, that my career had improbably bifurcated into two starkly different tangents. There seemed to be an unmovable wall between what I had done as a young artist in New York City and what I had done since in my self-imposed exile on the island of Bali, coincidentally or not, almost precisely the antipodean point on the planet to New York. It was apparently such a schism that there were actually two groups of people: one who thought the work I had done decades before in New York was tough, rigorous, and game-changing, whereas the work I had done on the island was decorous, fluffy, and overwrought tripe; and, conversely, a second set of folks, more or less equal in number to the first, who fiercely loved the Bali work and when exposed to my earlier efforts responded with a resounding "Meh!" Both groups had thoughtful and serious players, so that wasn't the reason for the division.

Now, while others might have been polarized, I never had any doubt that what I had been doing over the past quarter century in Bali was exactly the same thing I had done in New York all those years before. The same intellectual mechanisms, the same mischievous inclinations, and the same bemused and equivocal ways of slicing the universe were all in place. So, while the outer theatrics might have shape-shifted something serious, the motor remained unchanged. Getting others to see this was the challenge.

Shortly before my show at FLAG, I had a large retrospective in London at the Newport Street Gallery. While this exhibition covered thirty-five years of work in six large galleries, it was consciously chronological, and thus didn't allow any real direct juxtaposition of the apparently confusing transformations my work had undergone. But it was precisely because that exhibition was done in a more traditional way that at FLAG we were able to throw chronology clean out the window.

It was not intentional; the galleries at FLAG pretty much dictated our first moves, and the rest just seemed to fall into place. The intimate space generated amplification that I had not expected. It begged one to consider juxtapositions of works that I would never have dreamed of placing in direct proximity to one another. Even though it had long been my wish to flesh out the overarching and unifying impulses that have defined the overall work from the beginning, the idea of placing such divergent strains in direct dialogue seemed like madness at the start.

Well, we went wild and ripped history to pieces, tossing the fragments into the wind like so many dry leaves. Once we started, it became infectious, even perverse and gleeful, to come up with the most outlandish segues and sequences. And here I have to thank FLAG's stellar team, who granted such free rein and broadly encouraged these tendencies. It was through these collaborators and their intimate feel for the space that we were able to craft such improbably flowing cadences out of discordant shards. The result was the best that any artist could hope for: a chance to learn completely new things about their own work, about their own voice, their language, and to see musty old things, long entrenched in their epistemological furrows, with completely fresh eyes.

In the first excited moments upon finally completing the installation, it felt like everywhere I turned there were jarring collisions of past best intentions; yet as the nerves began to calm, it became clear that my worst fears—that this would look like some motley grouping of random strays—had not come to pass. It was quite the opposite: even the most startling juxtapositions began to harmonize, and for the first time ever I began to hear the tune. People often talk about the privilege of getting to know an artist's work, but I can assure you that the greatest privilege is that of an artist having the opportunity to get to know their own work.

—Ashley Bickerton

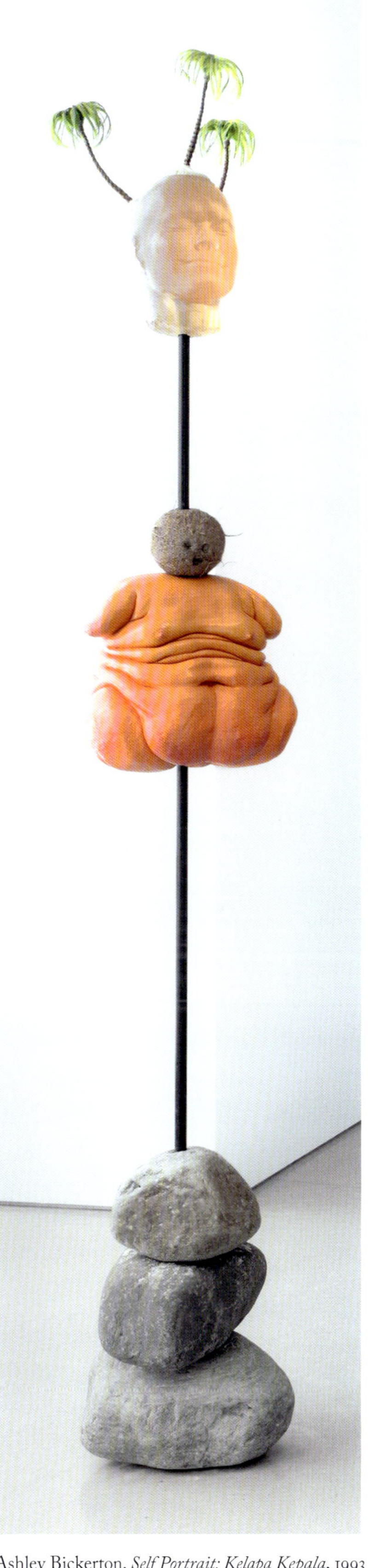

Ashley Bickerton, *Self Portrait: Kelapa Kepala*, 1993

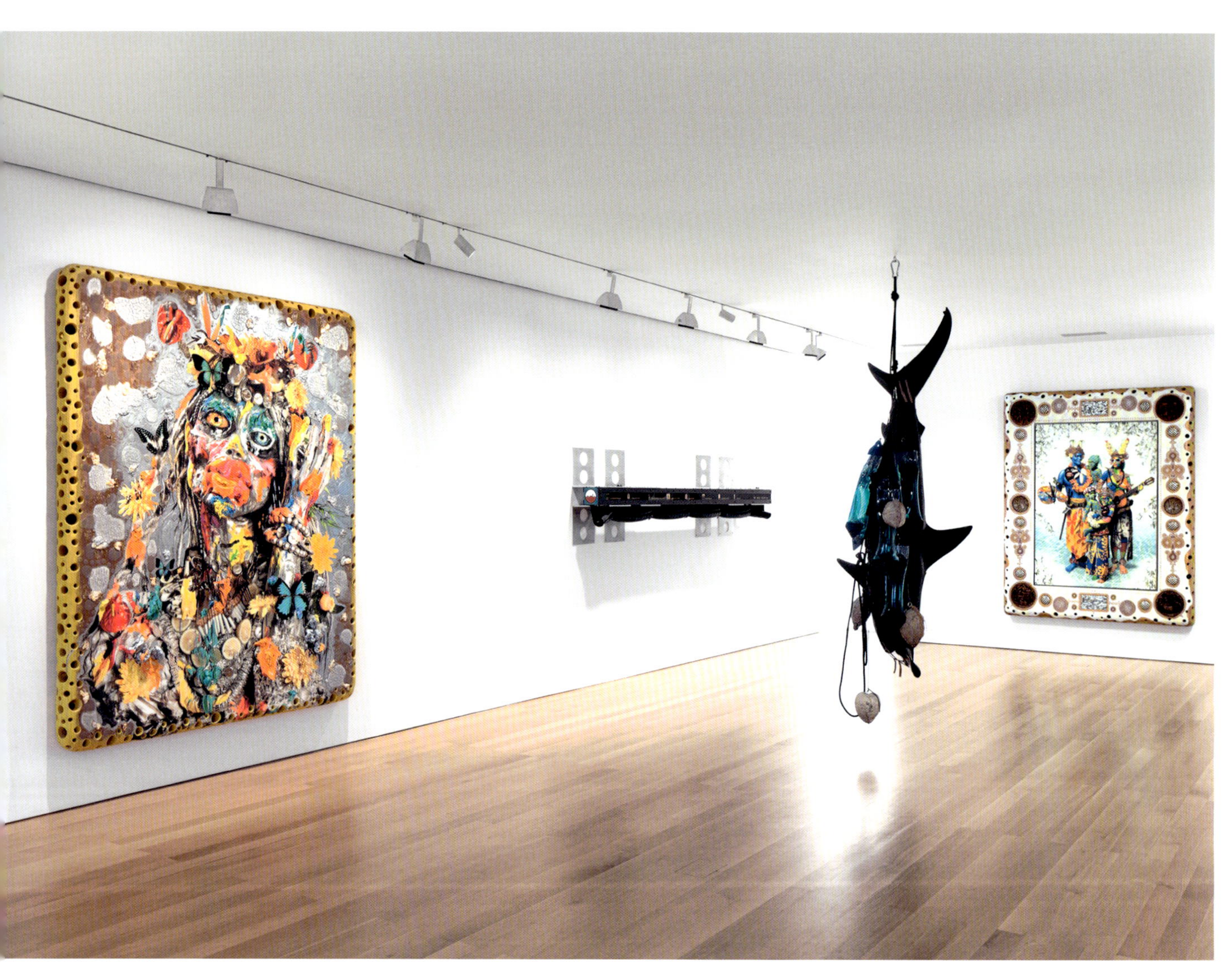

Left to right: Ashley Bickerton, *m-DNA_eve 1*, 2013; *The Ideal Collection*, 1988; *Solomon Island Shark*, 1993; and *Famili*, 2007

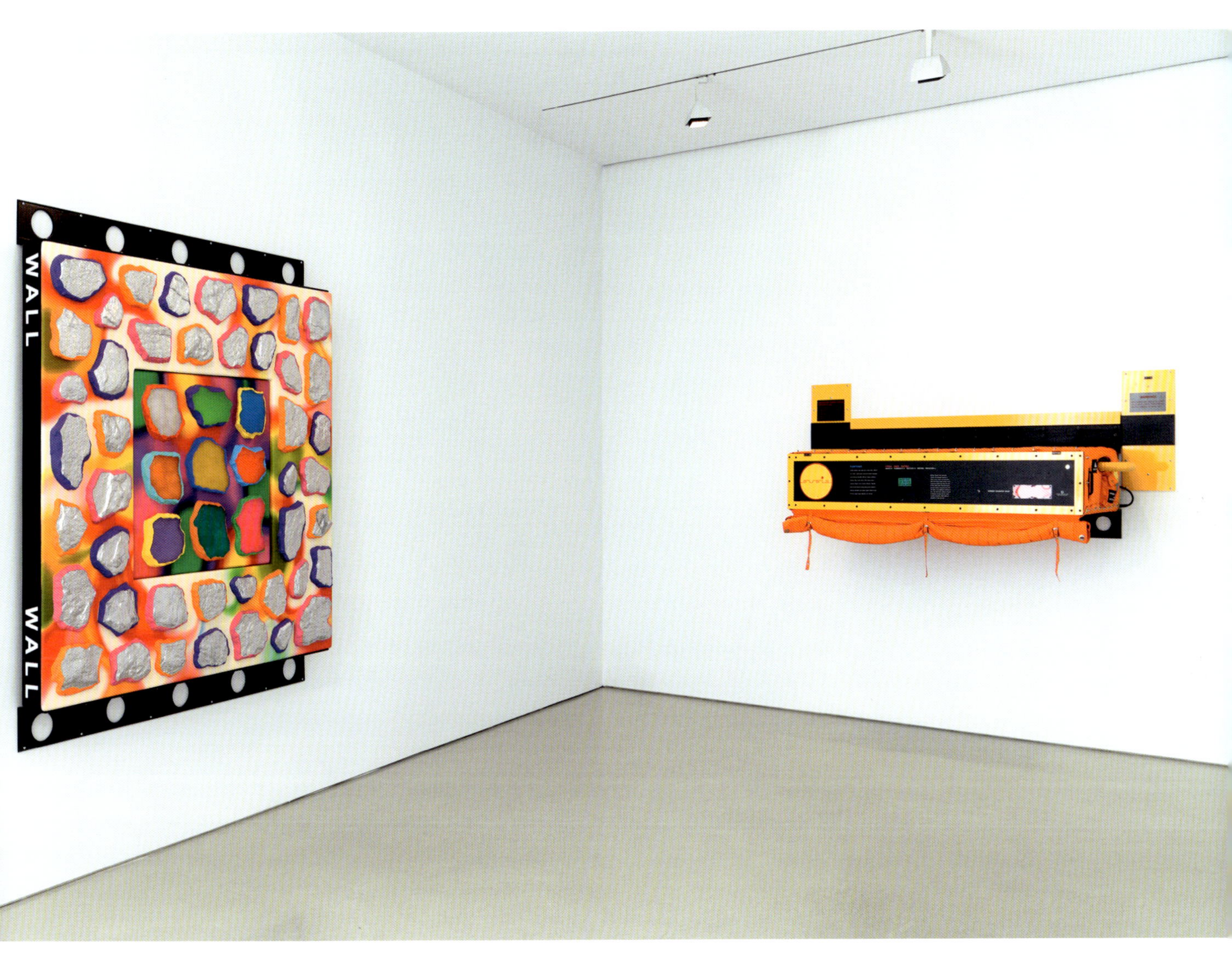

Left to right: Ashley Bickerton, *Wall-Wall SnS-S 2*, 2017; *Still Life (The Artist's Studio After Braque) #2*, 1989

ELLSWORTH KELLY: BLACK AND WHITE WORKS

February 23–May 19, 2018
Curated by Jack Shear

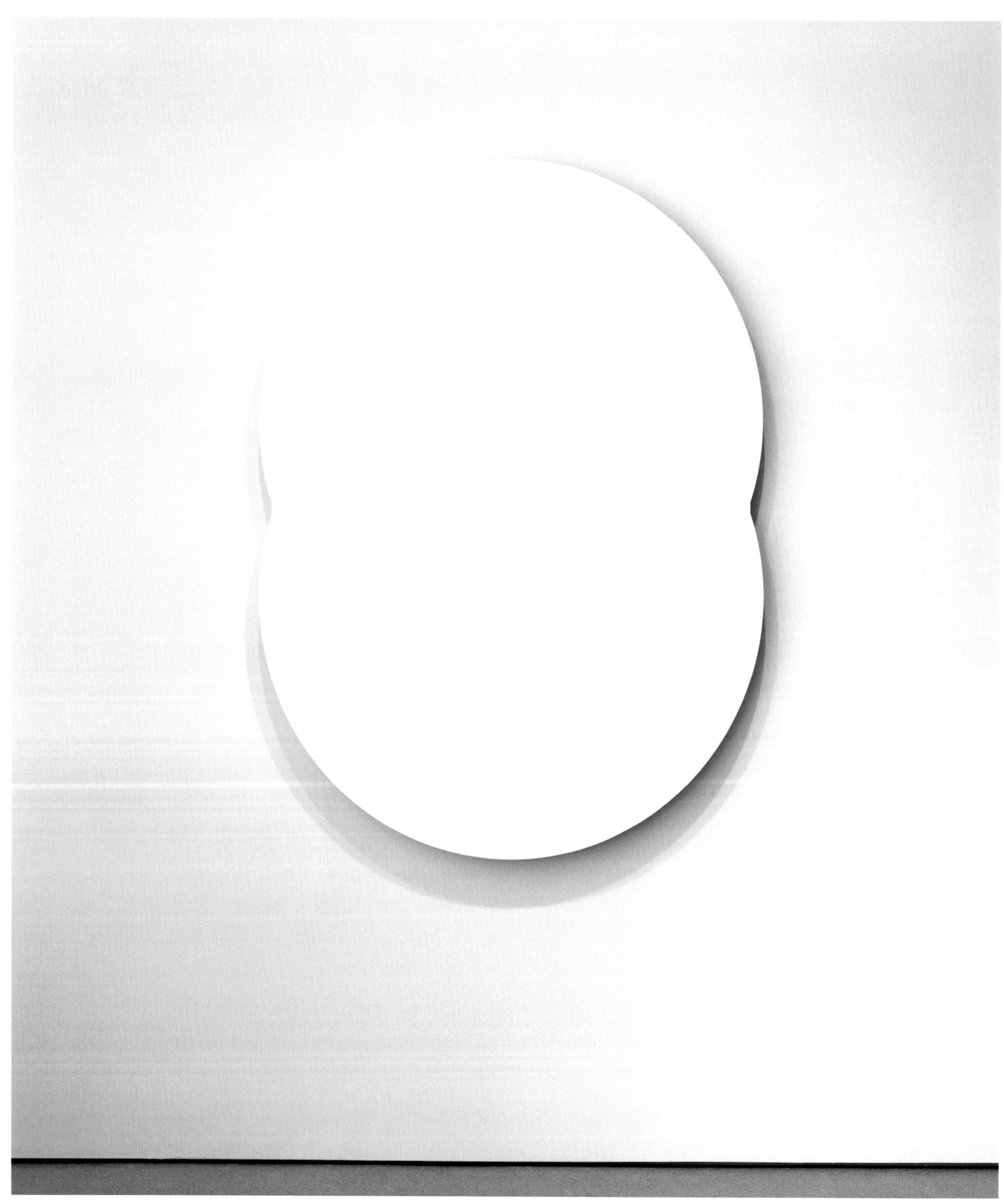

Ellsworth Kelly, *White Plaque: Bridge Arch and Reflection II*, 2011

Ellsworth often said, "Everything begins with drawing," and he was relentless in his drawing. Throughout his career, he created paintings, sculpture, and works on paper in black and white.

There are so many different aspects of Ellsworth's work that one can gravitate toward. People who grew up with him often focus on his paintings from the 1960s; they see him as a proto-Minimalist or a precursor to Pop art. Others think of his Matisse-like colors from France, or his plant drawings. Having been part of Ellsworth's artistic and personal life for thirty-two years, I certainly have a unique perspective.

For this exhibition, I wanted to show Ellsworth as an "experimenter." Perhaps because major exhibitions in the last fifteen years or so have primarily focused on his later, more serial works, often highlighting groups that are connected in some way, people might not think of Ellsworth in this way. However, early on, Ellsworth was decidedly *not* interested in making overt connections between pieces; he would solve a problem in one painting and move on to another.

My objective was to contrast those early works with what he produced in later years, and to demonstrate the range of his conceptual practice and the role that experimentation played in it.

—Jack Shear

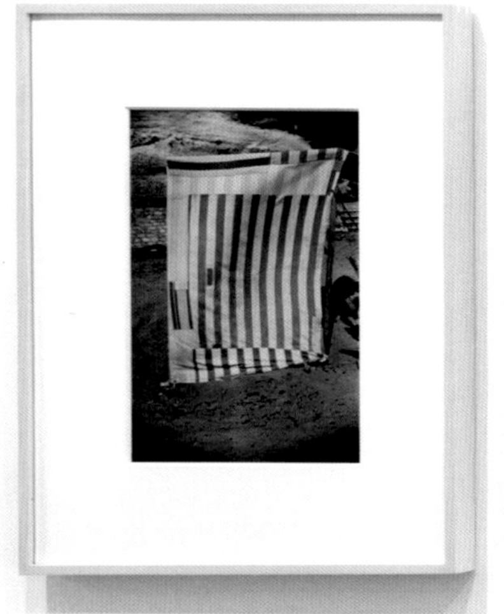
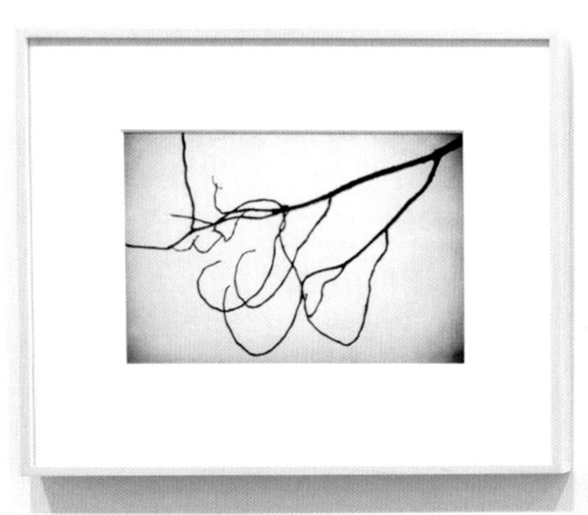
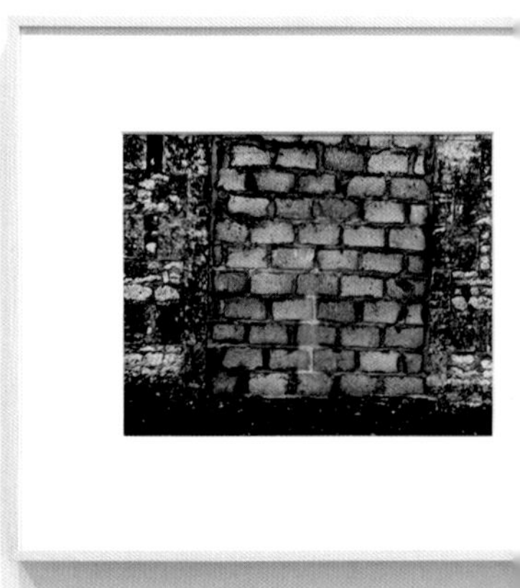

Installation view

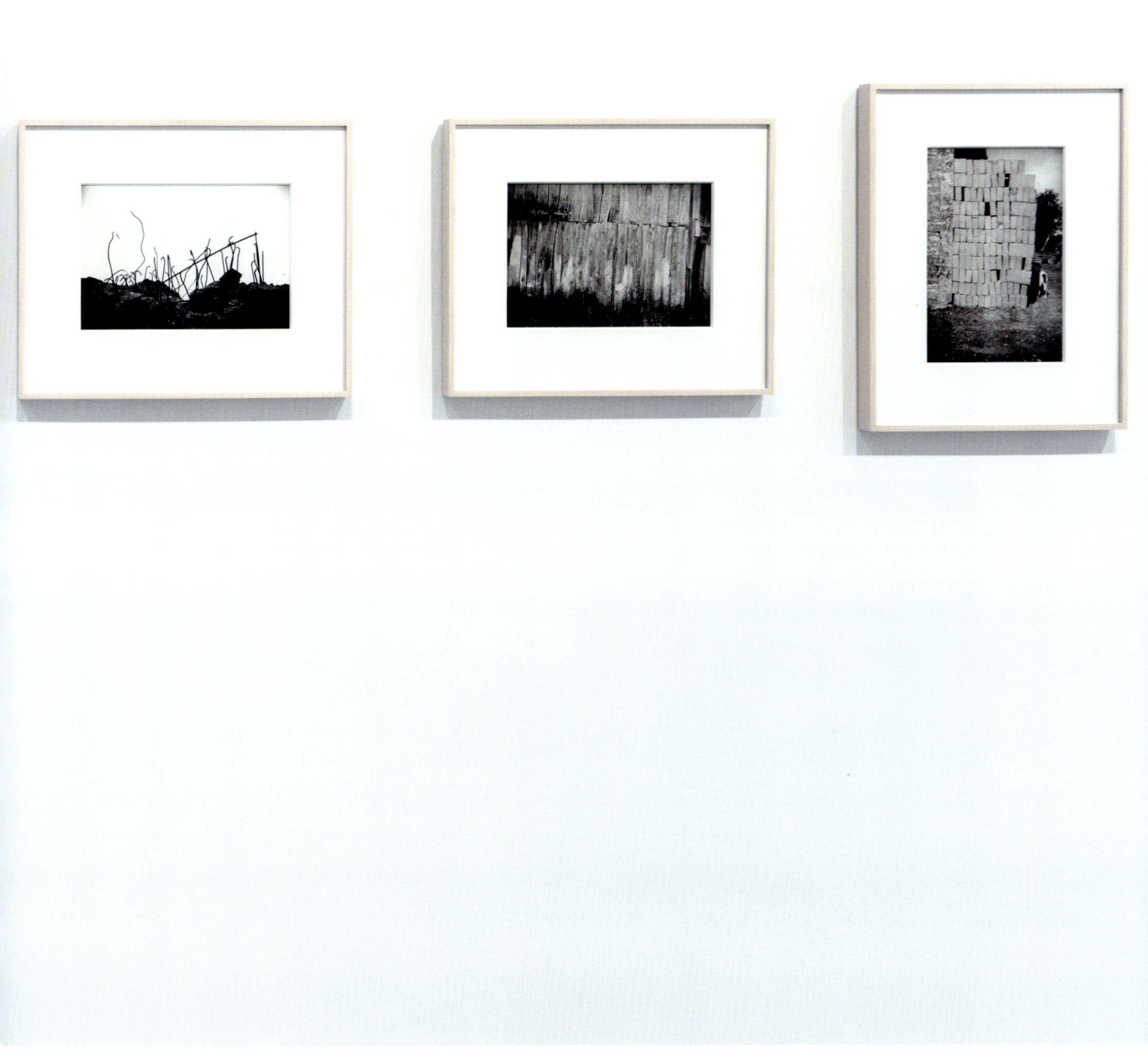

Following pages, left to right: Ellsworth Kelly, *River II*, 2004; and *Black Relief with White*, 2005

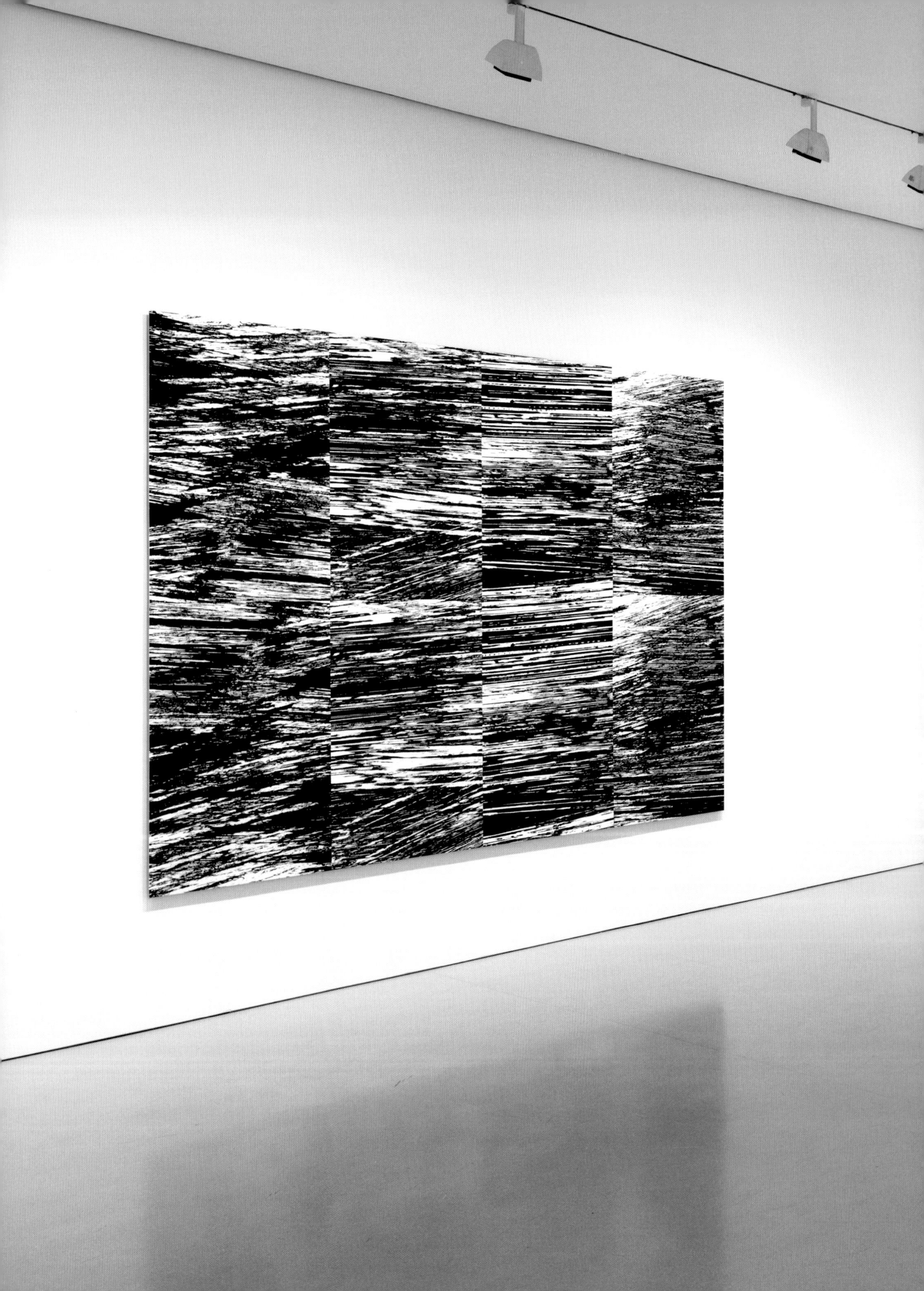

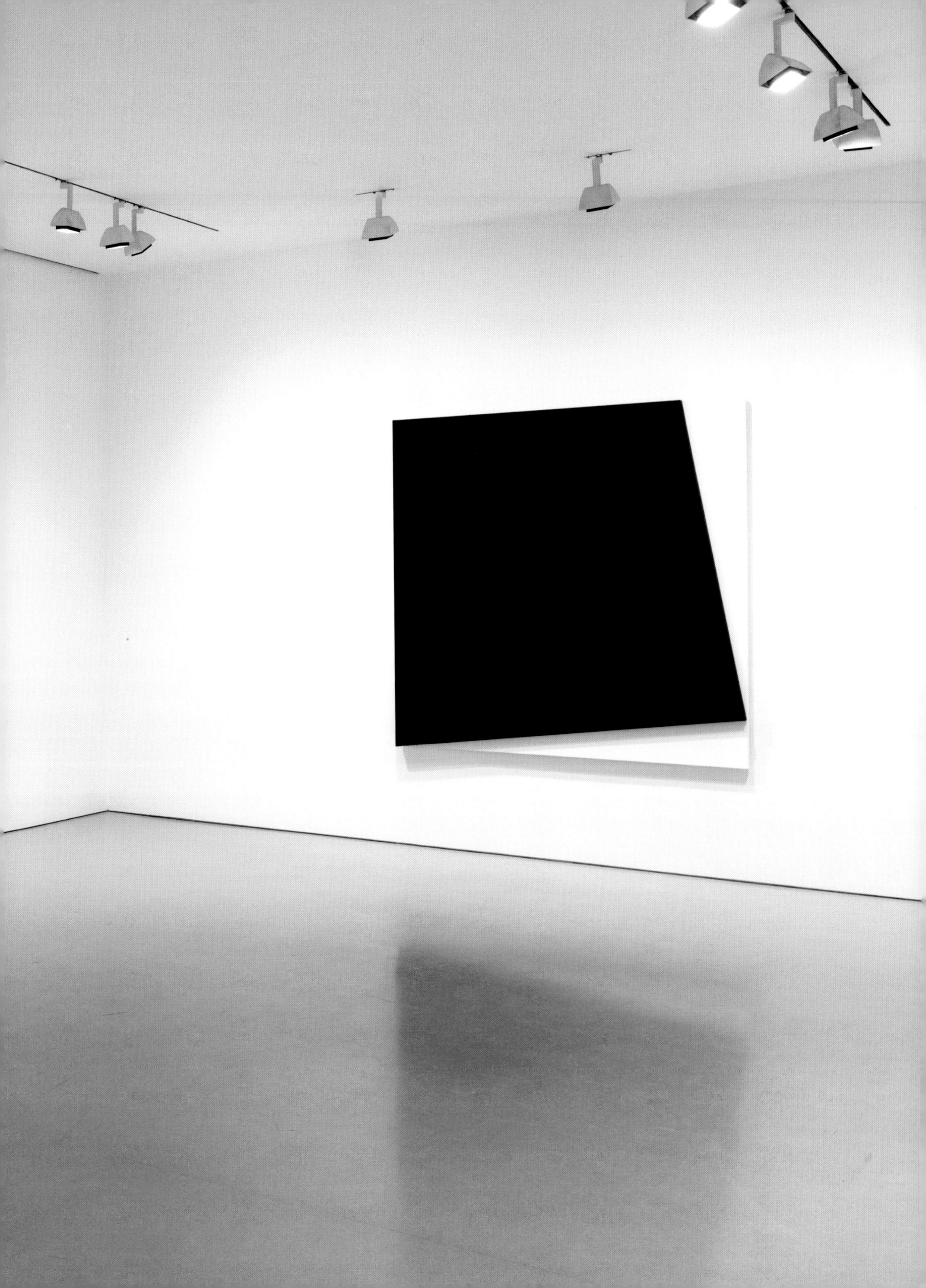

PAINTING/OBJECT

February 23–May 19, 2018

Artists
Sarah Crowner
N. Dash
Sam Moyer
Julia Rommel
Erin Shirreff

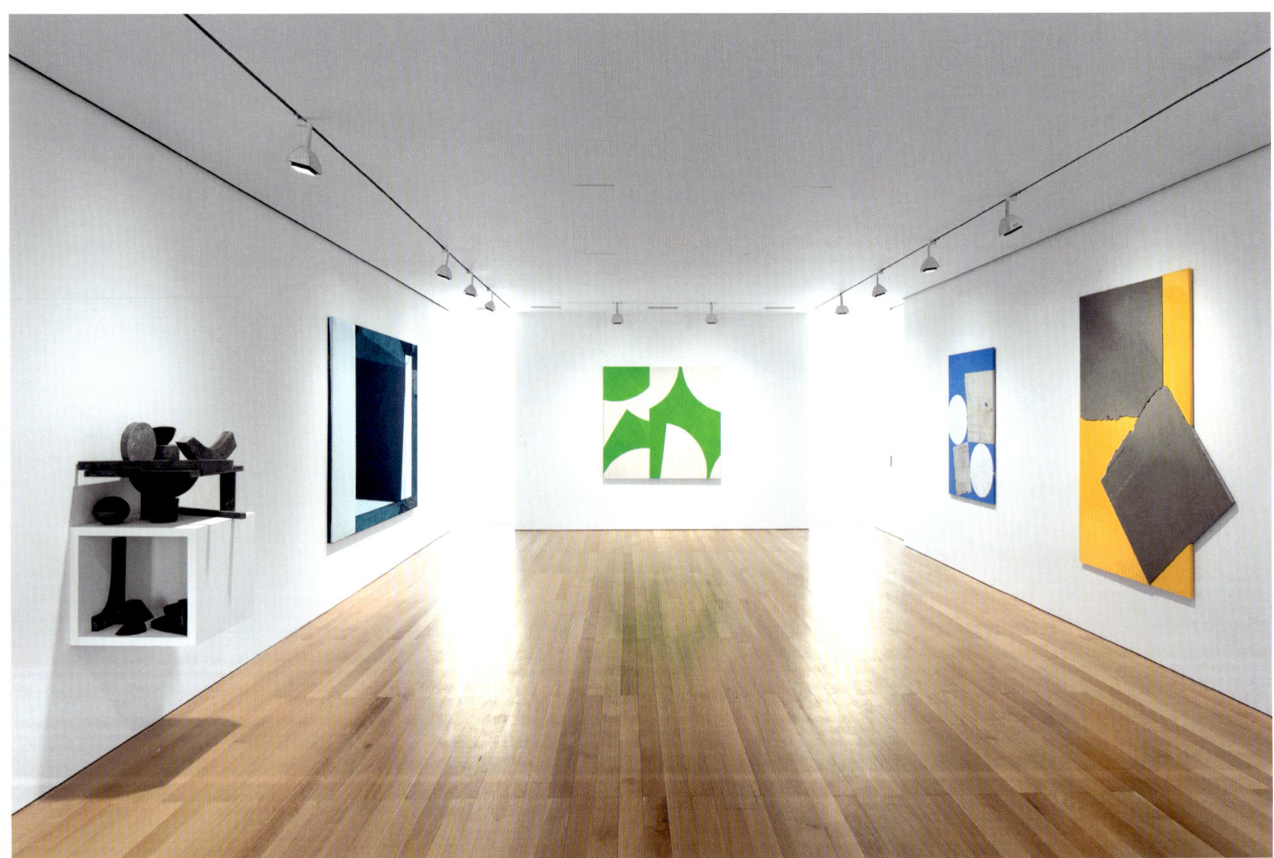

Left to right: Erin Shirreff, *Catalogue, 21 Parts*, 2016; Julia Rommel, *The Unbelievers*, 2016; Sarah Crowner, *Sliced Greens*, 2018; Sam Moyer, *Spencertown*, 2018; and *Rye*, 2018

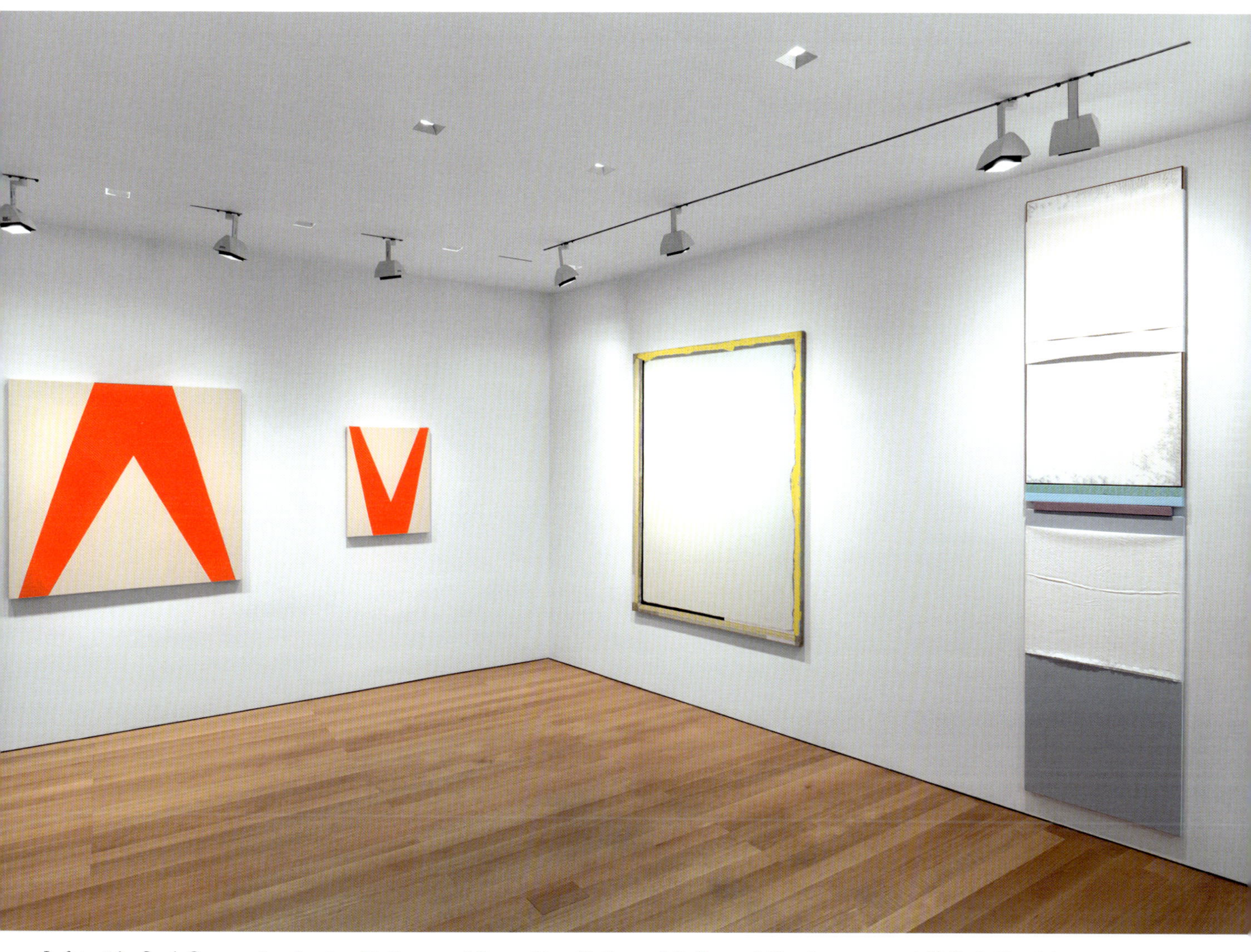

Left to right: Sarah Crowner, *Standing Legs (Red)*, 2017; and *Reversed Legs (Red)*, 2017; Julia Rommel, *Two Apartments*, 2016; N. Dash, *Untitled*, 2018

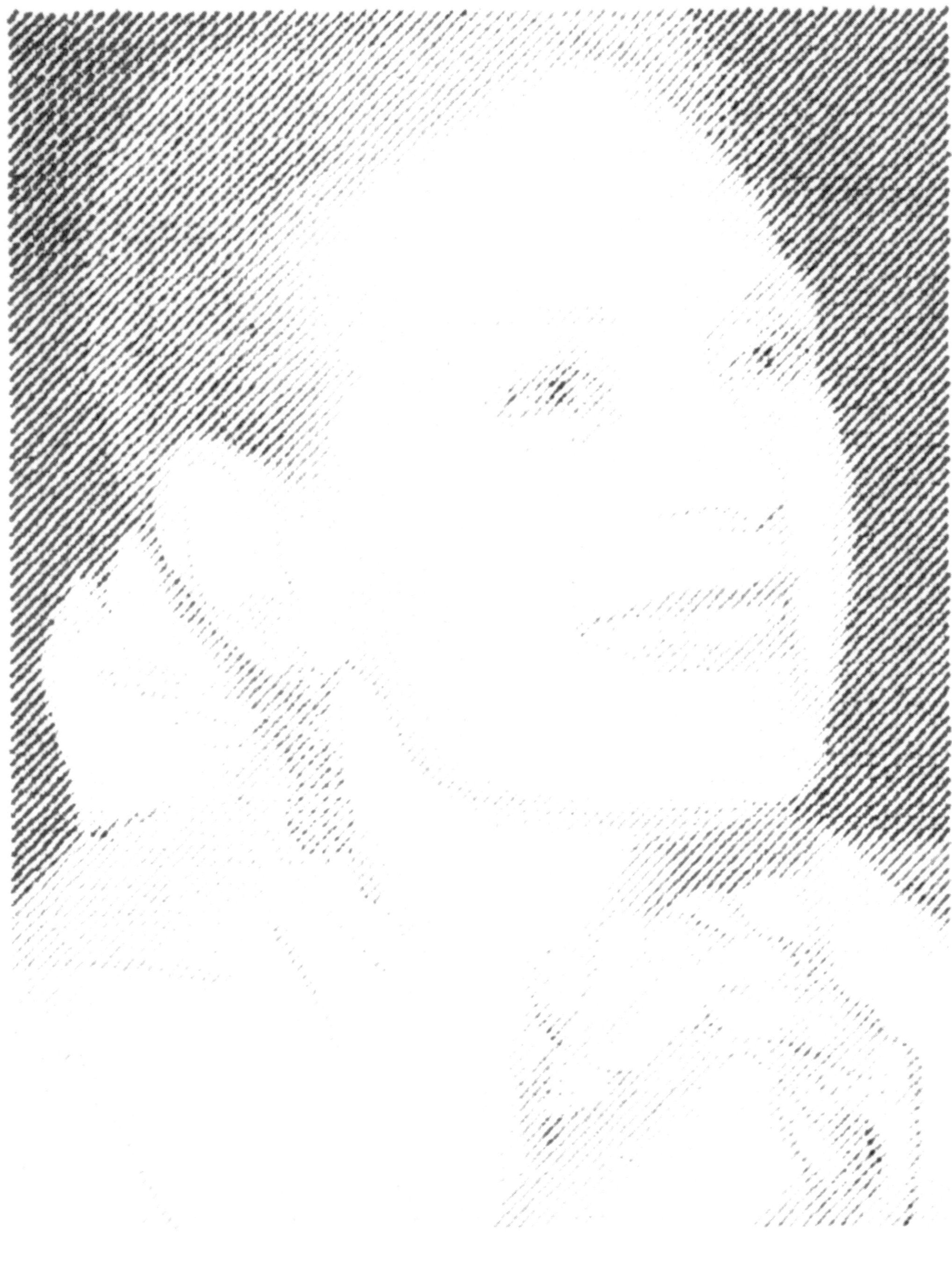

HOW EWAN MET GLENN

Carolyn Twersky

We sit down at a wooden table in Ewan Gibbs's kitchen, sipping wine and picking at nuts and chips.

"Glenn is my fairy godfather," Ewan says, standing up to prepare dinner.

"When you called me, you said you wanted me to be your Lorenzo de' Medici," Glenn clarifies.

Or is Ewan Glenn's artist in remote residence? Right now, they're just host and dinner guest.

Twelve years after Ewan emailed Glenn Fuhrman, asking for an art partnership, the two sat down for dinner at the artist's house in Faringdon, England, a small town outside Oxford, accompanied by Glenn's sister, Laura, and me, his niece. The menu consisted of roast chicken and assorted vegetables, cooked at the hands of the artist. The wine was provided by Glenn.

We get up to try to help cook, but Ewan kicks us out of the kitchen, banishing us to the table with the snacks and wine. My mother and I sit down with Glenn, hearing the story we are about to be told for the first time.

Ewan says, "You sat opposite me at dinner and we were drunk and I said, 'Who do you collect?'" In between cutting veggies and opening a bottle of wine, the pair recalls their first interaction, on September 10, 2003, in the Chelsea neighborhood in Manhattan. "You said, 'Gerhard Richter and Chuck Close,' so I asked if you had rich parents because you were only thirty-seven."

"And I said no," Glenn responds.

Just three months later, Ewan would bump into Glenn again, this time in the context of his own show at Paul Morris Gallery in New York. While Glenn couldn't make the opening, he purchased two

Opposite: Ewan Gibbs, *Arlene*, 2010

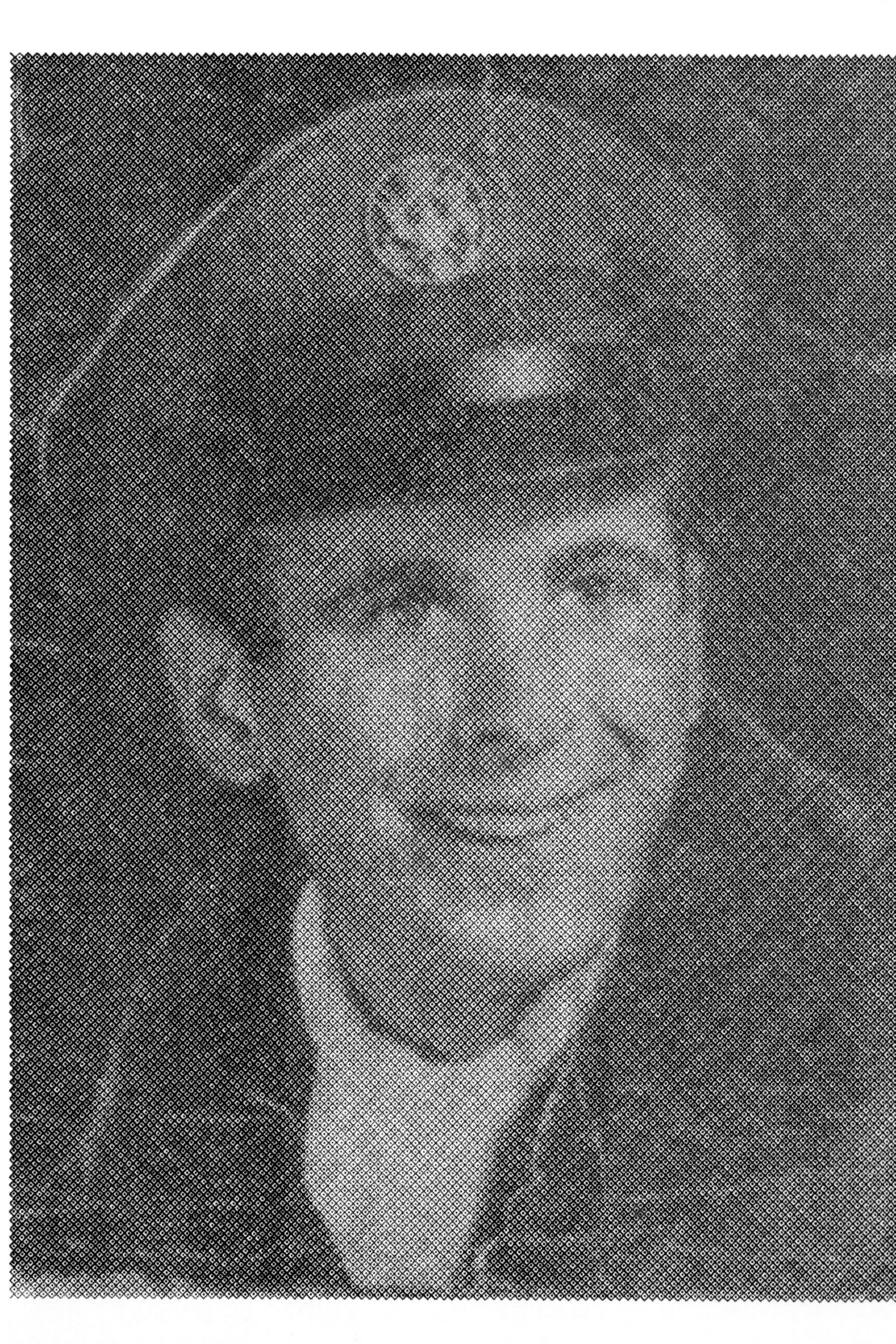

drawings prior, and he invited the artist and his wife to breakfast the next morning.

From there, a relationship grew, and come February 2005, it would undergo an interesting development. Paul Morris Gallery closed suddenly, and Ewan didn't feel secure in his relationship with the London gallery he had worked with for nine years. On top of that, his wife, Helen, was expecting. Ewan was looking for a change, so he reached out to Glenn.

Ewan didn't ask for much, simply to sell his work so he could continue to make it. "It is not my ambition to become rich and famous," the original plea to Glenn reads. "I am surer than ever that I only want to work with people who I respect and who respect me as an artist and person."

So, Ewan laid out a plan: Glenn would get first choice of Ewan's work every year at a 25 percent discount, and Ewan wouldn't have to split the commission with a gallery.

At this point, Ewan pauses from his cooking and leaves the room, returning a few minutes later with a binder. "Every piece of paper represents one month of Glenn sending me some money."

"You save all of the wire transfers?" Glenn asks.

"Yeah."

But Glenn has his own, less organized, catalogue: an album on his phone with all the works he has purchased from Ewan over the years. The content of the drawings spans from the "Bean" sculpture in Chicago to a gallery owner's dog in Aspen, but they all feature Ewan's signature crosses, circles, and slash marks.

Ewan began using the crosshatching style when he was twenty and happened upon some knitting charts at a flea market. With that inspiration, he started breaking down his scenes into grids, a technique he has used ever since. Going through every line, he remakes a photograph with little Xs, /s, or Os of varying thickness. After an hour hunched over his desk, Ewan emerges to find the Xs beginning to come together to create a scene.

No matter the original photo, Ewan approaches each work the same way: with a cup filled with perfectly sharpened pencils, a ruler,

Opposite: Ewan Gibbs, *Leon*, 2018

and a grid. The technique may seem simple, and Ewan may agree: "It's not my skill, it's just like looking at each square and it adds up."

Glenn, however, would not: "I'm going to call a little bit of bullshit. That's not your skill?"

"I'm not thinking, I'm drawing an eye," Ewan backtracks. "I'm just thinking, this square is a darker tone. So, in a way it doesn't matter what I'm drawing. As long as I'm looking after each square, it will add up."

Ewan describes the process as "economic." After eight hours of work, an average day for the artist, the eight hours are visible on the paper.

Despite working with simply a pencil and paper for so many years, Ewan never feels the urge to pick up paint and a paintbrush.

"It's weird, when I see a sunset or something beautiful I just think, I can't compete with that no matter what," he says. "With the drawings, no one questions why it's black and white because it's drawn in pencil. When a painting is black and white, it becomes a deliberate act."

So, Ewan goes out into the world with his camera, capturing images like Big Ben and the Statue of Liberty. He then returns to Faringdon, walks up the three floors until he reaches his attic, a tiny little room, filled with books on artists and CDs. He sits down at his desk, turns on the overhead light, and gets to work.

While, back in 2005, Ewan was producing twelve drawings a year, now, with the addition of two kids running around the house and with the works becoming more nuanced and labor-intensive, this number has reduced to around five. The drop is fine with Ewan, however, who believes that his legacy will be decided by retrospectives, not one year of work: "However much you make, you'll probably be judged in the end on about a hundred pieces. So, if you have a fifty-year career and you make two really good things a year, that's fine."

When it is finally time for Ewan's retrospective, the curator can just call Glenn, who, thanks to the system created by Ewan in 2003, in theory has two of the strongest drawings Ewan makes every year. A Ewan Gibbs retrospective would undoubtedly look like no other: black, white, and Glenn all over. One hundred black-and-white drawings depicting scenes from cities, Glenn's name on all of the labels, like postcards from around the world. From: Ewan, To: Glenn.

Every image is iconic, or "generic," as Ewan describes them. "I try to take fairly traditional, touristy photographs. My hope is that you go to the site and it's almost like the image is a trap to pull you in because you're familiar with it," he continues. "Then it's about how the structure is made and the perception of it. I'm not trying to use imagery that's all about me in some way." That's why you won't find a drawing of Ewan's kids anywhere, but you will find plenty of Glenn's.

The food is ready, and Ewan sits down to join us as we continue to scroll through Glenn's phone, looking at a fourteen-year relationship depicted in drawings of baseball pitchers and military graveyards.

I take in a drawing of a pitcher. His leg is bent up behind him and his chest is parallel to the ground. From far away the /s come together and then disappear. "You can look at it and think it's a photo." Two heads nod in agreement.

Apparently, I hit a nerve. After a career of drawing, Ewan has heard this before.

"Well, this is the interesting failure," Ewan begins. "What you're sort of saying is it looks really naturalistic." I nod, trying to explain that I meant it as a compliment. Ewan continues, "In a photo, there's detail we don't see in the real world. We're so used to looking at photography and thinking about photography as the real world—we think of that as realism—but in so many ways it's unreal."

"So, it looks real?" Laura says, catching on and amending my compliment.

"Yes. In photography, often the blacks are so black, but if you look outside, nothing is that black." We cut into our chicken. "Or, if you're looking at that bush, you're not looking at every twig. Your brain just says, 'bush,'" Ewan adds.

Wine is sipped, vegetables nibbled on. Ewan continues: "I was walking the other day and there were all these white things on the floor and a lump and it looked like a little bird had been attacked." He pauses to take a bite. "I got up close and it was a blossom and a log. From farther away, I physically felt a little bit ill because I thought it was a dead bird, but up close it was a beautiful thing. Essentially the same thing I was looking at kind of transformed just by getting a little bit closer and seeing a bit more detail."

Similarly, Ewan's work transforms as one gets closer. The leg of the pitcher turns into /s, the hunched stance turns into Ewan working at his desk. It happens with every one of his pieces; the Statue of Liberty is reduced to Os, the Colorado mountains fold too, even Glenn's own family, which Ewan drew for Glenn's fiftieth in 2015. The drawing depicts a photo from 1980 of Glenn, Laura, and their parents before there was Amanda, kids, FLAG, or Ewan. Along with the work, Ewan enclosed a note:

"I have spent many happy hours most days over the last month with family Fuhrman," he wrote. "In my drawing, the four of you blend into one another and it is difficult to say where each of you ends and the other begins. . . I would like to think that the order and rigorous structure and strength of the grid combined with the softness of mark and gentle touch of the pencil are akin to the combination of qualities your parents may well have exhibited as they nurtured you and Laura through your childhoods."

Ewan's works can be many things: rows of Xs, drawings, "just like photographs." They can be Glenn's or someone else's. They're generic or iconic or touristy. They are real, they are a bush, a dead bird, a log. They are one thing from up close and a whole different thing from far away.

The one thing they are not? Glenn reminded everyone constantly on that night in Faringdon. Much to Glenn's dismay, Ewan's drawings have never been . . . pornographic.

"He doesn't want to do naked girls," Glenn mentions for the last time.

Ewan looks at his fairy godfather and shakes his head. "I never had any interest."

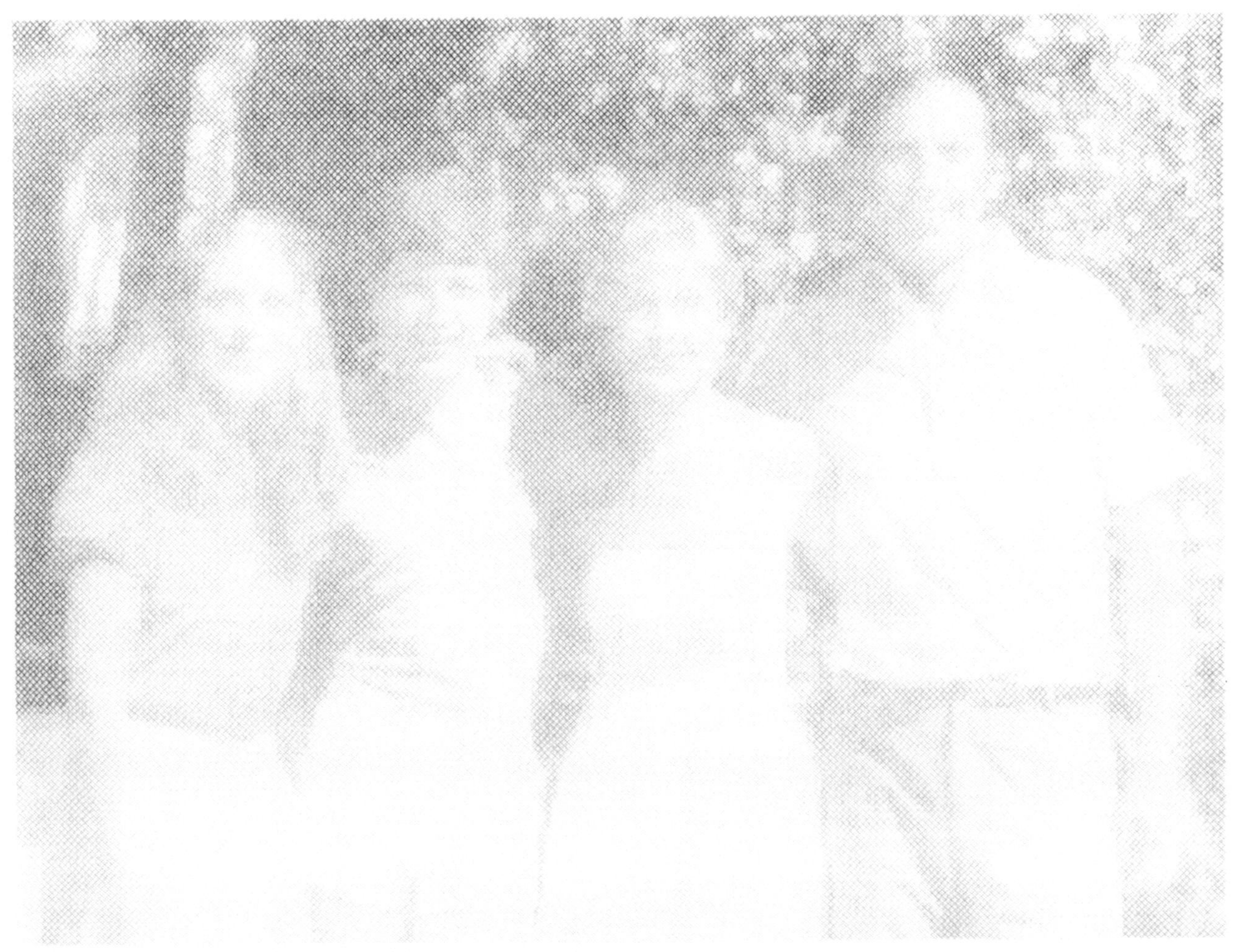

Ewan Gibbs, *The Fuhrman Family*, 2018

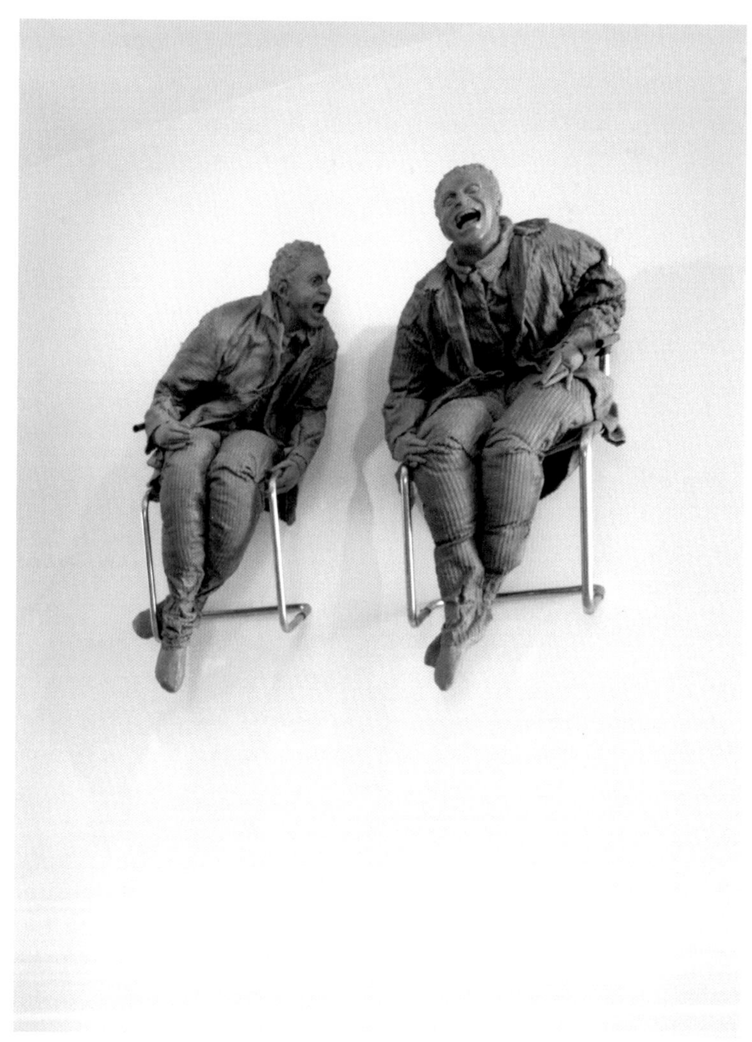

Juan Muñoz, *Two Laughing at Each Other*, 2000

A CONVERSATION

Sarah Douglas, Glenn Fuhrman, and Stephanie Roach

SARAH DOUGLAS: Let's get this out of the way: Why have you been so reticent to speak about FLAG, yourself, or your collection over the years?

GLENN FUHRMAN: I don't know. I've always observed that a lot of the people I most respect are press-shy. The less you talk, the higher the probability that a positive perception could develop. I think that once you do start talking, it can get addictive and then you will do it more often and pretty soon you will be in the papers all the time. I definitely don't want that!

STEPHANIE ROACH: Do you think this is especially true in the financial services industry, where you spend most of your time?

GF: Yes, but I think that's true about most industries.

SD: Fair enough. Let's start with FLAG's name. I've always wondered: What does it stand for?

GF: I always tell people the name means nothing. I didn't want it to be called The Fuhrman Art Foundation, so I played around with the names of my family, and FLAG includes all the initials of all my family members: Fuhrman; my dad's name is Leon; my sister's name is Laura; my mom's name is Arlene; and my name is Glenn. It includes the original members of my family, though it was nice that [my wife] Amanda and [my daughter] Annabel both start with "A." I wouldn't have married Amanda if she didn't have a letter that worked with FLAG. [laughs] She passed the test.

SD: That's interesting, because your family wasn't quite as into art as you are.

GF: No, but I'm really close to my family; I love my family. I have a pretty firm view that everything I am and everything good I've done is because of things my parents did for me growing up. Even though they're not a collecting family, they appreciate art. My mom used to take me to museums all the time. My parents obviously influenced my appreciation for art, even if it was through early osmosis.

SD: In the foreword for the catalogue of your 2014 Roy Lichtenstein exhibition you did at FLAG, you mentioned that when you were growing up, you had a Lichtenstein poster in your bedroom. I hoped we could go back there, and talk about how you first became interested in art.

GF: When I think about my childhood and growing up, I remember my bedroom so well. It had this shiny, bright red wallpaper, and on the wallpaper I had a handful of things: one was the iconic Farrah Fawcett poster that I think every boy had back at that time, and then I had this Roy Lichtenstein poster for Aspen Winter Jazz.

SD: Did your parents have a connection to Aspen?

GF: No, my parents must have thought it was a beautiful work. My parents did have an interest in art. They weren't collectors, but they obviously liked art. We had a [Tom] Wesselmann poster in the basement. We had a couple of [David] Hockney things, we had Alex Katz—all posters or lithographs. I remember going to museums with my parents, and I didn't hate it, but I don't remember loving it either.

SD: You did a project in second grade about [Andy] Warhol and Lichtenstein.

GF: Yes, and I know it still exists somewhere in my home because my parents saved it. I remember I used blue, yellow, and orange construction paper in that 8½-by-11 format; one page would have a picture of a beautiful Warhol and one would have a Lichtenstein. I don't remember what points I was making, but that was my book project.

SD: And your parents had no connection to art—I mean, professionally?

GF: My father was a carpet salesman/entrepreneur, and my mom was a retired teacher at the time.

SD: When did you first take art history?

GF: When I decided to go to Wharton for undergrad, I knew I would be taking finance, statistics, and accounting, and I thought there weren't going to be that many girls in those classes. So, I took Art History 101—and maybe I'd meet some girls. [laughs]

I took it first semester freshman year. It was a giant four-hundred-person seminar class. I took it pass/fail because I didn't want any pressure, and I ended up loving it and got an A+. Then I took Art History 102 or 101B the next semester for a grade, and I got an A in that too. I fell in love with the art stuff. I graduated with a finance major having taken three finance classes and eleven art history classes, including a semester in London, where I studied nothing but art history.

SD: Where did you study in London?

GF: At UCL [University College London], and one of my professors was [National Gallery of Art curator] Lynne Cooke. She was an amazing teacher.

SD: That must have been before she was at the Dia Art Foundation.

GF: Oh, way before—this was in the '80s. And I also had the very well-known British art historian John White as a professor, and he was spectacular.

SD: Were you specializing in a particular period of art history?

GF: My favorites were basically Renaissance and Flemish; I loved the Flemish artists Hans Memling, Jan van Eyck, and Rogier van der Weyden. It was mostly Christian iconography, so I was learning about all this Christian stuff, which was kind of fun and fascinating. I ended up taking the very famous Leo Steinberg class on Michelangelo at Penn, which was three hours long, once a week; it was brilliant, unbelievable. Every class was based on completely new research that he had done, and it was spellbinding to be in his class. I think that was the highlight of my art history studies. I even remember my mom came down from New York for one class, and we went together. That's a great memory for me.

SR: You interviewed Leo years later. I went to that interview when I was a senior [at the University of Pennsylvania].

GF: Five or six years after I graduated, when I became a trustee of the ICA [Institute of Contemporary Art, Philadelphia], I started a lecture series at Penn and Leo Steinberg came back to speak at one of them.

SD: At the time you were taking Steinberg's class, you were majoring in finance. Did you think eventually you'd become a collector? When I was studying art history in college, I asked a fellow student if she was going to continue in art history and she said, "No, I'm going to go into finance so I can collect the stuff." Is that something you were thinking about then?

GF: Definitely not. I don't think I even knew what a collector was. I had worked at Salomon Brothers, in finance, after my freshman and sophomore years and enjoyed it, but I obviously was developing this passion for art history, and I thought I should work in art because maybe I would want to do that after I graduated. So after my junior year, I got a job as a summer intern at Sotheby's. [The art dealer] Marianne Boesky was in my intern program. I had a great summer, but I didn't enjoy it as a job. There was something about it that felt impure to me. The part of art that I really loved wasn't about selling it, it was more about being around it. I didn't want to work in the art world, but it was very important to have had the experience at Sotheby's to help me realize that. After my junior year, I went to get my MBA at Wharton Business School—I never had a senior year in college—and started working at Goldman Sachs in between my two years in business school. After I graduated, I worked at Goldman Sachs full-time.

SD: Was it at Goldman Sachs that you discovered you wanted to collect?

GF: I was surrounded by all these photographs at work because both Bob [Mnuchin] and Dick Menschel were these incredible collectors of photography. They had their collection on the walls of Goldman Sachs, and they happened to be all around my office. It wasn't an office—I was a peon—it was a cubicle.

SD: Which is interesting, because these days you show a lot of your collection in your office.

GF: Exactly. Among the works that I really loved, beyond the Flemish and Renaissance works, I loved the New York School. I loved [Mark] Rothko, Clyfford Still, and Franz Kline. And there was one group of photographs that was of all those artists, so I saw portraits of Clyfford Still, [Jackson] Pollock, and Rothko, and they were all taken by this guy Arnold Newman, who I had never heard of, but I saw on the wall plate who he was. I really wasn't enjoying my job at that time; in fact, I hated my job at Goldman.

SD: This was when?

GF: I graduated from business school in 1988 so this was '89/'90.

SD: Why did you hate it?

GF: The job function. I was in high-net-worth sales, and I was cold-calling rich people. I wasn't cut out for it. But having said that, one day I cold-called Arnold Newman (I got his number from the phone book). I said, "Hi, is this Arnold Newman?" And he said, "Yes." And I said, "Are you a photographer?" And he said, "Yes." And I said, "Well, my name is Glenn Fuhrman and I'm twenty-three years old and I'm surrounded by your work at my office every day, and I would love a chance to come say hello. Would that ever be possible?" He kind of paused and said, "Okay, well, do you want to come over today at 5:00?" I said, "Okay, great." He was living on the Upper West Side. I was living in a studio apartment, and I went up there that afternoon. We totally hit it off, it was like hanging out with my grandparents; he was in his seventies. He introduced me to his wife. She said, "You're staying for dinner." I said, "Okay, great. I'm staying for dinner."

He walked me through his whole history; he showed me all of these images. He had taken pictures of every president since [Franklin] Roosevelt and had spent time with the Beatles and Martin Luther King, Jr.—everybody and every artist you could ever imagine. And so, the next day I bought two photographs from his dealer. I knew that you don't buy directly from the artist, so I called up. One was a portrait of [Pablo] Picasso and one was of Franz Kline. I still have them up in my office. And I was like, this is cool, how fun was that? I got to meet the guy and now I have two great works hanging in my apartment.

SD: So how did that become an interest in contemporary art?

GF: Well, you couldn't call up Rogier van der Weyden and say, "Hey, can I come over and say hello?" And I loved that direct contact with the artist. So I started calling other photographers whose work was on my floor at Goldman Sachs. I called Duane Michals. He said, "Come on over." I didn't buy anything at the time, but I had a great time with him. I eventually called Roy Lichtenstein. I couldn't touch anything there as a collector, but it was a magical experience—I went into that famous studio. He was so warm and engaging. From there, I started going to galleries every weekend and seeing a lot of art.

SD: For a newbie collector it's difficult to get access to dealers these days. What was it like then?

GF: It was pretty closed then as well—even more so, I would say. When I went to galleries, they literally wouldn't talk to me. I would walk in and ask how much a work cost and they would be like, "We don't know the prices." They wouldn't even have a conversation. Going to galleries in New York was painful; I was slowly becoming a collector, and they wouldn't even talk to me.

My real collecting started when my friend Lora Reynolds said that I needed to come to [Art] Basel, in Switzerland, because that is where all the action happens. I went to Basel and I was blown away by it; I had never seen anything like it before. She introduced me to Anthony d'Offay, and then everything changed. He really took me under his wing because he saw the passion that I had. I also met other dealers at the fair.

For the next several years after that, I was collecting very actively. I was buying a lot of things from dealers in Europe because they were happy to sell to me. They were fantastic. They had access to great work, and I paid quickly. And I wasn't buying super expensive works.

SD: Art fairs were different back then . . .

GF: It wasn't quite the event it is today. Now it's the opposite; now I don't love going to art fairs at all. For me, I don't think that there are as many great new things to buy at fairs—or it's very rare that there is. It was much more so twenty years ago.

SD: Could you talk more about your relationship with Anthony d'Offay?

GF: Anthony was fantastic to me. We had this close bond, and he recognized a passion in me that, in his opinion, was legitimate. He started off doing some great things for me. I sat next to him at every art auction in New York, at Christie's and Sotheby's. For years, I never bought anything, I just watched him and learned by watching and asking him questions. It was incredible.

He introduced me to a lot of his artists, and I started collecting them. We celebrated Rachel Whiteread's fortieth birthday together. I had a lot of unique art experiences with him. I got to know Ron Mueck well through him. I had become interested in some of the YBAs [Young British Artists] when I was studying at UCL in 1986. I think I'm the same age as Damien [Hirst], plus or minus, and Rachel Whiteread. All these artists were making art at the same time I was in London, and I was going to [Charles] Saatchi's gallery to see all his great art. Every time I went to London for Goldman when I worked there in the early '80s and '90s, I went to see Saatchi's shows and I was blown away. I went to Saatchi, not to the ICA or the Tate. Of course, there was no Tate Modern at that time—you just didn't see contemporary art in museums. Maybe in a gallery you would see one show and they were trying to sell you stuff, but not in the way that Charles put those beautiful shows together. There's definitely a connection between that and FLAG. I saw all of that happening and I had that in the back of my mind for a while, that I would like to do something like that—less my own collection, but wanting to put on great shows.

SD: But you've never worked with an art adviser?

GF: No, never.

SD: Or a personal curator? Why?

GF: I never felt I needed one. I wanted to make all my own mistakes if I needed to make any. I spend my free time going to galleries, building relationships with dealers, and traveling to see shows; I've enjoyed the process of being involved and making selections myself. Some people use an adviser if they don't live in New York or don't see enough shows and someone can help them see what they're not seeing; I've never needed to do that. I want to be the one involved from the ground up wherever I can. You need to develop the relationships with the dealers, and it takes a lot of effort, because for most good shows there are more people who want to buy than there is supply. You need to work with dealers and the people who work at the gallery and know the timing of upcoming shows, when works are going to be available, if they can send you JPEGs (or not), and when they are going to be installed. It takes a lot of work. I'm not as active as I used to be because I don't have as much time. I prefer to spend time with my kids on the weekends now. Also, I'm not collecting as voraciously as I used to. If I miss something, it's not the end of the world.

SD: When did you begin collecting individual artists in depth?

GF: From the very beginning, I wanted to collect artists in depth. Even that Arnold Newman experience: I bought two, I didn't buy just one. I wanted to tell a story and stay with each artist over time. Anthony introduced me to Ed Ruscha early on, and I was buying a lot of Ruscha. Every time he had a show, I would buy something.

The only change with my collection, as my walls have gotten filled and I've gotten older, is just to refine my art selection. And the marginal purchase is a bit tougher for me, because I already have every wall covered. And now that things are so expensive, you have to limit your purchases. You can't be as casual as I was earlier on.

SD: Gerhard Richter is an artist you have collected in depth—not an easy task. What was the first Richter you acquired?

GF: It was from Barbara Mathes at Basel; it was a spectacular abstract painting. It was on the secondary market, and it was a ton of money to me at the time. I thought it was ironic because Barbara Mathes Gallery was literally two blocks from where I was living at the time on Fifty-fifth Street—her gallery was on Fifty-seventh. I loved this painting and I bought it, and I still love it.

Then not too long after—maybe he had heard that I had bought it or something—[art dealer] Perry Rubenstein called me and said, "I have a great Richter and you should definitely buy this." It was a giant, red, incredibly beautiful abstract painting that was amazing. It was way above my budget, and I said that I just couldn't get it—I didn't have the money. And to his credit, Perry said, "You know, I think that this painting is perfect for you and I think that you can afford it. I'm going to send it to your apartment tomorrow. Live with it for a week, I'll pay for shipping, and if you don't buy it, I'll pick it up. But if you do, you don't have to take if off your wall." And I said, "All right, sounds like a fair deal." After living with it a few days, I said this is pretty spectacular and I ended up buying it. It's one of the most significant things I own. It's certainly something that has never not

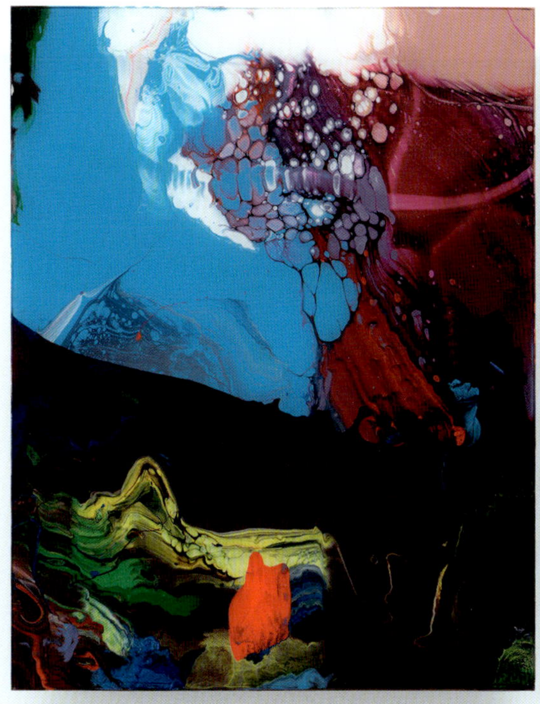

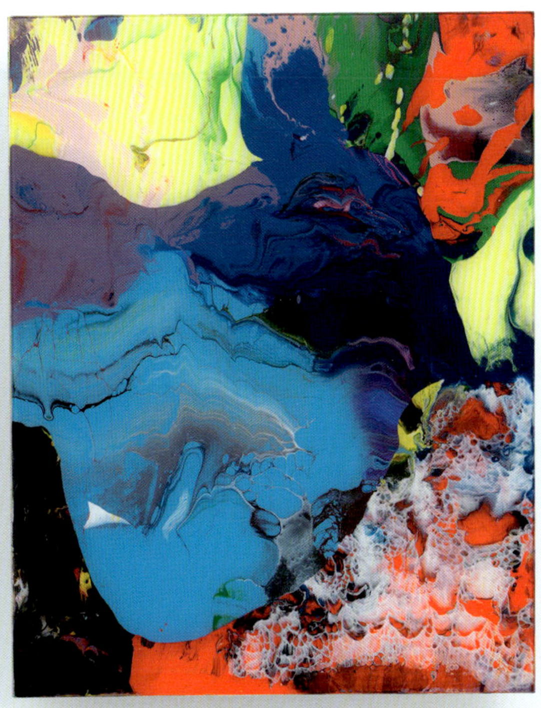

Detail, Gerhard Richter, *Sinbad*, 2008

been in my apartment, other than when it was at FLAG for one season. It's been there every day of my life since.

Back then, [Richter's dealer Marian] Goodman wasn't selling me anything, and I couldn't get in the door there. But you have to be your own advocate. I was, and I think I am still, a good salesman for myself as a buyer of contemporary art. The term "salesman" in that context sounds awful, but I'm a believer in the power of art. I love art. I love living with art. I think my intentions are good, and I'm able to convey that enthusiasm to dealers and artists in a way that comes through. Of course, this also works in bad ways where people personally advocate for themselves and buy something and then sell it at Phillips the next year. And they don't get to buy something again. You only have one chance to ruin your reputation, and thankfully I have never done that.

SD: As a collector, do you feel very separate from the pressures some feel to sort of play the art market?

GF: Very. Keep in mind, I recently sold the first thing ever after twenty-five years of collecting; for the most part, I've never sold anything. I recently sold some things because I wanted to buy something else, so I did a swap, but in general I don't sell. So, a lot of dealers call me and say, "Hey, I can sell you this hot artist and it will be worth twice as much tomorrow, massive demand, and I want you to have it because I want to start a relationship with you." And I say, "Thanks, but I'm not interested in that artist and I have no interest in buying to sell in six months for more money." That approach to collecting never had any appeal for me.

SD: When I first saw your collection, during the Armory Show in 2005 or 2006, I remember vividly that in the living room there were these blue-chip masterpieces. I went down this hallway and there in an office or den was a piece by an emerging artist, Alex McQuilkin, a very edgy video, this new, untested thing among this solid blue-chip stuff.

GF: I paid $500 for that video, and I still love looking at it. I've made it a goal to collect both blue-chip artists and less well-known ones, but always in a very targeted and in-depth way. I don't collect a thousand young artists hoping that 10 percent become successful. I'm not disparaging that type of collector, but that's not what I was doing. There were younger artists who I liked that I bought in depth. I still to this day collect the same way. Awol Erizku is a young artist who I collect very actively. Ewan Gibbs is also an artist I collect actively—not a super well-known artist. He makes great works, only makes five or six pieces a year.

SD: You mainly buy from dealers, rather than auction.

GF: I mainly work with dealers, and it's a shrinking number of dealers because you can only be important to so many people. Now, Larry [Gagosian] is one of my favorite people to buy from, because I have a very good relationship with him and it's always no-nonsense. I feel like I have a very straight relationship with him. Just like in my business, I like a "fast no" over a "delayed maybe." He runs it like a business; if your schedule is weird and you want to go see something in the gallery at 4 a.m., he won't even think twice. It's not just for me or a big collector—they operate to accommodate clients. I stopped into another favorite gallery of mine today to see a particular show I had been excited to see, and the person at the desk said, "Sorry, you can't come in. We're closed on Mondays." I wasn't going to mention my name or try to "pull strings," but my feeling is that I'm here, you're here, and I can take a fast look. She said, "No, you can't come in." Fine. I don't think that would happen at Gagosian.

I also have great relationships at Matthew Marks, the most artist-focused dealer I've ever met. No matter what I want, if it's better for the artist to sell it to someone else, I have no shot with Matthew. Having said that, I get to buy more than my fair share, and he has helped me shape my collection more than any other dealer. When I recently analyzed my collecting history, I found that I've bought significantly more art from Matthew than any other dealer.

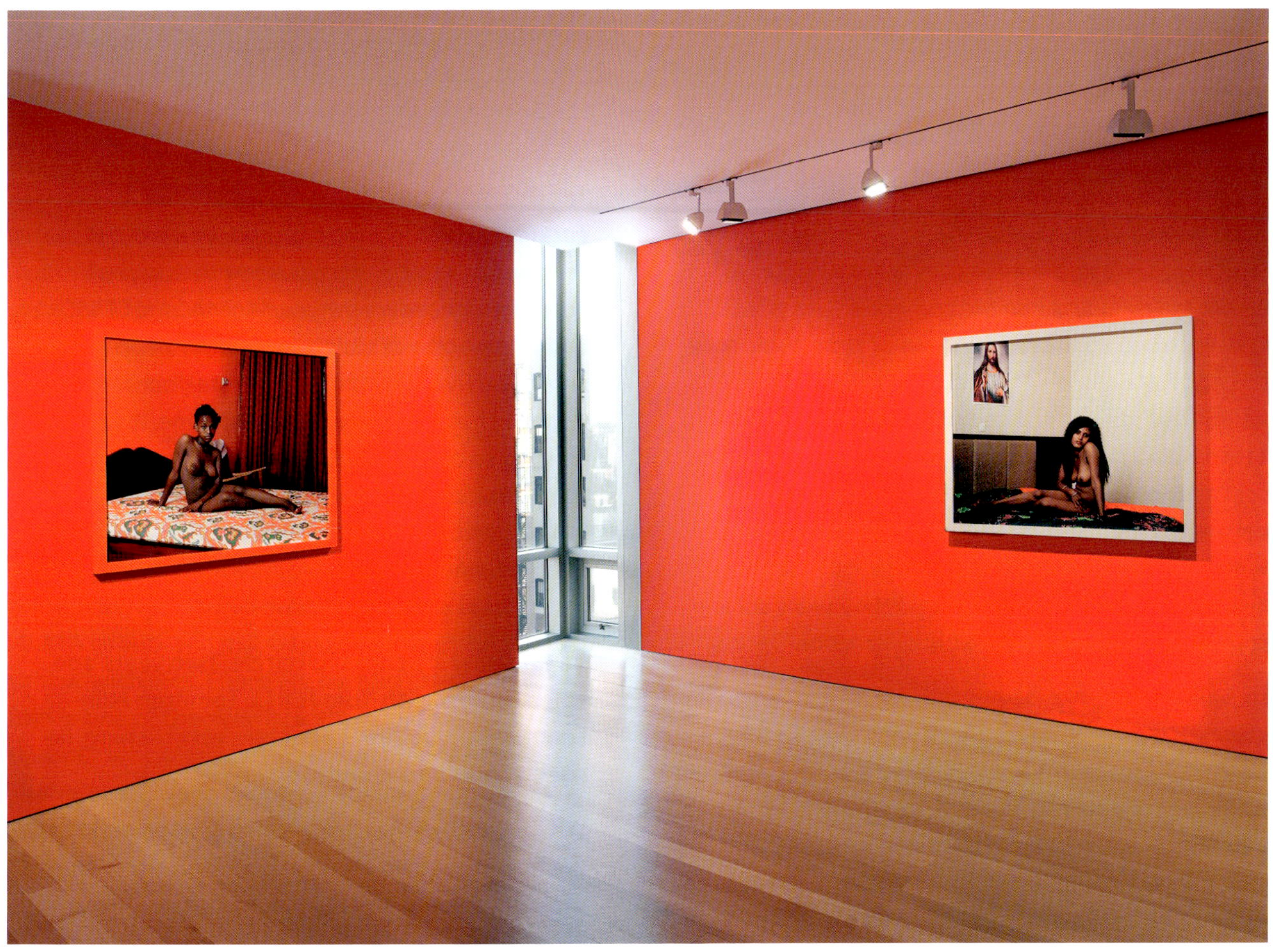

Installation view, *Awol Erizku: New Flower / Images of the Reclining Venus*

Marian Goodman is also super supportive, and I love dealing with her—a class act in every way. I've had similar great experiences with Jay Jopling, who sold me many fantastic pieces over the years.

The list of dealers I enjoy buying from is actually quite large, and I consider myself very lucky to be able to say that. That includes many younger gallerists who are in the earlier stages of building their businesses.

SD: When you had the idea for FLAG, what type of space were you looking for, and what was the search like? Did you always know you wanted it to be in Chelsea, or were you looking at other neighborhoods?

GF: FLAG became more and more of a real possibility in 2005–06. At that time, maybe because I had more success and more financial ability to consider opening something like this, I heard about a building in Chelsea that was not even built yet. It was an empty parking lot at the time, and I thought it could be interesting. I then spoke with Jack Guttman, who was developing the building,

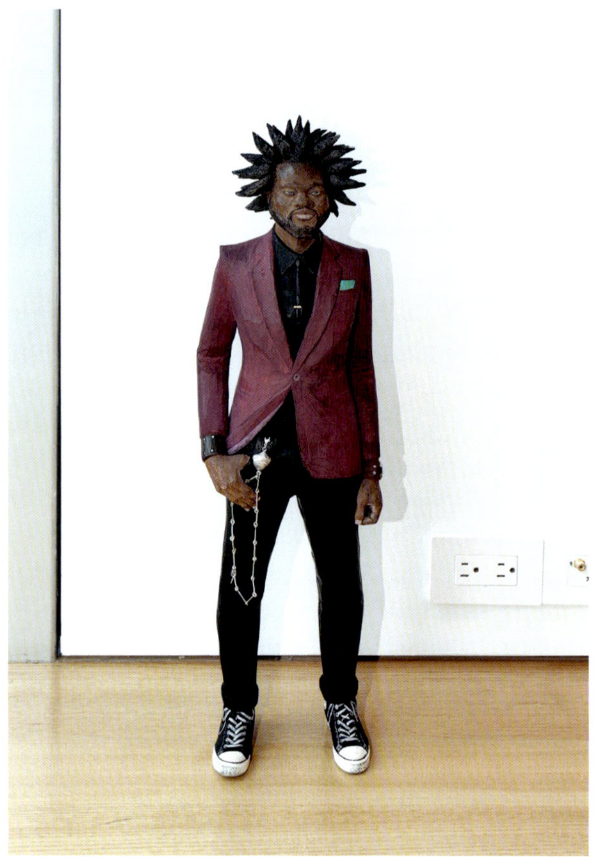

Installation view, *SIZE DOES MATTER*, showing Tomoaki Suzuki, *Shaka*, 2010

I love the Jim Hodges/Felix Gonzalez-Torres show [*Floating a Boulder: Works by Felix Gonzalez-Torres and Jim Hodges*, 2009]; that was very special. The Ashley Bickerton [2017] show was great because it was a solo show and he's never had a big survey like that in the United States. He and I did that all via Facebook, because he's in Bali.

I also loved the Cynthia Daignault show [*Cynthia Daignault: There is nothing I could say that I haven't thought before*, 2017]. Hers was certainly among the most fun shows I've done in the past ten years. She's a brilliant person and an incredibly talented artist. She put together a beautiful show, and we worked very intimately together on it. FLAG is totally summed up in that exhibition. To hear myself say that my seminal show was Cynthia Daignault, versus the Ed Ruscha show [*WALL ROCKETS*, 2009] or the Chuck Close show [*Attention to Detail*, 2008]—and those were all spectacular as well—is kind of telling even to me. That's what it's all about: working with an artist who is not as well known, who put together a spectacular show that had huge attendance and everyone really enjoyed, and it made them think. It was a great four months.

SD: How did the Hodges/Gonzalez-Torres show come about?

GF: We wanted to work with Jim as a curator, because I've collected him in depth and he's become a close friend. I knew he had had this great relationship with Felix, and a lot of Jim's work is in direct dialogue with some of Felix's. We had worked with some great artist-curators before; as I mentioned, Chuck Close curated our first show. I asked Jim if he would be willing to curate a show, and I had to work a little bit to convince him why I thought it was a good idea. He eventually was excited about it. In dealing with any great artist, you have to be prepared to work with them on their terms. I don't think there was anything Jim wanted to do that we weren't able to accomplish for him, including having a live go-go dancer on a regular schedule.

SR: That was a big moment in our history and we were able to secure loans from MoMA, SFMOMA, the Art Institute of Chicago, and the Cleveland Museum of Art. There were also works from

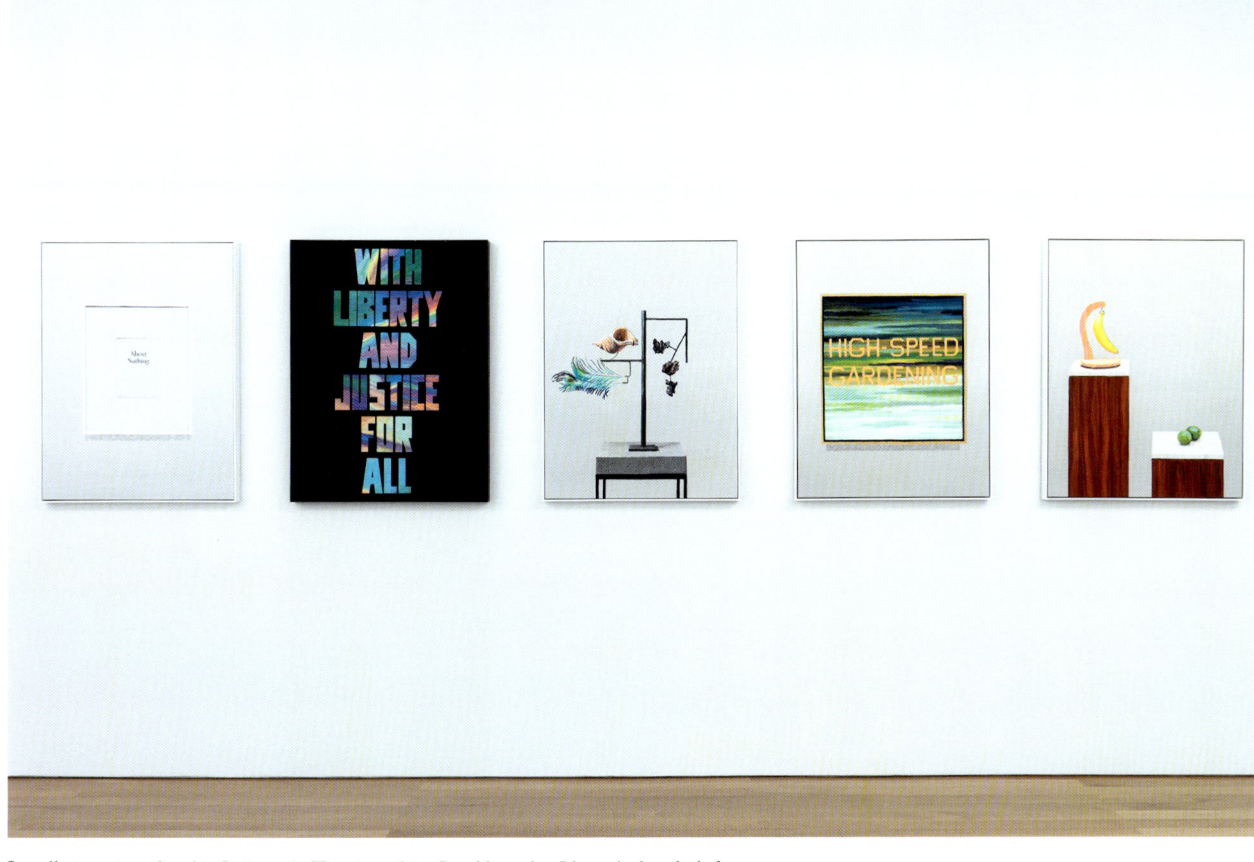

Installation view, *Cynthia Daignault: There is nothing I could say that I haven't thought before*

private collections. That was a big turning point in terms of our credibility and being able to branch out and do bigger loan-based shows.

SD: You identified the writer Linda Yablonsky as someone you wanted to curate a show; she had never curated before.

GF: This is directly related to my career and building MSD Capital with my partner, John [Phelan]. The most important thing we focus on in the success we've had at MSD is our ability to identify talented people and work with them to allow them to do the things they want to do—supporting them and collaborating on success. I had gotten to know Linda; I really liked her, and I thought she was fun and kind and eclectic and would be fun to work with. And I said, "Linda, why don't you curate a show for us?" And she laughed and said, "No one has ever asked me to curate, and I've kind of always wanted to curate." And I said, "This is your chance. Let's do it."

SD: And, of course, you don't exclusively do exhibitions of artists you collect. For instance, you did a big survey of Ashley Bickerton, whom you haven't collected. How did it come about?

GF: I've always liked his work dating back to the '80s, though I've never bought anything. We're

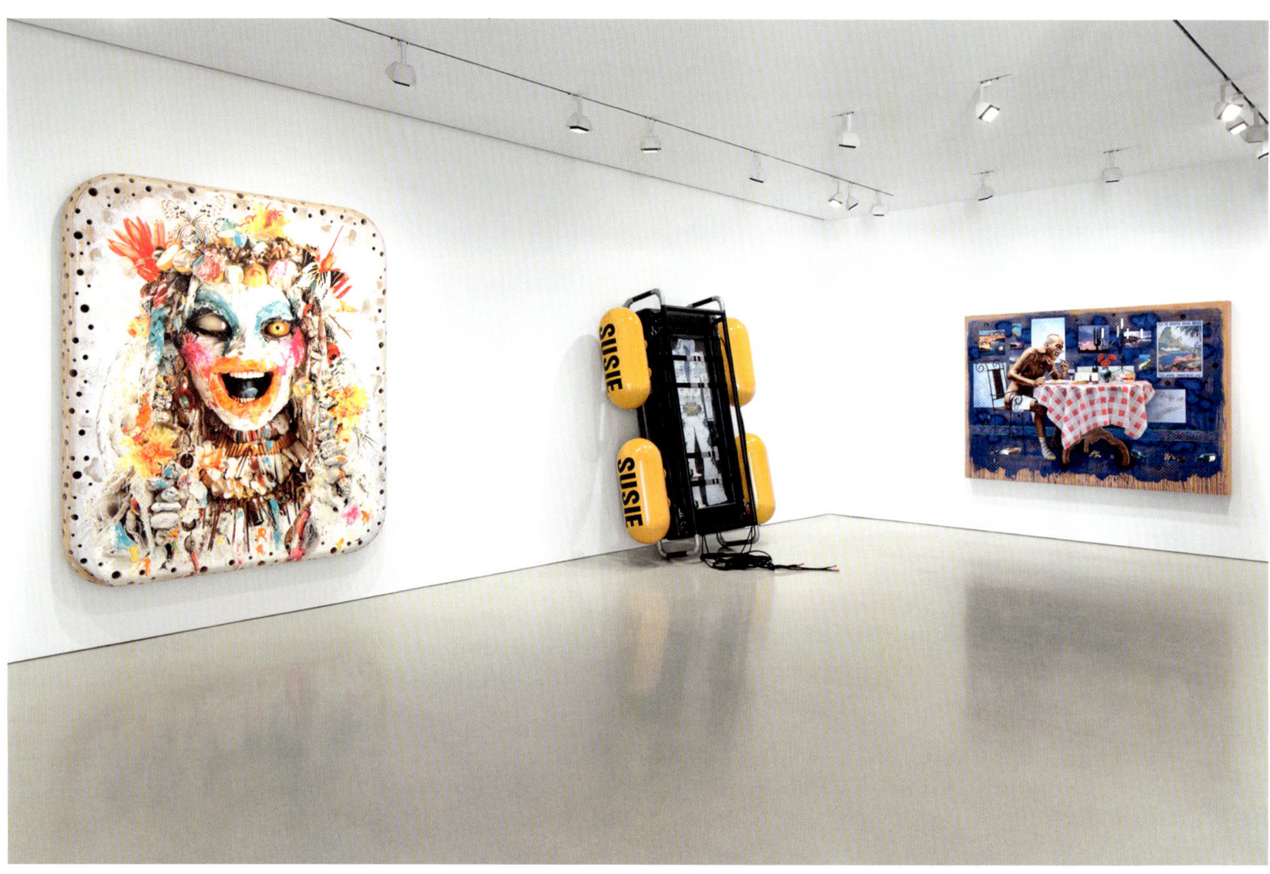

Installation view, *Ashley Bickerton*, showing *White Head II*, 2012; *Seascape: Floating Costume to Drift for Eternity III (Elvis Suit)*, 1992; and *L.W.S. 1*, 2000

friends on Facebook—he's very active on Facebook. I mean, he lives in Bali, so I wasn't going to go visit him at the studio. We developed this chitchat over Facebook, and he mentioned that he had never had a retrospective in America. I thought wow, FLAG could really do a good show for someone who has never had a major noncommercial show here. And I said, "Let's work on it." And he said, "Well, I want you to know Damien Hirst is working on something in London." [Hirst opened a show of Bickerton's work at his Newport Street Gallery in April 2017.] I thought, "Well, okay, that's far away from New York, so it's not really relevant." And then it all came together.

SD: What about Louis Grachos [Executive Director and CEO of The Contemporary Austin]—how did you get him involved with curating for FLAG?

GF: I meet people through being involved in the art world. I was on the board of the Hirshhorn, am on the board of MoMA, the ICA Philly, and I go to a lot of museums; I know almost all the museum directors. I was on Dia's board, so I know Michael Govan from there. I've respected Louis for a long time; I met him when I was involved at the Hirshhorn. I took a group of artists up to the Albright-Knox in Buffalo, which was a super fun time. The impetus was to see a major Jim Hodges outdoor sculpture they had just unveiled. The artists and Amanda and I went to Niagara Falls,

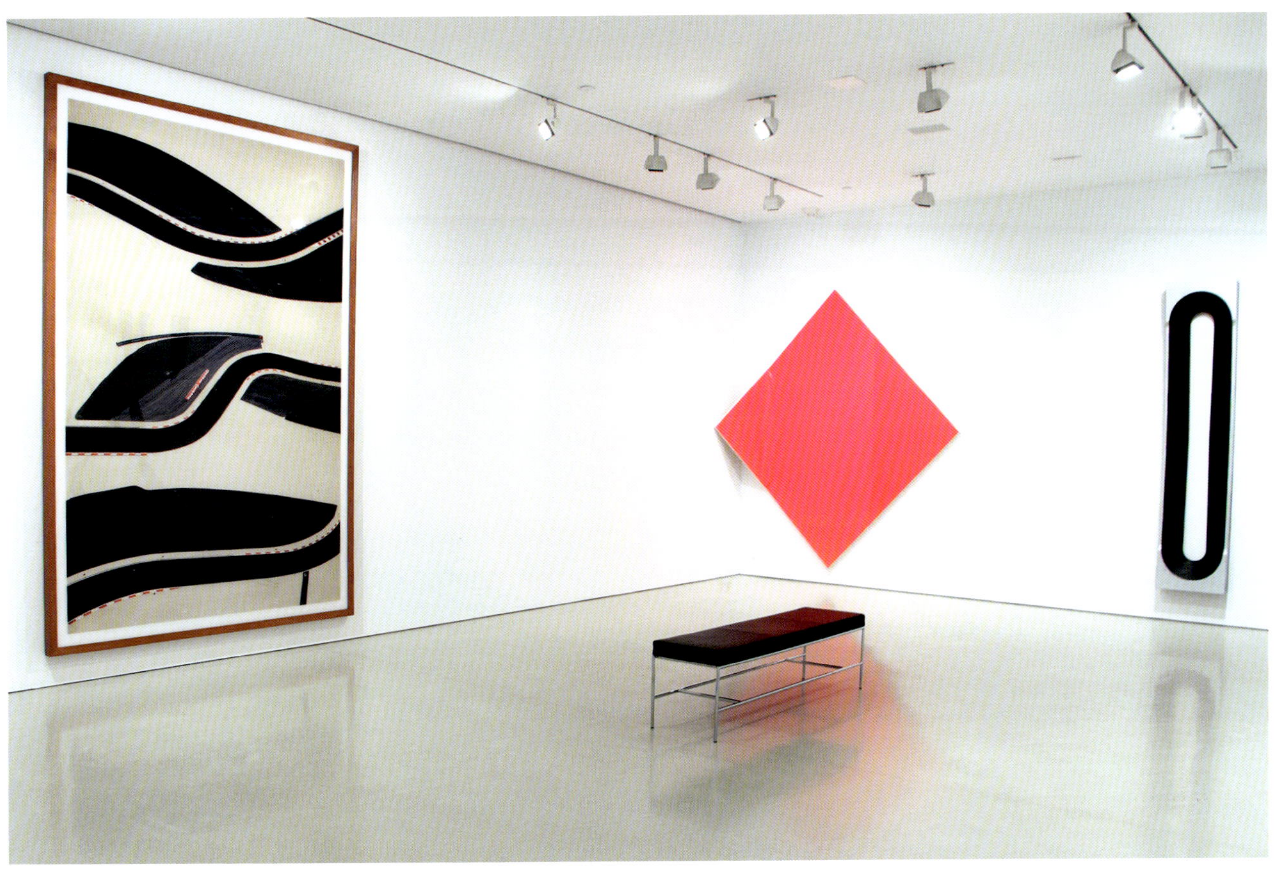

Installation view, *Space Between*, showing Andreas Gursky, *Bahrain II*, 2007; Kaz Oshiro, *Untitled Still Life*, 2013; Blair Thurman, *Mr. Freeeze*, 2015

spent the weekend together, and looked at Frank Lloyd Wright houses, and Louis arranged these great collection visits. It was a fabulous weekend and solidified a great relationship with Louis.

When he went to The Contemporary Austin—I was involved as a reference to help make that happen, though that sounds more involved than I was—we stayed in touch and did different things, naturally. I know Olga Viso because she was the director at the Hirshhorn when I was on the board. I love Annie Philbin from the Hammer. I don't know exactly how I know Annie, but our paths have crossed a hundred times. I have a lot of respect for her. Overall, the art world is pretty small, and you almost feel like you know everyone.

SD: Grachos curated *A Secret Affair: Selections from the Fuhrman Family Collection*, which opened at The Contemporary Austin [2014] and traveled to FLAG [2015]. In the catalogue, he wrote, "The primal need to connect with ourselves or others and the volatile nature of intimacy, complicated by protection and imprisonment, tenderness and aggression, isolation and togetherness are themes explored throughout the artworks in *A Secret Affair*." Does that ring true to you, in terms of the artworks you've collected?

GF: Those are all issues that are definitely relevant to my life—and all of our lives—and definitely my collection. Collecting contemporary art is an opportunity to collect things that speak to you in some way, that reflect on your own existence and your own experience in this crazy world of ours. It's for sure a part of why I collect the art of my lifetime. It resonates with me more about my world than collecting something from a hundred years ago, for example.

SD: Tell me about one of the most challenging exhibitions you've put on at FLAG.

GF: The Shaquille O'Neal show [*SIZE DOES MATTER*, 2010] was challenging. Shaquille is a super busy guy. He lives in Orlando. It was difficult to coordinate. He was an active player at the time with the Cleveland Cavaliers. I remember our first meeting was after one of their games. To his credit, he showed up on time without any entourage—literally just meandered into the restaurant to eat dinner with Stephanie and me after he had finished a game. We also had to borrow a piece [by Ron Mueck] from the Hirshhorn—one of the museum's prize possessions. And the Robert Therrien [*Untitled (Table and Six Chairs)*, 2003] was challenging to get into the space. We rigged it in—not the whole piece, but the top part. They had to close down a portion of Twenty-fifth Street to accommodate an entire crew to lift it up to the terrace.

SD: I can think of two FLAG exhibitions that were built around one artwork. In one case, it was an Ellsworth Kelly [*Space Between*, 2015], and in another a Robert Gober [*personal, political, mysterious*, 2013]. Are there others?

GF: Even I would admit that the Shaquille O'Neal show really started because I wanted to do a show with the Robert Therrien huge table and chairs. It was the first and it might be the only piece I've ever bought that I knew I could never live with. So I came up with the idea of "size does matter" before we had Shaquille O'Neal, and it was largely to show that piece. Then we found the curator to fit that piece. The photo of Shaq sitting in the giant chair is probably the most "famous" FLAG photo we have.

SR: If you look at Linda's show [*Something About a Tree*, 2013], *Disturbing Innocence* [2014–15] with Eric Fischl, and the Heidi Zuckerman show [*Funny.*, 2012], those are instances in which we selected the curator and let them have free rein, which marked a transition in our approach.

Eventually, we started thinking beyond curator-driven shows, which is also a testament to Glenn's style of collecting. How could we deepen a relationship with a specific artist and help them realize their vision? In 2011, Josephine Meckseper's show was our first major solo exhibition in which we fabricated a lot of the work. That was a major commitment. There are certain artists since then who we have chosen to provide with that level of support.

GF: And to have artists curate. Even for artists that I know, it's nice to work with them in a different way. Like Eric Fischl—I had known him a long time, I'm friendly with him personally and we used to play tennis together, but I don't collect his work. Having him as a curator was a nice way to work with him in a new context.

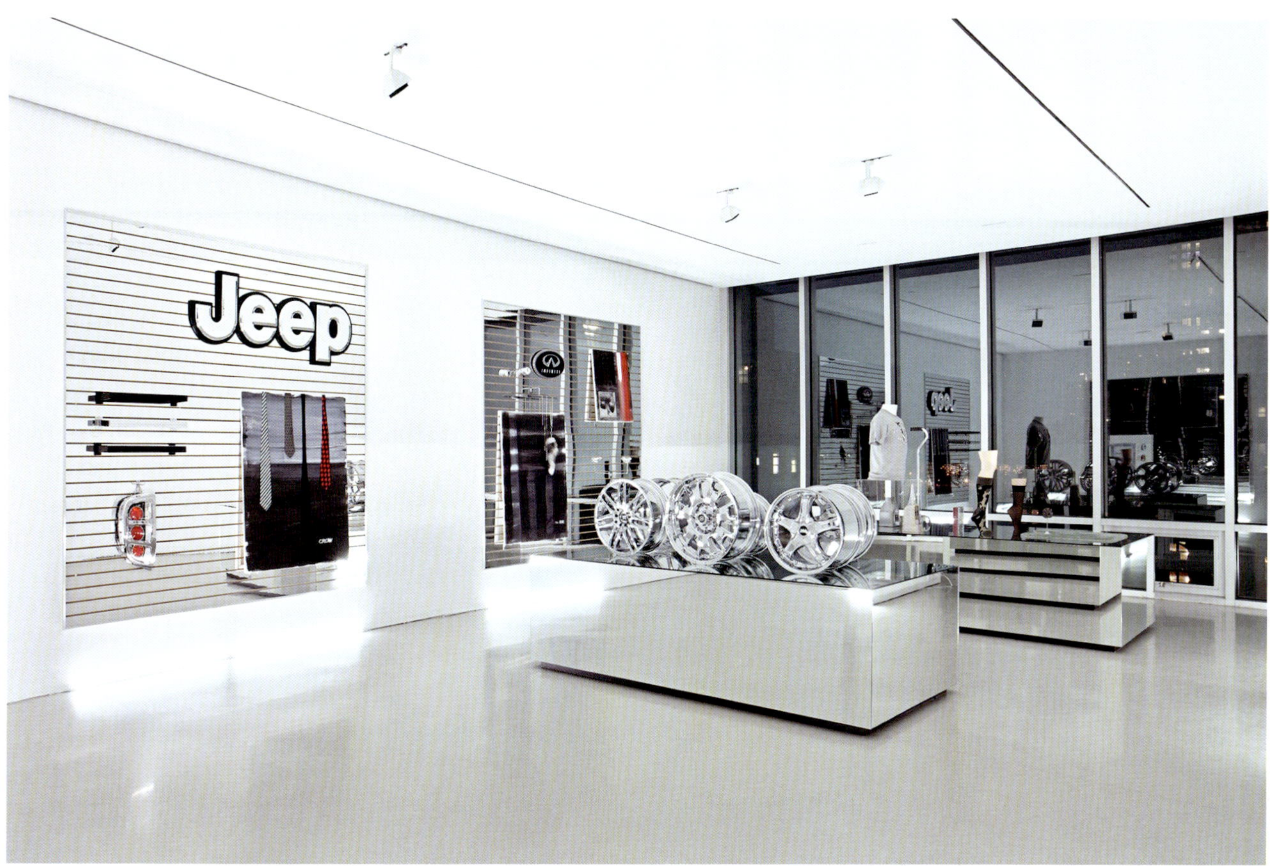

Installation view, *Josephine Meckseper*

And back to your other question, when we built a show around that Gober sink [*Untitled*, 2012], I had bought that work and wanted it to be in a show at FLAG, and so that was part of the process.

SD: It's a really interesting sink.

GF: It is unusual. The Richter hundred-panel painting—we also wanted that in a show, and so that's been in two shows. I love that work, and I can't put it in my apartment with our little children, so it was great to have it up at FLAG.

SD: The first time you showed it was on FLAG's second floor, and there was this couch positioned right in front of it and a table where a person could really contemplate the painting. I have to think that that was a conscious decision to have a contemplative environment.

GF: Very much so. As I was saying about your earlier question about Richter, when I first walked into that exhibition at Marian Goodman Gallery, I said to Marian, "That's the piece I'm really in love with." It wasn't an obvious choice, because it was something that had never been seen before—Gerhard had never done that before, the super colorful painting on glass. It was one hundred separate panels. It was a giant commitment. And she said, "Okay, it's not sold and it could be great for you. I'll have to talk to Gerhard, but it shouldn't be a problem." So I got excited, and she told me the price and said I got it. And then she called me and said, "Glenn, I need to talk to you about something," and I said, "Okay." And she said, "Gerhard thinks you're too young to own that piece." And I said, "What does that even mean?" And she said, "Well, he likes you a lot, but you're very young and he thinks it's really a museum piece or it should be in an institution and you're just too young." I was really devastated. I said, "Marian, I'm coming over to talk to you." I ran over to talk to her because her gallery is five blocks from my office, and I explained it. I said, "Marian, I'm really in love with this piece and you have to figure out a way. You know Gerhard, and you have to explain to him that I'm not that young. I look younger than I am. I'm not that young!" I really had a spirited conversation with her, and she said, "Okay, I'll see what I can do."

Ultimately, she called me back and told me, "Gerhard will let you have the painting." But now there's an additional component to that piece: when something like that happens, you feel an extra level of obligation, and I wanted that piece to be shown publicly at FLAG. I think it's one of the most important pieces he's made, and I'm very passionate about that work. But I also feel an extra sense of devotion to him for letting me buy it. Even though that sounds crazy, I'm particularly pleased that he let me buy it.

SD: One of the single greatest artworks that I remember seeing at FLAG was a stunning late Cy Twombly.

GF: That's another reason I created FLAG. I don't own that painting, I'll never own that painting—I would love to own that painting—but it was a chance for me to live with that painting for three months at FLAG. I remember that piece when it was shown at Gagosian Athens in the debut show there. I got an advance preview of those works. I called Larry and said, "Larry, I want one of these paintings, these are beautiful." And he said, "Glenn, you have to go to Athens. I'm only selling to people who go to Athens." I said, "Larry, I can't go to Athens. I have to work," and he said, "I'm sorry, then I can't sell you the painting." I knew there were other beautiful paintings, and this one wasn't meant to be. Then this opportunity came, and I could borrow it and have it in this show, and it looked amazing. It radiated off the wall.

The dealers have been really supportive of FLAG since the beginning. Cynical people might say that those dealers were selling art to me, and that may or may not be true, but we still couldn't put on these exhibitions without the loans, and the loans can't happen without the dealers. We don't know where anything is. So, we have to call the dealers and say we want to borrow that Etel Adnan or we want to borrow that Cy Twombly, and they have to help us figure out where the pieces are.

SD: You visited Cy Twombly shortly before his death. What was that like?

GF: Amanda and I have had two back-to-back personal visits to the homes of older artists who sadly died shortly thereafter. Cy Twombly invited us to his home in Gaeta in Italy, where Amanda

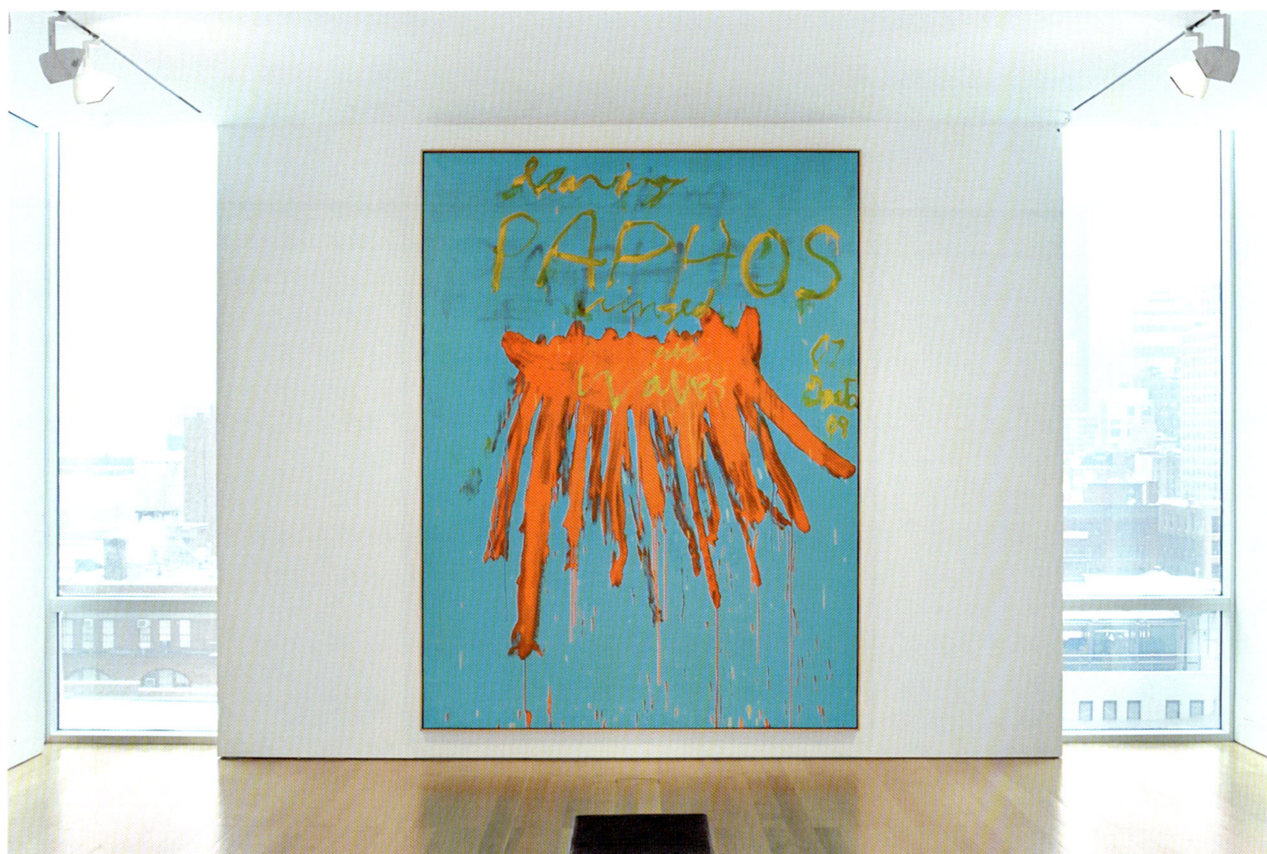

Installation view, *In Living Color*, showing Cy Twombly, *Leaving Paphos Ringed with Waves (IV)*, 2009

and I visited him and had an incredible experience. And we had gone to see Louise Bourgeois in her home/studio in New York; she died shortly thereafter as well. Both of those experiences were truly magical. The Edge and Bono joined us for the Bourgeois visit, and they sang to her a cappella. Hard to describe how amazing it was.

SD: You obviously enjoy speaking with artists.

GF: FLAG is a way for me to spend more time with artists. I really enjoy the company of artists, and I've always said it's a lot more fun to hang out with a group of artists than a group of bankers from Morgan Stanley.

SD: I've always been impressed that when you have events where an artist is interviewed onstage, you are doing the interview yourself.

GF: I love it, because it forces me to really prepare and educate myself on their practice, more than I would normally. You can't mess around. You have to do your homework, or it's not going to go well. It's fun to get to know an artist in a way that you might not have realized before, or hadn't fully appreciated. Over the years, I've interviewed almost every major artist out there: Ruscha, Ellsworth, Gober, John Currin, Lawrence Weiner, Alex Katz, etc. Only one artist has ever declined, literally only one: Cindy Sherman. She doesn't like to do interviews with anyone.

SD: There is this infectious sense of enthusiasm and curiosity when you are interviewing an artist.

SR: One of the first things Glenn wrote to me when I started to work with him was, "What we lack in experience we will make up for with enthusiasm and passion." He would always say to me, "Steph, you're the CEO—figure it out." There were a lot of different things that I learned on the job, and he really got his hands dirty alongside me.

He was and still is a laser-focused doer in every area of his life. I remember during one of the reviews of ideas for exhibitions he said, "You have to do a cost-benefit and ask yourself: what's the worst thing that can happen if I make this judgment?"

SD: How hands-on are you with FLAG? And how has that changed?

GF: It has definitely evolved. At first, I was very hands-on, but as time has gone on, I've had the luxury to be less hands-on because Stephanie and the team have done such a great job. I'm proud to say there have been some shows that I've seen for the first time at the opening. I still want to be connected and involved in certain ways, but I understand the power of delegation and empowering other leaders to do their job and do it well. I'm still involved in how we select shows and curators.

SD: Since FLAG started, it's done shows that don't just display art, but that respond in some way to, and support, the art ecosystem. It's not only about showing the art; it's about an interest in how the art world functions in supporting that ecosystem. When FLAG opened, in 2008, it was a dark time in the art world, during the global economic meltdown. Around that time, FLAG presented *Re-Accession: For Sale by Owner*, which dealt with how artists interact with the art market. In 2014, FLAG did *East Side to the West Side*, which was curated by dealers Rachel Uffner and James Fuentes, along with Brennan & Griffin, and emphasized collaboration during tough times for young and emerging galleries.

GF: There's no doubt that there's a culture and a family that exists within the art world and within FLAG: both artists who have shown with us, and curators with whom we've worked. We get a tremendous amount of support from the art community. And artists love coming to our shows, whether they've been in exhibitions at FLAG or not. They want to see good art, meet other artists, and be a part of the conversation. A great aspect of having FLAG is getting to work with artists in so many different contexts.

Jane Hammond, for example, who we had a show with years ago [2011], is a tremendously loyal visitor and comes to almost all our shows. She's one of many artists who keep coming and supporting us. You can't have a successful program without people coming and supporting the shows. And a lot of the people who come to the shows are from the art world and the art community, artists in particular. Part of that is because we've shown a lot of the same artists more than once. There's a little bit of a community that comes from that.

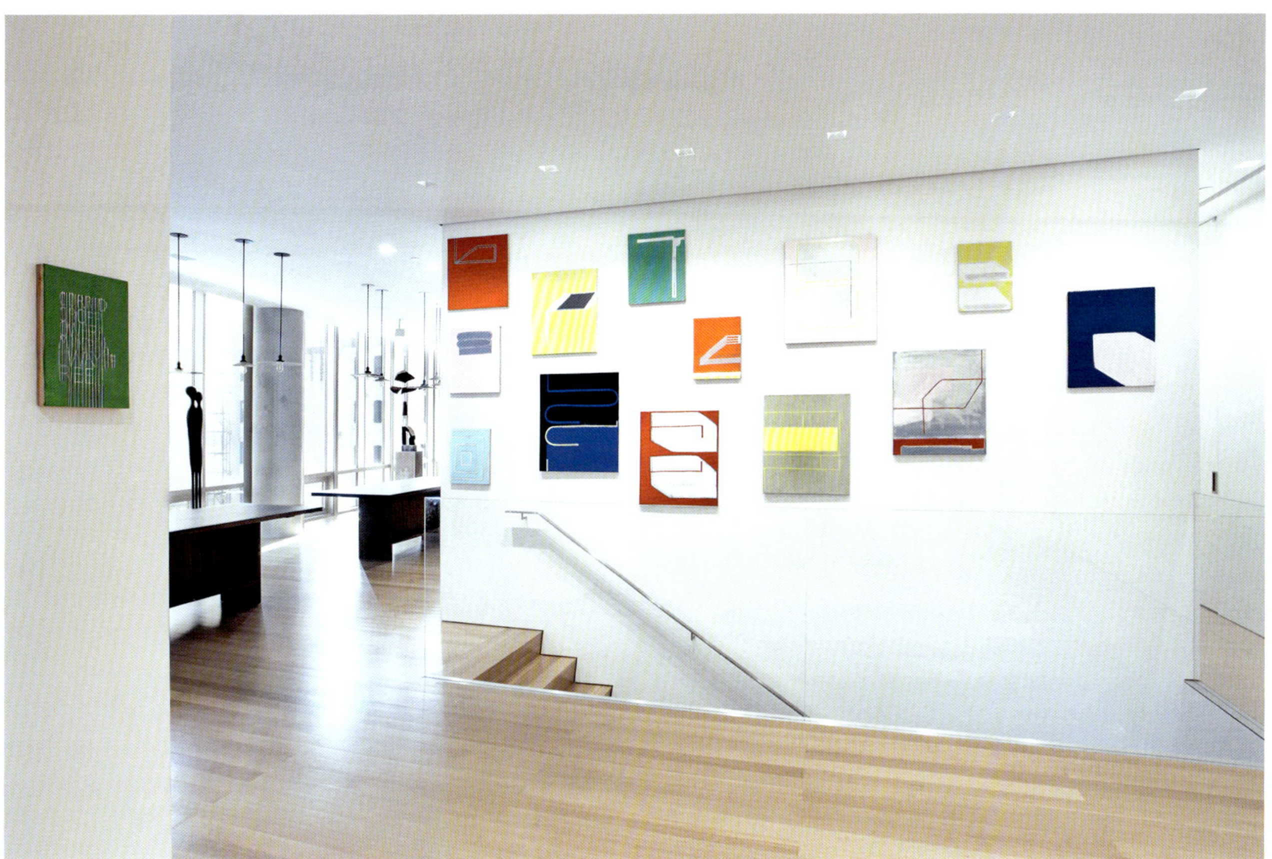

Installation view, *Re-Accession: For Sale by Owner*

SD: There's a group of artists you've had in many, many exhibitions at FLAG. Do you see yourself as a patron in the traditional sense?

GF: Not really, but I think that Ewan [Gibbs] sort of pitches it that way. As I advocate for myself with collecting, artists can be advocates for themselves. Ewan very specifically contacted me and said he wanted me to be his Lorenzo de' Medici. I had collected his work. He had two or three galleries at the time, but one went out of business and one he fired. He thought he had a great career with three galleries, and then he woke up one day and he had only one gallery, a young family and a wife, and he was worried about his ability to make a living. And that's when he said, "I love the idea of you being my Lorenzo de' Medici. Would you pay me a monthly stipend and you'll get first pick of everything I make? We'll both be happy because you'll get great works and I'll have a monthly income that I can rely on and use to support my family, and you obviously like my work because you've bought several works already." It seemed like a pretty sensible solution, and at that time, I liked the idea that I could support a good artist whose work I really loved. Not very long thereafter, I introduced him to [dealer] Tim Taylor and he said, "I love this artist," and he picked him up.

And then I introduced him to [dealer] Lora Reynolds, who picked him up—she has a gallery in Texas—and then Richard Gray Gallery picked him up, and Baldwin Gallery in Aspen. He was picked up by all these great galleries, so I said to Ewan that we could end this monthly situation. And he said, "Glenn, you don't understand. I really want this monthly thing to go on for the rest of my life. I love the fact that you get a piece from every show, but I also like the monthly income"—and we've raised the income over the years. It's a very powerful and great relationship. And I do now really consider Ewan a friend first and foremost.

SD: How else has FLAG changed over the past decade?

GF: Our audience has grown. We have a tremendous social media following—over 100,000 Instagram followers from all over the world—so now people get to experience FLAG and our perspectives without having to physically come to our space to see our shows. So that's cool.

SD: Instagram is not exclusively filled with pictures of what FLAG is doing; it's about going around and looking at other things.

SR: FLAG's associate director, Jon Rider, and I develop social media content together. If Glenn sees something great when he's at a gallery in London, or if I'm in LA, or Jon goes to the Met, we all try to find beauty in various places and different types of art spaces. It can go beyond art, too—it could even be fashion.

GF: On Instagram we recently started #WomeninFocus and #WomeninFocusatFLAG on Wednesdays to highlight current shows by women artists and curators. We feature women artists every day, but on Wednesdays it's only women. Our Instagram is basically a place to see contemporary art, and I think people like to follow us because it's a way for them to say, "Oh, I should go see that show." We don't have an MO.

SD: So, it's an exploration of visual culture through the eyes of FLAG?

SR: Yes, that's a great way of putting it.

SD: Would you say that FLAG's sensibility is synonymous with your sensibility?

GF: FLAG's sensibility has certainly been influenced by Stephanie, just as she has influenced my sensibility. Stephanie, for example, does a great job literally counting the number of women in every group show and highlighting to me how many we have. And if the artist list isn't balanced, we try to balance it, and we make sure our shows are as diverse as possible. I'm honestly happy we consider this; it leads to better shows. It's important that all institutions do that, because if we're not focusing on diversity and equal representation, it's too easy to fall back and have a bunch of white men putting up their work, which is not beneficial to anyone.

You shouldn't have a balance just to have a balance, but you need to have representation. I was extremely excited that when we were

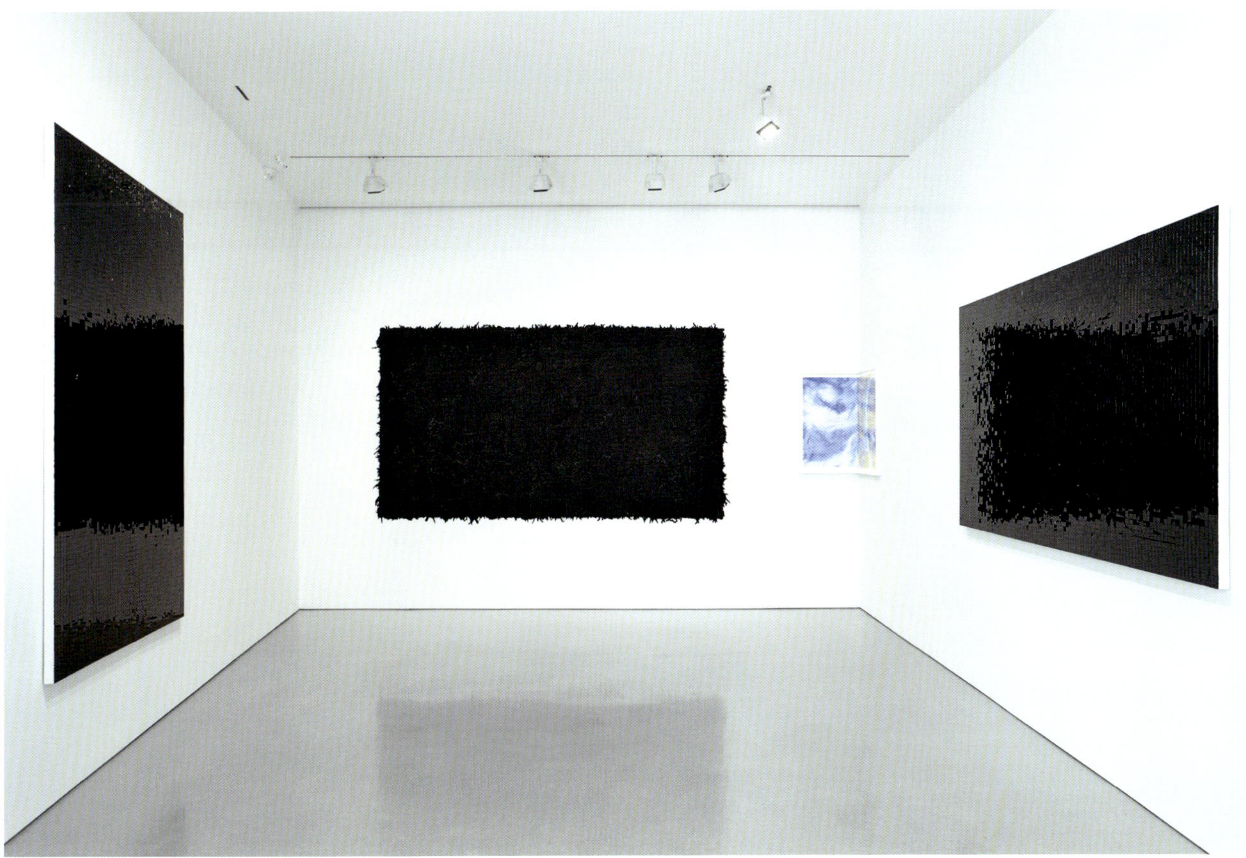

Installation view, *FLAG's 5th Anniversary Group Exhibition*, showing Jim Hodges, *First Light (Beginning of the End)*, 2010; *end of time (black)*, 2008; and *a passing gate (for Meredith)*, 2009

designing our most recent show of young artists working in the spirit of Ellsworth Kelly, it ended up being an all-women show. We hadn't planned it as a statement, it just happened that all the artists we felt fit into the show were female.

SR: To his credit, Glenn's been involved in the Modern Women's Fund at MoMA for years, and has been very involved in supporting female artists. We hosted a whole panel of female artists [Nancy Grossman, Marilyn Minter, Laurie Simmons, and Betty Tompkins, on May 6, 2016] at FLAG. I think it's a necessary conversation to have.

SD: Museums are in a tough spot with all these changes and political and cultural sensitivities, and it's something all institutions, even ones like FLAG, have to think about. You have to think about everyone who could potentially walk into the space and how they're going to react, without censoring anything. It's a tough balance that everyone is facing.

SR: From some of the curators and museum directors with whom I've discussed this, if you are going to take risks, you must address it with your staff and talk about why. You can't say, "Oh well, we did it." You want to be able to defend it.

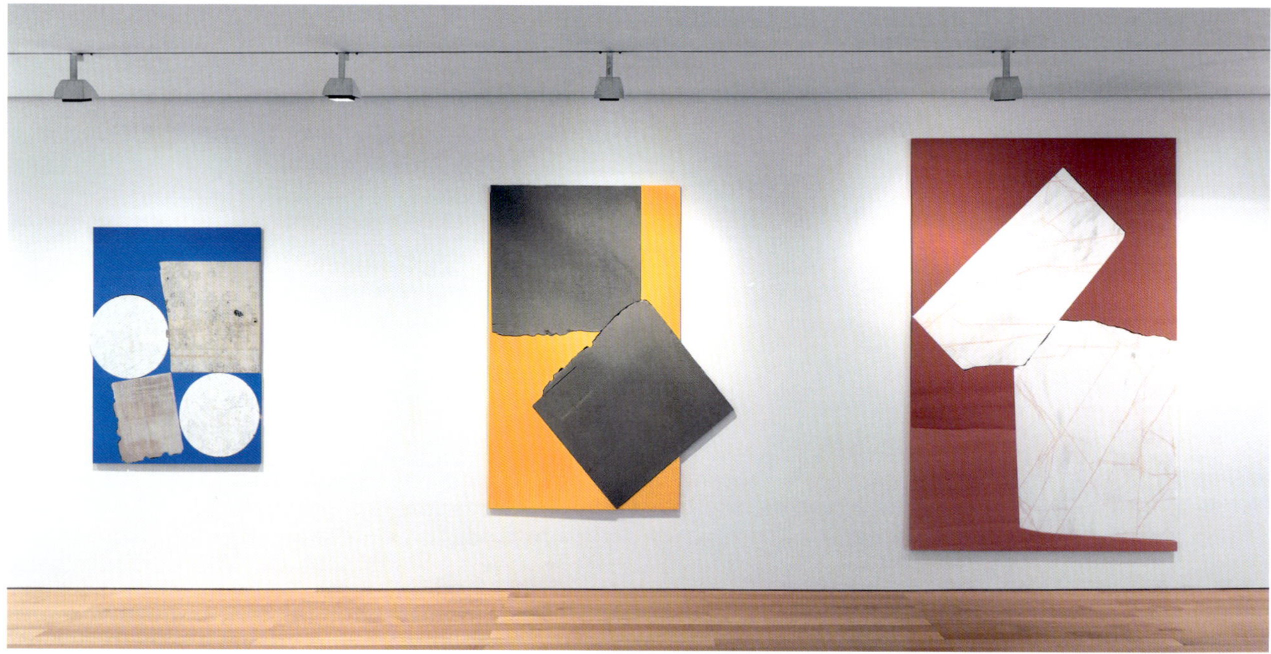

Installation view, *Painting/Object*, showing Sam Moyer, *Spencertown*, 2018; *Rye*, 2018; and *Coenties Slip*, 2018

For our recent Ashley Bickerton survey [2017], the artist's original concept for our opening wall was an oversize, floor-to-ceiling vinyl of his *Bad Painting* (1988), which had a swastika in it. This was all happening in the aftermath of the white supremacist rally in Charlottesville, Virginia, and we, as a team, discussed the pros and cons of keeping the swastika in the piece. We were willing to stand behind it, but we wanted to make sure that Ashley considered this particular moment in history, and that he was willing to stand behind it. The original piece was made in the '80s—it was a different time and context—and he ultimately decided to replace the image of the swastika with a biohazard sign instead.

GF: Was Ashley all for it?

SR: He said, "I don't feel the need to stand behind the swastika. Let's do the version with the biohazard." I talked to different museum directors—Amy [Sadao] from the ICA Philadelphia, Heidi Zuckerman [from the Aspen Art Museum]—and they each have their own way of dealing with this. Their common thread is that you have to really know what you're getting yourself into as an institution, be aware of that, and talk to your staff. Do your due diligence. I don't think Glenn ever vetoed something outright just because we thought it might be offensive.

GF: We had an exhibition of nude Ethiopian sex workers [*Awol Erizku: New Flower | Images of the Reclining Venus*, 2015], which resulted in a great show and led to a lot of conversations.

SD: You're saying it could have been controversial—for instance, it could have been seen as aestheticizing the profession?

GF: Yes, it could have been controversial; it could have been more of an issue. We talked about it. I wasn't at all hesitant to do that show.

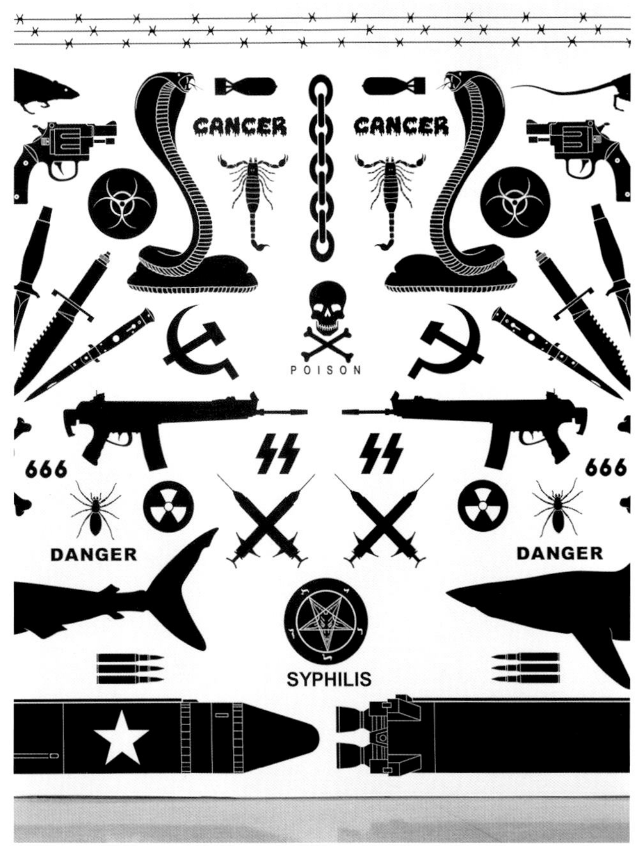

Installation view, *Ashley Bickerton*, showing *Bad Wall*, 2017

SD: In response to the times we live in, do you see FLAG's program engaging in political issues going forward?

SR: Well, *The Times* exhibition [2017] definitely did that.

GF: I'm personally a little bit more of a person that likes to create a forum for people to talk about things. I'm not interested in being didactic or saying, here's my perspective.

SR: When we were putting the show together, Glenn said, "Go for it. Invite artists to do this." But he didn't want the narrative to be told in a specifically biased way.

SD: How did that show come about?

SR: I wrote Glenn a pretty pointed email the day after the U.S. presidential election saying we needed to do something in terms of programming. Jon, our associate director, and I were throwing around ideas. I said maybe we ask artists what their vision is for the future. Jon said, "What about the *New York Times*?" and we merged those two ideas. I sent it to Glenn, and we had dinner with Jon, and Glenn said, "Great, let's do it."

SD: The *New York Times* has been a focal point, shorthand for the mainstream media.

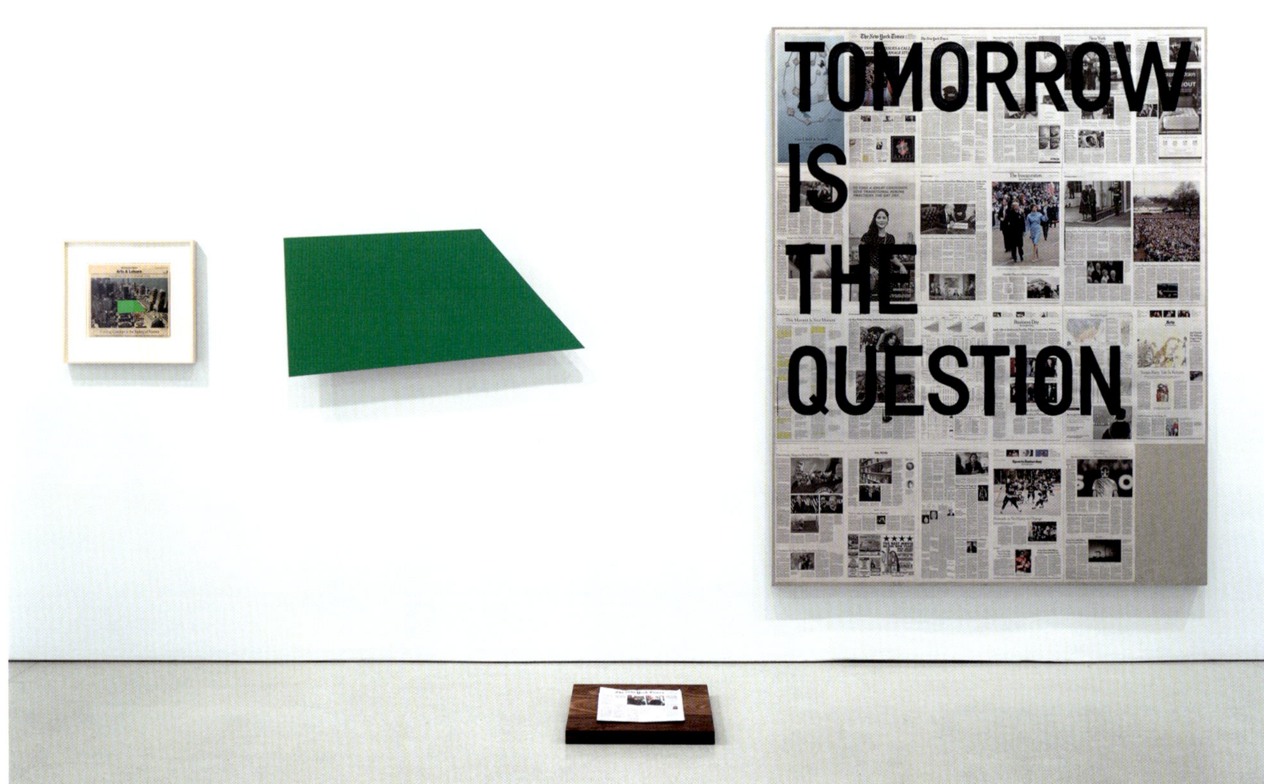

Installation view, *The Times*, showing Ellsworth Kelly, *Ground Zero*, 2003; and *Green Panel (Ground Zero)*, 2011; Dave McKenzie, *Yesterday's Newspaper*, 2007; and Rirkrit Tiravanija, *untitled 2017 (tomorrow is the question, january 21, 2017)*, 2017

SR: We had a preliminary list of artists. Glenn reached out to Fred Tomaselli (whom Glenn eventually did a talk with), and he agreed to make a new work. But we started to realize that we were going to have all the usual suspects, and all the artists were saying, "Have you looked at this person's work?"

GF: The open call for that show was a brilliant idea. In general, it's not my sensibility to have super confrontational, political, unattractive works that have a message—it's not what I'm interested in. We showed that spectacular Jane Hammond work [*Fallen*, 2011], with leaves representing all the fallen U.S. soldiers [killed in Iraq, 4,455 leaves at the time the exhibition began]. That was a political work done in an incredibly thoughtful, beautiful way. It's owned by the Whitney; we borrowed that.

SD: Where do you see FLAG in ten years?

GF: We would like to continue growing as an institution and expand our vision. Not expand physically, but continue to do different kinds of shows, new shows. Working with different artists, working with the same artists in different ways. I don't think there's going to be any major shifts.

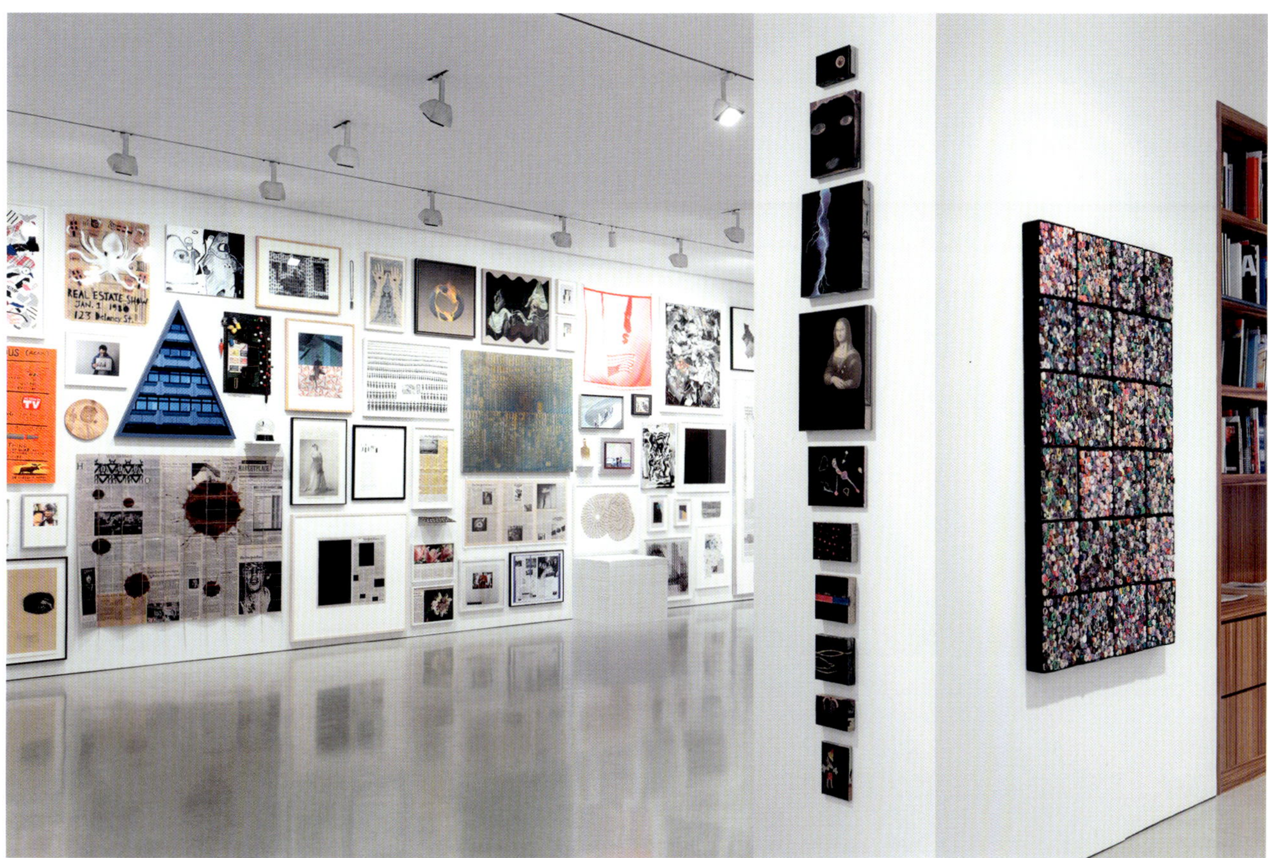

Installation view, *The Times*

SD: Is it important to you that your kids have any kind of appreciation for art?

GF: They'll develop their own areas of focus and passion, which may have nothing to do with art. I do think they'll grow up with an appreciation of art, but I think it's unlikely that they'll develop my same passion for art. We'll see.

SD: They live around it.

GF: They live around art, and they've had fun with it. They've met a lot of artists and have even been given drawings and gifts from artists they love. Jim Hodges is the godfather to our twins. Hopefully, they'll all appreciate art more and more as they get older. But I have no delusions—all of them may grow up saying, "That's mom and dad's thing; I'm not into it."

SD: Have you thought about your long-term plans for your collection, for when you are no longer around?

GF: I think about it a lot, but I haven't made any decisions. I have a lot of art—more art than anyone, or any museum, would want.

SD: They would love to pick and choose.

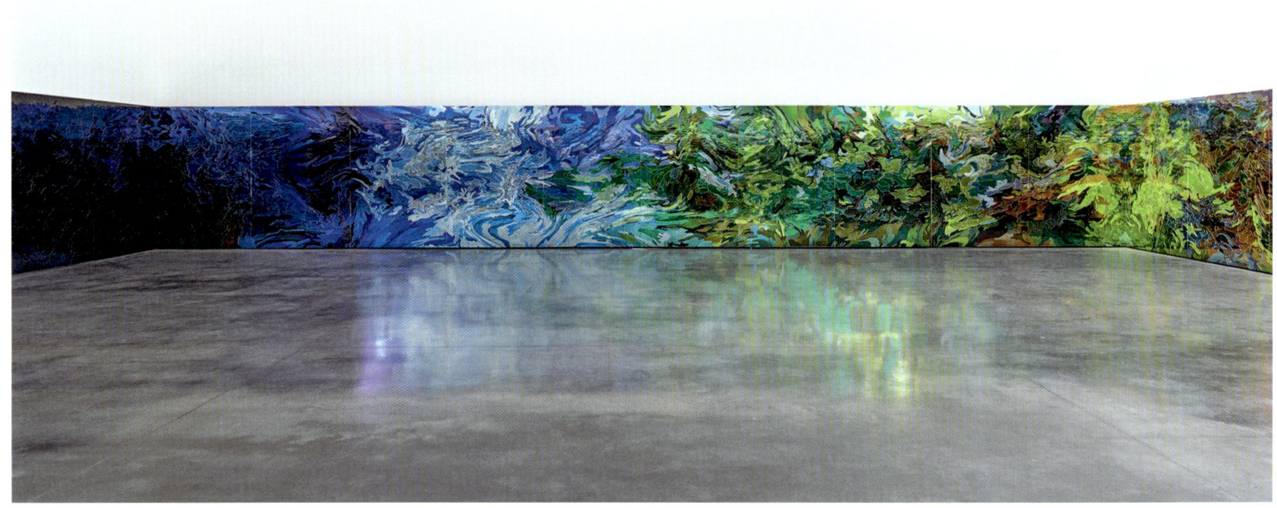

Installation view, Gladstone Gallery, Jim Hodges, *I dreamed a world and called it Love.*, 2016

GF: They would definitely like to pick and choose, and of course they'd like many of the most valuable things. For sure, I will give things to MoMA, Tate, and the Philadelphia Museum of Art, which have all had a huge impact on my collecting and helping to develop my love for art.

On one hand, it's nice to think that MoMA or the Met, or another preeminent institution, can have a group of works from my life that would live in their collections for posterity and that people could enjoy forever. That said, there is the reality that no matter how fantastic the work is, if it goes to a museum, it's going to be in dark basement storage, in a crate, for most of eternity—not on the wall. So, as much as I love living with the art and having people see it all the time—not just me, but museum groups and friends—I could sell a significant portion of the collection during my lifetime or when I die, and do something really beautiful with all the money: donate it to charity, health causes, children's causes, funding scholarships for college, whatever, and that would have a bigger impact than a bunch of works in the basement. All the works that would be sold, people would buy them, and live with them, and enjoy them. And, of course, some museums might buy some, and the works would keep living and having more exposure. If an artwork is in a dark basement for fifty years, does it even exist anymore? I'm not saying I'm going to do either of these things, but I think about the options all the time.

As a trustee of MoMA, I always advocate for contemporary art to be seen as much as possible. We should have a room filled with Jasper Johns,

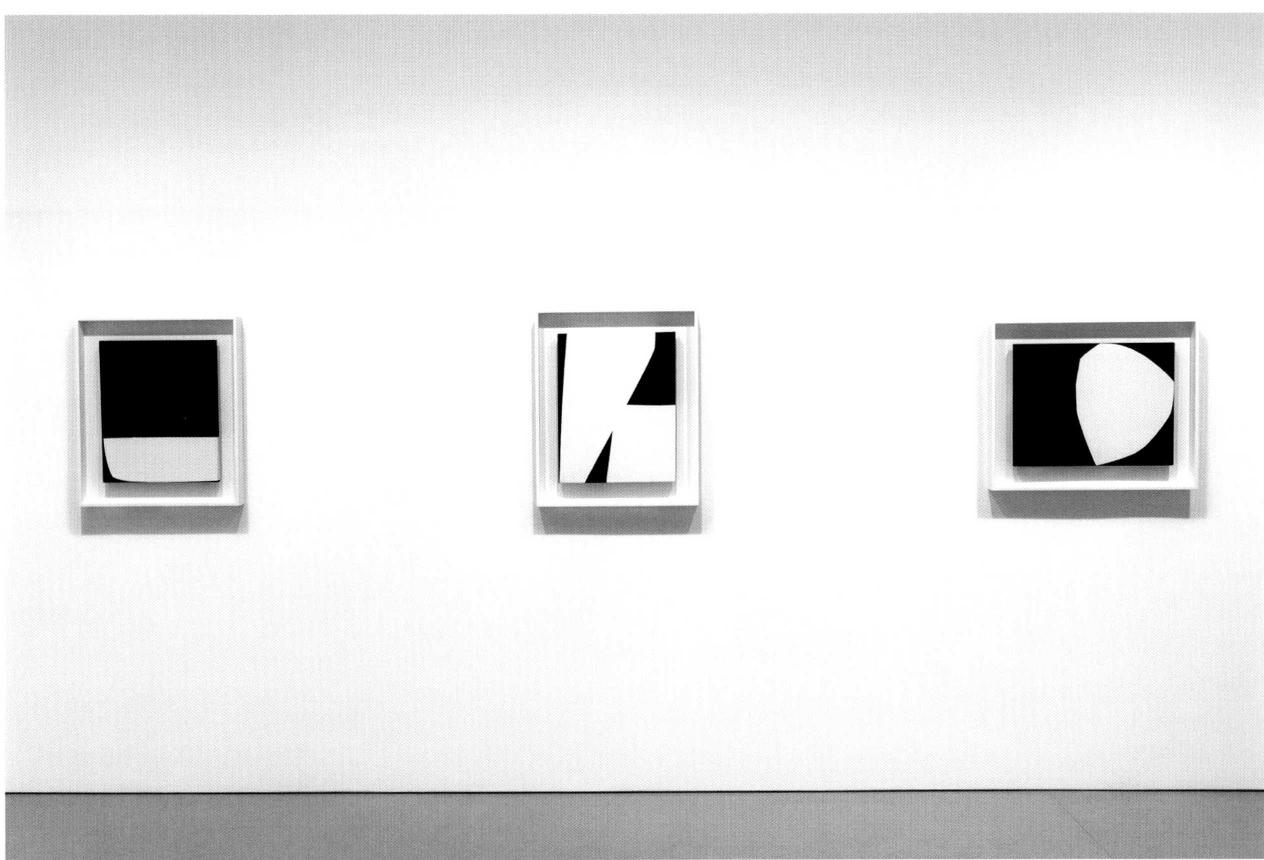

Installation view, *Ellsworth Kelly: Black and White Works*, showing *Slip Study*, 1959; *Falcon Study*, 1959; and *York Study*, 1959

Ellsworth Kelly, Cindy Sherman, Ed Ruscha, Brice Marden, Jenny Saville, and some of the many unbelievable works by Cy Twombly, but none of them are on long-term display or at least not nearly as many as I think most people would like. It's a bevy of riches, and the museum only has so much wall space. I understand the math of the size of the collection and the square footage of wall space available.

That said, I have absolutely no interest in starting my own museum to show my collection. The number-one fun thing about FLAG for me is actually almost the exact opposite phenomenon. We get to enjoy, albeit temporarily, all the amazing art FLAG gets to borrow in executing its mission as an exhibiting institution. I love that. I can dream with our incredible team all we want about which works we would love to borrow and then try to make a great enough show to entice the owners to lend us their works.

SELECTED EVENTS AND PUBLIC PROGRAMS

2011
Dance of the Gallerinas
July 22

2012
Awol Erizku in conversation with Glenn Fuhrman for Harlem Children's Zone
February 12

Lesley Vance in conversation with Glenn Fuhrman and Stephanie Roach
December 18

2013
Hilary Harkness in conversation with Glenn Fuhrman and Stephanie Roach
January 29

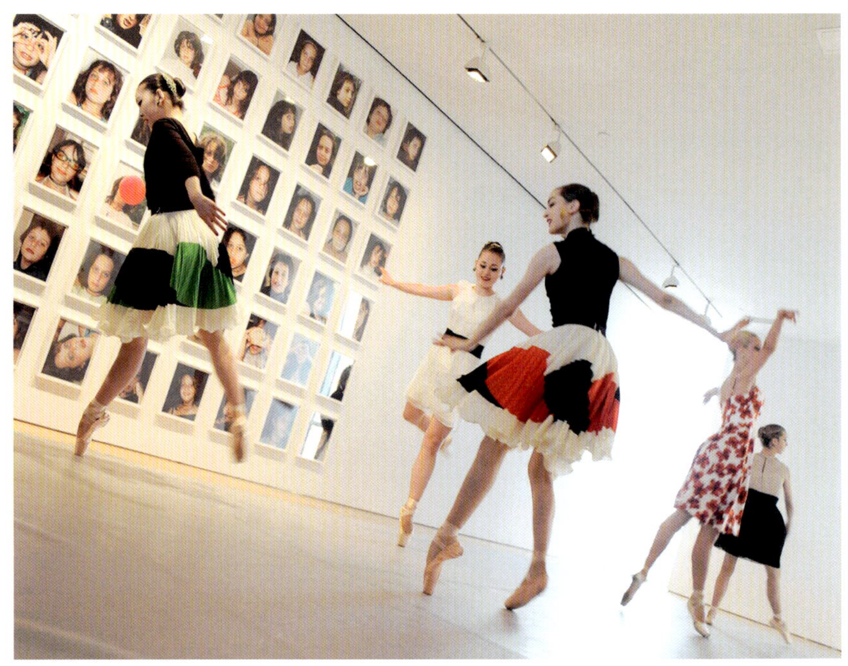

Dance of the Gallerinas, 2011

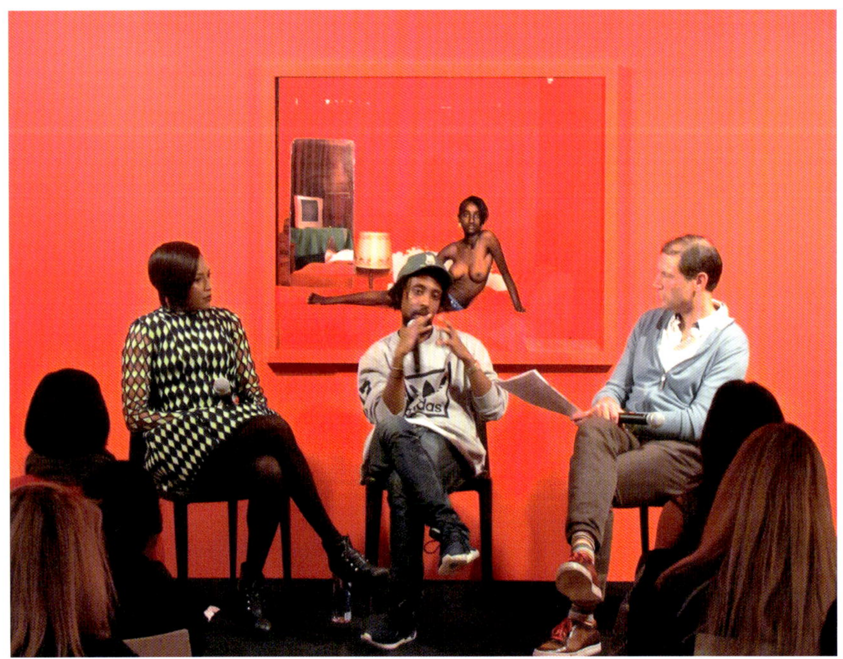

Awol Erizku (center) in conversation with Glenn Fuhrman and Alicia Quarles, 2015

Baby Art History, hosted by
Hilary Harkness
March 9

Drawing a Nude, hosted by
Will Cotton
October 13

Wayne Lawrence in conversation with Glenn Fuhrman for Harlem Children's Zone
November 7

Poetry reading with Joanna Fuhrman, Thomas Devaney, Jeanine Oleson, and Kenneth Goldsmith
December 4

Lawrence Weiner in conversation with Glenn Fuhrman, followed by a Scotch tasting
December 12

2014

Baby Art History, "Coloring Books and Roy Lichtenstein"
March 1

Inbal Segev, cello performance
May 21

2015

Artist-led walkthrough of *Disturbing Innocence*, curated by Eric Fischl
January 31

Jim Hodges in conversation with Glenn Fuhrman
May 16

Awol Erizku in conversation with Glenn Fuhrman and Alicia Quarles
November 13

Sean Scully in conversation with Glenn Fuhrman
November 20

2016

Betty Tompkins, *Words on WOMEN* performance
March 23

"A Woman's Greatest Weapon Is Her Tongue," Betty Tompkins in conversation with Alison Gingeras
April 6

Jeff Koons in conversation with Glenn Fuhrman
April 20

Heidi Zuckerman in conversation with Glenn Fuhrman
May 4

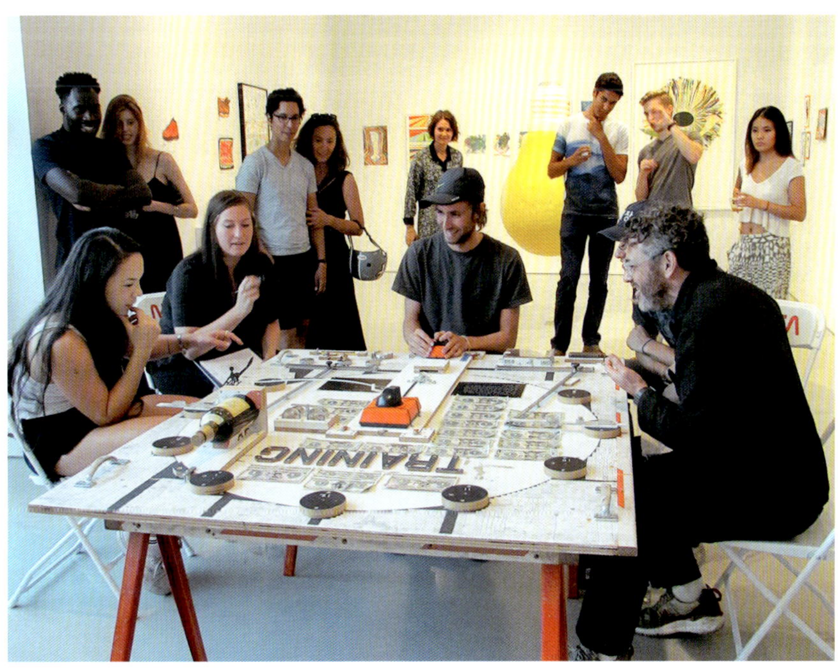

Training Tournament, hosted by Tom Sachs, 2016

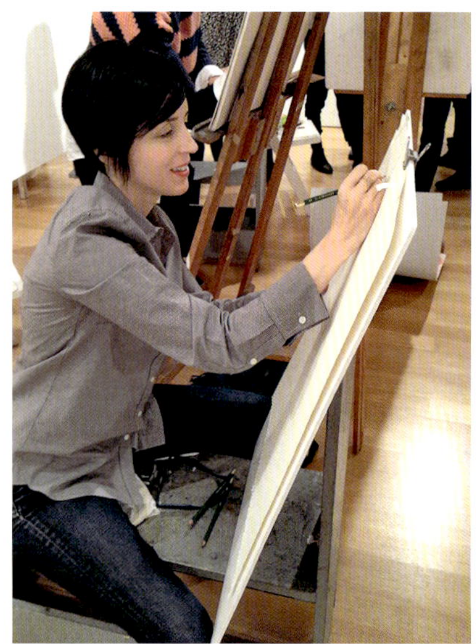

Hilary Harkness, Drawing a Nude, 2013

Nancy Grossman, Marilyn Minter, Laurie Simmons, and Betty Tompkins in conversation with Glenn Fuhrman
May 10

Training Tournament, hosted by Tom Sachs
July 6

Workshop with Harlem Children's Zone, led by Gina Beavers
July 27

Patricia Cronin in conversation with Maura Reilly
July 26

2017

Cynthia Daignault in conversation with Matthew Israel
February 16

Elmgreen & Dragset in conversation with Glenn Fuhrman
March 14

Cynthia Daignault in conversation with Glenn Fuhrman
March 31

Cynthia Daignault, Mark Loiacono, and David Kennedy Cutler performance
May 13

Fred Tomaselli in conversation with Glenn Fuhrman
July 25

Agnieszka Kurant, Dave McKenzie, William Powhida, and Hunter Reynolds in conversation with Antwaun Sargent
August 3

Artist-led walkthrough of Ashley Bickerton survey
September 28

2018

Jack Shear in conversation with Glenn Fuhrman
April 3

Sarah Crowner, Sam Moyer, Julia Rommel, and Erin Shirreff in conversation with Jacoba Urist
April 25

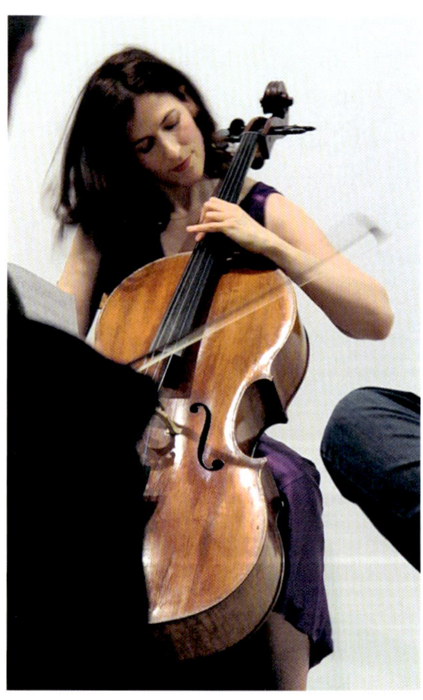

Inbal Segev, cello performance, 2014

ADDITIONAL PROGRAMMING

Since 2003, Glenn Fuhrman has hosted a series of artist conversations and art world talks for the Museum of Modern Art's Contemporary Arts Council.

2003

Thomas Struth
February 10

Amy Adler
April 18

Richard Patterson
September 29

Delia Brown
October 29

Anthony d'Offay
November 13

2004

Paul Pfeiffer
February 26

Cecily Brown
March 18

Roni Horn
April 27

Philip Taaffe
May 18

Chuck Close
September 13

Robert Gober
October 26

Gregory Crewdson
November 18

2005

Jim Hodges
January 5

Lawrence Weiner
February 8

Yinka Shonibare MBE
March 8

Brice Marden
March 15

Thomas Demand
April 18

Tom Friedman
May 10

Christian Marclay
June 28

Inez van Lamsweerde
September 23

Ed Ruscha
November 15

John Currin and Rachel Feinstein
December 15

2006

Lisa Yuskavage
March 15

Fred Wilson
May 25

Martin Eder
June 6

Vik Muniz
September 11

Kehinde Wiley
October 4

Matthew Marks
December 15

2007

Richard Phillips
February 14

Jeff Wall
February 21

Marc Quinn
May 1

Howard Rachofsky
September 18

Sarah Lucas
November 7

2008
Martin Creed
March 25

Ken Solomon
April 16

James Frey
November 12

2009
Sarah Thornton
March 13

Ugo Rondinone
December 1

2010
Charles Ray
February 18

Jeff Koons
April 7

Mickalene Thomas
December 15

2011
Ellen Gallagher
January 25

Agnes Gund
September 21

2012
Barry X Ball
February 23

Glenn D. Lowry
March 29

Klaus Biesenbach
September 13

2013
Wolfgang Laib
January 31

Jim Hodges
November 20

2014
Glenn Brown
May 9

Dorothy Lichtenstein
December 17

2015
Katy Moran
March 9

Ed Winkleman
October 29

2016
Alex Katz
January 28

Arlene Shechet
October 25

Carol Bove
November 10

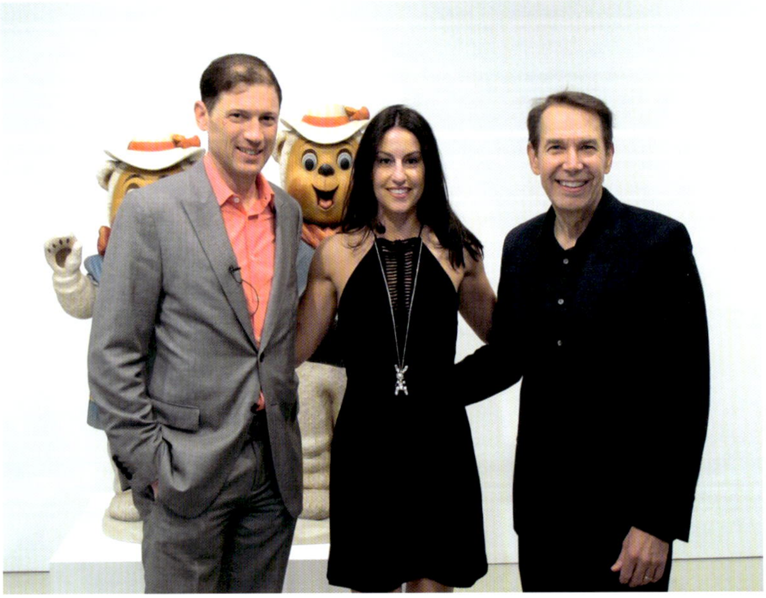

Glenn Fuhrman, Stephanie Roach, and Jeff Koons at the opening of *Cecily Brown, Jeff Koons, Charles Ray*, 2016

2017
Simone Leigh
February 6

Cynthia Daignault
May 2

Ashley Bickerton
September 26

Tom Sachs
December 12

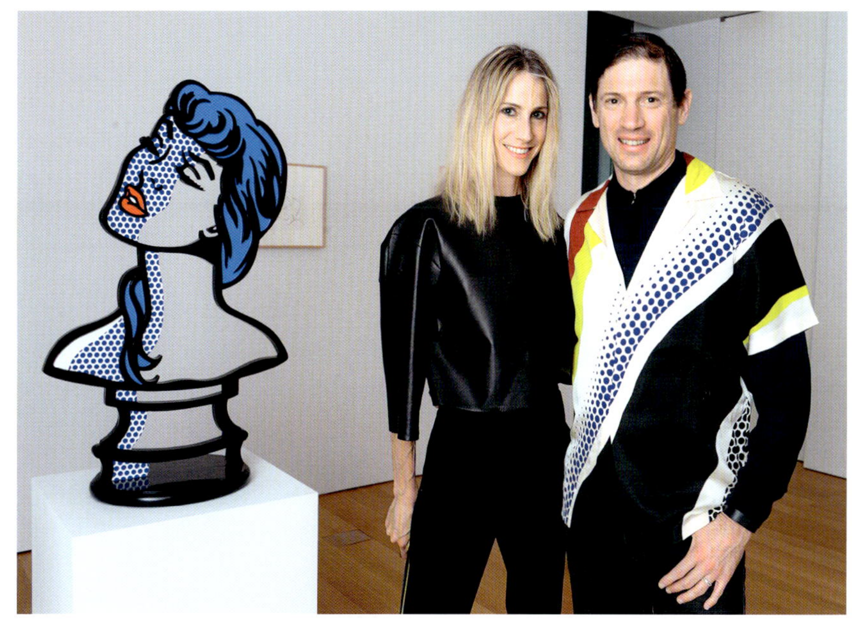

Glenn and Amanda Fuhrman at the opening of *Roy Lichtenstein: Nudes and Interiors*, 2014

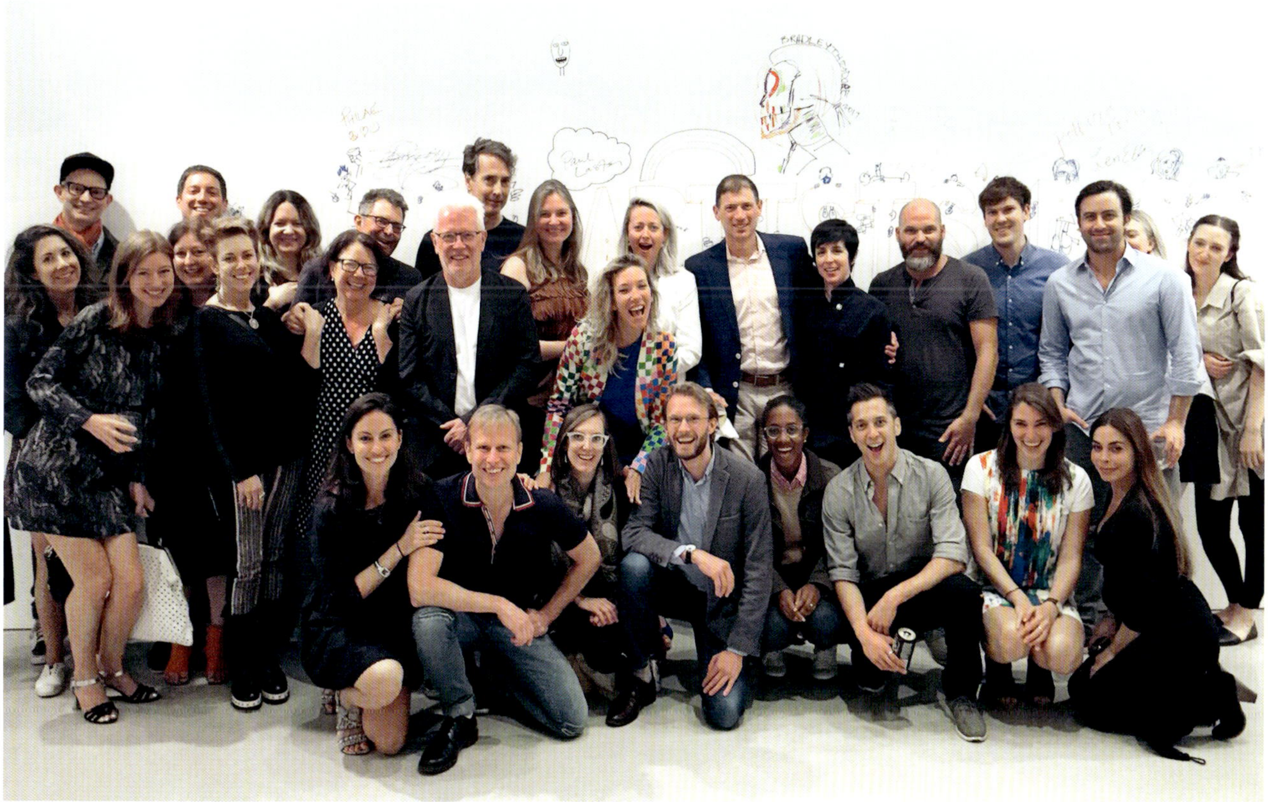

Autumn Artist Party, 2017

THE FLAG ART FOUNDATION STAFF

Stephanie Roach
Director

Jonathan Rider
Associate Director

Risa Daniels
Exhibitions and
Programs Manager (2013–18)

Caroline Cassidy
Exhibitions and
Programs Manager (2018–)

ACKNOWLEDGMENTS

The FLAG Art Foundation would like to acknowledge the contributions of our dynamic interns from 2008 to 2018:

Nicole Ahn
Amanda Albanese
Lauren Anderson
Kayla Barbera
Sophie Berg
Jennifer Billard
Kelsey Brow
Molly Butcher
Alice Centamore
Megan Chan
Chi Chen
Canada Choate
Mary Claire
Lauren Clark
Connor Cole
Hudson Cooke
Madeline DeFilippis
Nicole DuPerry
Alexa Eagle
Danyelle Elysée
Erzen Erez
Leah Falk
Mary Francis Flournoy
Jane Frost
Constanza Galindo
Yasmin Gee
Suzannah Gerber
Lauren Gidwill
Claire Gidwitz
Laura Glasser
Yixin Gong
Julia Gottlieb
Michellé Hoban
Lowery Houston
Ella Huzenis
Ana Isales
Emery Jenson
Cheryl Johnson
Hea-Mi Kim
Maddie Klett
Margaret Knowles
Cody Rae Knue
Joanna Knutsen
Stephanie Kryzak
Emma Laramie
Fiona Laugharn
Madeline Lazaris
Eumi Lee
DadryAnn Lee-Morris
Phoebe Leshay
Kachun Leung
Alexandra Liggett
Elena Light
Gabrielle Lipton
Bobbi Lutes

Christine Ma
Nicole McMurphy
Kaitlin Meese
Arianne Milhem
Grace Milligan
Natalie Ng
Katherine Ojeda
Dennis Orlov
Caitlin Parker
Amanda Platek
Veronica Quinlan
Jessica Riddiford
Brandon Schell
Misha Sesar
Danielle Sheppard
Jamie Shi
Vivienne Shi
Noel Shipp
Clare Smith
Minna Son
Simone Sutnick
Francesco TrejoMorales
Stacey Villafuerte
(Addison) Tate Waddell
Angela (Danchen) Wang
Xueli Wang
Yangxingyue (Rita) Wang
Andrew Wellborn
Rebecca Winn
John Zinonos

The FLAG Art Foundation would like to recognize this diverse range of individuals and companies for their collective efforts over the last decade:

Alba Brothers
Alchemy Paintworks
ARTA Shipping, Inc.
Artcore Fine Art Services, Inc.
Art Crating, Inc.
Artex Fine Art Services
Artifact Studios
Atelier 4, Inc.
Audio Video Crafts, Inc.
Boxart, Inc.
Albert H. Brand II, Eurostruct, Inc.
Contemporary Conservation Ltd.
Crozier Fine Arts
Jamie Forehand and Seth Hernandez, Acumen Fine Art Logistics
Richard Gluckman, Gluckman Tang Architects
Blerti Hajdari, Chelsea Arts Tower Building Manager
Genevieve Hanson, Art Echo LLC
Jerry Kelly
Maquette Fine Art Services Inc.
Amy Mees, X-ing Design
Minagawa Art Lines Inc.
More Specialized Art Transport and Logistics
Peter Muscato Framing
Object Studies LLC
Polich Tallix Fine Art Foundry
Steven Probert
Betty Rexrode and Michael Chirigos, Rexrode Chirigos Architects
Safe Art Transport
SecurAmerica LLC
Maureen Sullivan, Red Art Projects
Rafael Talavera, Chelsea Arts Tower Building Manager
Transcon International Inc.
UOVO
U.S. Art Company, Inc.
Craig Watson

PHOTOGRAPHY CREDITS

4. Jeff Koons. *Cat on a Clothesline (Red)*, 1994–2001. © Jeff Koons. Photograph: Genevieve Hanson, ArtEcho LLC. **6.** Courtesy the artist and VG Bild-Kunst, Bonn. Photograph: Genevieve Hanson. **16.** © Cecily Brown. Courtesy Paula Cooper Gallery, New York. **18–19.** Gerhard Richter. *MUSA*, 2009. Jacquard woven tapestry, 108$\frac{11}{16}$ x 148$\frac{13}{16}$ inches (276.1 x 378 cm). Edition 4/8, 2 APs. Private collection. Courtesy the artist and Marian Goodman Gallery. Photograph: Object Studies. **23.** © Tom Friedman, Courtesy the artist, Luhring Augustine, New York, and Stephen Friedman Gallery, London. **25 top.** Ron Mueck. *Spooning Couple*, 2005. Mixed media, 5½ x 25⅝ x 13¾ inches (14 x 65 x 35 cm). Installation view: Fondation Cartier pour l'art contemporain, Paris, November 19, 2005–February 19, 2006. © Ron Mueck, Courtesy the artist, Anthony d'Offay, London, and Hauser & Wirth. Photograph: Patrick Gries. **26.** Mark Bradford. *Ridin' Dirty*, 2006. Mixed-media collage on paper, 109 x 336 inches (267.9 x 853.4 cm). Courtesy the artist and Hauser & Wirth. **27.** Ellsworth Kelly. *Self-portrait*, 1948. Graphite on paper, 18 x 14⅛ inches (45.7 x 35.9 cm). Private collection. Artwork © Ellsworth Kelly Foundation. Image courtesy Matthew Marks Gallery. **32.** © Ugo Rondinone, Courtesy the artist and Gladstone Gallery, New York and Brussels. Photograph: Genevieve Hanson. **33 top.** © Ed Ruscha. **34–35.** © Andreas Gursky/Artists Rights Society (ARS), NY/VG Bild-Kunst, Bonn. Courtesy Gagosian Gallery. **35.** Thomas Demand. *Clearing*, 2003. C-print, 75½ x 195 inches (192 x 495 cm). © Thomas Demand/Artists Rights Society (ARS), NY/Courtesy Matthew Marks Gallery. **37.** © Barry Frydlender, Courtesy the artist and Meislin Projects. Photograph: Genevieve Hanson. **39.** © Conrad Bakker, Courtesy the artist. Photograph: Genevieve Hanson. **41.** Courtesy the artist and Charlie James Gallery, Los Angeles. Photograph: Genevieve Hanson. **42.** *Background:* Felix Gonzalez-Torres. *"Untitled" (Go-Go Dancing Platform)*, 1991. Wood, light bulbs, acrylic paint, and go-go dancer in silver lamé bathing suit, sneakers, and personal listening device; overall dimensions vary with installation, platform 21½ x 72 x 72 inches (54.6 x 182.9 x 182.9 cm). Installation view: *Floating a Boulder: Works by Felix Gonzalez-Torres and Jim Hodges*. The FLAG Art Foundation, New York, October 1, 2009–January 31, 2010. © Felix Gonzalez-Torres, Courtesy of The Felix Gonzalez-Torres Foundation. *Foreground, right:* Felix Gonzalez-Torres. *"Untitled"*, 1989. Framed silkscreen on paper, 16½ x 21¾ inches (41.9 x 55.2 cm). Edition of 250, 10 APs. Published by Public Art Fund, New York. Installation view: *Floating a Boulder: Works by Felix Gonzalez-Torres and Jim Hodges*. The FLAG Art Foundation, New York, October 1, 2009–January 31, 2010. © Felix Gonzalez-Torres, Courtesy of The Felix Gonzalez-Torres Foundation. Photograph: Genevieve Hanson. **42–47.** © Jim Hodges, Courtesy the artist. **45.** Felix Gonzalez-Torres. *"Untitled"*, 1991. Billboard, dimensions vary with installation. Installation view: *Floating a Boulder: Works by Felix Gonzalez-Torres and Jim Hodges*. The FLAG Art Foundation, New York, October 1, 2009–January 31, 2010. © Felix Gonzalez-Torres, Courtesy of The Felix Gonzalez-Torres Foundation. Photograph: Genevieve Hanson. **46.** *Left:* Felix Gonzalez-Torres. *"Untitled" (Perfect Lovers)*, 1987–90. Wall clocks, original clock size 13½ inches diameter (34.3 cm). Edition of 3, 1 AP. Installation view: *Floating a Boulder: Works by Felix Gonzalez-Torres and Jim Hodges*. The FLAG Art Foundation, New York, October 1, 2009–January 31, 2010. © Felix Gonzalez-Torres, Courtesy of The Felix Gonzalez-Torres Foundation. Photograph: Genevieve Hanson. **47.** *Foreground:* Felix Gonzalez-Torres. *"Untitled" (We Don't Remember)*, 1991. Print on paper, endless copies 8 inches at ideal height x 29 x 23 inches (20.3 x 73.7 x 58.4 cm) (original paper size). Installation view: *Floating a Boulder: Works by Felix Gonzalez-Torres and Jim Hodges*. The FLAG Art Foundation, New York, October 1, 2009–January 31, 2010. © Felix Gonzalez-Torres, Courtesy of The Felix Gonzalez-Torres Foundation. Photograph: Genevieve Hanson. **48–49.** *Left:* Ron Mueck. *Big Man*, 2000. Pigmented polyester resin on fiberglass, 80¼ x 47½ x 80½ inches (221.6 x 120.7 x 207 cm). Courtesy of the Hirshhorn Museum and Sculpture Garden, Smithsonian Institution, Washington, DC, Museum Purchase with Funds Provided by the Joseph H. Hirshhorn Bequest and in Honor of Robert Lehrman, Chairman of the Board of Trustees, 1997–2004, for his extraordinary leadership and unstinting service to the Hirshhorn Museum and Sculpture Garden. *Right:* © R. J. Patterson, Courtesy the artist and Timothy Taylor gallery. Photograph: Genevieve Hanson. **50.** © Robert Therrien/Artists Rights Society (ARS), NY. Photograph: Genevieve Hanson. **51.** Photograph: © Richard Baddeley. **52.** *Left:* Richard Phillips. *Michelle Angelo*, 2010. Oil on linen, 114 x 83 inches (289.6 x 210.8 cm). Private collection. Courtesy Richard Phillips and Gagosian Gallery. *Right:* © Tom Friedman, Courtesy the artist, Luhring Augustine, New York, and Stephen Friedman Gallery, London. Photograph: Genevieve Hanson. **53.** Maurizio Cattelan. *Untitled*, 2001. Stainless steel, composition wood, electric motor, electric bell, electric light, paint, and computer in two parts, 23½ x 33⅝ x 18⅝ inches (59.7 x 85.4 x 47.3 cm) overall. Edition of 10. The Steven and Alexandra Cohen Collection. Courtesy the artist and Marian Goodman Gallery. Photograph: Genevieve Hanson. **54–55.** © Robert Lazzarini, Courtesy the artist. Photographs: Genevieve Hanson. **56.** © Noriko Ambe, Courtesy the artist and Lora Reynolds Gallery. Photographs: Genevieve Hanson. **57.** Courtesy the artist and Charlie James Gallery, Los Angeles. Photograph: Genevieve Hanson. **58.** Courtesy the artist and VG Bild-Kunst, Bonn. Photograph: Genevieve Hanson. **59 top.** © Damián Ortega, Courtesy the artist and Gladstone Gallery, New York and Brussels. Photograph: Genevieve Hanson. **61–65.** © Cary Kwok, Courtesy the artist and Herald St, London. Photographs: Genevieve Hanson. **66–71.** © Josephine Meckseper, Courtesy the artist and Timothy Taylor gallery. Photographs: Genevieve Hanson. **72.** Gerhard Richter. *905/1-48 Sinbad* (detail), 2008. Lacquer behind glass plate, 11$\frac{13}{16}$ x 19$\frac{11}{16}$ inches (30 x 50 cm). Private collection. Courtesy the artist and Marian Goodman Gallery. Photograph: Genevieve Hanson. **73.** Gerhard Richter. *905/1-48 Sinbad*, 2008. Lacquer behind glass plate, 98 panels, 11$\frac{13}{16}$ x 19$\frac{11}{16}$ inches (30 x 50 cm) each. Private collection. Courtesy the artist and Marian Goodman Gallery. Photograph: Genevieve Hanson. **74.** Roni Horn. *This is Me, This is You*, 1997–2000 (detail). Mounted and framed C-prints, 96 pieces, 12½ x 10¼ inches (31.8 x 26 cm) each. © Roni Horn. **75.** Roni Horn. *Double Mobius, v. 1*, 2009. Two pure gold ribbons and plastic peg; ribbons 2½ x 60 x 0.0008 inches (6.4 x 152.4 x .002 cm) each, plastic peg 1⅞ x 1⅛ inches diameter (4.76 x 2.86 cm). © Roni Horn. **76.** *Left:* © Diana Al-Hadid, Courtesy the artist and Marianne Boesky Gallery, New York and Aspen. Photograph: Genevieve Hanson. *Right:* © Artists Rights Society (ARS), NY/VEGAP, Madrid. **77.** *Top:* Rachel Whiteread. *Untitled (Pair)*, 1999. Bronze and cellulose paint, 35⅜ x 30$\frac{5}{16}$ x 80$\frac{5}{16}$ inches (89.9 x 77.1 x 204.1 cm). Edition of 12. © Rachel Whiteread, Courtesy the artist, Luhring Augustine, New York, Galleria Lorcan O'Neill, Rome, and Gagosian Gallery. Photograph: Genevieve Hanson. **79.** *Background:* Courtesy the artist. *Foreground:* © Richard Prince, Courtesy the artist. Photograph: Genevieve Hanson. **81.** Courtesy the artist. **84–89.** Jane Hammond. *Fallen*, 2004–ongoing. Assemblage of Inkjet prints with matte medium, adhesive, fiberglass, ink, acrylic, and opaque watercolor, dimensions variable. Whitney Museum of American Art, New York; purchase with funds from Sarah Ann and Werner Kramarsky, The Schiff Foundation, Melissa and Robert Soros, Marion C. and Charles Burson, Toby Devan Lewis Foundation, The Judith Rothschild Foundation, Nora and Guy Barron, Pam Joseph and Rob Brinker, Greg Kucera and Larry Yocom, Ted and Maryanne Ellison Simmons, and The Stanley Family Fund of the Community Foundation of New Jersey. © 2004–ongoing Jane Hammond. Photographs: Genevieve Hanson. **90–91.** *Far right:* © Cy Twombly Foundation, Courtesy Gagosian Gallery. Photograph: Genevieve Hanson. **92.** © Dan Colen. Photograph: Genevieve Hanson. **94.** Richard Forster. *American Pastoral/Ostalgie Pattern with tape*, 2011. Graphite, watercolor, and acrylic medium on Bristol board, 11$\frac{13}{16}$ x 16$\frac{11}{16}$ inches (30 x 42.4 cm). © Richard Forster, Courtesy the artist. **95.** Richard Forster. *Incoming Sea's edge on fourteen consecutive occasions at random time intervals. Saltburn-by-the Sea, January 5th 2010; 11.30–11.37am*, 2011. Drawing no. 9 of a 14-part sequence. Graphite and acrylic medium on board, 17$\frac{11}{16}$ x 11$\frac{13}{16}$ inches (44.9 x 30 cm). © Richard Forster, Courtesy the artist. **96.** © Patricia Cronin, Courtesy the artist. **97 top.** *Background:* © Polly Apfelbaum/Artists Rights Society (ARS), NY. *Foreground:* © Michael Phelan, Courtesy the artist. **97 bottom.** *Left, background:* © Tara Donovan, courtesy Pace Gallery. *Left, foreground:* © Richard Serra/Artists Rights Society (ARS), NY. *Center:* Felix Gonzalez-Torres. *"Untitled" (A Corner of Baci)*, 1990. Baci chocolates, endless supply; overall dimensions vary with installation, ideal weight 42 pounds. Installation view: *Watch Your Step*. The FLAG Art Foundation, New York, June 7–August 24, 2012. © Felix Gonzalez-Torres, Courtesy of The Felix Gonzalez-Torres Foundation. *Right:* © Tom Friedman, Courtesy the artist, Luhring Augustine, New York, and Stephen Friedman Gallery, London. **98.** *Left:* © Rob Pruitt, 2018, Courtesy the artist and Gavin Brown's enterprise, New York/Rome. *Right:* © Mike Kelley Foundation for the Arts. All Rights Reserved/VAGA at ARS, NY. Photograph: Genevieve Hanson. **99.** Peter Fischli and David Weiss. *Rat and Bear (Sleeping)*, 2008. Cotton, wire, polyester, and electric mechanism, dimensions variable. © Peter Fischli and David Weiss, Courtesy Matthew Marks Gallery. **100.** © Richard Prince, Courtesy the artist. Photograph: Genevieve Hanson. **105.** Lesley Vance. *Untitled*, 2012. Oil on linen, 17 x 13½ x 1 inches (43.2 x 34.3 x 2.5 cm). © Lesley Vance. Courtesy David Kordansky Gallery, Los Angeles. Photograph: Fredrik Nilsen. **106–7.** Courtesy the artist and Lora Reynolds Gallery, Austin, TX. **108–13.** © Hilary Harkness, Courtesy the artist and Mary Boone Gallery. **124.** *Left:* © Artists Rights Society (ARS), NY/DACS, London. *Right:* © Marc Dennis, Courtesy the artist. Photograph: Genevieve Hanson. **125.** *Left:* Gerhard Richter. *YUSUF*, 2009. Jacquard woven tapestry, 108$\frac{11}{16}$ x 148$\frac{13}{16}$ inches (276.1 x 378 cm). Edition 4/8, 2 APs. Private collection. Courtesy the artist and Marian Goodman Gallery. *Center:* Julie Mehretu. *Fever graph (algorithm for serendipity)*, 2013. Graphite, ink, and acrylic on canvas, 96 x 120 inches (243.8 x 304.8 cm). Private collection. Courtesy the artist and Marian Goodman Gallery. *Right:* Gerhard Richter. *MUSA*, 2009. Jacquard woven tapestry, 108$\frac{11}{16}$ x 148$\frac{13}{16}$ inches (276.1 x 378 cm). Edition 4/8, 2 APs. Private collection. Courtesy the artist and Marian Goodman Gallery. Photograph: Genevieve Hanson. **126.** Wayne Lawrence. *Yari*, 2011. Digital C-print, 30 x 37 inches (76.2 x 94 cm). © Wayne Lawrence, Courtesy the artist. **127.** © Wayne Lawrence, Courtesy the artist. Photograph: Genevieve Hanson. **128, 129, 134–35.** © Richard Patterson, Courtesy the artist and Timothy Taylor gallery. Photographs: Genevieve Hanson. **131.** © Richard Patterson, Courtesy the artist and Timothy Taylor gallery. Photograph: Kevin

Todora. **136–41.** © Roy Lichtenstein Foundation/© Estate of Roy Lichtenstein. Photographs: Genevieve Hanson. **142.** © Awol Erizku, Courtesy the artist. Photograph: Awol Erizku. **143.** © Genevieve Gaignard, Courtesy the artist. Photograph: Awol Erizku. **144.** © Joanne Greenbaum/ Artists Rights Society (ARS), NY. Courtesy the artist and Rachel Uffner Gallery. **145 bottom.** *Left to right:* Anya Kielar. *Feather*, 2013. Fabric dye and fabric, 72 x 45 inches (182.9 x 114.3 cm). Courtesy the artist and Rachel Uffner Gallery. Anya Kielar. *Sweater*, 2013. Acrylic on canvas, 74 x 52 inches (188 x 132.1 cm). Courtesy the artist and Rachel Uffner Gallery. Anya Kielar. *Accessories*, 2013. Fabric dye and fabric, 72 x 45 inches (182.9 x 114.3 cm). Courtesy the artist and Rachel Uffner Gallery. **146.** Roy Lichtenstein. *Mirror II*, 1977. Painted and patinated bronze, 59¾ x 30 x 12 inches (151.8 x 76.2 x 30.5 cm). Private collection. © Estate of Roy Lichtenstein. **147.** Roy Lichtenstein. *Cup and Saucer II*, 1977. Painted and patinated bronze, 43¾ x 25¾ x 10 inches (111.1 x 65.4 x 25.4 cm). Private collection. © Estate of Roy Lichtenstein. **148.** © Awol Erizku, Courtesy the artist. **149.** Photograph: Cheri Eisenberg. **151.** Tony Oursler. *Half (Brain)*, 1998. Two Sony CPJ 200 projectors, two videotapes, two Samsung VCRs, polystyrene foam, and paint, 14 x 13 x 13 inches (35.6 x 33 x 33 cm) each, plus equipment. Performance by Tony Oursler. Courtesy the artist and Metro Pictures, New York. **152.** © Charles Ray, Courtesy Matthew Marks Gallery. Photograph: Yangxingyue Wang. **153.** *Top:* Jim Hodges. *picturing: my heart* (detail), 2004. Cast pink crystal, two parts, 9½ x 22 x 16 inches (24.1 x 55.9 x 40.6 cm). © Jim Hodges. Photograph: David Regen. *Bottom:* © Matthew Barney, Courtesy the artist and Gladstone Gallery, New York and Brussels. **154.** *Left:* Felix Gonzalez-Torres. *"Untitled"*, 1995. Silver-plated brass, 16½ x 33 inches (41.9 x 83.8 cm) overall. Edition of 12, 4 APs. Published by Patrick Painter Editions, Vancouver. Installation view: *A Secret Affair: Selections from the Fuhrman Family Collection*. The Contemporary Austin, Austin, TX, May 3–August 31, 2014. Curated by Louis Grachos with Danielle Nieciag. Catalogue. [Travels to: The FLAG Art Foundation, New York, February 21–May 16, 2015]. © Felix Gonzalez-Torres, Courtesy of The Felix Gonzalez-Torres Foundation. *Right:* Felix Gonzalez-Torres. *"Untitled"*, 1992. Light bulbs, porcelain light sockets, and extension cord, overall dimensions vary with installation. Edition of 2. Installation view: *A Secret Affair: Selections from the Fuhrman Family Collection*. The Contemporary Austin, Austin, TX, May 3–August 31, 2014. Curated by Louis Grachos with Danielle Nieciag. Catalogue. [Travels to: The FLAG Art Foundation, New York, February 21–May 16, 2015]. © Felix Gonzalez-Torres, Courtesy of The Felix Gonzalez-Torres Foundation. Photograph: Brian Fitzsimmons. **156.** Ellsworth Kelly. *Blue Relief over Green*, 2004. Oil on canvas, two joined panels. 80 x 74 x 2¾ inches (203.2 x 188 x 7 cm). Private collection. Artwork © Ellsworth Kelly Foundation. **160.** Jim Hodges. *Toward Great Becoming (orange/pink)*, 2014. Mirror on panel in two parts; left panel 71¾ x 44 5/16 inches (182.2 x 112.6 cm), right panel 60 x 48⅜ inches (152.4 x 122.9 cm). Private collection. © Jim Hodges. Photograph: David Regen. **161.** Sadie Benning. *Red and White Painting*, 2013. Medite, plaster, milk paint, and acrylic, 48¾ x 60½ inches (123.8 x 153.7 cm) overall. Courtesy the artist and Callicoon Fine Arts. Photograph: Chris Austin. **162–67.** © Awol Erizku, Courtesy the artist. Photographs: ArtEcho LLC. **168.** El Anatsui. *Telesma*, 2014. Mixed media, found aluminum, and copper wire, 99 x 107 inches (251.5 x 271.8 cm). © El Anatsui, Courtesy the artist and Jack Shainman Gallery, New York. Photograph: ArtEcho LLC. **169 top.** *Left:* Lesley Vance. *Untitled*, 2015. Oil on linen, 19 x 22¾ x 1 inches (48.3 x 57.8 x 2.5 cm). © Lesley Vance. *Right:* Sam Gilliam. *Out*, 1969. Acrylic on canvas, 113½ x 152½ x 2 inches (288.3 x 387.4 x 5.1 cm). © Sam Gilliam/Artists Rights Society (ARS), NY. **169 bottom.** *Left:* Sean Scully. *Landline Deep Blue Sea*, 2015. Oil on aluminum, 98⅜ x 78 11/16 inches (249.9 x 199.9 cm). © Sean Scully. *Center and right:* Courtesy the artist. Photograph: ArtEcho LLC. **170–71.** *Background:* © Charles Ray, Courtesy Matthew Marks Gallery. *Foreground:* Jeff Koons. *Cat on a Clothesline (Red)*, 1994–2001. © Jeff Koons. Photograph: Genevieve Hanson, ArtEcho LLC. **172–73.** *Background:* Jeff Koons. *Sling Hook*, 2007–09. © Jeff Koons. *Foreground:* © Charles Ray, Courtesy Matthew Marks Gallery. Photograph: Genevieve Hanson, ArtEcho LLC. **174.** *Left:* © Cecily Brown, Courtesy Paula Cooper Gallery, New York. *Right:* © Charles Ray, Courtesy Matthew Marks Gallery. Photograph: Genevieve Hanson, ArtEcho LLC. **175.** *Left:* © Cecily Brown, Courtesy Paula Cooper Gallery, New York. *Right:* Jeff Koons. *Winter Bears*, 1988. © Jeff Koons. Photograph: Genevieve Hanson, ArtEcho LLC. **176–77.** © Betty Tompkins. Photographs: Genevieve Hanson, ArtEcho LLC. **180–85.** © Patricia Cronin, Courtesy the artist. Photographs: Genevieve Hanson, ArtEcho LLC. **186–91.** © Artists Rights Society (ARS), NY/VISDA, Copenhagen. Photographs: Steven Probert. **192–93.** *Left:* © Etel Adnan, Courtesy Galerie Lelong & Co. *Right:* Gerhard Richter. *Abstract Painting (744-1)*, 1991. Oil on canvas, 78¾ x 63 inches (200 x 160 cm). Private collection. Courtesy the artist and Marian Goodman Gallery. Photograph: Object Studies. **194.** © Etel Adnan, Courtesy Galerie Lelong & Co. Photograph: Object Studies. **195.** Gerhard Richter. *MUSA*, 2009. Jacquard woven tapestry, 108 11/16 x 148 13/16 inches (276.1 x 378 cm). Edition 4/8, 2 APs. Private collection. Courtesy the artist and Marian Goodman Gallery. Photograph: Object Studies. **196–201.** © Cynthia Daignault, Courtesy the artist. Photographs: Object Studies. **202–7.** © Rebecca Ward, Courtesy the artist and Ronchini Gallery. Photographs: Steven Probert. **209.** Felix Gonzalez-Torres. *"Untitled"*, 1990. Print on paper, endless copies 25 inches at ideal height x 29 x 23 inches (63.5 x 73.7 x 58.4 cm) (original paper size). Installation view: *The Times*. The FLAG Art Foundation, New York, June 1–August 11, 2017. © Felix Gonzalez-Torres, Courtesy of The Felix Gonzalez-Torres Foundation. Photograph: Steven Probert. **210–11.** *Foreground:* Ashley Bickerton. *Good Painting*, 1988. Mixed-media construction with neoprene covering, 90 x 69 x 18 inches (228.6 x 175.3 x 45.7 cm). Private collection. Courtesy Sonnabend Gallery, New York. Photograph: Steven Probert. **213.** Ashley Bickerton. *Self Portrait: Kelapa Kepala*, 1993. Translucent turquoise rubber head, dyed human hair, steel, coconut, hydrocal, river rocks, and enamel paint, 88 13/16 x 12 x 11 inches (225.6 x 30.5 x 27.9 cm). Rachel-Art Ltd. & Lehmann-Art Ltd. The Rachel and Jean-Pierre Lehmann Collection. Photograph: Steven Probert. **216.** Ellsworth Kelly. *White Plaque: Bridge Arch and Reflection II*, 2011. Painted aluminum, 64 x 48 x ½ inches (162.6 x 121.9 x 1.3 cm). Artwork © Ellsworth Kelly Foundation. Photograph: Steven Probert. **218–19.** *Left to right:* Ellsworth Kelly. *Beach Cabana, Meschers*, 1950. Gelatin silver print, 14 x 11 inches (35.6 x 27.9 cm). Edition of 6. Artwork © Ellsworth Kelly Foundation. Ellsworth Kelly. *Pine Branch and Shadow, Meschers*, 1950. Gelatin silver print, 11 x 14 inches (27.9 x 35.6 cm). Edition of 6. Artwork © Ellsworth Kelly Foundation. Ellsworth Kelly. *Stonework, Meschers*, 1950. Gelatin silver print, 11 x 14 inches (27.9 x 35.6 cm). Edition of 6. Artwork © Ellsworth Kelly Foundation. Ellsworth Kelly. *Shelled Bunker, Meschers*, 1950. Gelatin silver print, 11 x 14 inches (27.9 x 35.6 cm). Edition of 6. Artwork © Ellsworth Kelly Foundation. Ellsworth Kelly. *Barn Wall, Meschers*, 1950. Gelatin silver print, 11 x 14 inches (27.9 x 35.6 cm). Edition of 6. Artwork © Ellsworth Kelly Foundation. Ellsworth Kelly. *Bricks, Meschers*, 1950. Gelatin silver print, 14 x 11 inches (35.6 x 27.9 cm). Edition of 6. Artwork © Ellsworth Kelly Foundation. Photograph: Steven Probert. **220–21.** *Left:* Ellsworth Kelly. *River II*, 2004. Two four-color lithographs on Rives BFK paper mounted on aluminum, 80 x 109 inches (203.2 x 276.9 cm). Edition of 9. Artwork © Ellsworth Kelly Foundation. *Right:* Ellsworth Kelly. *Black Relief with White*, 2005. Oil on canvas, two joined panels, 72½ x 73⅞ x 2¾ inches (183.2 x 187.6 x 7 cm) overall. Collection of Larry Gagosian. Artwork © Ellsworth Kelly Foundation. Photograph: Steven Probert. **224.** Ewan Gibbs. *Arlene*, 2010. Courtesy the artist. **226.** Ewan Gibbs. *Leon*, 2018. Courtesy the artist. **231.** Ewan Gibbs. *The Fuhrman Family*, 2015. Courtesy the artist. **232.** Juan Muñoz. *Two Laughing at Each Other*, 2000. Metal, resin, polyester, and oil, 39⅜ x 21⅝ x 19⅝ inches (100 x 55 x 50 cm). Courtesy the Estate of Juan Muñoz and Marian Goodman Gallery. **239.** Gerhard Richter. *905/1-48 Sinbad* (detail), 2008. Lacquer behind glass plate, 11 13/16 x 19 11/16 inches (30 x 50 cm). Private collection. Courtesy the artist and Marian Goodman Gallery. Photograph: Object Studies. **241.** © Awol Erizku, Courtesy the artist. Photograph: ArtEcho LLC. **243.** *Top:* © Rachel Whiteread, Courtesy the artist, Luhring Augustine, New York, Galleria Lorcan O'Neill, Rome, and Gagosian Gallery. *Bottom:* © Tony Matelli, Courtesy the artist and Marlborough Contemporary, New York and London. Photograph: Genevieve Hanson. **244.** Courtesy the artist and Corvi-Mora, London. Photograph: Genevieve Hanson. **245.** © Cynthia Daignault, Courtesy the artist. Photograph: Object Studies. **246.** *Left to right:* Ashley Bickerton. *White Head II*, 2012. Oil, acrylic, coral, and found objects on digital print on plywood, 92 x 80 x 7 inches (233.7 x 203.2 x 17.8 cm). Courtesy of the Morton G. Neumann Family Collection. Ashley Bickerton. *Seascape: Floating Costume to Drift for Eternity III (Elvis Suit)*, 1992. Suit, glass, aluminum, wood, caulk, fiberglass, enamel, and canvas webbing, 92 x 81 x 41½ inches (233.7 x 205.7 x 105.4 cm). Private collection. Ashley Bickerton. *L.W.S. 1*, 2000. Acrylic, oil, aniline dye, pencil, and collage on wood, 66 x 96 inches (167.6 x 243.8 cm). Private collection. Courtesy of Sonnabend Gallery. Photograph: Steven Probert. **249.** © Josephine Meckseper, Courtesy the artist and Timothy Taylor gallery. Photograph: Genevieve Hanson. **251.** © Cy Twombly Foundation, Courtesy Gagosian Gallery. Photograph: Genevieve Hanson. **255.** © Jim Hodges, Courtesy the artist. Photograph: Genevieve Hanson. **256.** © Sam Moyer, Courtesy the artist and Sean Kelly, New York. Photograph: Steven Probert. **257.** Ashley Bickerton. *Bad Wall*, 2017. Wall vinyl, dimensions variable. Photograph: Steven Probert. **258.** *Far left:* Ellsworth Kelly. *Ground Zero*, 2003. Collage on newsprint, 8 x 12¾ inches (20.3 x 32.4 cm). Private collection. Courtesy Matthew Marks Gallery. Artwork © Ellsworth Kelly Foundation. *Second from left:* Ellsworth Kelly. *Green Panel (Ground Zero)*, 2011. Painted aluminum, 23⅝ x 50 x ½ inches (60 x 127 x 1.3 cm). Private collection. Artwork © Ellsworth Kelly Foundation. Photograph: Steven Probert. **259.** Felix Gonzalez-Torres. *"Untitled"*, 1990. Print on paper, endless copies 25 inches at ideal height x 29 x 23 inches (63.5 x 73.7 x 58.4 cm) (original paper size). Installation view: *The Times*. The FLAG Art Foundation, New York, June 1–August 11, 2017. © Felix Gonzalez-Torres, Courtesy of The Felix Gonzalez-Torres Foundation. Photograph: Steven Probert. **260.** © Jim Hodges, Courtesy the artist and Gladstone Gallery, New York and Brussels. **261.** *Left to right:* Ellsworth Kelly. *Slip Study*, 1959. Oil on linen, 21 x 18 inches (53.3 x 45.7 cm). Artwork © Ellsworth Kelly Foundation. Ellsworth Kelly. *Falcon Study*, 1959. Oil on linen, 22 x 18 inches (55.9 x 45.7 cm). Artwork © Ellsworth Kelly Foundation. Ellsworth Kelly. *York Study*, 1959. Oil on linen, 18 x 24 inches (45.7 x 61 cm). Artwork © Ellsworth Kelly Foundation. Photograph: Steven Probert. **267.** Clint Spaulding/Patrick McMullan

Published in 2018 by The FLAG Art Foundation, New York, and Gregory R. Miller & Co., New York, on the occasion of the tenth anniversary of The FLAG Art Foundation.

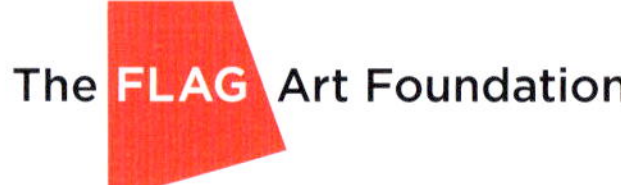

The FLAG Art Foundation
545 West 25th Street
New York, NY 10001
flagartfoundation.org

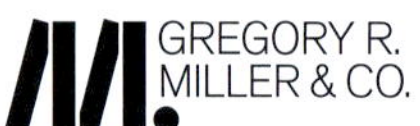

Gregory R. Miller & Co.
62 Cooper Square
New York, NY 10003
grmandco.com

Distributed worldwide by:

ARTBOOK | D.A.P.
75 Broad Street, Suite 630
New York, NY 10013
artbook.com

Design and production by Miko McGinty, Rita Jules, and Claire Bidwell
Editing by Kate Norment
Proofreading by Lynn Scrabis
Printed by Puritan Capital, New Hampshire
Typeset in Caslon and Mallory

Library of Congress Cataloging-in-Publication Data

Names: FLAG Art Foundation, author. | Fuhrman, Glenn, writer of foreword. | Bickerton, Ashley, 1959–
Title: The FLAG Art Foundation : 2008–2018 / with contributions by Ashley Bickerton, Delia Brown, Chuck Close, Patricia Cronin, Cynthia Daignault, Lisa Dennison, Sarah Douglas, Elmgreen & Dragset, Awol Erizku, Eric Fischl, James Frey, Ewan Gibbs, Louis Grachos, Stamatina Gregory, Prabal Gurung, Jane Hammond, Hilary Harkness, Jim Hodges, Philae Knight, Cary Kwok, Josephine Meckseper, Shaquille O'Neal, Richard Patterson, Jack Shear, Carolyn Twersky, Lesley Vance, Rebecca Ward, Linda Yablonsky, and Heidi Zuckerman.
Description: New York : The FLAG Art Foundation and Gregory R. Miller & Co., [2018]
Identifiers: LCCN 2018042607 | ISBN 9781941366219
Subjects: LCSH: The FLAG Art Foundation—History. | Art, Modern—21st century—Exhibitions.
Classification: LCC N6496.N4 F594 2018 | DDC 709.05—dc23
LC record available at https://lccn.loc.gov/2018042607

Front cover: Detail, Jim Hodges, *I dreamed a world and called it Love. #7*, 2016
Back cover: Detail, Jim Hodges, *I dreamed a world and called it Love. #6*, 2016
© Jim Hodges. Photograph: Ron Amstutz

Page 2: Foreground: Marc Quinn, *Sphinx (Fortuna)*, 2006; background: Rachel Whiteread, *Cabinet V*, 2006; Tony Matelli, *Successful Weed*, 2006

Page 4: Installation view of *Cecily Brown, Jeff Koons, Charles Ray*, showing Jeff Koons, *Cat on a Clothesline (Red)*, 1994–2001

Pages 18–19: Installation view of *Etel Adnan/Gerhard Richter*, showing Gerhard Richter, *MUSA*, 2009